The Life and Sermons of Dr. Ichabod Spencer

Volume Two

Doctrinal Sermons

Solid Ground Christian Books
PO Box 660132 ~ Vestavia Hills AL 35266

SOLID GROUND CHRISTIAN BOOKS
PO Box 660132, Vestavia Hills, AL 35266
205-443-0311
sgcb@charter.net
http://www.solid-ground-books.com

The Life & Sermons of Dr. Ichabod Spencer, Vol. 2
Ichabod Smith Spencer (1798-1854)

Published by Solid Ground Christian Books

Classic Reprints Series

First printing April 2003

ISBN: 1-932474-04-8

Manufactured in the United States of America

CONTENTS.

———•••———

I.

PAGE

THE LIGHT OF NATURE 7

II.

VANITY OF THE WORLD'S WISDOM........................... 29

III.

THE TRUTH HELD IN UNRIGHTEOUSNESS....................... 59

IV.

THE MAGNIFICENCE OF GOD.................................. 83

V.

THE DIVINE CHARACTER PRE-EMINENT...................... 99

VI.

ON KNOWING GOD... 120

VII.

WISDOM OF GOD IN MYSTERY................................ 136

VIII.

ELECTION... 154

IX.

ATONEMENT... 173

X.

MYSTERY APPROPRIATE IN REDEMPTION...................... 192

XI.

LEGAL AND EVANGELICAL JUSTIFICATION DISTINGUISHED.......... 211

XII.

PAGE
VANITY OF MAN IF NOT IMMORTAL............................ 229

XIII.

THE MERCY OF GOD.. 249

XIV.

THE MERCY OF GOD, CONTINUED............................. 266

XV.

GOD NO PLEASURE IN THE DEATH OF SINNERS................. 285

XVI.

GOD NO PLEASURE IN THE DEATH OF SINNERS, CONTINUED....... 305

XVII

GOD NO PLEASURE IN THE DEATH OF SINNERS, CONTINUED....... 325

XVIII.

HELP IN GOD FOR SINNERS................................. 345

XIX.

FORGIVENESS... 360

XX.

THE DEPTHS OF SALVATION................................. 375

XXI.

SKETCH OF THE PLAN OF SALVATION......................... 391

XXII.

CHRIST STRICKEN... 412

XXIII.

CHRIST DELIVERED UP..................................... 432

XXIV.

REJOICING OF FAITH,..................................... 449

XXV.

THE LAMB SLAIN WORSHIPED IN HEAVEN...................... 464

The Light of Nature.

The Law of the Lord is perfect, converting the soul.—PSALM xix. 7.

THERE is something not a little remarkable in the manner in which this expression is introduced by the inspired author. He had been up on the mount of contemplation. Standing on its loftiness, his mind felt the grandeur of the things around him. He was wrapped in the study of the stupendous works of God; and on that lofty eminence, where every breath must be poetry, he breathes forth a strain of sublimities and beauties, like one of the fondest admirers of the works of nature. The very first thought is poetry; it is the genius rush of a lofty imagination. Hear him: *The heavens declare the glory of God, and the firmament showeth his handy work.* His mind took in the compass of the heavens. It roved among the worlds of light hung out on the firmament above him. These worlds, their order, beauty, and movement, were instructive. They told him something: *day unto day uttereth speech, and night unto night showeth knowledge.* They told every body. These heavens, these illuminated worlds above us, suns and stars, carry their tuition to every child of mortality: *there is no speech nor language where their voice is not heard. Their line* (of instruction, their lucid lesson) *is gone out through all the earth, and their words to the end of the world.* Yes, for *in them hath he set a tabernacle for the sun, which is as a bridegroom coming out of his chamber, and rejoiceth as a strong man to run a race. His going forth is from the end of heaven, and his circuit unto the ends of it, and there is nothing hid from the heat thereof.* Thus he talks about the heavens. He is moved by their sublimity; and commends their instruction in a style of impassioned ardor, which that Deism, that so much extols the light of nature, can very well afford to admire.

But he was no Deist. After all this poetry about nature, *the heavens,* the *tabernacle of the sun,* he knew what it was all good for, and knew where its utility stopped. He comes back from this venturesome flight to read a lesson in another place : *The* LAW *of the Lord is perfect, converting the soul.* It was not in the material heavens, with all their grandeur, that he found the lesson of perfection. He turned from them to the *Law of the Lord,* and there he found it. This LAW is perfect : it *converts the soul.* This is the remarkable connection and instructive sense of the text.

History furnishes us with many remarkable confirmations of its accuracy. Among all that poetic excursiveness, which has delighted to roam over the " works of Nature" (as they are called); and all that sedate philosophizing, which has often boasted of its pure reasonableness and its practical utility, there have been no well-attested instances of a *regenerated spirit* in the poet or the philosopher, coming from the influences of the mere book of Nature. Poetry could sing in life and health ; but her voice faltered and her lip quivered in death ! Philosophy could speculate, and then expire in despair ! Human nature never took a promise from even the *taber-*

nacle of the sun, that would do any good to a dying man. The damps of the sepulcher put out its light; neither poetry nor philosophy can make it burn and shed light on that dark pathway by which a mortal travels to another world.

The truth is, these " works of Nature" were *not made to last:* they shall be burnt up; and a reasonable man ought not, therefore, to *expect* them to teach him lessons for his immortality. They may furnish him useful hints while here; but they never put into his hand or his heart a promise to carry out of the world with him. They may aid his piety, too, if he has gone to the foundation of the Prophets and Apostles, and, by yielding to Divine truth and seeking the Holy Spirit, has got his *soul converted*. But without this, the "light of Nature" will never cultivate piety. It never did. Hope has ransacked history for an example. So has Deism. So has a proud philosophy. But they have found none. The world has been barren of piety wherever there has been no revelation of God, or none of its light remaining among the glimmerings of tradition. Man needs *the Bible* to convert him to God and fit him to die.

This is our theme: the absolute necessity of special communications from God himself, to teach human nature those truths about God, about man's self, his duties, and his destination, which are necessary to his virtue, peace, happiness, and stable hope.

God's Word, as sole authority and guide in religion, is, in some places around us, getting jostled out of its place; and religion is judged of, its regeneration and cast of character, not by inspired thoughts, so much as by something to tickle human fancy and please human pride. Among statesmen, politicians, there seems to be

a growing disposition to forget Divine Revelation, the
just foundation of law and obligation, and to exalt
human wisdom and dreams about human progress into
its place. Our scientific and literary institutions, not
always destitute of pride, nor always superior to a passion
for novelty which endangers truth, fond of speculation,
and fond of talking about "the progress of the human
mind," have some of them too much forgotten the
difference betwixt human science and divine teaching
—forgotten where the one ends and the other begins
—forgotten, too, that religion is not a human science,
and can not, therefore, be improved like all human
sciences.

A growing error seems to be rapidly creeping into
many writings, professedly religious, and which, formed
for youthful minds, are the more perilous to truth and
the salvation of souls. "The *Light of Nature*" is an idea
that beams out largely in some of these modern productions. Their authors do not, indeed, all of them, affirm
its sufficiency to save men without the Bible; but they
represent it as teaching many fundamental truths, and
their mode of thought is such as to invite us to study religion *in* the Bible, only so far as Nature confirms it;—
while they are so much afraid of offending a disguised
infidelity, or half-infidel philosophizing, that they will
not tell the truth about reason's pretended "DISCOV-
ERIES," and plainly call them what they are,—*pre-
tences, impositions*, every one. The danger is, that our
delicate, and gentle, and illustrative, and what is called
"philosophical and natural" method of teaching Christianity, will utterly undermine her foundations, and convert her so-called disciples into a race of Deists.

We maintain that the Light of Nature is insufficient:

Reason reading it will not do. Man needs an immediate revelation beyond Nature. Let us see.

We know of only *three* great sources of proof to bear on this proposition. Let us examine them, and decide the question.

I. The first is *Fact, History.* We call your attention to what men HAVE DONE in studying religion by the Light of Nature, through the powers of their own reason and without any special revelation from God.

Glance at the heathen world. Let travelers tell you. Ask the missionaries of the Cross now scattered round the world. What will all these tell you? Do they say that the heathen know God? that they have any just ideas of his providence, of his government, or their own duty? that they have any tolerable system of morals? nay, that they have any tolerable notions of those very works of nature, which are so much relied upon as going far to teach them religion? It is all contrary to this. These people are in *gross darkness.* And, what is very noticeable, that which they call religion is the very worst thing there is among them! (not universally, I admit, but generally.) Their religion is baseness! It is cruelty! It is crime! Their very gods have the attributes of devils! And this is the "religion of Nature!"

Now travel back into heathen *antiquity.* It has always been so. Not a nation can be named, among all those that have come up in the long march of centuries, who ever had any clear ideas of the living and true God, or the duties they owed their Creator. What could any one of them tell you about the soul of man? Had they found out whether it was mortal or immortal? Did they know what holiness is? what is "the chief end of man"? Not one! Your child that answers the first question in the Catechism knows more theology than they.

The plain matter of fact is, these nations without the Revelation of God *never had any natural religion!* Their religion was all *un*natural, monstrous, absurd, as distant from the teachings of the Light of Nature, as it was from the meekness and sweet hopes of a blessed Christianity. Reason *has failed,* there; always failed, and every where! The Light of Nature has been no better than nothing! Not a people can be found, on the wide map of nations and during the long roll of centuries, whose religion, without the Bible, ever did them any good; made them any better to live, or any happier in dying. Be it remembered, they had no natural religion. Their religion was all *un*natural, unreasonable, superstition, vanity, and lies, which never could make men any better.

One thing more. Scholars have been accustomed to extol some of the sages of heathen antiquity. I will not say too highly. There were master-minds among them. Aristotle, Plato, Euclid, Cicero, deserve still their standing in the libraries of the learned. But mark: When they studied science, they excelled; when they studied religion, they were fools! They could not take a step rightly. They stumbled and fell at the very threshold. Cicero says, in his celebrated treatise, " Concerning the nature of the Gods," "those who affirm that there are such beings as Gods, have such strange varieties and contradictions of opinion, that it is impossible to classify them." On the primary article of natural religion, therefore, the very being of a God, these master-spirits were full of absurdities, conjectures, and confusion. They knew nothing, certainly; not an article; not a single truth. If heathenism *ever had* a creed, it was a creed of follies, absurdities, and contradictions.

But still, scholars will call to mind some of the dignified sentiments scattered through the classics; expressions of high morality, as they call them, and some expressions which sound like piety; and modern religious literature is making a foolish use of them. True, there are such expressions. In reference to them, we have these *seven* things to say; and scholars will allow us to condense when we answer their assumption.

1. All these expressions put together, all that scholars can rake up, are not worth so much for the religion of man, as these four words in the Bible,—*there is one God.*

2. Most of these ideas so much commended came, probably, not from the Light of Nature, but from *tradition,* handed down from Noah or Abraham; or they were derived from intercourse with the Jews. They could have been so derived; they probably were. The advocate for natural religion has no right to assume that they were deductions of reason made from the Light of Nature. It is more probable that they were derived from the Jews. Pythagoras traveled much in the East. He lived for years on Mount Lebanon, where surely he must have learnt much about religion from the people of God. Herodotus, the father of history, traveled. Plato traveled. The Jews themselves were scattered the world over, and carried their religion along with them. Horace sneers at their credulity; " credat Judeus, non ego." And it is a matter of astonishment to any good scholar, how it could have come to pass, that *the learned,* at least among the heathen, were as ignorant of religious truth as they were. The Christian knows very well how it came to pass; he knows *they did not like to retain God in*

their knowledge. (Rom. i. 21.) They lost as sinners what they had learnt as scholars, by testimony and tradition.

3. The knowledge which men need to have of God, if it had been gained (as it was *not*) by the scholars and sages among the heathen, and gained from the Light of Nature by reason, would not prove that to be a sufficient light for the religion of man. ALL men need to know God. It would not be enough, when we are inquiring, for the sake of the whole race of humanity, after some sufficient guide in religion, if you *should* be able to hunt up some instances of great men, of great minds, great leisure, great opportunities, who have found such a guide. Little men die, as well as great ones. A man does not need to be a scholar in order to have a soul. You must not, then, bring up your *scholars* as examples. Here every human being has an equal interest. If there lives a man, or ever did, who, by the common exercise of his powers, cannot attain the knowledge of God, that fact is fatal to the scheme of a natural religion. Such knowledge needs to be as universal as souls. It needs to be clear to the weakest understanding.

4. It needs to be well *proved.* *A guess* is bad foot-hold for an immortal soul! And if you could make it out (as you cannot) that some of your sages guessed right, that will not do; that will not demonstrate the sufficiency of the Light of Nature.

5. On a matter of so much moment as our chief interests, our duties, our destiny in another world, and how our God will judge us, we can not afford to have a single lingering particle of uncertainty on vital points. If we have, it may be fatal to us. We may imagine we are pleasing God when we are displeasing him. We may think we are going in the way of life while we are only on

the down-hill of perdition. The uncertainty, the lack of proof among your sages, makes chaff of their speculations.

6. Our knowledge needs to be extensive. A hint or two flung out in the dark cannot answer our purpose. Those *other* points, of which we are ignorant, may be the *vital* ones; the very points essential to our duty and our everlasting peace.

7. If scholars will search a little, they will find demonstrations, thick and dark enough, of the entire *inefficacy* of all this boasted knowledge of heathen sages and scholars, to turn them from the grossest indecencies and immoralities; things so gross, that there is not a promiscuous assembly in Christendom that would endure even the mention of them. The light which only leads to such a religion cannot claim any excellence or even efficacy.

These seven ideas are enough to silence every word that can be spoken about some of the expressions of ancient heathens, which sound like religion, and which are taken to prove the great extent to which nature can conduct men in the knowledge of God and their own duties and destinies.

Now let us gather up the substance of all this, and bring this argument to a conclusion. The substance is FACT—HISTORY—the record of human nature. And it is this: *mankind never* HAVE *learnt any thing about true religion from the Light of Nature*—not an article, not the very being of a God, not the most necessary vital truths. This is the premises. The conclusion is irresistible; *they never can learn in that way.* It is folly to maintain, that men in all ages, and of all degrees of intellectual advancement, can learn what no man ever yet did. The revelation of God is, therefore, indispensable, and indispensable every where. The sage, the scholar among his books, needs it, as really and as much, as the boor over his mattock. All FACT—the history of human nature, proves that men can learn nothing at all of religion by the Light of Nature alone.

II. The second source of proof is the Scriptures themselves. We call your attention to the fallacy of those ideas about the Light of Nature, into which so many of the well-meaning, but weak, (in the Church and out of it,) have fallen. If we have in one article corrected their history, let us have a second to correct their Scripture interpretations.

These men open the Bible and read,—*the heavens declare the glory of God.* But they forget, while they thus summon Scripture witness, two very important matters. One is, that the Scriptures do not say that men are *converted* by the declaration of these heavens. They attribute conversion, all religion, to the Divine revelation, accompanied by the Divine Spirit. The other is, that the Scriptures never say that men *see* and *understand* what these visible heavens *declare.* Our stripling philosophers, and poet Christians, proud of their so-called "Light of Nature," and disposed to teach Christianity to men very much as they would teach botany or astronomy, must not think to press the Bible into their service, to make it countenance their errors. It neither says that Nature's light *converts* men, (makes them religious,) nor that men *understand* nature.

The fallacy of the conclusions drawn from Scripture by these dreamy natural religionists, may be detected by any example. How often is that passage in the Epistle to the Romans quoted, only to be perverted for bolstering up a conclusion directly the opposite of its own. *The invisible things of him, from the creation of the world, are*

clearly seen, even his eternal power and godhead. What is
the Bible conclusion? It is this: *so, then, they are without excuse.* Excuse for what? For having a knowledge of God? That would make the apostle talk like a
a madman! No. *Without excuse* for *not* knowing God.
But what is the conclusion of our poetic and naturaliz-
ing Christians? It is that the Light of Nature, the
creation, the *things that are made*, are quite sufficient to
give men a knowledge of God! And this conclusion
they take as a foundation for theories, and songs, and
lectures; though directly in the face of the conclusion
stated in the text itself. The text plainly affirms the
practical inefficacy of the works of God to teach men
religious truth. It says they are not taught—they are
without excuse. They are only condemned, instead of
being enlightened and saved. They do not read nature
rightly.

This text and its misinterpretation may stand as an
example of all the passages in the Bible which have
been pressed into this bad and mistaken service. Every
one of them has been perverted. The case is simply
this : the Bible tells us of the evidences of himself which
God hath imprinted upon the works of his hands. It
does *not* tell us, that men, unaided by *another* revelation,
have ever read one of these evidences rightly, or ever can.
It does *not* tell us that man, corrupted, fallen, blinded by
sin and in love with darkness, can ever read and understand those lessons of light, which illuminate the
heavens, and lie, more or less clear, over all the works of
God. Mistaken men have concluded that, because there
is light *in* Nature, therefore men could see it. They forgot that men had no eyes! The Scriptures, and God
their author, did not forget it. This Bible came out

from behind the curtain which hides invisibles, to *open the eyes of the blind*, and teach men how to read those lessons about God, which are scattered over creation, and echoed so often in the language of Divine Providence. Without this special Revelation, however effective these lessons might be to a *sinless* man, to link him to the Deity in light and love, they have utterly failed to profit sinful man.

These lessons are clear. We will not yield to the most poetic naturalist in admiration of them. For our part, we cannot conceive how God Almighty could have fitted up a material machinery which should have more clearly unfolded his wonderful power and wisdom, than this moving, visible universe. But men *see* this machinery and know not God. The sun is in his *pavil-ion* above them by day, and the stars roll in the gorgeous heavens of midnight; but men look out upon all these things of materiality and movement, and, until the Bible tells them how to understand them and reason about them, and guards them from error at every step, they never learn a single religious truth rightly! And the clearness, the multitude and glory of these bright lessons about God, only ought to serve to convince us, therefore, to what an awful depth of degradation and darkness sin has flung man. The firmament that bends above him—the sun in his pavilion of glory, does him no good! He can *see* it all; he does see it; he has seen it for centuries; he has seen it from New Zealand to Nova Zembla—from Labrador to Patagonia; and, without the Bible, has remained an idolater still! The Bible never says that the Light of Nature alone can lead man a single step in religion. It says only that men ought to be instructed by it, but are not. Let not our moral philosophers, and our tasteful Christians, misinterpret it. Let them remember that the Bible appeals to the works of Nature, for the purposes of *impression*, not for those of *instruction*—for devotion, but not for doctrine.

III. The third source of proof is found in the inconclusiveness of the arguments employed by the disciples of Nature. We take it for granted, that they have done the best they could; and if their arguments are not sufficient, no sufficient ones are to be found. Turn, therefore, your attention to those premises, processes and conclusions of reasoning, by which the Light of Nature is said to be shown as sufficient to teach a reasonable man some important religious truths.

This is a wide field. We cannot examine the whole of it. We select only a few prominent matters. Take six articles.

1. The existence of one God, the Creator and Ruler of the world. Men have said, that this is one of the plainest truths of natural religion, demonstrable without the Bible. I deny this assumption. I demand the proof. Speak, thou disciple of Reason: tell me how you know there is one God, and not twenty, till the Bible has taught you.

The disciple of reason gives me this answer: He says there is a unity of design in all the works of creation and providence; and he says, it is just, reasonable, unavoidable, to infer, from this unity, the unity of God, the Author of creation and providence. But I am not ready for that inference: three difficulties lie in my way. Lift out these stumbling-blocks from my path, and I will go along with you.

First Difficulty. I do not see that unity of design,

(unless you allow me to take the Bible explanations.) I never did. I cannot. What do I see? I see trees growing up in the forest; but, lightnings rive them! hurricanes dash them down! Where is the unity there? I see health and beauty mantling the cheek of youth; but they fade away while I look! disease, death have done their dreadful work! Where is the unity there? I see nations living in harmony, and happiness growing out of it; but soon my ear is startled with the trumpet-summons, and the next post brings me the tale of blood, under some such name as Cerro-Gordo, or Marathon, or Waterloo, or Bosworth fields!—These things do not look like unity. The world is full of them. And I am ready, therefore, to fling into the face of this disciple of Reason, this strange question: Is it not more reasonable to infer, that there are two Deities, a good one and a bad one? He is dumb. He cannot answer that question, till he calls the Bible to his aid.

The *Second* Difficulty about the inference of the unity of God, from the unity of design seen in the operations of Nature, is the *link* that joins these two unities together. I do not see it. If there was a unity of design seen in the world, how would that demonstrate the unity of God? Why, says the reasoner, (very acute,) " different Deities could not harmonize." Ah! who told you that? How do you know it? If there are *twenty* Gods, must they necessarily quarrel? especially if they are good ones? Why is it at all unreasonable to suppose that several Deities should perfectly agree and act together? The reasoner is baffled again! He can not lift the stone of stumbling out of my way, till the Bible puts the lever into his hand.

The *Third* Difficulty is, that men without the Bible

never made this inference. They never did. I defy you; you can not find it. If the unity of God is such a plain inference of common sense, how came it about that common sense never made this inference *alone?* The disciple of Reason is confounded again. He cannot answer. This fact annihilates his theory.

We dismiss this article. Unaided reason cannot prove there is but one God. Man needs the Bible.

2. A second Article; *the attributes* of Deity. The same processes of examination may be applied to all of them. We name two, as examples—immutability and goodness.

First, the immutability of God. How does the Light of Nature demonstrate this attribute? It needs to be demonstrated. If God is one thing to-day and another thing to-morrow, we have no firm foothold—no ground of hope or peace. But reason alone can not demonstrate it. The government of the world certainly *appears* unstable. Examine it. Ancient cities have crumbled down: arts have been lost: oceans sometimes gain upon the dry land, and sometimes the dry land pushes back the ocean: barbarism reigns now, where once science built her temples: the bones of animals are dug out of the earth, belonging to races now utterly extinct, perhaps: aye, and a sensation of mournfulness comes over the heart from the distant heavens, when we remember the *lost Pleiad!* There is no rock here to stand upon, to demonstrate the unchangeableness of God. Reason can not prove it.

Second; the goodness of God is a still greater difficulty. For, behold! Wars follow peace: famine treads on the heels of plenty: earthquakes shake down cities, and, amid their shock, all that felicity which you relied

upon to prove the goodness of God, perishes in an hour!
The rich yellow harvest, ripe for the sickle, seems like
a proof of goodness; but what will you say, when mil-
dews have blasted it, or agues hinder the strong men
from the gathering? The Light of Nature cannot tell
us, how a God of infinite goodness can inflict so many
woes upon the world. And if you take a step more and
try to tell, the existence of the very moral evil you
mention, as deserving chastisements, introduces you into
a worse difficulty. How came sin? How does its very
existence comport with the goodness of the Deity? The
mere disciple of Reason cannot touch the question! he
stands aghast and dumb! and he will stand thus forever,
if revelation does not help him!

We dismiss this article. Unaided Reason staggers,
when attempting to demonstrate the attributes of God.
She needs the Bible.

3d. A third article—the *mode* of the Divine existence.

If the knowledge of the true God is essential to our
religion, to our duty and happiness, we ought to know
something about the Father, Son, and Holy Ghost.
Creation says not a word about this,—Providence not a
word,—Reason alone never even ventured a conjecture.
And if the reasoner should affirm, that this knowledge of
the Trinity is not necessary to true religion, we might beg
his permission to affirm, that it is; and who, then, shall
decide betwixt us? We need the Bible to decide, after
all. But, how does he know it is not necessary? How
little may a man know about God, and yet have true religion? Whatever he might respond to this question,
the great fact remains, that the Light of Nature gives

not even the faintest glimmering about the Trinity of the Godhead. Man needs the Bible.

4th Article—the knowledge of God's will.—Probably none but an Atheist will deny, that, in order to our having any religion, we need to know the will of God ; and that our religion must consist somewhat, at least, in a designed conformity to that will. But Nature's light does not teach it to me. It does not tell me how to worship my Maker, or how to act towards mortals like myself. If any one says I must seek a knowledge of God's will in his works, I look abroad on the earth and upward to the heavens, and confess that I behold splendid and innumerable proofs of power, of design, of wisdom unfathomable. I see how God wants *matter* to act; but what good does that do to my immortal soul? I do not see how God wants *mind* to act. His works do not tell me what to do to secure the favor of God, and my own eternal happiness. I cannot find in them the record of his will. I want his favor. If there *is* a God who hath made me, and who hath spread out these visible heavens and laid the foundations of the earth beneath my feet, I dare not have him up in arms against me! But *where*, in the Light of Nature, do I perceive any atonement for sin?——*where* any proof of its possibility, or of its acceptance? *where* any ground of certainty, that God will not yet embark all his power to make me miserable, do what I may? Nowhere! nowhere! The whole Universe has not a hint visible to man! Man needs the Bible.

5th Article—the penalty of transgressing against the will of God, and the results of conformity to it.

If I am to act in religion, in an intelligent manner, I wish to know what is before me. If I act on a mistake, my mistake may be fatal. If I act on a mistake, my religion may all be false. Penalties and rewards form an important part of a system of moral government; and the governed need to know something about them. Now, what says the Light of Nature? Not a syllable! Felicity, it is true, as a general thing, follows one class of actions *in this* life, and infelicity another. But I wish to know if this is all. If not, what rewards and punishments are reserved in another world, and how long the one and the other are going to last. If your conjecture should whisper in my ear that punishment will come to an end, my fears, my hopes will both urge the inquiry, how can I be certain, then, that rewards will not come to an end? show me some bond of security to spread over my eternity! You perceive we are afloat— out of sight of land; and thick darkness is around us, not a star to twinkle on our midnight, when we study these matters in the mere school of Reason! Man needs the Bible to give him unfoldings of futurity.

Yes, of futurity altogether: for the 6th article is, the utter insufficiency of Nature's light to demonstrate even *the immortality of the soul.*

Such a demonstration, the disciples of Reason tell us, is to be found in its *capacities.* Their argument is this: these capacities are not fully unfolded here, and the Creator never would have formed them, to have them perish at death. But this is no proof. It is miserable conjecture, and nothing but conjecture—a mere assump- tion. Besides, there are thousands of things, having valuable properties, which are never permitted to be unfolded. Seeds rot. Gold is hidden in the bosom of the earth. Not human beings only, but brute ones, die in infancy. And does the reasoner tell us, that these seeds, this gold, these perished young brutes, are going to have an immortality for the unfolding of their properties? And more: talk about valuable properties? what are our little capacities to the infinite God? If he should annihilate us, he could easily fill our place with more noble beings. Where does Nature tell us he will not do so?

But the disciples of Reason muster a little poetry, and tell us of

> "This pleasing hope, this fond desire,
> This longing after immortality."

And this desire for perpetual existence, they take as demonstration that the soul is immortal. The argument runs thus: God would not have implanted such a desire to mock it with disappointment. The argument is weak. Three ideas are each one of them enough to overthrow it: First, it is only an assumption. It does not belong to man to tell what God would not do. Second, this very desire for immortality may be one of the fruits of sin: Nature does not prove it is not, and how can she prove that the desire itself may not fall under the displeasure of God? And the third idea is, that men have other longings, besides that after immortality, which God does utterly disappoint. They long for power, for honor, for wealth; and the longing often goes for nothing. Death finds them longing to live longer; and if the longing could demonstrate the immortality of the soul, it would demonstrate the immortality of the body too; and we should have few friends to bury and

few tombs to build. And if it should be granted, that
the longing proves there is an immortality *somewhere*, it
does not prove that immortality is for me. It may be
denied to me, as are many things I long for.

But again, these disciples of Reason resort to "philosophy," (as they call it,) and tell us the soul must be immortal because it is "immaterial"—a spirit, and *cannot*
perish. This argument might be sufficiently answered
by asking, if it applies to *all* spirit? to the ox in his
stall, and the oyster in his bed of mud? are their spirits
to be immortal? and by asking, if it just brings us down
to a level with the theology of the poor Indian—

> " Who thinks, admitted to that equal sky,
> His faithful dog shall bear him company " ?

Is the immortality of man on a level with the immortality of horses, in this natural religion? But we have
another answer. Our spirits came from God. He can
annihilate them if he please : at least, Nature's light is
unable to show that he can not, and unable to show that
he will not cast back our immaterial spirits into their
original non-existence. Perhaps he has some unknown,
but wise purpose to answer by us for a little while; and
then will order that we exist no more! Where, in
Nature, do you find any thing to demonstrate the contrary? Nowhere! God has not assured us by this
earth, or these heavens, that the immaterial spirit shall
not perish for ever! And once, once the boastful "reign
of reason" did write over the entrance to the grave-yards
the strange words—"death is an eternal sleep!" It was
an impious falsehood; but its authors were the disciples
of "reason" and "philosophy," and talked proudly about
the advance of mind. Man needs the Bible to teach him
his immortality.

We have done. As much as possible we have condensed these arguments. You see how it is. The history of what man has done in attaining religious knowledge without the Bible's aid, by the mere Light of Nature; the use which the Bible itself attributes to that light; and the weak, sophistical, and unsatisfactory arguments of Reason about religion, all of them put together, not enough to furnish the least satisfaction to sinful and dying man; demonstrate to us the insufficiency of Nature, and our need of the Word of God. Speculation will not do. You must have faith to take God at his word, and die on the pillow of the promises.

The real utility of all the Light of Nature on the subject of religion consists in this: that it demonstrates its own insufficiency for teaching us a single important truth, and thus turns us over to the Word of God; and having done so, shines as a constant witness, and every where *to impress* the lessons of Bible-teaching upon us. It strikes the Infidel dumb, and aids the devotions of the Christian, living or dying. But *alone* it teaches nothing. It never did. God never said it could. And its reasonings, proudly called in the schools "science" and "philosophy," vanish into smoke when we touch them. That philosophy is good for nothing. It cannot teach religion. All it can do is to demonstrate its own darkness, and turn you over to the Word of God for every truth and every certainty.

You will never read God's world rightly, till his Word teaches you how. After it has taught you, you may gather proofs of religion from Nature, which you could not gather before. If we take his Word first to teach us, we may understand the Light of Nature rightly, and may derive some advantages by appealing to these *heavens*

which *declare the glory of God.*   The lesson is *in* Nature;
but Nature is a sealed book to a sinner.   Alone, though
it may silence a skeptic, it cannot satisfy a soul.   If we
do not take God's Word to guide us, we shall grope our
way to eternity in the dark.   Reason cannot support the
staggering footsteps of humanity on the dark mountains
of death.   She has no Christ to tell of, no atonement, no
pardon, no firm foothold on immortal rock, no friend to
take us from the grasp of death upward to

" Jerusalem, our happy home."

Man needs the Bible.   Under lucid skies men are
perishing without it.   The Light of Nature does not
suffice to make them wise, or good, or happy ; to pacify
conscience, or light up the eternal world with the certain-
ties of a blessed hope.   But, *the Law of the Lord is perfect, converting the soul.*

Vanity of the World's Wisdom.

For after that in the wisdom of God the world by wisdom knew not God, it pleased God by the foolishness of preaching to save them that believe.—1 CORINTHIANS, i. 21.

THE grandeur of Christianity and its value very much consist in the two facts, that it reveals a peculiar system and accomplishes peculiar effects. Christianity is unlike every thing else. It is not a matter of nature, and is not to be explained by nature. It is a miracle from beginning to end; it is all miracle. It is an interposition of God, doing what he has no where else done, and among the ravages of sin setting up the signals of recovery.

He who approaches this system, therefore, either to understand it or be saved by it, must not approach it as he approaches an ordinary subject. He must give to it its own high place and the distinction of its own high peculiarity, else he cannot be saved by it—he cannot understand it.

This idea enters into the text before us. It pervades it. The apostle draws a distinction betwixt the attempts of men and the revelation of God. Such attempts, without revelation, accomplished nothing; *the world by wisdom knew not God.* This was one side of the matter. On the back of this failure came the other side: *it pleased God by the foolishness of* PREACHING *to save them that believe.* This was no failure. The thing was accomplished by preaching which could not be accomplished by all the wisdom of men. A new system came in. Divine revelation was different from all human wisdom, and its results were different.

The general idea of the text, therefore, is the peculiar superiority of Christianity over all human Science on the subject of religion. But, in order to understand the meaning of the apostle, let us,

I. Explain the terms and clauses of the text.

II. Let us explain and demonstrate the general principle it lays down—the superiority of Revelation.

III. Let us glance at some items of application.

I. In explaining the terms of the text, let us take them in their order.

In the wisdom of God: This clause is employed here just to account for a thing mentioned in the next. It was *by the wisdom of God, that the world by wisdom knew not God.* A large portion of mankind had been left for centuries, (as some are left still,) destitute of Divine Revelation, to try their power and follow the dictates of their own boasted reason. The apostle gives no other account of this, than that it was done *by the wisdom of God.* He does not assign any reason for it. Probably he did not know any. *He* knew how far to go in his explanations, and where to stop. He does not speculate: he merely states a matter of historic fact, and says this occurred *by the wisdom of God.* It was a matter of Divine sovereignty and Divine wisdom; a thing of the Infinite One, and not to be complained of, or even understood, except as a naked fact.

Why men were left then, and some are left now, without revelation to try the powers of their own reason, is a mystery we cannot penetrate. Paul did not try to penetrate it. He only refers it to the wisdom of God, and leaves it there. This is characteristic of him. I do not recollect a single instance in all his Epistles wherein he attempts to speculate. He explains; he reasons like a giant to demonstrate the great doctrines of Christianity; he embarks all his severe logic to convict men of sin and persuade them to fly to Christ; but in reference to any of the matters which he discusses, I recollect no instance wherein he ventures a conjecture, or attempts a single step of unfolding, by any reasoning powers of his own, a single step beyond the revelation which was given to him. He knew the peculiarity of Christianity, and was willing to let it remain peculiar. He did not aim to level it down to the reason, the sciences, the philosophy of men. Nobody ever knew better than Paul knew how much the feelings of human nature will sometimes rise in opposition to facts transpiring under the Divine government, and in opposition, too, to the doctrines of Divine grace. But in all such cases, the apostle's answer is just like the clause in the text before us; he refers the matter to *the wisdom of God*. If, for example, he is proclaiming the Divine sovereignty in election, and a man chooses so to pervert or misapply the doctrine as to cast off the matter of personal accountability, *why doth God yet find fault? who hath resisted his will?* then Paul's ready response is, *nay, but, oh man, who art thou that repliest against God?* If, *e. g.*, again, Paul is proclaiming the doctrine of the resurrection of the dead, and some one reasoning on the mere principles of Nature (like our infidel, Bush), and knowing that the body is decomposed by putrefaction in the grave, chooses to ask, (Bush's question,) *with what body do they come ?* the ready answer of Paul is, *thou fool ! God giveth it a body as it pleaseth him.* It is *God* with Paul—not Nature, but God—as in the text, *in the wisdom of God.*

The next clause is : *the world by wisdom knew not God.* This was the thing which Paul affirms to have come to pass *in the wisdom of God.* It was an inscrutable wisdom, and there we must leave it. We cannot explain it. Perhaps our limited minds could not understand it if it were explained. We must leave it to the wisdom of God, just where we leave a hurricane, an earthquake, a pestilence, Herculaneum, Pompeii, and the graves of ten thousand infants born only to die.

The world by wisdom. The word *wisdom* is not to be taken here, perhaps, in the same sense as in the preceding clause, where the *wisdom of God* is spoken of. The sense may be —*after that in the wisdom of God*, the world by *Philosophy* knew not God, it pleased God to save men in his own way.

The wisdom of the world, therefore, of which Paul speaks, means simply human reason and speculation, in which the Corinthians so much gloried, as they extolled their " age of improvement," as they called it, and wanted to introduce their improvement into the churches, where Paul did not want them.

It was not Philosophy that founded Christianity or reasoned it out—Philosophy *knew not God*, and now let Philosophy keep her own place and mind her own business, and leave Christianity to the *wisdom of God* which originated it. This monition and advice of Paul were not more needed then than they are now.

Knew not God. Unquestionably the Apostle means by this expression, that the world, with all its boasted reason and proud learning, had not derived from all the works and Light of Nature any true knowledge of God, or any sufficient principles of true religion. Men are accustomed *now* to extol the "Light of Nature," (as they call it,) the power of Reason, "improvements," "the march of mind." And some Christian ministers sometimes think to do Christianity a very good service, by philosophizing it to make it keep up with the times. In all this, they do Christianity no other service than rob it of its power by robbing it of its peculiarity, and do no other service to the "philosophic minds" which they say they would influence, than just to mislead them, and keep them away from true faith in Christ and reliance on his great atonement.

It is a historic fact, *the world by wisdom knew not God.* Reason had tried her powers and failed. She was foiled in every attempt. She *knew not God.* And this simple fact, a matter of history, of history spread over centuries, ought to be enough to silence for ever every claim of Philosophy to teach a sinner any thing which could benefit his soul. That Reason should now pretend to be able to make independent discoveries in religion, or dare to arraign Christian doctrines at her bar and explain away their old-fashioned peculiarities, is such a combination of foolishness and impudence as is to be found no where else, but in the range of a proud, boastful and superficial Philosophy. Surely a religion which *knows not God* is a very contemptible religion. It will do sinners no good. But it is all that Philosophy can furnish.

But there is another thing to be noticed in this clause: It is *the nature* of the expression, *knew not God.* This was the sum and substance of the matter with Paul. He does not say, *knew not principles*, or doctrines, or deduc-

2*

tions, or *truth* even. He says, *knew not God.* The
Apostle, in all he has written, shows in what order he
was wont to consider the things of religion. He did not
begin with man and reason upwards—he began with
God and reasoned downwards. The world by wisdom
knew not God. That was enough. That fact was fatal
to all their schemes. The starting point, the heart of all
true religion, was wanting in their speculations; and
through whatever courses their speculations might run,
therefore, or on whatever landing-place they might stop,
both courses and landing-place would be error.

Men like the Corinthians are alive yet. It is not uncommon, yea, it is very common, to find even in the
Church, men who are very much enamored with a speculative Christianity. They want speculative sermons,
philosophical, philological, natural, some importation
from Germany, or some *invention* more fit for the patent
office than the pulpit. They are not willing to begin
with God. As they would know how to be saved even,
they are unwilling to have us tell them that they must
obey only the written Word, must take every lesson and
every step by prayer, must turn directly unto God on
the revealed foundation of an infinite atonement, and by
faith, not in Philosophy, but in a revealed redemption,
must learn to know the *only true God and Jesus Christ
whom he hath sent, for this is eternal life.*

The next clause proves this: *it pleased God by the foolishness of preaching to save them that believe.*

It pleased God. No other account can be given of it.
All nature is silent. The universe has not a hint any
where in all its matter and movements. *It pleased* God
—it came from infinite sovereignty and infinite love.

By the foolishness of preaching. Paul never quarrels

about names. He is too much in earnest for that. If he can get the *thing* he wants, men may call it by what name they please. He consents even himself to call the Gospel by a name not at all descriptive of its own nature, or the views *he* entertained of it; but by the same name which the men of the world gave to it, and which was expressive of the views which they entertained of it. On this principle he speaks of the *foolishness of preaching*—just because men of the world called it foolishness. In another place he calls it the *foolishness of God*, and says, *the foolishness of God is wiser than men.* And he says, too, *God hath chosen the foolish things of the world to confound the wise.* In another place he says, *the natural man receiveth not the things of the Spirit of God, because they are foolishness unto him.* Paul, therefore, calls the utterance of the Gospel, *the foolishness of preaching*, just because other men called it so; and the man without any religion is apt to esteem it such, if the preaching will not take his speculative turn and put on the literary taste which suits his refined ears. It was foolishness to the Greeks to speak of *Christ crucified*, of the great atonement, because their philosophy was dumb, utterly and for ever dumb, on the whole subject. Reason could not touch it. She could not take a step in it, or utter a syllable on the whole matter. The Greeks might call the fundamental doctrine of the Gospel foolishness if they pleased, they might reject the atonement of a crucified Christ; but Paul assures them that in this way God was pleased to save them that believe. Thus the Apostle brings round the whole matter to *faith*—just to faith. No man need speculate. No Philosophy would do him any good;—no efforts of a mustered and proud reason would land him in the kingdom of heaven.

The sum of the whole matter then is, that all the efforts of human reason are utterly insufficient for attaining the knowledge of religion; and after the lapse of centuries had demonstrated their insufficiency, God gave the Gospel to do for man what Philosophy could not do—to reveal to man what Reason could not discover, and by a peculiar system to lead those to eternal life, who would trust the Bible to lead them there. Lay your pride in the dust. Dismiss your vain philosophy. Cease to dishonor Christianity by attempting to conform it to a fashionable literature. Obey it. Flee to Christ. Rest on the great redemption; for it *pleases God to save them that believe.*

II. We proposed to explain and demonstrate this great principle of the text.

The submission of reason to faith, is one of the difficult things for human pride and depravity to endure. Science is not to be despised. Human reasonings are not to be undervalued. But though they are of vast moment when they are confined to their proper place, they become sources of error and danger when they are extended beyond it. This is one of the present dangers of the Church. The boast of human progress leads many a one of the proud boasters to undervalue the old truths of Divine Revelation. Under the pretense that philosophy and reason have made great advances, revelation becomes pushed out of its place—Divine doctrines are proclaimed as obsolete and behind the age. We propose to defend the sense of the text. We propose to show that the wisdom of men, unaided by Divine Revelation, can learn nothing in religion, and, therefore, that speculation is out of its place, when it brings in its innovations, and discards our old doctrines. We name par-

ticular items : A future state. Human duty. The character of God. The pardon of a sinner.

1. We call your attention to the matter of a *future
state*. What does mere Philosophy know about it?
what can Reason alone teach you? Reason, you know,
must have some materials to work with—some grounds
to go upon—some premises of truth to start with. But
in respect to another world, another life beyond this,
what materials has she got? what ground to stand
upon? what sure premises of truth to start with? A
dark, deep gulf separates this world from another. We
can not pass it—we can not see over it. From that other
world, (if there is one,) no man can bring forth, with all
his philosophy, a single fact for his philosophy to work
upon. Our question is about another world : *is* there
one? Show me a fact to prove it. Show me one of its
inhabitants—one of its productions—one of its operations—one of its *any thing* that shall constitute to me a
demonstration that such a world exists. If Philosophy
will only furnish me one solitary material, one single
fact, clear and unquestionable, which shows me that
there is such a world beyond this; then I shall feel that
I have got something to begin with—and I consent to
take that fact and make the most of it in reasoning from
it to reach something else. But Reason has no such fact.
She has nothing to start upon. She has got no foothold
upon the shores of eternity, (if there is one.)

If you take up any of the materials or existences of
this world, you have a perfect right, I admit, to reason
from them to conclusions which lie in this world. But
how can you reason upon them to reach conclusions
which lie in another. You yourself admit, (for you
cannot deny,) that that other world is most *un*like this—

that vast and mysterious changes are to transpire before you shall be an inhabitant of another world. Your blood is to stagnate—your breath is to stop—your immaterial spirit is to come out of its earthly temple—it is to have new powers of perception given to it, (if its future existence is to be of any value,) for its organs of perception, its sight, its hearing, and all its instruments of perception and knowledge, are left behind it. How shall it talk, to tell other spirits what it thinks? How shall it hear, to receive any knowledge or idea from them? How shall it become acquainted with either matter or spirit, or whatever it is that goes to make up the world to come? And if such wonderful changes are to take place, how *can* you reason from any thing *here* to reach any certain and indubitable conclusion about any thing *there?* How can you be certain that there *is* any thing there, and that the spirit itself does not become extinct, instead of passing into another state of existence—a state confessedly mysterious and inexplicable?

How shall Reason demonstrate that the soul survives the death of the body? There is so close a connection betwixt all the known operations of the soul and the operations of the body, that when one set of operations ceases, it would seem reasonable to suppose that the other set of operations ceases also, and all the philosophers in the world cannot furnish a particle of certain proof to the contrary. A body is in perfect health, and the mind is regular: in a few days that body is disordered, and the mind suffers more or less of disorder also. If anger ruffles the mind, it also ruffles the blood. If fever burns in the veins, the brain is soon disturbed, and the mind loses its regularity. If melancholy settles upon the soul, the appetite is irregular, the blood slow, the body becomes sluggish and lean. As years creep on, and the joints become stiff, the pulse low, the muscles rigid, the blood cold; the soul, at the same time, true to her sympathy, puts on the equal signals of decay—the memory fails, the imagination becomes inactive, the wings of fancy are folded or broken, and even the judgment becomes feeble and loses its soundness. And, finally, death comes and dissolves the body to dust—and now, what does Reason say? how can she demonstate that that soul, which, all along from infancy to age, was affected so intimately with every fortune of the body, shall not be dissipated into nothing when the body crumbles back into dust? or, at least, when the body returns again to form a part of its original earth, how can all the philosophers in the world give any certain proof that the soul does not return to its original, to be absorbed and lost in it, retaining no more individuality than the crumbled body that mingles with the common earth?

You perceive Reason can do nothing with the question of a future existence—she has no materials to work with. She cannot give an item of certainty whether the soul survives, or becomes involved in the ruins of matter. Reason cannot bridge the gulf that lies betwixt this world and another.

But the philosopher tells us there are some grounds of *probability*, if not of certainty, that the soul shall survive death and inhabit another world. And this probability, this perhaps, this lean and trembling peradventure, is Philosophy's security for another life! This is her foothold on eternity! I appeal to the wants and aspirations of any soul that ever lived, if this is not an insult to it. What! die on a probability? my soul staked on a per-

haps! my whole eternity hanging on a mere, uncertain
probability! If that foundation meets the wants of any
human soul, that fact alone would make me doubt
whether such a soul can be immortal: if it has no more
reason in it, than to be willing to die on a bed of "*probability*," it seems hardly worthy of an immortal existence, or reasonable to suppose it shall have it.

But, says the reasoner, the soul has some qualities
about it—qualities of reasoning, of enjoyment, of advancement indefinitely in knowlege and felicity—which
would seem to make it worth preserving for ever. What
does this mean? Worth *whose* preserving? Who wants
it to live in eternity? Who *needs* it, and would suffer a
loss if it should cease to exist? You talk of God as if
he were a man, and would lose some of his property or
advantage if a soul should go into non-existence! Let
it go, and God has lost nothing. He can instantly make
another soul as valuable, as noble, and with as high and
far-reaching aspirations. You cannot reason for God.
For aught you know, the infinite Creator has some mysterious purposes to answer by the soul's existence here
for a little while; and when those purposes have been
accomplished, will annihilate it. We solemnly protest
against your *reasoning* about God as if he weré a man—
reasoning that something is so valuable to him that he
will take care to preserve it! Reason cannot touch the
matter. Your very probability trembles and shrinks
into a corner before that great truth, the infinitude of
God, the incomprehensibility of his plans and purposes.

But Philosophy (unwittingly, I believe, very often
undesignedly, not knowing that she is giving the first
lesson to make her disciples materialists, or some other
kind of infidels) does not like to have the nature of God

come in, and therefore she takes her appeal to the "nature of things." She says, *e. g.*, the soul must be immortal because it is immaterial, and therefore indivisible, and therefore indestructible. She says we have no idea of destruction but by division—as a tree is destroyed when it rots down—as a rock is destroyed when the lightnings, the frosts, the winds and rains have shivered it into pieces, and allowed it to be rock no longer—as the human body is destroyed when the putrefaction of the grave has dissolved it, and divided it into particles among the common dust. Division, she says, is indispensable to destruction, and as the soul is indivisible it must be indestructible. How can she prove that division is necessary to destruction? She cannot. It is an assumption. For aught we know, any existence, body or spirit, can as easily perish all together as perish by division. Yea, division, as far as Reason knows, can make nothing perish. Divide your tree. Has any of it perished? Divide it again. Has any of it perished? Keep on with your division till the minuteness of the particles makes further division impracticable. Has any of it perished now? Not a particle. Every atom exists somewhere, or at least you cannot prove the contrary. You said the soul must be immortal, because it is indivisible; but now it appears your argument does not even touch the question of perdition at all—or if it does, you have as much proved the eternity of *matter* as of mind, and so far established an equality betwixt the two. This is the result of appealing from the nature of God to "the nature of things," as Philosophy is fond of doing—and, I must add, heresy is fond of copying her example.

This appealing from faith to "the nature of things,"

as it is called, is a very delightful affair to two classes of minds—superficial ones, and skeptical ones. It is not the *nature* of the soul that makes it immortal. Matter is as much eternal by its nature as the soul is eternal by its nature. Neither of them has any thing wrapped up in its *nature* which secures it an immortality.

The argument for our future existence, which is taken from the *spiritual* nature of the soul, is another of the attempts of the *wisdom of the world*. We need not expand the argument. To state it will be quite enough. It is this: The soul must survive the dissolution of the body, because the soul is capable of ideas, conceptions, thoughts; and a thing of such capabilities is altogether superior to matter, and can not, therefore, be involved in the dissolution of the body. What an argument! How do *you* know it is superior to matter? It is to *you*, but how do you know it is to *God?* It seems so to you, but who can tell how it seems to Him? Your reason knows nothing about it. This is one link in the argument. But there is another. Beasts think. Nobody would venture to affirm that they are mere machines, self-moved. What, then, becomes of them when they die, on your ground that nothing capable of ideas and thoughts can perish? Ah! the reasoner, full of his philosophy, stands in his study among his books, and specimens, and apparatus, and contemplates his hold on future existence. He says: I know this *body* will die. It is doomed to the dust, and cannot avoid it. It will be taken to pieces—dust returning to dust, and ashes to ashes. But within it there is an indestructible principle. It *must* be indestructible, because it thinks—it is spiritual —it has ideas and conceptions, and therefore qualities of inconceivable value, far too precious to perish. So he meditates and reasons. Then let him leave his books, and go out into the fields among the herds that crop the grass, and meditate and reason there. This ox, says he, this ox—yes, I know his body will die; it is doomed to the dust, and cannot avoid it. But within him, this ox has an indestructible principle—it must be indestructible, because it thinks, it has ideas and conceptions, and therefore qualities of inconceivable value, too precious, far too precious, to perish. This ox and I, precious creatures—this ox and I are the children of immortality, destined to an imperishable existence in another life. This is the argument of spiritual value. If it is good in the library, among the books; it is just as good in the field, among the cattle. The proud reasoner, therefore, finds what level his immortality stands upon. As an immortal being, to survive death, and live beyond it in some future state, he stands on the same level, according to his own argument, as a beast. With a mere philosophy, after all her thirsting for a future existence, and attempts to demonstrate it, darkness and perplexity hang round the bed of death, and rest like an ocean of midnight over all the eternity beyond it. *The world by wisdom knew not God.*

The doctrine of Immortality which the Bible advances, is not founded on any metaphysical ideas—not on any ideas of valuable qualities in the soul, even. Far from it. Our revelation founds the doctrine on a basis firm enough to sustain all that rests upon it. That basis is simply the will of God. I recollect no other idea than this in the whole Bible. The Bible assures us of a future existence, because such is the will of our Creator. This is all. Immortality hangs solely on the naked will of God.

The disciple of Christ, therefore, is not condemned to tremble amid a few items of probability, gathered from the nature of things, every one of which sinks into nothing the moment the mind recurs to the nature of God, which gives him an infinite supremacy of will above all that is or can be in the nature of things. The disciple of Christ is not compelled to float and fluctuate betwixt hope and fear, doubt and confidence, and be tossed about upon a shifting ocean of probabilities, and possibilities, and conjectures, at one moment seeming to have got foothold upon the rock, and the next moment dashed off again by some wave of uncertainty, or some dark billow of doubt. The disciple of Christ rests his immortality upon the rock. Such is the revealed will of God.

2. We turn from human duration to human *duty*. Every body will admit there is such a thing as duty. Every reasonable man acknowledges that religion has an intimate connection with it. It is an important part of religious instruction to tell us what our conduct should be.

Now, on this important matter, how far can the unassisted wisdom of man go. She can not go into eternity, certainly, for her materials, for we have just seen that she can not reach eternity with even her conclusions. She must take her stand here upon the earth, then, and from what is visible around her, she must find facts to teach what is duty, to teach it in the way of a reasonable conclusion.

We admit, she may do something by a mere philosophizing. Man is a social being. As such, obligations rest upon him. Truth is beneficial to society, and therefore men ought to speak truth. Kindness is beneficial, and therefore men ought to be kind. Gratitude is beneficial, for if men will be ungrateful, they will discourage a beneficence and charity which are very much needed in such a world as this; and therefore men ought to be grateful. Thus Reason can argue for a little way, we admit; and we have no disposition to quarrel with her conclusions. But there is a weak point in her argumentation, and there is a spot beyond which she can not conduct us; and beyond that spot (it may be) lie our most important duties and interests. Let us see.

There is a weak point in her argumentation. Just notice on what her argumentation turns. It turns on benefit—as truth is beneficial, gratitude is beneficial, kindness is beneficial, to society; therefore truth, gratitude and kindness are duties. This is the reasoning.

But now, let me put a very plain question to this *wisdom of the world:* May I do whatever I deem beneficial to society? or if I may not be the judge of what is beneficial, who shall be? If benefit or utility is to be the criterion of duty—here is a man a great deal richer than any man ought to be for the good of society. He has vast possessions—vast amounts of lands, houses and gold. But he keeps all to himself; he gives away nothing; he lives at ease, though very well able to work; he receives rents which his tenants can very ill afford to pay, and which he can very well dispense with; he rides in his carriage, though strong and vigorous enough to go on foot; he has vast grounds around him, which he keeps covered with a forest, and which might furnish food enough to feed a hundred poor families around him, if he would allow them to go in with axe and cut away the trees, and bring the plow, and the hoe, and the sickle, to produce and secure a crop. But

he will not allow it. He will neither do it himself, nor
allow them to do it. Besides, though he has got a thousand-fold more than he needs—more than he uses—he
is growing richer and richer every day, and never does
any other good with his riches than to live at his ease,
and perhaps in a luxury which will ruin his health and
shorten his life. Manifestly, it is not useful, not "beneficial to society," that this man should have so much
wealth, particularly when he makes such a use of it.
May I, therefore, just take some of it away from him?
May I enter his grounds, and cut down his trees, and
sow wheat, and plant corn, and thus turn his useless
forest into a useful field? Or if I may not do it alone,
may Society do it? May the government of the State,
just for the general good, lay hands upon his wealth,
and divide it among those that need it, and leave him
only such a portion as they judge best, on the whole, for
him to possess? If this philosophy of "utility" says
"no," I ask, why not? Her argument turned on the
point of benefit, of utility ; and since it would be beneficial to have this old miser's wealth divided among the
people, where it would do some good, why not divide it,
since he never will? How far is this argument of philosophical utility to go? where shall it stop? who shall
enforce its conclusions? You perceive there is a weak
point in it—there are several weak points. And I have
never yet heard of any natural religion which could
ever suit itself in the application of its own reasonings,
even on mere social duties and obligations.

The ancients, full of the world's wisdom, tried it.
First, they maintained that a private man had no right
to deprive such an affluent man of his affluence, because
that affluence had been of no detriment to any one private

man in particular, and, because, if private men should undertake to do it, they would be sure to quarrel among themselves in the division of the spoils. So they concluded society or government might do it; and then kings, who had power enough, took advantage of the philosophical conclusion, and very beneficently robbed the rich, just for the general good.

But when it was discovered by these ancient philosophers (who tried to find out duty by the mere light of nature) that the argument of utility had a difficulty about it, because there were many actions which might be useful and still were very objectionable, they invented another criterion of duty to join with this utility, and thus aimed to make a perfect rule of moral duty. They said, an action must not only be "beneficial" in order to be right, but it must also, at the same time, "look well;" it must be "decorous:" they had their "τὸ πρεπόν," and their "τὸ αγαθόν," the beneficial and the beautiful. They dragged in this idea of beauty to help their philosophy out of a "useful" difficulty. They found that human nature possessed within itself something which revolted from many of the conclusions to which the mere argument of utility would lead. It might be useful to deprive a rich man of his wealth when he had too much for the general good, but then it did not "*look well*," when he had committed no other offense than to be industrious, and ingenious, and frugal, and thus get rich. It might be useful (and this is their own example) for a child to take away the life of a parent when too old and infirm to do any good in the world, but they confessed there was something in such an action which did not "look well"—was not decorous. And, therefore, in order to make a perfect rule of duty, they just joined the beneficial and the beautiful together; an action was right where it was both "useful" and "decorous." This was their religion of nature.

But this, again, was a very troublesome rule to apply. Whose eyes should be used, in order to tell what did "look well," was a difficult question which they could not solve very clearly; but when they finally came to the conclusion that what looked well in every body's eyes must certainly be beautiful, every body chose to think war, slavery, and suicide, and revenge, looked well enough to be free from any moral blame. Reason made bad work, you perceive, even in Greece and Rome, in teaching morality ; *the world by wisdom knew not God.*

I am quite willing that the natural religionist should make the most of it, as he finds that man carries along with him in his own soul something which compels him to respect virtue and contemn vice. But as he attempts to *employ* this fact, he labors under two difficulties :

First. This fact only proves there *are* such things as virtue and vice without telling us what they are, so that we are none the wiser about our duties and obligations than we were before; and,

Second. Where shall we stop when we attempt to reason unto righteousness from the innate feelings of man ? If, in spite of all my sinful indulgence, I am still compelled to respect virtue, and, therefore, you draw the conclusion that my Creator designed I should be virtuous, because he compels me to respect it by an implantation of his own, let me apply your species of reasoning to another implantation within me, thus: If, in spite of all my aims to be virtuous, I have that within me which still makes me love vice, may I, therefore, draw the conclusion that the Author of my being will never punish

me for obeying the impulses of his own implantation—
the dispositions with which he was born? If *you* reason
from one implantation, why may not I reason from another? Is not the God of my nature, the God of my religion also? Will the God of religion forbid that conduct to which the God of my nature inclines me? and if
I follow the inclinations which come from the God of
nature, am I to be punished for so doing by the God of
religion? Thus, you perceive, that when we would
apply the argumentation of our natural religionists, it
just leads us into immorality as fast as into good morals ;
or, at least, it brings us into a difficulty from which philosophy can never extricate us. *The world by wisdom*
knows very little. Philosophy can not reconcile the God
of nature and the God of virtue.

But, I spoke of a limitation. Suppose you could find out
by your philosophy, the duties which lie upon you in regard to one another, and as inhabitants of this world; what
can your philosophy, and light of nature, and reason,
teach you about your duty to your God, and as a being
moving into eternity to meet him? I think it reasonable
to suppose these latter duties are the most important.
God is a more important being than my fellow creature.
He made me, as my fellow did not. He owns me, body
and spirit, as my fellow does not. Therefore, my obligations respecting him, who can dash me to pieces when
he will, surely rise above any obligations to my neighbor
over the way, who, at most, can but *kill the body, and
after that hath no more that he can do.* Tell me, then, by
the lamp of your reason, what duties do I owe to my
God? How, where, will he punish me if I omit them?
Where, how, when, how long, will he reward me if I
perform them? Shall I worship him? *How* shall I

3

worship him? How shall I *serve* him? Where *is* the code of my duty? Show me the rock on whose engraving I may read it. Show me the grass, the field, the sky, the cloud, the sea, the clod of earth, the *any thing*, which shall answer any one of these questions, and unfold to me the most important of all duties and obligations which rest upon me. Natural Religion can not do it. However she may be able to grope her way along among men, by some little twinklings of light flung out just to render her darkness visible, she can not take one single step towards God, without walking right into the bosom of a double midnight! *The world by wisdom* can only grope in darkness in respect to the most momentous obligations.

3. From *duty*, we turn to the *character of God.* Men who reason from the mere Light of Nature, certainly present to us some very pleasant ideas. They tell us of the order of this vast universe—how one star does not dash upon another—how day and night succeed each other, exactly adapted, the one to our necessity for labor, and the other to our necessity for repose—how the eye, made to love beauty, may riot upon a landscape, upon the evening cloud, upon the tints and touches of the flower garden, and how the ear, formed for melody, may teach us to say—

> "Sweet is the laugh of girls, the song of birds,
> The voice of children and their earliest words."

All very pleasant: all very good poetry. And the conclusion from all this is, that *God is a benevolent being.*

But there are some difficulties standing in the way of this argumentation. Look at it. A large, very large

portion of mankind are so poor, so oppressed, so hungry,
or so dissatisfied, that they never stop to enjoy the
beauties you mention; and they would be very well
satisfied to have you remove the beauties of the landscape, the tints of the flowers, and the melody of the
bird's song, if you would give them an atmosphere never
loaded with the pestilence, food that never deranges
while it supports, a body never tormented with pain,
and keep their hearts from being pierced through with
many sorrows. They would spare you all the poetry, if
you would take all their pain. If this world does present to our view some things which would seem to prove
God to be a beneficent Being, it also presents other
things, which, to mere Reason's eye, seem to conflict
with that conclusion. To consider human disappointments, human pains, and sorrows, and dissatisfactions,
how few are happy, how many are miserable, how often
we are incapacitated in old age to enjoy the things for
which we labored and studied, and met the buffetings of
the world through all our youth and manhood—and then
to consider how death robs us of all, bows every head to
the dust, and brings us to the spot where the bones are
scattered at the grave's mouth—I say, to consider these
things is enough to make a serious doubt with a reasonable man, (who has not the Bible,) whether it was a benevolent disposition or an opposite one, which inclined the
Author of our being to bring us into existence. How
can the *world's wisdom* solve this doubt? how prove God
benevolent? at least, how *dis*prove that this attribute of
God is very imperfect—disprove that God is of a mixed
disposition, sometimes delighting in our happiness in
years of plenty and health, and at other times delighting
in our misery in years of pestilence and famine? *The*

world by wisdom knows not God.   His character is a
mystery to Philosophy, if not a contradiction.

Take any other attribute of God—yea, *any* other, and
mere natural religion can get along no better. To see
here, unjust princes driven from their thrones—avarice
working out its own punishment—idleness cursed into
beggary—injustice punished by the scorn of the world
without, and the stings of conscience within—ambition
punished by sliding down to the bottom of the hill—
voluptuousness finding its pleasures turned into poisons;
this sight might almost lead to the conclusion, that the
God and Governor of the world is a *righteous* Being, and
has so made us and made the world, as to demonstrate
that he is in favor of righteousness by the punishments
he has affixed to iniquity.   But here comes up another
difficulty out of which the world's wisdom is insufficient
to extricate us.   Not every tyrant's throne is dashed to
pieces—not every avaricious man is gnawed to death by
his avarice—not every idle man is in rags—not every
unjust man is either scorned or stung—not every ambi-
tious man fails of his wish—not every voluptuous man
torments himself first, and kills himself afterward by
his voluptuousness: haughtiness sometimes lives in high
places, and humility in mean ones; unrighteousness
stalks abroad in robes of honor among a community,
where there is not virtue enough to scorn the wicked
holder of a bribe, and make that scorn burn and blister
upon him, till it drives him out of all society but that of
villains like himself; in one word, holiness itself, the
love of God and his truth, brings many people into
intolerable afflictions, and the opposite brings others to
exaltation and felicity.   A man, by the mere Light of
Nature, therefore, will never be able to solve this diffi-

culty, and justify God amid the darkness which enwraps his equity. *The world by wisdom knows not God.*

4. *The pardon of a sinner* rests in the same darkness. Man *is* a sinner. He knows *that;* he feels it. But is sin pardonable? *Is* there—is there *any where,* in all the field of Natural Religion, among all her materials, growing out of all her arguments, is there any proof that a sinner can be forgiven? Where is it? what is it? Show it to me, and lift the intolerable burden from a sinner's soul. Such a demonstration of a sinner's forgiveness is nowhere to be found in all the field of Natural Religion. It is not beamed from the sun; the stars do not twinkle it; the winds do not whisper it; the fields do not promise it; it is not penciled on the bosom of the flower, nor engraven on the bosom of the rock; *the sea saith, it is not in me, and the depth saith, it is not in me.* You can not find a single intimation of *pardon,* where the world furnishes most to exult in, among the bounties and beauties of a smiling earth! And certainly, pardon is not promised by our *calamities:* the storm doth not speak it; the pestilence doth not bring it on her death-wing; the thunder doth not mutter it; it is not hymned in the hurricane; it is not shrieked on the bed of death; it doth not come up in the hollow moan from the deep, damp vault of the grave, the voice of putrefaction and dead men's bones! and you can not hear it in the deep anthem of the ocean, beneath whose waves in the coral cavern, the sailor-boy sleeps with the *sea-weed wrapped about his head*—the waters his winding sheet, the deep roar of the ocean his dirge!

Do you say, *you* would forgive a sinner? Presumptuous man! daring creature! You are not God! Irreverent wretch! how dare you set yourself as a pattern for God to follow? But how do you know you would forgive a sinner, if you sat on the throne? Have you seen all the results of such an act of forgiveness? Can you tell the effects of it upon the government of all worlds? Can you be assured that such an act would not do more evil than good, and that you would not feel bound, if you were on the throne yourself, to execute punishment with the exactest justice upon every offender? You have no right to say you would forgive a sinner; and if you would, you have no right to conclude that the great Ruler of the universe will do as you would. You can not prove that it would not be an *imperfection* in God to forgive a sinner. The innumerable benefits of God go a little way, I admit, to assure us that God loves to bestow favors upon us; but the attributes of God are unfathomable, boundless oceans. You can not traverse them. All nature can not measure them. And it is evidence of impiety and unreasonableness in man, when he thinks to gauge the dimensions of the mind and will of the Eternal One, and, by the mere efforts of his puny reason, come to conclusions for Him who *sitteth upon the throne*. Do you say you have intimations all around you, that God is kind, and you only want him to be infinitely merciful? Do you not want him also to be infinitely just? If his justice gives way, what *security* have you against dropping into hell, however innocent you may be? Do you say you want him to be infinitely merciful and infinitely just at the same time? This idea may be sufficiently answered by the remark, that you have very often yourself found that God will not be what you want him to be, and will not do what you want him to do; but there is another answer: how does it appear in any of the wisdom of your philosophizing, that infinite justice and infinite mercy are compatible with one another, and *can* exist in the same Being? If justice is infinite, where is mercy? If mercy is infinite, where is justice? If either of them is *not* infinite, where is God? And if mercy is not infinite and *alone* too, justice sunk and forgotten, where is your hope, thou sinner against God? You perceive the *wisdom of the world* must be dumb for ever before such questions. The forgiveness of a sinner has neither certainty nor intimation in all that mere reason can reach.

But all these difficulties vanish in an instant the moment Divine revelation comes into our hands. The most reasonable thing, therefore, which a reasonable man can do, is to fling away his Philosophy and cleave to his Bible. The submission of Reason to Faith is the demand of this discussion.

III. *The application* of this subject is extensive. We name only a few items, briefly.

Be on your guard against a style of reasoning on moral and religious subjects, which is fast creeping into our literature and lectures, and, I am compelled to say, into many of our sermons. Every thing is coming to be *philosophized*. Many a minister in the pulpit—shame on him—betrays his trust to the Bible and his God, by teaching religion very much as if it were a mere matter of reason, and human progress, and human discovery, instead of taking God's Word as his authority and instructor, and uttering in the ears of the people, like the old prophets, *Thus saith the Lord God.* Beware of such proceedings. They tend to infidelity. Learn duty from God. The Bible is safe. Philosophy is blind.

Be attached to the great distinctive *doctrines* of the

Bible.   These old doctrines are now sneered at in some
quarters and slided over in others.   But they are foundations.   For true religion, indeed for a decent morality,
you can find no other.   Such doctrines as the depravity
of man, the sovereignty of God, the necessity of the
Holy Spirit, the need of faith in the atonement, of repentance, not simply because sin is against nature, and
society, but more especially because it is against God—
in one word, those doctrines which begin with God, and,
unfolding his character and high sovereignty, place
every thing beneath the infinity of his attributes—these
doctrines, old-fashioned and unchangeable, and these
only, will teach you your right place and guide you to
truth and eternal life.   In his own Word God has revealed his mercy and the mode for our securing it.   It
admits of no innovations, no new developments.   Woe
to us, if we heed not his revelation!   Woe to us, if we
refuse to *bring every thought into captivity to the obedience of
Christ!*   Woe to us, if forsaking these *fountains of living
waters*, we attempt to *hew out for ourselves broken cisterns*
of speculation and *the wisdom of this world!*   Our philosophy can teach us nothing to solace or save.   It
can not know God.   It can not leave duty.   It can not
gild with a single ray of light the bed of death.   It can
not write a promise upon the grave.   It can not bridge
the gulf that yawns betwixt this world and another, and
furnish light and a landing-place on the shores of eternity.

Prize the pure Gospel.   Never say that you can
accept and sign any creed that you ever saw: a sillier
expression never fell from the lips of a fool.   Value the
truth.   It gives you an inestimable privilege, *life and
immortality.*   You are not compelled to say what Cicero
said about future existence: "I do not pretend to say

that my idea is infallible as the Pythian oracle—I speak only by *conjecture.*" Conjecture! probability! what a pall to hang over eternity! what a word to tremble on a death-struck tongue! *The world by wisdom knew not God!* You are not compelled to talk to your families as Xenophon says Cyrus, the king of Persia, spoke to his children: "I know not how to persuade myself that the soul lives in this mortal body, and ceases to be when the body dies. I am *rather inclined to think* that after death it acquires more penetration and more purity." Rather inclined to think! What an idea to wrap round futurity! How insufficient for a *soul*—a soul approaching—perhaps *immortality*—perhaps annihilation! If one of your children dies, you are not compelled to say, as Tully said, in his grief at the death of a favorite daughter, "I hate the gods." You are not compelled to say, as the learned philosopher, Socrates, said to the judges who had sentenced him to death: "And now we are going to part; I to suffer death, and you to enjoy life; and God only knows which is best." You need not die with your soul whelmed in such a sea of uncertainty. If you have faith, you may say, *I am ready to be offered up.* *I know that my Redeemer liveth; and though after my skin worms destroy this body, yet in my flesh shall I see God.* Such is your privilege. Immortality is vouchsafed by the will of God.

But it is a strange thing—yes, it is passing strange—that after the *sure word of prophecy* has been given to us, *as a light shining in a dark place*—after God has made duty known to us, redemption known, salvation, heaven known, and cleared away all the difficulties and darkness which trouble speculation, confound reason, and make mere natural religion useless, leaving us as it does *without God and without hope*—it is passing strange to see here so many immortal souls who have never heeded the words of God's redeeming mercy! Many of you have never obeyed the Gospel! Oh, sinner! impenitent sinner! blind unbeliever! I warn you, in the name of reason and of God, I warn you it is a solemn thing for you to live under the Gospel and not obey it—to have in your hands the book of life, and make it to your immortal soul the book of death! If you obey it, you will live for ever. If you only hear it, and cast off its faith from your heart, its duties from your conscience, and its promised grace from your soul, the day is coming when your Bible will be your accuser at the tribunal of God, and demonstrate your desert of the condemnation of those who *love darkness rather than light;* yea, and your very minister will be to you *a savor of death unto death!* Stop in your mad career! Take not another step towards hell! God, your Maker, calls to you. You *must* believe. You must trust Christ· You must be *born of the Spirit.* Lay your pride in the dust. Dismiss your vain philosophy, for it *pleases God to save them that believe. To-day, if ye will hear his voice.* God grant you ears. *Amen.*

The Truth held in Unrighteousness.

For the wrath of God is revealed from heaven against all unrighteousness and ungodliness of men, who hold the truth in unrighteousness.—
ROMANS, i. 18.

JUST before this text, Paul had affirmed that those only could *live*, that is, could be *saved*, who were justified by faith. He meant to declare what he has elsewhere declared so often—that no righteousness, except that which is of God, through faith in our Lord Jesus Christ, can avail for the justification of men. In this verse he proceeds to assign the reason. The reason is, that God is just. Men must be justified by faith in Christ, if they are justified at all, FOR *the wrath of God is revealed from heaven against all unrighteousness;* that is, God's disapproval of sin, and determination to punish it, are things clearly made known, *revealed from heaven.*

The Apostle does not here tell us *how* this is made known. In other places he has told. He has given us two explanations of it. One is, that the Divine revelation discloses it. The other is, that it is made known by nature—that is, by the natural conscience and reasonings of man, as he studies the things of the universe around him, and studies his own heart. But here he does not stop to explain the method of the revelation. He had just asserted the necessity of faith in Christ, in order to any sinner's justification with God; and in this verse he

assumes it as a fact forced upon the full conviction of
the sinner, that God will punish sin. This is the reason
why the sinner must believe in Christ. He can escape
wrath in no other way.

That man is a sinner, and that God will punish sin,
are among those manifest truths which are proved in so
many ways, and which lie so clearly in man's own convictions and conscience, that they may fairly be assumed
as already known, and beyond the necessity of demonstration.

Paul's reasonings all proceed upon the ground of
God's retributive justice. If such justice forms no part
of the Divine character and Divine dominion over sinners, then it may be admitted that they are ever so sinful, and yet may be consistently maintained that their
justification is possible in some other way than by faith
in Christ who died for them—possible by any work,
moral or ceremonial, by outward rights or their own
good works, as God may appoint. But if sin must be
punished, then pardon, dispensed to the sinner, must
not only be perfectly free and gratuitous to him, but it
can never be bestowed upon him even *as* a gratuity,
only on the foundation of a sufficient atonement. Such
punitive justice, Paul says, is *revealed from heaven*, and
therefore faith is indispensable. The sinner must accept
the atonement which alone God will accept for him *as* a
sinner.

This justice is *against all unrighteousness and ungodliness of men*. It condemns and will punish all immorality
and all impiety. Men who *hold the truth*, even if they
hold it *in unrighteousness*, can not escape.

In the sacred Scriptures, the word *truth* is often used
to signify the system of true religion, all its doctrines,

and all its duties. It is so used here; that is, it is used to signify true knowledge about religion, whether that knowledge is more or less extensive. Such knowledge many do possess, but they *hold it in unrighteousness;* they are unrighteous still, they do not *obey* the truth, and they are not justified and saved.

There may be some doubt whether the apostle, in this latter clause, has reference to the heathen, (as manifestly he refers to them in the twenty-first verse,) or has reference to those who have the written Word of God. We will not attempt to decide that question. But if the heathen are justly condemned because they do not obey the little truth which they *do* know, certainly those under the Gospel may expect a *much sorer condemnation* if they *hold the truth in unrighteousness.*

To *hold,* sometimes means merely to *possess;* and sometimes it means to *confine,* to *hinder,* or *impede.* Its sense can not be mistaken here. Those spoken of are said to *hold the truth in unrighteousness;* they are not benefited by it—they are not justified and saved. It is manifestly implied, that the due influence of the truth which they *do* understand would lead them to righteousness, if they would consent to be influenced *by* truth; and, therefore, their *holding it* must mean that they *hinder it*—they limit its influence—they deny to it its just sway over them.

To this latter clause, with the interpretation we have thus given it, we now invite your attention. We are going to maintain the following proposition:

That the truth, which establishes the religion of Jesus Christ, has no defects which can account for the rejection of that religion; but that its rejection is attributable solely to an *unrighteous* disposition, which refuses to truth its due influence.

This is our theme. We maintain, that, on this ground, so many immortal souls under the Gospel's light are still in darkness, and hasting awfully onwards to the bar of a just God, having no other prospect before them than the *wrath* mentioned in the text.

To substantiate this proposition, we select from a multitude which occur to us, twelve ideas respecting this rejected *truth*:

1. Its powerful nature.
2. Its clearness.
3. Its strong evidence.
4. Its important matter.
5. Its reasonable terms.
6. Its manifest obligation.
7. Its ease of acceptance.
8. Its frequency of solicitation.
9. Its felicity in obedience.
10. Its adapted motives.
11. Its striking arguments.
12. Its feeble antagonists.

These are the items to occupy us now. It would be easy to compose a whole sermon upon each of them. But sometimes it is beneficial to condense and group together into a small space those particulars which would naturally fill up a larger one. Our memories are not very retentive; and most of all do they fail us when we are called on to remember for God and our own salvation. As the preacher expands one idea, the hearer loses the influence of the one which preceded it; and thus the very perfection of the logician diminishes the force of his arguments. We condense, therefore, to mere hints, what might well afford materials for elaborate discussions.

1. The *powerful nature* of truth. The human mind is so formed, that to it truth is omnipotent. The mind has no ability to resist it. The mind is, and must be, in respect to its convictions and conclusions, perfectly passive under it. If the mind only understands it, it can not disbelieve it. Evidence compels assent; demonstration conquers, controls, and carries the mind captive at its will. Just the moment that truth is perceived, and it is perceived to be the truth, the mind can no more refuse its convictions, than the body refuse to feel the fire that burns it, or the frost that freezes it; no more than the opened eye can refuse to see the light of the sun poured on its naked ball; or the ear refuse to hear the thunder that bellows in the heavens. No volition, no purpose, no fixed resolution, has any influence *directly* in the matter. Man can avoid conviction by truth, just as he can avoid burning by fire—getting out of its way, refusing contact with it—and in no other way. So of the frost, so of the light of the sun, so of the thunder. These may be shunned, but not directly resisted. The truth is just like them.

Such is truth to the mind; and such is the means appointed by God for man's salvation. If, therefore, men did not *hold the truth in unrighteousness ;* if they did not, by evil disposition, refuse to it its due influence, it would be impossible that they should be lost. But they avoid truth. They refuse to open their eyes to its evidence. The heart of sin leads the mind off. And even when the mind is vanquished, as often it must be, the sinner will scarcely undertake a single duty of religion, even in external form. He limits truth's influence. He does it in *unrighteousness,* from the evil of his own disposition.

Nothing but such intentional iniquity can resist the powerful nature of truth.

This is the first argument. We could write a book to illustrate it. Let us name to you the outlines of some of the chapters.

One chapter should treat of those whose minds are solicited by different themes of thought, whose libraries contain different kinds of books, who have opportunity to hear different kinds of discussions, but whose indisposition to obey God in righteousness leads them to lend their attention to themes which they know will never influence them towards religion, and deny it to the truths of God.

Another chapter should treat of infidels. It should show that men like Gibbon, and Voltaire, and Volney, and Bolingbroke, and Paine, and Hume, and even Herbert, were ignorant of the contents and evidences of the very Bible they attacked; or else filled their writings with intentional misrepresentations and falsehoods.

Another chapter should treat of men's practices. It should show that society is filled with men, who have Bibles in their houses, and seats in the churches, who acknowledge the truth of Christianity and the obligation of its duties, but who rarely or never attempt to discharge them. Some of them indulge avarice, some sensuality, some pride, some never pray in secret, some never in their families!

Another chapter should treat of men's different tastes in the things of nature. It should show how strangely they use the world. It should tell of the astronomer among the stars, the geologist among his rocks and fossils, of the painter and the poet enraptured among the beauties and grandeur of creation, catching delight and breathing ecstasy every where; and *all* of these minds suffering but ONE KIND of truths to escape them, those truths that lead to God !

These should be some of the chapters. And all of them, combined or singly, we are sure could be made lucid illustrations of the point before us, that nothing but an evil disposition can account for the inefficacy of those truths about duty and about God, which lie in the Bible, and which are scattered every where over creation, and which would vanquish mind, if a heart of sin would allow mind to touch them.

2. The clearness of the system of religious truths.

For the use and influence of mind, according to the very nature of mind, it is not enough that truth should be powerful. It must be clear. No man can justly expect its influence to be quick and common, if it is wrapt in obscurity. But religious truth is not. It is very remarkable, how all the duties of morality and piety are made perfectly plain in the Bible. No man can mistake them, except by evil disposition. Who ever doubted the meaning of the first commandment? Who was ever misled by our Saviour's golden rule? What sinner on earth is ignorant of what prayer means? or ignorant of its duty and its necessity for salvation? Is there a single accountable creature in the universe who can not see, as clearly as he can see any thing, that honesty is right? dishonesty is wrong? that revenge, cruelty, debauchery, irreverence, and disobedience towards God, his Maker, are sins? Not one! No, never a man! They can as soon doubt the light of the sun, or the sound of the thunder. Well, so it is. All the essential truths of morality and piety are clear. We do not know as God could make them any clearer. We do not know as eternity itself shall ever do it. Mind, if a wicked heart does not in *unrighteousness* hold it back from the study, shall understand all the truths essential to salvation, with as much clearness as its very nature will admit. Nothing could make them clearer. In eternity, in heaven, or in hell, a man will not, probably, perceive that he ought to obey God and love him, any more clearly than he perceives it now. He perceives it, or can, and ought to perceive it, as clearly as he perceives his own existence.

What, then, is the conclusion? It is, that *unrighteousness holds truth*, limits, hinders its influence! That an evil disposition, and not any lack of truth's clearness, keeps sinners from morality, piety, and salvation.

This is the second argument. We could write another book to illustrate it. Let us name to you some of the items in its table of contents.

One chapter should compare the science of religion with human sciences. It should show, that there are none of the human sciences (no, not even the science of mathematics) so clear. Some of you are scholars. You recollect the mathematical demonstration of the continual convergence of two extended lines, which can be infinitely extended, and always approaching each other, and yet, in all that infinite extent, never meet. Your mind sees no defect in the demonstration; every link of its chain looks firm as steel. But think of it. Your converging lines were, at first, but a single inch from one another. They are extended onwards and onwards, and perpetually approaching each other to an infinity. What have you, then, but *an infinite inch?* a single inch in measure, which you shorten for ever and ever, and never exhaust your diminutive little inch? Our chapter should show, that there is not a single essential truth in religion so difficult for the human mind to perceive with clearness, as this. And yet, men act in difficult sciences, and refuse to act in an easy religion.

Another chapter should be entitled, "Commerce." It should show that men of trade are acting every day, and must, (if they act at all,) act on the basis of information, whose clearness has no comparison with the clearness of the most difficult truths in religion. Yet, they neglect a clear religion, and attend to a cloudy commerce.

Another chapter should be entitled, "Political Economy." It should have two sections in it. The first one should attack the very foundations of Smith and Malthus, and the rest, maintaining that the "wealth of nations" consists in the *piety of the people;* and that this truth about the value of religion is more clear, (substantiated, as it is, in all the history of human poverty and competence,) than are those truths on which these writers have founded their systems, and on which men are constantly acting.—The second section should illustrate the fact, that there is no principle of Political Economy so clear, as is the sense and propriety of that question of Jesus Christ, *what shall a man be profited, if he shall gain the whole world, and lose his own soul?* And all the chapters of this book should combine to show, that men in every department and occupation of life are constantly acting on systems of truth, which are less clear than all the truths essential to salvation.

The cause, therefore, of your impiety, if you are an impious man, is not that religious truth is not clear, but that your evil disposition *holds* it in, limits it, denies to it its due influence.

Mind has light enough. Religious truth is clear enough. Its light shines on infancy, manhood, and old age. It shines on us in society and in solitude, at home and abroad, in the field of work and on the bed of pain. Its light shines every where. It is on Sinai, on Calvary; it beams upon Lebanon, and along the vales where molder the bones of the prophets. It shines along the track of the Apostles. It enters their jails. It reaches every hut of poverty and ignorance; and there is not a mind so dark, uncertain, and untutored, among human kind, but it may have knowledge enough. If man can know any thing clearly, he can know how to be saved. *Unrighteousness* alone can hinder him.

3. The *strength of evidence* which belongs to religious truth. Mind needs this. It is not enough that the meaning of truth is clear. In order to its proper claim for acceptance, its character *as* truth needs to be evinced to us. And so it is. It is evinced powerfully and variously.

Here is the Bible. I ask history where it comes from? who wrote it? when? where? History takes me back into the shades and among the relics of antiquity. It brings up ancient Chaldea and Persia, ancient Syria and Egypt, and Greece and Rome—their kings, and generals, and conquests—their commerce, arts, and battles. She points me to Horeb, still there with its rock; to the wilderness of sand; to the ruins of cities; to the Lake of Gennesaret; to the Mount of Olives. And thus she compels me to confess, that, if pen ever wrote facts to be believed afterwards, this Bible is to be believed.

Here is the Bible. It is full of prophecies. Every body knows there is but one eye which can penetrate down into the mysteries of the Future. God, not man, can write the history of cities and kingdoms in advance. I ask the traveler what Tyre is now? what Babylon? what Nineveh? what Jerusalem? Tyre, Babylon, Nineveh, Jerusalem, are just what the Bible said they should be. Titus, though its conqueror, could not save Jerusalem's Temple; and Julian, though Emperor, could not rebuild it. Jesus Christ had said, *one stone should not be left upon another.* Ah! this is God's Word. And as centuries march on they are constantly fulfilling more and more of the predictions recorded here, and rolling up an accumulation of evidence down to the period when *time shall be no longer.*

Here is the Bible. Who loves it? The good, the moral, the kind, the honest, the sober; the men of mind and heart such as mind and heart should be; the men of prayer. Who hates it? The bad, the immoral, the revengeful, the dishonest, the men of sin. This evidence is clear. Good men do not love falsehood; and bad men are prone to hate propriety and truth.

Here is the Bible. It takes more venturesome steps than any book that was ever written. It ventures into the inside of every man's heart. It foretells every man's moral history and habits, if left without the Holy Spirit. It tells all man's character, all his wants. It tells what shall comfort him. It tells what it is, that shall satisfy man's conscience, as he is a sinner; shall soothe his fears; gild the curtains of his death-bed; make his grave light, and put alleluiahs into his lips, as his spirit forsakes its clay. This is evidence enough. Every man knows the truth of the Bible, just as well as he knows his own heart and the real wants and woes of his own moral and immortal being.

It is hardly conceivable in what manner the truth of our religion could be evinced to us with more strength of evidence. Miracles could not do it. They have done what they could. Bad men said, when they saw them, that Jesus Christ wrought them by the power of the Devil, and bad men would say it again. *If ye believe not Moses and the Prophets, ye would not believe though one rose from the dead.* The truths of religion have such a strength of evidence that they would perfectly vanquish every mind in the universe, and control all the hearts, and habits, and hopes of sinners like us, if an evil heart did not unrighteously limit their influence.

4. The importance of its matter. This is a thing of necessity, in order to just claim for influence. Man can not be expected to give himself up to the influences of truth, evinced to him ever so clearly, if the matter of the truth is a thing of little moment to him. But religious truth is of moment to him. He sees something of its moment here; and he shall see more of it when the hand of death shall lift the curtain which hangs over the entrance-gate into eternity! Every man knows the importance to human happiness that the morals enjoined in the Bible should prevail. Every man knows, or may know, if he is willing to know it, that the most of the ills which afflict men in health, which diminish their felicities, and enhance their woes, come from their own disregard, or the disregard of other people, for the morality of the Bible. Its truth *is* of moment. If obeyed every where, we should have no murders, no thieves, no bank-robbers and swindlers, no jails, no gibbets, no angry law-suits, no cruel slavery, no slanders, no locks, and bars, and bolts on our houses. May we ask you to study the question, when you have leisure,

how much of the present misery of man is entirely unnecessary—entirely of his own creation? and how great an amount of misery would be no more, if Bible piety and morality prevailed? It is admitted, men would still have religious trials, and fears, and despondencies; men would be sick; men would die. But if true religion prevailed with all men, there is not a living man whose felicities would not be doubled. It would gild every path of life, and make the world and life in it more valuable. But death is in it! And heaven and hell, built for eternity, are separated from us only by a few hours of mingled smiles and tears, and a few death-struggles. In one or the other of them we shall dwell eternally! As far as nature will permit, we shall resemble God or resemble devils! All the felicity of eternal glory, or the wrath of God, revealed from heaven, awaits us! The importance of the matter, therefore, which religious truth brings before us cannot be enhanced. Its matter is more important to men here than any other system to make life happy, from the cradle to the coffin. And after coffins shall be emptied of their tenants, its importance lies out beyond the resurrection of the dead —immortal weal, or immortal woe! All this God says; the mind can understand, the heart fear or hope. Nothing, therefore, but a heart of unrighteousness can breast the influence of such truth as this. It would overwhelm mind, it would control the habits, hopes and aims of every dying sinner on earth, if he were not *unrighteous* in his treatment of it.

5. Its *reasonable terms*. It is difficult to conceive how any body can quarrel with them. Their whole nature is formed on this principle, namely, to make every sinner on earth as happy as he is capable of being, and lead

him to heaven in the best way he could ever get there. The account of their origin is, *God so loved the world that he gave his only-begotten Son.* Let God tell us the terms themselves: *Let the wicked forsake his way, and the unrighteous man his thoughts, and let him return unto the Lord, and he will have mercy upon him, and to our God, for he will abundantly pardon. If any man thirst, let him come unto me and drink, without money and without price. The Spirit and the Bride say, Come; and let him that heareth say, Come; and let him that is athirst, come; and whosoever will, let him take of the water of life* FREELY. What say you, sinner? These are the terms, and what quarrel have you with them? God hath made a free grant of his Son to every sinner that wants him. And if the sinner will turn from his sins (through offered grace), and take God at his word, he need do no more. Are not the terms reasonable? And if you would let reason, and not unrighteousness, prevail with you, this system of kind and blessed truth would instantly bear sway, and set you out on the way to the final city of God.

6. The *manifest obligation* of the truth. Every body can understand that the obligation is perfect and infinite. Man is a creature. He is dependent, sinful and helpless. God is the proprietor of his being. He has made him with a conscience, and a heart of sensibilities, as well as with a mind of intelligence. And (to greater or less extent), sinner and dark as he is, all these faculties, and all this feebleness and dependence, conspire to show him, that if any one obligation is more incumbent upon him than another, that obligation is, *to do as God bids him.* It is impossible that any other obligation should equal this. None ever can; the sinner must have another

God and another Maker first. If he will not obey God, he is doing the worst thing he can do He is a rebel against his Maker. He is unjust, ungrateful! He is battling his own mind, his own conscience, and the better sensibilities of the heart within him! Truth of such obligation would instantly dash the weapons of rebellion out of his hands, if he did not love to be a rebel against God. His *unrighteousness* hinders its influence.

7. Its *ease of acceptance*. We are not going to maintain that it is an easy thing to become a Christian. But we do maintain, that the only great difficulty in the way, lies simply in this, namely, *really desiring to be a Christian*. Nothing hinders a sinner from accepting easily and willingly all the truths of God and all the terms of salvation, except that one thing we have mentioned so often in this sermon—his own *unrighteousness*, his evil disposition. That *is* a difficulty. That is the only great difficulty. God is willing to save him. Jesus Christ is willing to accept him. And the Holy Spirit's influence, if he had not resisted it, would long since have subdued his stubbornness, and brought him to rest sweetly on the mercy of God. But he never *will* rest there, without the special influences of the Holy Ghost. His need of Divine aid is an infinite need. He can do nothing without it. He is a dead man. But he is dead *in sin*. *Unrighteousness* makes him need the special influences of the Holy Spirit infinitely, and in every thing. Oh! that he knew it—realized it. Then he would rely no longer upon his own shattered strength, vain purposes, and unaided attempts to master the sturdy rebellion of his dreadful heart. He would fall into the hands of God. All the sinner has to do, is simply to let God have his

4

heart, and lie down on the everlasting arms stretched out to receive him.   Salvation is so easy, that if a sinner's whole heart seeks it, if he is really willing to have it, the promise of God puts it into his hands.   *Ye shall find me, when ye shall search for me with all your heart.*

8. Its *frequency of solicitation.*   It would be impossible to give you any adequate description of the frequency with which we are solicited towards God and salvation by the truths that meet us.   We are solicited every where.   In every object of vision, in every subject of thought, there is something which would naturally bring religion to mind.   *Consider the lilies of the field,* and their beauty shall teach you, that *Solomon in all his glory was not arrayed like one of these;* the penciling of God's fingers is upon them.   The sparkling diamonds of a summer's morning ask you the question, *Who hath begotten the drops of the dew?*   It rains: How natural the question, *Hath the rain a father?*   It snows: How natural to ask, *the hoary frost of heaven, who hath gendered it?*   It is midnight: You may look upon the orbs of light that lie out on that bosom of blue, and ask of any being but God, *Canst thou bind the sweet influences of the Pleiads? or loose the bands of Orion?   Canst thou bring forth Mazzaroth in his season? or guide Arcturus and his sons?* You are a child, and the lessons of piety are poured into your ears.   You are a youth, and the Bible is put into your hands.   You are a man, and resort to the house of God; and, no older than I am, I am now preaching to you the four thousand five hundred and fourteenth sermon that I have been permitted to preach.   It is impossible to go on with this illustration.   Let me say, and ask you to remember it, that there is no other class of truths

in existence which is so frequently soliciting your attention as the truths of religion. Religion is the lesson of the universe. God's fingers have written it every where. It solicits you at every step, in every breath, in every beating pulse. From this frequency of solicitation, nothing can escape, but a willing *unrighteousness*. This universe of truths, this life of lessons, would gather every body into heaven, if every body was willing to be right. No other thing has any thing like such frequency of suggestion to the human mind as the subject of religion.

9. Its *felicity in obedience*. If it made men miserable, we could not so readily expect men to embrace it. But look at the world. Judge for yourself. Who are the happiest people? You must be blinded indeed by sin, if you can not see that even present felicity is increased by obedience to God. But, go ask the men of God. Moses will tell you that he chooses affliction in godliness before royalty in Egypt. Paul and Silas will tell you that they love that midnight song in the prison. Ask where you will, the poorest, lowest, most miserable disciple of Jesus Christ on earth, and he will tell you that he would not exchange the felicity of his hope in God for all your wealth, and pride, and power, could give him. Why, then, will not *you* be a Christian? You would; the truths of Christianity would vanquish *mind* if the heart of sin would allow mind to touch them. That heart *holds them in unrighteousness*, limits their influence, or their attraction would draw every living sinner to the felicities of forgiveness.

10. Its adapted motives; and,

11. Its striking arguments. (We are compelled to fling away half our materials, and, even then, blend these two ideas together.) Adapted motives—striking.

arguments. That the motives of religion are most perfectly adapted to our condition, and that its arguments
for acceptance is most striking, need scarcely be mentioned to a dying man. Death is an idea which strikes
the mind as no other earthly idea does; and death is a
motive for religion. Religion changes death from an
enemy into a friend. He comes to the believer only to
put him into the arms of Jesus Jehovah, while his stiff-
ened lips are saying, *Come, Lord Jesus, come quickly.*

It is a striking idea, that all these living bodies of this
great congregation, now animate with life, and elasticity,
and vigor, shall be crumbled down into the dust; and,
after moldering among the clods of the valley, shall be
flung up, perhaps, by the spade of the grave-digger, and
scattered to the winds! But what a motive for religion!
God shall gather the scattered particles. The resurrection morning shall reanimate the believer's body; while
those that have done evil shall come forth from their
graves *to shame and everlasting contempt*—the resurrection
of damnation!

If some visitant, from some distant planet where sin
never was, should light on this miserable world, probably nothing would strike him more forcibly, than the
wants and the woes that are in it. That *is* a striking
idea. Strange, strange world! Fears fill it! Tears
are streaming from the eyes of its inhabitants! Hearts
bleed! And, as this race of humanity tread on, covered
with crape, towards the spot where they have buried
their kindred, the most awful of all ideas is the anger of
God—*after death the judgment!* But how adapted the
motives of religion here. Religion tells you, too, of
the strangest things in the universe. One is, that God
can forgive a sinner, and love him, and save him! The

THE TRUTH HELD IN UNRIGHTEOUSNESS.

other is, that if the sinner will accept his love and his
Son, all his miseries, from that very moment, shall be
turned into mercies; he never shall have a sorrow too
deep, or shed a tear too much, or die too painfully, or too
quick! *All things* shall *work together for his good.* God
will lead him to heaven in the best way.

For my part, I can not, after repeated trials, think of
any other subject which has such striking arguments
for attention, as religion has ; or think of a single point,
wherein its motives are not perfectly adapted to such a
creature as man. Why, then, does not man attend to
it, and yield to the motives which grace brings down
to his miseries, his sin and his sepulcher, and stretches
out on the bosom of eternity beyond it? There is but
one answer, and the old one: these truths are *held in
righteousness.* Nothing, nothing but wickedness hinders
their influence from urging every dying sinner to repentance and salvation. Who can doubt, that this sturdy
rebellion needs the direct influence of the Spirit of God?

Finally ; the *feeble antagonists* of this truth. The rejection of true religion would not be so wonderful, if the
things which oppose it were not of such meanness.
Wherever you find them, you find they are little in
themselves, mere trifles, the veriest dreams.

We have already alluded to that infidelity, which
openly denies the truth of Christianity, and whose most
gifted champions, in every chapter of their arguments,
expose either their contemptible ignorance, like Herbert
and Bolingbroke, or their intentional falsehood, like
Paine and Gibbon, or both ignorance and falsehood
together, like every flippant fool, who glories in dogma-
tizing over others, as weak and wicked as himself. All
these have expended their force, and the strongholds of

Christianity are unshaken. A mere scholar in the Sunday-school can often confute the champions of infidelity. But that opposition to true religion, which is most influential, is to be found in the pleasures and promises of sin. And, let any man think, what are these? How strong an argument for irreligion do you find in the oaths that come from the blasphemer's lips? in the dishonesty, which ends usually in disgrace and prison? in the rags, poverty, and death, of the drunkard? in the little and vanishing pleasure of the theater, the dance, the honors of ambition, and the coveted wealth of the world? For these, and things like these, men neglect religion! And what do they gain? What does any sinner on earth gain, that ought to weigh a feather in that scale of judgment, whereby he decides for the present against religion, and concludes to live on, without prayer, without piety, and without Christ? Hearer, what are *you* gaining, for which you continue to offend God, and expose, every moment, your immortal spirit to his final anger? What would you *lose*, if you should now obey God and live? Ponder it, ponder it well! It does seem to me, that one of the most marvellous things in the universe is this, how a rational being can, for all that sin, and Satan, and the world can give him, neglect, for a single hour, to set his heart fully to seek God! *Is* he rational? Is he *not* a madman or a fool? See what trifles he is after! what dreams! what bubbles! what vanishing visions! what nothings! And these are the antagonists of religion! For these he lives! for these he dies for ever, smitten with the frost *of the second death!* Truth would have saved him, if his wicked heart had allowed it.

We have done. As much as possible, we have condensed these articles, and the argument is closed. It shows, that there is no defect in religious truth; and the rejection of the religion of Christ, of pardon, of holiness, and heaven, is to be accounted for only on the ground of a sinner's own loved and voluntary wickedness of heart. Let the rejecters remember, that *the wrath of God is revealed from heaven against all unrighteousness and ungodliness of men, who hold the truth in unrighteousness.*

My hearers, you ought not to reject this truth and its salvation. Be persuaded to yield to it. In order to eternal life, this truth must prevail. You must heed it. It must conquer your mind, and heart, and will, through the Holy Ghost, and lead you in a new and living way. It is the instrument of all the good that God has to bestow upon sinners. *Sanctify them through thy truth, thy word is truth*, is a passage in the Saviour's prayer.

For proclaiming this truth, this ministry exists, and we come here this day to set over you, in the gospel of Jesus Christ, the man of your own choice.* With his full heart's consent we give him to you, in the name *of our God and your God, our Father and your Father.* We know he will be an able and faithful minister of the New Testament. We know he will love you; and both our faith and our knowledge of you would be at fault, if we did not add, we know you will love him.

Come, hear his words. Standing on the high vantage-ground of this truthful Gospel, with trained mind and holy lips, he will demonstrate to you the justice and the mercy of God. He will tell you the best news your ears can hear. He will prove to you that God loves to save sinners, loves to forgive them, to adopt them into his

---

* Preached at the installation of *Rev. J. M. Sherwood*, at Bloomfield, N. J., and also at the installation of *Rev. Wm. Van Dyke*, at Brooklyn.

family, and invite them to pour their sorrows into his
bosom. He will render you familiar with such names
as Bethlehem, and Bethany, and Nazareth, and Jerusalem; and, pointing you to the blood-dyed wood, the
vinegar and the gall, the nails and the spear, he will
demonstrate to you that the most needless of all calamities in the universe is the loss of a poor sinner's soul!
He will go with you along the path where Joseph of
Arimathea bore the mangled body of the Son of God,
and lead you down among the bloom and roses of that
garden where *there was a sepulcher*. And then, leading
you away over Mount Olivet to Bethany, and pointing
you to the glory that lingers around the ascension-track
of the Redeemer of men, he will aim to conquer you by
the love of God, and allure you up to brighter worlds
on high. His argument will defy your despair;

> "*Sav'd!* the deed shall spread new glory
>   O'er the crowds, the throne above;
> Angels tell that blissful story,
>   A sinner sav'd—our God is love."

And, having pointed you to that bright ascension-track,
he will invite your ear to listen to that mingled melody
that comes floating down from the lips of saints and the
lyres of angels—

> "From the highest throne of glory
>   To the cross of deepest woe,
> All to ransom guilty captives—
>   Flow my praise, for ever flow."

Would you go up in that bright track, and join in that
happy song? Come in hither from Sabbath to Sabbath,
and hear the minister we give to you to-day. From the
Bible truth, if you will not *hold it in unrighteousness*, he

will give you such consolations as dying sinners need—
as deathless spirits long for.

Come here, ye guilty children of the fall, be made
heirs of God, and joint-heirs with Jesus Christ.

Come here, ye pious, love truth more, and Jesus Christ
more. Pour your prayers around these altars, and
depart with the song, *I shall be satisfied, when I awake
with thy likeness.*

Come here, ye worldly, never-satisfied and often miserable ; let this Gospel of truth correct your error—*love
not the world, neither the things that are in the world.*

Ye rich, often-tempted, and tried, and miserable, bit-
terly learning how hard it is for a rich man to enter into
the kingdom of God; come, hear this truthful Gospel;
it shall tell you of *durable riches, even righteousness.* Ye
may be saved, for *with God all things are possible.*

Ye poor, oppressed with daily toil, and afflicted and
tearful, come, hear this Gospel, for *God hath chosen the
poor of this world, rich in faith, and heirs of the kingdom.*

Ye strangers, separated from the homes and churches
of your childhood, while

"Mountains rise, and oceans roll between,"

we invite you to this house of God, and the hopes of
this Gospel. Though you worship not by the altars of
your fathers, and may not sleep beside them in the
sepulcher, come, learn *righteousness,* and you shall meet
the whole family of your pious kindred in heaven.

Come, ye ignorant, this Gospel is for you. The
words of Christ shall teach you, shall dissipate your
darkness, and bring the balm of comfort to your
troubled bosoms.

Come, blooming youth, this message is for you;

4*

come, make your home in this house of God; its ministry will proclaim to you the promise: *those that seek me
early shall find me.*

Come, little children, the Gospel is for you; here you
shall be told of that Saviour who took little children in
his arms and blessed them, and said, *Suffer little children
to come unto me, and forbid them not, for of such is the
kingdom of heaven.*

Come, ye aged, trembling with the palsy of the tomb!
come here and learn your departing song: *Lord, now
lettest thou thy servant depart in peace, for mine eyes have
seen thy salvation.*

Come ye, *holding the truth in unrighteousness*, ye pro-
fane, ye careless, ye bold and stout-hearted, be persuaded
to frequent this house of God, *make you a new heart and
a new spirit, for why will ye die? though your sins be as
scarlet, they shall be as wool; though they be red like crim-
son, they shall be made whiter than snow.*

Come, any sinner, of any condition, any dying mortal,
come; yield up your *unrighteousness;* this Gospel shall
pour words of comfort upon your ear. Obey it, and
you shall pass through life's trials, and through death's
dark stream, sweetly singing, *In the time of trouble* HE
shall hide me in HIS *pavilion; in the secret of his tabernacle
shall he hide me.*

God grant these blessings here, dwelling in these
courts, henceforth and for ever. *Amen.*

The Magnificence of God.

Thus saith the Lord, The heaven is my throne, and the earth is my foot-stool. Where is the house that ye build unto me? And where is the place of my rest?—ISAIAH, lxvi. 1.

IT is often beneficial, when we are studying the sacred Scriptures, to examine minutely all the circumstances under which the part we would understand was penned. Such circumstances may throw light upon the text. They may explain its imagery, and thus give it a vivid-ness and force unseen before; and they may unfold its design, and thus guide us into a just application of it. But this is rather the office of the scholar, than of the preacher. The Apostles, Jesus Christ himself, seldom labored much on the circumstances of the passages they quoted from the Old Testament, if we may judge from the specimens of their preaching recorded in the New. They took the fact, the command, or the promise, as it stood, and, without any elaborate display of scholarship, employed it for the purpose in hand.

We now follow their example. We have not time for any thing more than an attempt to lead you to understand and apply the sentiment expressed in this text.

Please to notice the subject of remark here, and the manner in which it is remarked upon.

The subject of remark is, God himself. The prophet

is sent to exclaim, *Thus saith the Lord, the heaven is my throne, the earth is my footstool.* The attention is turned simply, to God—his grandeur, his magnificence, if you please, his immensity, his omnipresence. He abides in heaven, he puts the earth under his feet.

The manner in which the remark about God is conducted, is that of a kind of contrast betwixt him and men. *Where is the house that ye build unto me, and where is the place of my rest?* God is unlike man. He challenges any comparison. *The heaven, even the heaven of heavens, can not contain him.* Ancient kings aimed often to impress their subjects with an idea of their magnificence, and surrounded themselves with a solemn and salutary awe, by rearing palaces of the most imposing splendor and magnificence. They wished to overawe the multitude. On this ground, God himself seems to have ordered the unequaled grandeur of the ancient temple. But in doing it, he took care that its dazzling beauty and stateliness should only be an aid, a stepping-stone, to assist the imagination in its upward reach towards the grandeur of God. In the prayer of the dedication, Solomon's devotion soars infinitely above the temple. Here, the majesty of God, and the littleness of man, stand side by side. After mentioning the *earth* and the *heaven*, God says, *All these things hath my hand made.*

But yet, lest dread should too much terrify the worshiper, or a high and just idea of God's infinite majesty should lead the humble into the error of supposing that such an august Being would not regard such an insignificant creature as man, he adds, *To this man will I look, even to him that is poor and of a contrite spirit, and trembleth at my word.* A turn of thought well worthy of our admiration. A contrite sinner has nothing to fear from God. His very majesty need not terrify him. Indeed, his majesty constitutes the very ground for his encouragement. It *can* condescend. It operates *by* condescension. Just as much does the *King of kings and Lord of lords* glorify himself, when he consoles, by the whisperings of his Spirit, the poorest and most unworthy sinner that ever felt the pangs of a bruised heart, as when he *thunders in the heavens* as the *Most High*, and *gives his voice, hail-stones and coals of fire.* With this idea, sinners should approach him and meditate his grandeur. In his kindness, in his pardoning mercy, in his condescensions of grace, he displays the ineffable majesty of his Godhead—reaching as far down to a penitent creature's littleness, as he reaches up above his imagination.

First, therefore, we direct your attention to the *style* of the text. What we mean is this: God speaks of himself. He seems to aim to fix the mind on *Him* as the subject of contemplation. *The heaven is my throne, the earth is my footstool.* This style of religious address is especially common in the Scriptures. We dare not undertake to describe it, and descant upon it. We can only give the fact in the language which no mortal pen has ever yet equaled, or ever will. There is something peculiar in this.

Hear *David*, when, in a style resembling the text, his mind soars to God: *O, Lord, thou has searched me and known me. Thou knowest my down-sitting and mine uprising: thou understandest my thought afar off.* . . . . *Whither shall I go from thy Spirit? or whither shall I flee from thy presence? If I ascend up into heaven, thou art there; if I make my bed in hell, behold, thou art there. If*

I take the wings of the morning, and dwell in the uttermost parts of the sea; even there shall thy hand lead me, and thy right hand shall hold me. If I say, surely the darkness shall cover me; even the night shall be light about me. Yea, the darkness hideth not from thee: but the night shineth as the day, and the darkness and the light are both alike to thee. For thou has possessed my reins; thou has covered me in my mother's womb. I will praise thee, for I am fearfully and wonderfully made: marvelous are thy works, and that my soul knoweth right well. What a chapter upon God! what an amazing chapter!

Hear *Job: I have heard of thee by the ear; but now mine eye seeth thee. Wherefore I abhor myself, and repent in dust and ashes.* Again hear him: *Canst thou by searching find out God? canst thou find out the Almighty to perfection? As high as heaven; what canst thou do? deeper than hell; what canst thou know?* (xi. 7, 8.) *Hell is naked before him, and destruction hath no covering. He stretcheth out the north over the empty place, and hangeth the earth upon nothing. He bindeth up the waters in his thick clouds, and the cloud is not rent under them. . . . The pillars of heaven tremble, and are astonished at his reproof. . . . Lo, these are parts of his ways; but how little a portion is heard of him? but the thunder of his power who can understand?* (xxvi. 6–14.) *Gird up now thy loins like a man; for I will demand of thee, and answer thou me. Where wast thou when I laid the foundations of the earth? . . . . when the morning stars sang together and all the sons of God shouted for joy? . . . Hast thou entered into the springs of the sea? . . . hast thou seen the doors of the shadow of death? Canst thou bind the sweet influences of the Pleiads? or loose the bands of Orion? canst thou bring forth Mazzaroth in his season? or canst thou guide Arcturus with his*

*sons ? . . . Canst thou send lightnings, that they may go,
and say unto thee, Here we are ?* What sketches of God!
what unequaled sketches! How diminutive and mean
does man appear before such an incomprehensible Being!

Hear *Isaiah: Who hath measured the waters in the
hollow of his hand, and meted out heaven with a span,
and comprehended the dust of the earth in a measure, and
weighed the mountains in scales, and the hills in a balance ?
Who hath directed the Spirit of the Lord, or being his coun-
selor hath taught him ? . . . Behold the nations are as a
drop of the bucket, and are counted as the small dust of the
balance. All nations before him are as nothing ; and they
are counted to him less than nothing, and vanity. . . . .
He sitteth upon the circle of the earth ; . . . he stretcheth out
the heavens as a curtain. . . . Why sayest thou, oh Jacob,
and speakest, oh Israel, My way is hid from the Lord, and
my judgment is passed over from my God? Hast thou not
known ? hast thou not heard, that the everlasting God, the
Lord, the Creator of the ends of the earth, fainteth not,
neither is weary?* (Chap. xl.)

These passages all have a resemblance to one another;
and they all resemble the text. They all speak of God,
and speak of him in a style which we can not attempt to
analyze. Their aim appears to be two-fold. First, to
lead us to make the idea of God himself the leading idea
in religion; to have it preside over the whole system
and pervade every part of it; just as if a correct idea in
religion could not even exist without it. And, second, to
have this idea, which we are to entertain about God, an
idea of the utmost grandeur, of the most amazing magnificence, and solemn sublimity. So the Divine writers
speak of God. So they aim to have us filled with the
awe of him. So they place his ineffable grandeur to

preside over religion and animate the whole. This is their style; this is the style of the text.

II. The design they have in view can not easily be mistaken. They would give us just ideas of God. The impression they aim to make is simply this, that God is incomparably and inconceivably above us—an infinite and awful mystery! We could name to you a philosopher, (and his name is too famous in history to be spoken of by us with any disrespect,) who has maintained that the mode in which men are to arrive at the most just idea of God, is to suppose a man clothed with every possible excellence of character, wisdom, equity, goodness, justics, and so on; and then to suppose these excellences all united in the same being, and extended and exalted beyond measure: that Being, he tells us, is God. There may be some truth in this. We are such creatures of littleness, that our imperfections seem to need some gradations, some stepping-stones, some scaffoldings, to conduct us up to the Deity. And in the sacred Scriptures, this mode may have some few exemplifications. But after all, this is not their ordinary style. More commonly, they adopt an opposite one. At a single dash they portray an infinitude. At once they introduce us to an infinite mystery. Instantly, when they would give us a just impression about God, they bring up something to show that he is beyond description, beyond mind, beyond all conception, *that high and lofty One who inhabiteth eternity.* This is their aim. They form no comparisons. They are not accustomed to conduct us on little by little; and, through steps and resting-places, and measuring of distances, tempt us to think that we have attained any thing like a comprehensive idea of the Infinite One. They rather fling us back from any such mental stair-case:

High as heaven, what canst thou do ? deeper than hell, what canst thou know ? They would impress upon us the inconceivable and awful grandeur of God. Just experience does the same thing.

III. The *call*, the *necessity* of this may exist on different grounds.

1. Our littleness. In the nature of the case, there can be no comparison betwixt man and God. All is contrast—an infinite contrast. At least, we arrive at the most just impression by that mode of conception. You can not form of human excellences any measuring-line for the Deity. You can not stretch it along his character, and apply it to such an extent, that you can ever pause and say, that you have come any nearer to the whole than when you first commenced. After all you can do, there is still an infinity beyond you—just as exhaustless and inconceivable as when you started. All you have measured is not God ; it is no comparison for God ; it is only a diminutive little something which lies in an inexpressible contrast with his immensity and magnificence. Our littleness renders this mode of the Scriptures, of the text, necessary to us.

2. So does our *sinfulness.* Sin never exists aside from the mind's losing a just impression of the Deity ; and wherever it exists, there is a tendency to cleave to low and unworthy ideas of him. Sinners do not think of him justly. Their ideas degrade him. This is the cause of their rejecting so often many of the vital doctrines of religion, and neglecting so many of its duties. For example, the doctrines of human depravity, and the necessity of being born again. They reject these, or think lightly and wrongfully of them, because their low ideas of God have sunk infinitely below the holiness and

spirituality of his character. They do not see their depravity, and see they MUST *be born again*, because they do not see God. Again, for example, the eternity of punishment for the wicked. Men are staggered on this, they doubt it, they sometimes reject it; and all this comes to pass because they have such imperfect and erroneous notions of God. They do not so perceive his ineffable grandeur, holiness, and immensity, as to understand the infinite ill-desert of sin, and understand that any thing short of an eternity of punishment would only be a burlesque on God's retributive government. What is it, in our assemblies, where the solemnity of our business ought to secure a solemnity of mind, where God speaks and we listen, where hang the interests of our immortal being, interests high as heaven and deep as hell; what is it here that allows so many wandering thoughts, so much levity of heart, such lack of homage, and allows so many worshipers to come up hither without earnest prayer, and depart hence, ready, as soon as they have crossed the threshold of the tabernacle, to take up their interest and employ their tongues in the veriest trifles of a contemptible, little world? The same answer comes back upon us. They have no just sense of the awful majesty of God, his magnificence, his ineffable grandeur. Our sinfulness renders the style of the Scriptures, the style of the text, necessary to us.

3. So does our *materiality*, the connection of our minds with material and gross bodies. This connection renders it difficult for us to soar beyond matter. We are in danger of introducing the imperfections of our existence into our religion, even into our ideas of God. Consequently, when God speaks to us of himself, he speaks in a manner designed to guard us from error. He speaks

with an elevation of thought which makes language labor. It is a distinctive mark of our littleness, dependence, and imperfection, when we are so united to matter that the east wind troubles our mind, that the flesh and blood of our mortal bodies has power over us, and often determines our purposes, and decides our happiness or misery, not to say virtue or vice. What more distinct mark could we have of our dependence, of our creature condition, of our helplessness, than when we find ourselves insecure against the very dust which rises from the footsteps of the passing traveler, and may put out our eyes? when the sun may smite us by day and the moon by night? when the change of a few particles of matter in our blood or in our brain, over which we have no control, and which we can not even understand, has an effect to fill our bosoms with hope or sadden them into despondency and gloom? We are such creatures, such beings connected with matter. Being such, it is very difficult for us to rise above the influences of our condition upon our religious conceptions. We are prone to feel them even in our conceptions of God. Consequently, few things are more labored in the Scriptures than the attempt to lift us above this. God will not allow us to think of him as we think of ourselves. We build houses to dwell in. He says to us, *The heaven is my throne, and the earth is my footstool. Where is the house ye build unto me?* We are limited to the world. We can not get foothold or resting spot any where else. We are circumscribed within very narrow limits. But God asks us, *Where is the place of* MY *rest?* He would elevate our conceptions of him above matter, beyond it, out of the reach of its bounds. And even when, in accommodation to our material connection, he speaks of himself as possessing a resemblance to any of our faculties or qualities, so that we may be able to have some little glimpse of his ineffable grandeur, he does it in a mode to carry a caution along with it, and give us, after all, more the impression of a contrast than of a comparison ; and an impression of himself, as a high and incomprehensible spirit. Listen to him. If he speaks of his eyes, they are eyes that *run to and fro through the earth ;* eyes to which the *darkness and the light are both alike,* to which *night shineth as the day.* If he speaks of his feet, they are feet before which *burning coals go forth* when he moves ; and when he rests, which reach from the throne of his loftiness to the earth—*heaven is my throne, and the earth my footstool.* If he mentions his hands, they are hands which take up the *isles as a very little thing,* which *mete out the heavens as a span,* which *weigh the mountains in scales and the hills in a balance,* which *measure the waters of* the ocean *in the hollow of his hand.* If he mentions his voice, it is a voice *full of majesty,* which *divideth the flames of fire,* which *shakes the heavens,* which wakes the *thunder,* which wields the *lightning,* which *breaketh the cedars of Lebanon,* which maketh them *skip like a calf, and maketh Lebanon and Sirion skip like a young unicorn.* Wonderful imagery ! amazing grandeur and magnificence ! God would evidently fill us with an awe of him, and represent himself to our conceptions as unutterably above us, ineffably unlike man, an amazing and incomprehensible Spirit. The influences of our bodily condition render this style of the Scriptures necessary.

4. So does the nature of God. Man is only a creature. He owes his existence to a cause without him. That cause still rules him. That cause allows him to know but little, and often drops the veil of an impenetrable

darkness before his eyes just at the point, the very point, where he is most desirous to look further, and it drops the veil there, in order to do him the two-fold office of convincing him of the grandeur of God and his own littleness, and of compelling him, under the influence of those convictions, to turn back to a light which concerns him, moré than the darkness beyond the veil can, to a light, where are wrapped up the duties and interests of his immortal soul. God would repress his curiosity, and make him use his conscience. Therefore, he makes darkness preach to him. Therefore, he speaks of himself in a mode to admonish every student of his perfections, that he must not think of God as he thinks of himself, but must think of him as un-caused, self-existent, and eternal—as having no derived ideas, but as having such an infinite supremacy that he has no need to observe any thing, in order to know every thing: in his own mind were treasured eternally the models of all that exist. Hence, the mode in which God speaks to man of himself is demanded by the nature of his perfections. His essence, the efficiency of his will, his spirituality, his supremacy, his justice, his mercy, all that belongs to him, demand the ideas of amazement, magnificence, and grandeur—the idea of the text, which we dare not attempt to explain, but only cite other passages to exemplify.

IV. But we must stop on the borders of this ocean of thought. We have only taken a little glimpse : Let us make some little application.

We have seen that God would impress our minds · with an idea of his amazing grandeur—that this object governs the style in which he speaks of himself to us. Hence,

1. Let us be admonished to approach the study of religion with an awe and solemnity of mind which belongs to it. It is the study of God; it is the science of his infinite perfections. He himself has emblazoned it before us, as we have seen, wrapped in the dark grandeur of an amazing imagery! Evidently he would make us tremble. The voice comes from the burning bush, *draw not nigh hither, put off thy shoes from off thy feet, for the ground whereon thou standest is holy ground.* How unlike all other subjects is religion! How differently we should approach it! How little should we expect to prosper in it, in the mode whereby we prosper in other studies; and make genius, judgment, and sagacity, and the talents of discrimination, perception, and other faculties, contribute to our success, on the same principles as they contribute to it in other studies! No, never! never! The first impression should be a solemn awe, mingled with a deep sense of our own insignificance and sin. No sinner need expect to understand religion without this. No sinner need expect to find his pathway up to the Cross, without the aid of the Holy Spirit. Never did a mind take a more unreasonable, more unappropriate, more unpromising course, than does that sinner who studies religion without prayer! Fall on your knees, mortal man! Prostrate yourself in dust, and lift up your imploring cry to the Infinite One, or you can not have either the attitude or the spirit which belongs to the subject, and without which all your endeavors will be vain!

2. This mode in which God teaches us—this grandeur and magnificence which belong to him—ought to remove a very common difficulty from our minds, and prepare us to receive in faith, those deep and dark doc-

trines, whose mystery is so apt to stagger us. What can we expect? God, the infinite God, is the presiding genius of religion. Religion takes all its nature from his nature. Religion is what it is, simply because God is such a Being as he is. If it had no depths about it, it would therefore be false: it would neither come from God, nor conduct to him: it would be infinitely unlike him, and would cultivate in us a set of ideas and impressions, which would be an infinite insult to his amazing magnificence.

It would be superstition, indeed, if we were to receive a doctrine, simply because it was deep and mysterious. But to reject it, for such a reason, when God hath revealed it, is infinitely unreasonable. Deep it must be, if it comes from God, accords with God, or conducts us towards him. As we contemplate the grandeur of God, as we look out on that boundless ocean, without a bottom or shore, nothing should surprise us, nothing make our faith stagger, if God has spoken it. Once lost in his immensity, and flung into our just place, by a just idea of his inconceivable greatness; we can not but understand, that religion can not teach us a single lesson about God, unless it teaches something beyond our abilities fully to comprehend. A reasonable mind will be willing to stand on the borders of this vast ocean, amazed and awed! After this—after God's magnificence, what word of God shall stagger us? After this—three persons in one God—the efficiency of a Divine control closely linked with man's perfect freedom—election linked with human accountability—the incarnation of the Son—the love to sinners which prompted it—Divine justice satisfied with a Divine atonement—none of these mysteries will trouble a reasonable mind; it will be willing to let

God *be* God; and standing, amazed, but comforted and satisfied, on the borders of this fathomless ocean of truth, will be willing to exclaim, *Oh, the depth of the riches, both of the wisdom and knowledge of God; how unsearchable are his judgments, and his ways past finding out.* On the infinite field of religion we are to expect the foot-prints of an infinite God.

3. Since God is so vast a being, how deep should be our humility! Proud man! what art thou? an insect, an atom, a worm of the dust! a vapor! a nothing!

4. How deep should be our homage! At what an inconceivable distance is God above us! We may approach him for ever, and be no nearer! With an unlimited awe it becomes us to regard him! The speculative worshiper, who examines here his truth as he would examine a question of trade, or science—the formal worshiper, with heart untouched and unamazed— the fashionable worshiper, here tempted to allow his thoughts to rove on every vanity—these must depart from these courts under a cloud, if not under a curse! What are they doing? What ideas and impressions have they of God? Let them laugh at the thunder— let them play with the lightning—let them dance to the howlings of the hurricane and over the heavings of the earthquake; and none of this shall be so unappropriate, or so untasteful and stupid, as their presence here, without a deep reverence for God, without the spirit of solemnity and supplication.

5. The greatness of God should gauge the depth of our repentance. Our sin is against him. It has provoked him. It has insulted his infinite majesty. It has poured contempt upon his law, that law which proceeded from his infinite rectitude; and, while it continues

without repentance and turning to God, it pours contempt upon his love, that love which produced the flowing blood of his Son!

6. The greatness of God should invite our faith. His greatness is so vast, that we know he can condescend to us: he can over-step every barrier, and reach down to every depth. Sin, do thy worst—law, muster thy thunders—hell, make thy claims; *if God be for us, who can be against us?*

7. The magnificence of God should be a motive to our service. He is able to turn our smallest services to an infinite account. He will. It will not be long before the poor disciple, who has nothing else to give, shall stand before the *great white throne*, and hear the King say unto him, because thou hast *given a cup of cold water in the name of a disciple*, thou *shalt have thy reward;* and then, on the harvest-field of eternity, he shall gather the fruits of his *sowing here to the Spirit*—fruit, *life everlasting.* The unsearchable God can accept the smallest service, and knows how to make vast and eternal benefits grow out of it, as easily as out of the most magnificent.

8. The greatness of God ought to encourage the timid. Miserable mortal! poor creature of tempestuous circumstances, tossed with fear, shipwrecked in storms, forsaken by friends, pained with sickness, and, after having aimed to live *godly in Christ Jesus* and maintain a good name, aspersed with foul slanders—poor mortal, fear not! The great God reigns! And because he *is* great, his regard reaches to every one of your annoyances. Your enemies can not hurt you. They may pain you; but God shall make them profit you. He *has his hook in their nose, and his bridle in their lips.* Be God's friend, and if your enemies touch you, *they touch the apple of his eye.* Be his

5

friend, and if poverty trouble you here, it shall not trouble you long.

9. The grandeur of God ought to rebuke our reliance upon creatures. All creatures are his. He made them. He governs them. He will govern. Not a sparrow falls, or an angel sings, or a devil blasphemes, without him! We have not, and we can not have, any resource but in him. All else shall fail us. They will soon fail. They are even now failing. Friends sink around us! Hopes perish! We carry the seeds of death in our mortal bodies! And this wide world, and these sweet heavens themselves, shall pretty soon vanish away at the sound of the final trumpet! "Our God in grandeur and our world on fire!"

Oh, give me hope and treasure *in God!* Give me some solid foundation to build upon! Give me my house founded upon the Rock of Ages! Give me this, and soon, when I stand a disembodied spirit on the ashes of a burnt world, and see the *heavens rolled together as a scroll*, I shall be able to say, I have lost nothing! And then, taking my way up to that *Mount Zion which can not be moved*, I shall be able to exclaim, I have gained every thing! Because God, speaking in the grandeur of power and grandeur of grace which belongs to him, has issued the promise to the poor and contrite spirit—*the mountains shall depart, and the hills be removed, but my kindness shall not depart from thee, neither shall the covenant of my peace be removed.* Would to God, that we could persuade every immortal soul here, to give up the treacherous world, and rest itself on the bosom of this vast and gracious God—immeasurably great and immeasurably good.

The Divine Character Pre-eminent.*

Render unto God the things that are God's.—MATTHEW, xxii. 21.

WE do not propose to examine with minuteness the occasion which gave rise to these words of Jesus Christ. It will be sufficient to remark, that they were uttered on an occasion when some of those who disbelieved in his Divine mission sought to *entangle him in his talk.* Passing by the matters of religion, and desirous to bring down upon him the displeasure of the civil government, the *disciples of the Pharisees and the Herodians* were sent to him to ask him, (after some empty and insincere compliments,) *is it lawful to give tribute to Cæsar or not?* Jesus knew their wickedness. He answered, *why tempt ye me? show me the tribute money. And they showed him a penny. And he said unto them, whose is this image and superscription? They say unto him, Cæsar's. Then saith he unto them, Render, therefore, unto Cæsar the things that are Cæsar's, and unto God the things that are God's.* He met their temptation by laying down a great principle. This principle was to give Cæsar his own, and God his own. Rights never conflict with one another. Duties never conflict with one another. Righteousness has no inconsistencies. It is error that is full of absurdities and contradictions, while truth has none

* Delivered before the Synod of New York, at Brooklyn, Oct. 20, 1851.

of them. Religion will blame no man for rendering *unto Cæsar the things that are Cæsar's*, but it demands of every man to *render unto God the things that are God's*.

The text, therefore, implies the necessity of knowing the character, standing or office of Cæsar, that he may receive his due; and the necessity of knowing the standing of God, what God is, that we may render unto him *the things that are his*. To this latter necessity we propose to attend in this sermon. *Render unto God the things* that are God's.

We have no special reference now to any civil or political duties; but we propose to consider the importance, in *religious* respects, of our having just ideas of the being and character of God.

We lay down this principle ;—that, for the purposes of correctness and security in our religion, it is an indispensable thing for us, that we know the character of God correctly, in order to know what to render to him, in homage, service and love—in every emotion and duty of religion. This is our doctrine. We proceed to substantiate it. We name to you only four general ideas: the purpose of creature existence—a correct conscience—the foundation of religion, and the manner in which religious character is formed.

I. God is the Head of the universe, in a sense peculiar and without comparison. He is not only supreme over it, but he made it *for himself.* It exists, all creatures in it exist, not for their sakes, but for his own. *He hath made all things for himself.* He took the motives for his work of creation from his own infinite existence and character, and planned the whole, when nothing existed but himself, standing alone in the solitude of his vast and unpeopled eternity—not a creature to praise him—not a being to move. There *was* nothing but God. Nothing else, therefore, could bring into action his creating power. The universe exists for the sake of God, its Author.

Over this universe he presides. And his *rule* is as peculiar, and as much beyond comparison with any other, as his existence is. He needs no machinery to aid his strength: his will is his power. He needs no study to perfect his wisdom—no experiments—no time. He is infinitely above all this. Indeed, he needs no inspection or examination in order to his knowledge. He has only to have recourse to his own plans—the eternal models of all things, which have existed for ever in his own infinite mind. His control, therefore, is peculiar and beyond all analogy. His volition is his omnipotence—his thought is infinite wisdom—and infallibly he directs all things under his government to the accomplishment of his designed ends.

Now, if we have not these and such like correct ideas of his character and attributes, how is it possible that we should render him his due? He is head over all. He is infinitely and peculiarly supreme. Every thing else may give way, but God will not. The universe must bend to him. He will not bend to the universe. If we have not just ideas of him, to give him his own place, we can not have just homage for his high and eternal attributes, nor take our own fit place in the humility of our littleness, and the unquestioning promptness of our obedience and faith. It would seem, certainly, that if it is important for us to know *any thing* correctly, it must be important to know *Him* correctly, under whose government we are, and who will dispose of us eternally just as he pleases. We want to know his character. We want to know what will please him, and what will displease him. We can not afford to be in ignorance on a point, whereon hinges every duty in time and every destiny in Eternity. Rule, he will. Nothing shall hinder him. The efficacy of his character shall be carried out in the destinies of our future life; and we must know what that character is, if, under his supreme government, and creatures as we are, we would have a single hope to cheer us, as our face is turned towards the opening portals of a never-ending eternity. Ignorance, error on any other point, may be endured; but not here. This is the supreme point. According to what God *is*, the universe must be treated. He is its head. He made it for himself. He will not give it up. It can not be plucked out of his hands. We need to know what that character of God is, on which hinges all that can interest us, as long as eternity shall roll on its vast and immeasurable ages.

We need to have just ideas of God, because he maintains and will maintain a supreme and peculiar headship over his universe and all that is in it. We could dispense with minor matters of knowledge, but not with this.

And just here, therefore, we can not but remark, how far from the proprieties of truth and the prospects of an ultimate benefit those persons do wander, who, in attempting exhibits of religion, fail to exhibit God as he is, and, in accommodation to the taste of the age, descant upon visible utilities merely, on what befits us according to the mere tuition of Nature or the injunction of our social relationships. A very tasteful and polite method of crowding *God* out of his world! In any foundation of moral obligation to be laid by such a mode, there is

nothing stable. Moral essaying, the dreams of an infidel socialism, the fancies of an utilitarian scheming, all
as superficial and silly as they are proud, will not do.
The character of God gone—all is gone! We are afloat
then—out of sight of land—on a sea of midnight—not a
star to steer by! Philosophy is not faith. The world is
not God. The little taper lights of time will go out. We
need the great *Sun of Righteousness* to illume the skies of
eternity. According to what God is, *we* must be, and
the world must be, or rectitude and happiness will
soon perish together.

II. As the creatures of God we are capable of moral
control. We have conscience. We know right from
wrong—not merely capable of discrimination betwixt truth
and error, but capable of discrimination on those moral
matters, about which conscience wields her energies, and
whereon the foundations of divine government do rest.
God is the infinite Governor, the infinite Legislator and
Judge. That system of government which he has ordained, expends its supremacy, not on natural or intellectual matters, things of science, taste or materiality,
but on moral (spiritual) matters; and the ultimate destiny of every being possessed of conscience hangs on
the simple question of the manner in which he uses it.
The felicities and the miseries of a future and interminable life are to be determined by the holiness and the
sin of God's moral and immortal creatures. Holiness
indeed may have much misery on this side the tomb, but
none beyond it. Sin may have much felicity in this life,
but none at all in another. Such are the Law and government of God that the question of *right and wrong*
will decide the destinies of eternity.

Now this law and government, (which are of so much moment to us, which shall fix us unalterably in weal or woe,) this law and government are *as* they are, simply for one reason, namely, because God is what he is. If God were different, law would be different. If we have unjust ideas of God, we shall have unjust ideas of law. If we have wrong ideas of God, we shall have wrong ideas of duty. Then, conscience will be misled, and the misleading will by no means be the worst of the matter : it will be a worse matter, that its exercise, its application, its purity and strength, will be hindered. For illustration—take a naturalist, (I know not what else to call him,) a man who has such ideas about God as to ascribe to him nothing more than a control over visible and material things, and giving laws to us only in respect to the duties begun and ended on these shores of time—a man who judges of God merely by what he sees, as he calls it, by Nature. Such a man may have a conscience about buying and selling, about decency, kindness, and all fit demeanor, down to the last breath of life, and deem it his duty to resign the last breath contented and peaceful. But he has limited his conscience. He has confined it very much to these little and temporary scenes. He has felt it his duty to live well with his fellow-men here, till he has filled up the little space allotted to him; but he has put this minor duty before a greater one—(if, indeed, he has not made it every thing) —he has *not* felt it to be his first and supreme duty to prepare his immortal soul to live well with God and the holy inhabitants of heaven, through the interminable spaces which stretch out beyond the resurrection of the dead, and reach down to the remotest distances of eternity. This is a naturalist's conscience. It is confined : it is trammeled and laid asleep on the *main* points. The man who only consults the rocks and trees, the skies and seasons, the relations of life here, and the results of action here, to teach him duty and impel him to rectitude, *ought never to die !* He is unfit to die. His moral principles and all the moulding of his moral feelings have done nothing more for him, at most, than make him a good citizen of the world, and prepare him to be a very bad citizen of the world to come. His false ideas of God have led him to all this. He did not think of God as enacting a law for us here, for much other reason than to affect our destinies here ; and especially, he did not think of him as enacting a law, which makes every thing beneath the sun subordinate to interests which shall swell out in ever-increasing magnitude on the bosom of eternity after the sun has gone out—extinguished for ever ! Consequently, all of this man's moral sentiments are confined to one field. He has only half, or less than half a conscience. He had false ideas about God to begin with, and they led him into this moral limitation and moral stupidity. He may be partly fit for time, but he is not fit for eternity. He may be fit for an earthly inheritance with men in temporal things, but he is not fit for intercourse with disembodied spirits and with God in the high society of an eternal heaven. He may be fit—partly—partly fit to have a wife here, but he is not fit for that society and those relationships, where *they neither marry nor are given in marriage, but are as the angels of God.*

Just so in all respects. False ideas about God will debauch human conscience. If our ideas about his purity are false, our ideas about his law of purity will be false. We shall never rise higher than our standard.

If we think of God as hating injustice only a little, we shall ourselves feel bound to hate it only a little. So of all else. False ideas of God, as far and as fast as they go, tend to the utter subversion of the conscientious principle. And if it is of any moment to us to understand and be influenced by that system of moral government and law, which shall dispose of the destinies of eternity, weal or woe; of the same moment is it to us, that we have just ideas of that character of God, which makes law and government what they are. His will is the foundation of right—right, never conflicting with the just decisions of science and nature indeed; but making all nature and all science subordinate to ends eternal. This world, this life, with all its delightful scenes—its scenes of poetry, taste, science, and affection; this world, this lifetime, constitute only a machinery, the issues of whose movements lie off beyond the valley of death. To be educated, and trained, and morally molded for this transient scene *only*, will not answer God's will. It will not be right. It will be a training of only half our moral sensibilities and principles, and a misguiding of them even in that half. We are not at home here. Our home lies in another country with God. We need just ideas of his infinite and presiding character.

III. Just ideas of the character of God are important also, because that character is the foundation of all religion. If there were no God, there would be no religion; and if God were different from what he is, true religion would be different from what it is; and if God should change, religion would change. True religion is that system which aims to bring our principles, feelings, and

habits into conformity with God. It is the stamping
of that image of God on the soul, which was effaced by
the fall. We have borne *the image of the earthly :* to be
saved, we must *bear the image of the heavenly. Be ye holy,
for I am holy. Without holiness no man shall see the Lord.
Be ye reconciled to God ;* not to nature, time, society, or
even law, but *to God.* Whatever it is that true religion
embraces within itself, it takes the whole of it from one
eternal fountain—from the depths of the character of
the Deity. We must obey *Him.* We must love *Him.*
We must serve *Him.* We must be like *Him.* To begin
to be so is the only beginning of religion, and advancement in it consists simply in being more and more trans-
formed into his likeness.

If, therefore, we have false ideas of God, we can.not
fail to have false ideas of the very foundation and
nature of religion. Error on this point is fundamental
error. It is error at the fountain-head, at the very
life-spring of the whole matter ; and, according to its
extent, will pervert and poison all the rest. It is not
like error on some subordinate part—some filling up—
or some outwork—or adjunct—some shade or coloring.
It is just building upon *the sand ;* and, when the winds
blow and the storms beat, the whole edifice must fall—
it *was founded upon the sand.*

It will never do for us to think of religion as founded
in the nature of things. It is not. It is founded in the
nature of God. *God is a spirit ; and they that worship
him must worship him in spirit and in truth.* " *Things* "
are only his machinery, temporary machinery. The
present relations of things shall soon be altered. Men
die. The world shall come to an end. The sun shall
go out in blackness. The purpose of religion is not

merely, or mainly, to guide our footsteps, so that we may
not stumble in the rough paths of this life, but to guide
our souls, so that they may enter upon the life to come, in
holy and happy relations and intercourse with God for
ever.   Just ideas of the character of God are important
and indispensable, because *there* lies the very foundation
of religion.

IV. This doctrine, perhaps, may become still more
clear to our mind, if we consider *the mode* in which the
religious character of creatures, like ourselves, is influenced.   We are susceptible of influence from various
quarters, indeed; but there is one fountain of influence
superior to all others.   It is the influence that comes
from our conceptions of God.   This is the supreme
matter in all true religion ; and not only so, but it comes
in to qualify all other influences, which are beneficial in
any part of true religion.   There will be a defect—a
signal if not fatal defect—in all other motives and
arguments, if this does not go along with them.   For
example, all the arguments which you weave to enjoin
the observance of the second table of the law, would be
defective, and could be but partially influential for good,
if you should *forget* that another table of law comes
before it.   The propriety and obligation of *loving your
neighbor as yourself* may have some salutary enforcement,
it is true, as you consider how much felicity would spring
from such an affection, and the acts which flow from it,
and how much misery would result from the opposite
affection.   But this enforcement is not all.   You are
bound to love your neighbor, not merely for his sake,
but for God's sake—not merely for time's felicities, but
for eternity's felicities.   You are bound to feel, and you

need to feel, that, if you injure your neighbor, you offend *him* not only, but God also. The main and most influential idea, therefore, is *gone*, if you only consider your relation to your neighbor, but do not consider that the high and infinite authority of God has itself flung a rampart around your neighbor's rights, which you may not scale. You are to remember, and you need to remember, that if you sin against him you sin against God. In your quarrel with him, if you were unjust to him, you might hope to get along without much trouble, and come off victorious in the end. But if you *are* unjust to him, you have another quarrel. It is a quarrel with God. He will call you to an account. And that idea is indispensable for the just influence of the law upon your heart, and conscience, and habits, and all your character. So that not only the supremacy, but the universal *extension* of the idea of God's character makes that idea a very momentous one. You can not spare it. You can spare it nowhere. It covers, and must cover, the whole field of duty. Blessed be God, if the wicked man would *devour widows' houses*, he must know that the infinite Power above him is the *widow's God and Judge;* if he would defraud the defenseless orphan, and have more courage to attempt it because he *is* defenceless, he must know that He who is the *Father of the fatherless* will hold him *doubly* guilty! I would not have his curse for all the sun shines on! And he would not dare to perpetrate his iniquity, if he had any just ideas of the character of God, and justly felt its influence.

Nothing else can be substituted for this idea. In no spot of duty, in no question of morals, can you bring in any other idea to take the place and answer the purposes of this. Nothing *can* hold its place for an instant.

Nothing can answer its purposes. If you would bring in the authority, and character, and wisdom of man—of any finite being—and hold them up as injunctions to any supposed duty, and tell the transgressor what an authority, what a wisdom, what a character, he comes into conflict with when he transgresses, you have diminished the power of your persuasion to duty, to an extent equal to the distance between finite and infinite— between a creature and God. If you would bring in the nature of things, philosophy, utility, to enjoin duty, and if, doing so, you would show that sin must and will, in the end, work out its own punishment, because of some pervading principle which, in the end, will bring it to misery, you have diminished the power of your persuasion to the full extent of the difference betwixt a principle and a person. God is more than a principle—he is a person. It was not a principle which built hell; God built it. It was not a principle which built heaven; God built it. To be punished by a principle is quite another matter than being punished by a person. To be rewarded by a principle—a principle of utility, of philosophy, of nature (call it what you will)—is quite another matter than being rewarded by a person. A mere principle has got no *heart* in it. It can not love you—it can not hate you—it can not sympathize with you. You can not hold any fellowship with it, as you can with a kindred spirit. You can not pray to it, as you can to God, and lose half your misery by the very act of praying, and the other half by God's answer to his child. Your principles will not do: they will never reach hearts. In morals, as in sociality, we want a place for hearts. What would your home be to you, with all its loaded table, its bed of down, its books, and

all its adornings, if there you could never meet the
smile of "wife, children, or friends"? Cold home! a
hermit's cell! worse than any cabin or cave, and but a
single crust to be shared with some loved one! Cold
religion, too, if we must put out of it that Father, God,
and in exchange for his person take only some *principle*
that can never love us. We want a *friend*—a friend to
lean upon, amid the duties and difficulties of life; and
when we depart out of it, we want something more than
a *place* to go to; we want what Paul had—the privilege
to be *with* CHRIST, evidently to him the best part of his
heaven. The heaven of a principle is only half a heaven,
at best—we want the heaven of a person. We must
not think, therefore, that in any part of our duties we
can take in some idea of utility or philosophy, or I
know not what, and dismiss the idea of God. We need
the whole influence of his character—of his understood
character—of his character known through Christ, who
loved me, and gave himself a ransom for me.

If you examine into the mode in which the Scriptures
aim to affect us, and form our religious habits, and hopes,
and emotions, you will find that they rely much upon
impressing upon our hearts right conceptions of the
Supreme Being. Naturalists, materialists, may quarrel
with them, but still they do it. The superficial, silly
philosopher, who imagines he can work out religion
enough, as he carries his taper into the wilderness of
this world's analogies, may quarrel with them, also, but
the Bible will go beyond all his analogies; it will let
him know there is no analogy for God—he can stretch
no measuring-rod upon the immensities of his being.
And nowhere else but in God himself can he find a sin-

gle gleam of light that shall shine down to the grave's depth, and give hope that

"Beauty immortal shall wake from the tomb."

Examine the Scriptures. How do they expect to affect us? In what mode do they attempt to form our religious character? It is very remarkable how steadily they insist upon the character of God; God revealed in Christ; Christ incarnate, and dying to save sinners through the great atonement; and, if at any time they employ the machinery of created things, they do employ it only *as* machinery. All their sublimity, and poetry, and tenderness, and taste, and kindness, about earthly things, are only smiles to lead us on. They employ the seas and mountains, the storms, and thunder, and stars, only as scaffoldings and stepping-stones to help us away towards that *high and lofty One that inhabiteth eternity.* The sea is HIS, HE *made it* Before HIM, the *nations are but as the drop of the bucket.* HE *taketh up the isles as a very little thing.* HE *weigheth the mountains in scales and the hills in a balance. God is a Spirit, and they that worship him must worship him in spirit and in truth. This is life eternal that they might* KNOW *thee, the only true God, and Jesus Christ whom thou hast sent. Thou thoughtest that I was altogether such an one as thyself, but I will reprove thee and set them in order before thine eyes. Now consider this, ye that forget God, lest I tear you in pieces and there be none to deliver. I remember* THEE *upon my bed; I meditate on* THEE *in the night-watches. It is good for me to draw nigh unto God. I shall be satisfied when I wake with thy likeness. Acquaint now thyself with* HIM, *and be at peace. The kindness and love of God our Saviour towards man hath appeared. Behold I, even I am* HE, *that*

*blotteth out thy transgressions for mine own name's sake.
Like as a father pitieth his children, so the Lord pitieth them
that fear him.   God now commandeth all men every where
to repent, because* HE *hath appointed a day in the which* HE
*will judge the world in righteousness, by that man whom he
hath ordained, whereof he hath given assurance unto all men,
in that he hath raised him from the dead.   I am the Lord ;
I change not, therefore ye sons of Jacob are not consumed.
Be ye holy, for I am holy.   Our God is a consuming fire.*
But we can not go on with such passages.   This principle of quotation would bring in literally more than half
the Bible.   We can not pursue it.   Not only are those
passages which would form our religious principles,
practices, and emotions, by the character of God, of
every possible variety, but the character of God is the
ONE IDEA which presides over all, and without which,
(whatever *you* may have,) the Bible has no reliance upon
any other.

You may find a thousand exemplifications.   When
Peter would silence the scoff of the skeptic, who thought
he could sneer very safely and philosophically, because
he imagined he could press the visible world into his
service—*where is the promise of his coming? for since the
fathers fell asleep all things continue as they were from the
beginning of the creation ;* Peter takes the poor fool from
things to *God*—*one day with the Lord is as a thousand
years, and a thousand years as one day.*   The poor skeptic
was going to vitiate a Bible "promise" by the "things"
of nature.   Because he did not see the sun growing
dim, or feel the earth giving way beneath his feet, he
supposed he could conclude triumphantly and with a
sneer, that the promise of Christ's coming and the end
of the world was contradicted or refuted by the "*things*"

that " continued as they were," by every solid mountain, by the burning sun, and by every glittering star. Peter lets him know that "continuance," *time*, is nothing to *God;* God never grows any older, any more than he grows wiser; years are nothing to him; ages are the same as moments. Just ideas of God would postpone his scoffs, till he could find some measure or comparison for God's eternity, and tell how old God is.

When Paul stood on Mars' hill, surrounded by the pride, and pomp, and taste, and philosophy of Athens, the most refined city in the world, whose learned men had invited the apostle to explain his religion, he did not commence with any refined disquisition about men or things, or the nature of the things, social right or visible utilities, as Aristotle would have done, or about moral agency, as certain of our theological professors, I am afraid, would have done. He broke ground with God: *God that made the world and all things therein, seeing that he is Lord of heaven and earth, dwelleth not in temples made with hands.* At a single dash the apostle goes beyond every spot where philosophy could reach him. He preaches God. He gives God the throne. He makes all men alike. He preaches repentance to all—not in view of the nature of things, philosophy, the utility of virtue, or moral agency—but in view of this God, his promised resurrection of the dead as Christ rose, and the final judgment. The mode of Peter and Paul was the mode of the Prophets before them. The Bible relies upon the character of God to teach men religion and turn them to it; God revealed in Christ and his cross.

It is just as plain that the character of God is the life-spring of influence in every part of experimental religion. For example:

There is such a thing as *conviction of sin*. Under its influence the soul has some unwonted emotions. It has realizations then which it had not before. What and whence is their peculiarity? Just this: God is better known; *against* THEE, THEE ONLY, *have I sinned*. THEE ONLY! Sin might be against other beings, but that was nothing with the convicted sinner. It was against *God*, and that was every thing with him: I have *done this evil in* THY *sight*.

There is such a thing as *repentance*. Whence does it spring? and how bear influence? *I have heard of* THEE *by the hearing of the ear, but now mine eye seeth* THEE, *wherefore I abhor myself, and repent in dust and ashes.* God's character laid him in the dust.

There is such a thing as *faith*. Where does it look?

> " The Lord 's my Shepherd, I 'll not want,
>   He makes me down to lie
> In pastures green. He leadeth me
>   The quiet waters by ;"

He restoreth my soul. Who shall lay any thing to the charge of God's elect? It is Christ that died; yea, rather that is risen again, who is even at the right hand of God.

There is such a thing as *love*. What kindles it? *We love* HIM, *because* HE *first loved us. If Christ so loved us, we ought also to love one another.*

There is such a thing as *hope*. And it casts anchor *within the veil, whither and because the Forerunner hath himself for us entered.*

There is such a thing as *resignation*. Whence comes it? *It is the* LORD; *let him do what seemeth good in* HIS *sight. Though* HE *slay me, yet will I trust in* HIM.

This is a strange world. We often tread in rough

places. Dark days will come. How different the lot of many of us, from what we expected when the sun of our youth rose smiling on us, and the blood of our youth leaped joyfully in the channels that God made for it. In times of the heart's desolation, our props knocked away, our comforts gone, the past too painful to remember, and the future promising to be more painful still ;— oh, we could not bear up under life's sorrows, much less be profited by them, if we might not learn to say, *in the time of trouble* HE *shall hide me in* HIS *pavilion, in the secret of* HIS *tabernacle shall* HE *hide me.*

This conviction, and repentance, and faith, and hope, and love, and resignation, and sweet confidence in God, all lie among the experiences which go most certainly to form our religious character; and they all exist as simply the results of just ideas of the character of God, imprinted upon the soul by the Holy Spirit.

As you trace (so far as it belongs to human sagacity to trace at all) the advancement of any human soul in holiness and ripeness for death and heaven, you will always find that advancement just connected with a clearer conception of God's character, and an additional intimacy of communion with him. In the infancy of religion, men think much of moral machinery to do them good. In the old age of religion, they think much of God. They have got beyond other reliances and resources. The whole history of their religious training and maturing has consisted very much in this, that they have learned to think of creatures less, and to know God better. More just and more perfect ideas of his whole character, as holy, just and good, as Governor, and Redeemer, and Guide, and Friend, have helped them on in the pathway of holiness, and now throw an additional light upon it, as it winds down to the tomb. To them God is every thing. They have learnt to know him better than they used to know him. His character has become more amazing, grand and good—more awful, but more sweet and attractive. The effect has been, that they lie before him more low in humiliation, but more happy in hope—deeper in reverence, but more satisfied to let God reign. They are glad he does reign. They are amazed at his mercy to them as sinners, but they know it all, they hope in it all, they rejoice in it all, without doubting or fear, because they know God— *grace reigns through righteousness unto eternal life, by Jesus Christ our Lord.*

Because God is the Head of the universe—because rectitude and good conscience are vital matters in religion—because all religion is founded upon the being and character of God—and because that character is the great moral and spiritual means for training all true piety—for these reasons, just ideas of God's character are of infinite moment to us. *Render unto God the things that are God's.*

The conclusions from this subject, such as the following, can only be named, and left to your reflection. We see from this doctrine:

1. That any error about the character of God is *vital* error. It changes the whole of religion. It may do for us to mistake his works, but it will not do for us to mistake his will. An error on nature, on providence, on science, on scholarship, is only a little matter, and can not corrupt every thing—it may leave a thousand other truths unharmed; but an error about God flings its evil over every thing else—every thing in both

worlds! It makes duty different, and holiness different; it makes heaven and hell different!

2. Therefore you need have little fear about any error in religion which leaves the character of God to stand in its own place, and unchanged. That one thing right will put every thing else right. That wrong, all else will be wrong. That character stands in the way of *all* falsehood and error.

3. Familiar expressions about the Deity are always utterly inappropriate and untasteful. Awe becomes us —solemn reverence before Him, our ideas about whom, just, shall help us toward heaven, unjust, shall help us toward hell. *Put off thy shoes from off thy feet, the ground whereon thou standest is holy ground.* It is no place to trifle, by the burning bush!

4. We see from this subject, that the fit mode of studying religion, even *intellectually*, is to begin with God, and keep the character of God the presiding idea at every step, and in every reflection. The Bible does this—you should do this. According to what God is, *you* must be—and all the universe must be. If ever you lose sight of him, you are afloat on an ocean of midnight —nothing to moor to, and not a star to steer by. The stars were not made for eternity.

5. Speculations, governmental or economical—socialism—utility—doctrines about human rights and duties, drawn from *the world merely*—all such things are so far from being Biblical or Christian, that they are unworthy of a sober Deist. God rules his world, and not his world him. The principles of his government are as high and deep as the attributes of his character; and to forget God and look at mere things and their relations, is to turn from the fountain of light to the bosom of

darkness. Ministers of the Gospel ought to feel that they stand upon firmer and loftier ground than those speculations which profess to learn truth and duty from mere visible things and earthly analogies. They have God's eternal Word. *That* is eternal rock. Visibilities go but a little way. The *lost Pleiad!* it has left a vacancy in the heavens! and what speculation or analogy could dare to conjecture, aside from the character of God, the duties of the beings who once inhabited it? We live for Eternity—for God! Preach God, my brethren, God in Christ, God more revealed, and more glorified, and more august and attractive in the great Redemption than in any thing else. Let the Divine character be your guide, and you may resemble the angel standing in the sun—you will be bathed in light, and light to reach *all worlds.*

6. Finally. For all and every one of the purposes of piety, you need much converse with God. Piety can not grow or be secure without it. Every plant of Paradise must be watered with the dews of heaven. Walk with God. Render him his due. See him every where, and reverence him every where. Love him and serve him in the faith of Christ, if you would have peace in the hour when *the dust shall return to the dust, as it was, and the spirit shall return to God who gave it. Render unto God the things that are God's.*

On Knowing God.

And this is life eternal, that they might know thee, the only true God, and Jesus Christ, whom thou has sent.—JOHN, xvii. 3.

THESE are the words of Jesus Christ. They occur in that intercessory prayer which he offered on the eve of his crucifixion. At such a time, his mind naturally lingered around the essential principles of that august mission which brought him into the world, and was now taking him out of it. Ready to shed his blood to give *eternal life* to as many as the Father had *given him ;* his prayers take hold on this principle of the eternal cove· nant, and then he adds, *This is life eternal, that they might know thee, the only true God, and Jesus Christ, whom thou hast sent.* The expression is remarkable. He speaks of *knowing God.* Omitting all other ideas and suggestions of the text, let us attend to this. He speaks of knowing God. It is not nature—system—destiny—contrivance—plan; it is God. The mind of the Saviour passes over all things else, and centers upon the Infinite One, and the Christ sent to reveal him, when he considers the method in which eternal life must come to his disciples.

The method of Christ and a Christian's heart is very different from the loved method of an unsanctified understanding. Christ and a Christian's heart find the essence of all that is desirable in the *knowledge of God.*

An unsanctified understanding, darkened and deceiving, is much more prone, even in religious investigation, to study man and what befits him, than to study the character of God, and thus be led to see, that all the universe must bend to the infinite and changeless nature of him who presides over it. But we must not stop in these minor truths; we must *know God*, if we would have *eternal life*. Hence, as the plan of this discourse, we propose,

I. To make some general remarks on this subject of study and knowledge. And,

II. To present some more direct arguments for inducing men to aim at knowing God.

I. We are to make some remarks of a general nature on the knowledge of God.

1. The first remark is, that the existence of God is that grand fact which lies at the foundation of all true religion; and therefore, the knowledge of God himself is the touch-stone of its principles. Error and falsehood are not going to yield to any science but that of Deity. Sin is not to be reasoned out of the world, or out of the Church, by any of those demonstrations which do not fling man, and all his reason together, in the dust, before the awful glories of the Infinite One. Religion will be superficial, proud, arrogant, worldly, and, therefore, corrupted and deceitful, if it is not first formed, and then tempered, and purified, and guided by the knowledge of God.

2. A second remark. It is the *lack* of this knowledge which sustains impiety. The stupidity of unconverted sinners would be gone if they saw clearly what God is.

It could not continue. Their hearts would trouble them. They would see they are more fit for hell than heaven. They would perceive themselves to be less like God, than like any other being! The depravity of their hearts would fill them with confusion and shame; and before the fears of a deserved condemnation, they would cry out, *What must we do to be saved?* But to avoid this distress, they choose to study religion (if they study it at all) by some other light and guide than the character of God. That one thing they shun. They do *not like to retain God in their knowledge.* Oh! how often, very often, they will abandon the ministry, which would teach them the only true God, and take refuge under that teaching which comports better with their erroneous feelings, and the equally erroneous and dangerous principles of their own dark and unconverted souls! If impenitent sinners knew what God is, their stupidity would be gone.

3. If Christians knew God better, their piety would be increased. Those ancient saints, whose happy attainments held them superior to the world, always nurtured their piety by much study and fellowship with God. They were nursed on the bosom of God. Very likely, they have not been eminent in mere speculative views of other things. Human science did little for them; and even religious systems of human coinage, though formed on the *foundation of the Apostles and Prophets,* lent them little aid in comparison with what they gained by direct contemplations on the Deity, and a holy intimacy with him. *Enoch walked with God,* is a description which intimates his manner of religious study and living. A Christian's piety is not to be nurtured, merely by considering the blessings he needs and receives, and the sins he repents of. Oh! no: it will be better nurtured when

he stirs up his soul to the study of God himself, and fixes his heart to come directly into the presence-chamber of the *King of kings.*

4. This subject of knowledge can never be exhausted. Piety on earth and piety in heaven will never exhaust it! A finite mind, perhaps, beginning here its study, and continuing it beyond the tomb, mastering one difficulty after another, may reach some point in its eternity, when it shall have compassed all other subjects, and be able to look down upon and over all other fields of knowledge without darkness and without a doubt. But God stills lies above it—beyond it! From that wonderful point in eternity, and that wonderful elevation, which not even an angel has yet reached, the soul will see depths in the ocean of the Divine Nature yet to be explored, and, sanctified and sublimated, will be invited to stir up its powers to more wonderful and blissful views of the Infinite One!

Let us begin now. Let us know God better. Many bright lessons are within our reach. They are lessons of eternal life. Acquaintance with God is the felicity and the security of heaven, and on earth our profit and bliss will bear a near proportion to the clear discernment we attain of his character.

5. This knowledge of God is not confined to the understanding. It occupies the understanding, but not that alone. There is a vital difference between all the knowledge of the Deity ever attained by mere speculation and that intended in the text. By a true knowledge of God, we shall have a clear and experimental discernment of his glory—of the excellency, and beauty, and grandeur, and loveliness of his character. Hence, we shall feel the desirableness of being like him. The

mind, the heart, will go out in delightful exercises; and we shall begin to realize how blessed and glorious a Being God is, and how blessed *we* should be, if we should cease to be sinful, and selfish, and worldly, and should be taken up into heaven, to dwell with him, and behold his face, and be like him for ever and ever! This is the knowledge of God. It takes hold on the heart. It is experimental. It is sweet, precious, solid, calm. It is what the most favored saint enjoys when, embracing Jesus Christ by a living faith, he sees the glory of the Father in the face of the Son, and delights to lay himself down in the hand of God, as a helpless, believing, and happy child!

This knowledge of God, therefore, includes clear intellectual discernment and right affections of heart. It is spiritual. It is the experience of a heart linked with God. It includes extensive understanding, and that understanding gained by the filial and family spirit of an adopted child. Mind and heart both know God.

6. That our relations to God are such that we ought greatly to *desire* to know him as he is—to know him well. He is our Maker, and therefore the proprietor of our being. From his fingers drop all our mercies. We have not a comfort but he gives it—and never shall have. He will be our final Judge. He holds our eternal destinies in his hand. To know *Him*, therefore, is of more moment to us than to know all other beings in the universe. We have more *to do* with him than with all others. We have to do with him every moment of our lives, and ever shall have in all our eternity. According to what he is, we must demean ourselves, or we must suffer. We are anxious to know the *men* we have to deal with, and how strange it is that we should

be indifferent about knowing the God we have to deal with! Did some earthly prince hold dominion over us, through the actions of whom we were daily receiving manifestations of kind disposition, mingled with tokens of no small displeasure against us, we should be anxious to know all about him, and learn what he was going to do with us at last. Should some unseen friend send us daily comforts, whose heart would not desire to *know* the individual whose daily kindness was a daily blessing? But this our God scatters his mercies all along our path. We have them in the earth, the air, the sea, the skies. Midnight and noon teach them. He blesses us with bounty in summer and winter. He makes the bird's song to cheer us, and the blushes and fragrance of the wild-flower to make us happy. He puts kindness into the hearts of the friends that take care of us when we are sick. It was he who guided the hand of the mother and the father, which wiped the tears of bitterness from our youthful cheek. Surely, if we ought to desire to know any thing, we should desire to know God.

II. Let us, then, in the second place, present some direct arguments for this study. We name five of them, and leave you to fill up the lesson for yourselves.

1. This knowledge of God tends, above all things, to humble us.

Humility, the true and happy humility of the Christian, comes, most of all, from a clear knowledge of God. It is when we know him best that we know ourselves best. It is knowing God that dissipates our delusions. We need to come near to him, to gaze directly at his character in all its glorious excellences—to see his holy and lovely purity, and justice, and mercy—to have an intimate and spiritual discernment of his spotless excellence, of his holy hatred of sin, of his infinite love of holiness—before we shall ever attain the due humility of a Christian. This humility is not going to be engendered by the considerations and glooms of guilt. All our tremblings at deserved and dreadful wrath, all the terrors of hell, are not enough. Remorse, its stings and terrors, a sense of guilt, and fears and tremblings, exist in hell—but there is no humility there. Man, as a Christian, as a sanctified and safe-guided sinner, is led to a true sense of sin far more by seeing what *God is*, than by considering the iniquities which he himself has committed. When one has a near view of God, a clear discovery of the excellency and majesty of his holiness, he sees most clearly the evil of sinning against him. Such a sight lays the soul in the dust, not so much by the sadness of guilt as in adoring and humble wonder at the mercy of God. This was the experience of David in his conviction: *Against thee, thee only have I sinned, and done this evil in thy sight.* The most humbling idea there is about sin is, that it is *against God.*

It is true, the Christian will find arguments for humiliation in the remembrance of his sins, and he ought never to forget them. But after all, his holiest and sweetest humility will come from his acquaintance with God, and contemplations on his character. There is a vast difference between the humility produced by contemplations of guilt and the contemplations of God. Views of our guilt may humble us (if we are Christians), but they are agitating; the soul is troubled, and agitated, and uneasy. Views of God, showing us what sin deserves, and what we are, make the soul calm—its mere feelings lie still, hushed and overawed by the holiness and excellences of God. As we contemplate our guilt, our humility is apt to be bitter and passionate; as we perceive the holiness and majesty of God, our humility becomes deep, still, subdued and satisfying. Views of our guilt give rise to feelings tormenting, desponding; and hence remorse, under the scorpion stings of a guilty conscience, sometimes drives one to violence against himself—Judas hangs himself, and plunges to his own place! But that humility which arises from a clear view of the nature of God, is solid, peaceful, *hopeful*. Yes, it cherishes hope, because the very views of God which flung the sinner in the dust teach him he can hope, and may hope. God was the leading object in the knowledge which humbled him, and he keeps on thinking of God, and loves to be humble. He sees the fitness of it, and sees *his* infinite perfections can reach down comfort to his sackcloth and ashes. Those very perfections of God which humble him most are the very perfections which tell him to say to his soul, *My soul, hope thou in God—I shall yet praise him.*

That kind of humiliation which springs from the mere contemplation of guiltiness and ill-desert, often gives rise to the sensibility, that one can not endure to feel so criminal, and unworthy, and vile: that which springs from the knowledge of God shows one the fitness of just such feelings: the believer would not have any other; he would lie in the dust, speechless and satisfied; and lifting a beseeching look to Christ, he loves to lie infinitely low before God, and be an infinite debtor to Divine grace. He loves to feel his unworthiness. The more he feels it, the happier he is. Views of God revealed it to him, and he saw the fitness of laying himself in the dust. He would not be any where else if he could. And a sense of guilt leads him back again, to adore and wonder at the precious mercy of his God and Saviour! Hence, in his humility he is happy in thinking of God; and he thinks of him, his character, and glories, and excellences, far more than he occupies himself about his own character or destiny. He is taken up with thinking of God. He loves to lie at his feet, a humbled, hoping, and happy spirit, and look up on the excellences of God, and let him do as he will.

Convicted sinners often try to humble themselves by recollecting and weighing their sins. Such a mind expects humility from the power of a remorseful conscience. Such a sinner calls himself base, unworthy, guilty; he multiplies epithets upon himself, and strives to feel the burden of all his deformity and guilt, and then wonders that his heart don't give way—bow or break! But such views are not going to break or bend it. Animal feelings may be crushed by them, and nothing but animal feelings. The spirit itself will yield up its self-righteousness and pride, not by a stronger sense of guilt, but by clearer views of God. A spiritual knowledge of the Divine character—to perceive God to be so holy and excellent, that eternal woe is due to the being who does not love him; to see with a spiritual eye, that God could not and ought not to do less than turn the sinning angels down to hell, and turn this sinning world into a place of groans and dying, and smite the head of his own Son to save a sinner from hell—these are views which will bring the power of the Divine character on the spirit of the sinner, and teach him to feel (if any thing will) that his humblest spirit can say,

> "If my soul were sent to hell,
> Thy righteous law approves it well."

But such a humbled soul does not much fear hell. There are mainly three reasons why he does not.

(1) He *loves* a sense of his guilt and ill-desert. He is never so happy as when he realizes his unworthiness and takes his place in the dust. It is his own place. It is fit he should be there. He would not be any where else before God. He would not desire to lose a sense of his guiltiness if he were in heaven, but sing on for ever, *Unto Him that loved us, and washed us from our sins in his own blood.* It is so fit, therefore, and so good to him, to realize with humbled spirit his pollution and guilt, that fears vanish; and the deeper his sense of guilt, the happier his humbled spirit is.

(2) A second reason why he does not fear hell is, that while he lies thus in the dust, and wraps his face in the sackcloth that covers him, he is just thinking of God— of *God*, and half-forgets himself.

(3) A third reason is, that while his mind is wrapt in the vision of his God, his humility consists very much in wonder and amazement at the patience and mercy of God that have spared him; and the same patience and mercy he sees can do *any thing*—can even save *him*, guilty as he is, if they could spare him so long. He sees the reason why he is not already in hell is to be found in the Deity, not in himself; and in that wonderful ocean, the mercy of God, he casts anchor for his ship-wrecked and troubled soul.

Hence, that mystery is explained, how the deepest humility is connected with the most enduring and un-yielding fortitude. Such a humility converses with *God*, and is indifferent to human distinctions and mere human rewards. And that other mystery is explained, how the humblest soul is the least fearful and the happiest.

6*

Such a soul is satisfied that God should do as he will. And that other mystery too, how the deepest sense of Divine things is without show, and makes one very modest, and retiring, and still. Such a one resembles Elijah on Mount Horeb. It was not the *great and strong wind, that rent the mountains and brake in pieces the rocks;* it was not the *earthquake,* nor the *fire,* that moved him; but he felt that God was in the *still, small voice,* and he wrapped his face in his mantle. It is always so. A true sight of God is most efficacious of all things to humble us. *Woe is me! I am undone.* Why! *Mine eyes have seen the King, the Lord of hosts.*

2. We name a second argument. This knowledge of God tends most of all things to crucify us to the world.

To have a spiritual understanding of the exceeding excellences of God, to perceive the delights of contemplating him and communing with him, makes the world seem but a very little thing. It shows us its emptiness, its vanity and nothingness. It lifts us above it; and thus does most to fit us to live for God and eternity. Considerations of another nature, designed and adapted to *crucify us unto the world and the world unto us,* often experience a very signal and sensible failure. There are such; and we are sometimes compelled to wonder that they have no more abiding power over the human mind. We can easily and vividly paint the littleness of the world, and all that is in it. Dismal facts, which form the burden of its history, are too numerous and too thick, to leave any doubt of the fidelity of the picture, which would represent its entire worthlessness as a portion for the human heart. It takes, moreover, but a moment to lead the imagination down to the general conflagration of the world. And there is scarcely a worldling in existence who does not know and feel that we speak truly when we paint his prospects—few smiles, and many sorrows, and a dark and dreadful end beyond them. But, after all, the worldly heart turns back; the cold Christian heart lingers and hesitates to step off, and let go of a world crumbling into nothing! Thus we are baffled. The world *will* attract—will appear lovely—and the power of the most appalling demonstration vanishes before the rising emotions of a worldly and deceitful heart.

But when we can get the eye turned on God, on the glories of his character—when we see his loveliness in being just such a God as he is, and the desirableness of being like him; then, the sweetness of his majesty, the friend we want attracts us—riches, honors, the world are dead, and the heart uses that new arithmetic, to *count all things loss for the excellency of the knowledge of God in Christ Jesus* our Lord. It is by the knowledge of God, and by nothing else. *Things seen and temporal* sink before the discovered excellences of *things unseen and eternal.* Not so much by discovering that the world is *not* worth our having, as by discerning that God *is*, are we ever *crucified unto the world and the world unto us.* You may make the worldling behold desolation stalk over all his pleasant fields; you may make him behold his honors withering at the touch of truth and time; you may force him to lift the bitterest chalice of *wormwood and gall* that ever cursed human lips; and after all, he will love the world and have his hopes in it. And so far as the Christian, in any undue sense, is worldly, he will be like him. He needs, therefore, to *know God.* He needs to feel the attractions of his character and his communion. He needs to lift his eyes from the top of Pisgah, and *feel*, that if he had not another portion or another friend in the universe, he would be happy: *Thou art my portion; whom have I in heaven but thee? and there is none in all the earth that I desire besides thee.*

3. This having a spiritual knowledge of God tends most of all things to purify the heart.

No sight is so transforming as that of God. When we can have our minds and hearts brought so as to *see with open face the glory of the Lord, we are changed into the same image from glory to glory.* When the believer has a clear spiritual discernment of God, he sees it is reasonable, yea the most delightful *duty*, to devote himself and all he has to God, the Father, Son, and Holy Ghost. He takes motives for holy living from God himself; sin puts on the appearance of ugliness, and the world, its honors and once coveted emoluments, lie dead and forgotten at his feet. Christians do not cease to sin, so much by the horrors of conscience and fear, as by the love of God. The attempt to beat sin out of the heart by a lash of scorpions, fails. Views of God are more purifying than all the fears, and glooms, and distresses of a convicted spirit. You can't reason sin out of the heart, or love into it. It must be faith in God as he is, *reconciling the world unto himself,* seeing him, knowing him as he is, that must purify the heart. This wins it. This delightfully fills, and satisfies, and attracts it. This brings the awe of the upper sanctuary down to hush the commotions of sin. Sin never appears of such horrid magnitude as when we see how it offends Deity, outrages all his loveliest attributes, and requires the labors, the life, and the death of the Son of God to atone for it. Sin never appears of such horrid deformity and unloveliness, as when God is so known, that sin is seen in malignant contest against all that is amiable and good.

4. This knowledge of God tends, most of all things, to confirm and establish the believer's heart. Speculation can not do it. Self-examination, submission to creeds and forms, and all study of doctrines, can not do it. One must be established, by a conscious and vital experience—such experience as shall make the soul feel that it rests on God, an everlasting rock. To have full views of God; to know him by direct fellowship and communion; to live in his presence, and lie down and feel that the everlasting arms are around him, shows to the believer the fullness and the faithfulness of God, and confirms his heart in something like the full assurance of hope. Now he can call God his Father. He can look at that house *not made with hands*, and call it his own. His heart, his whole soul, has gone directly to his covenant God in Jesus Christ, *drawn by the cords* of that *perfect love* which *casteth out fear*.

Hence, finally, such a knowledge of God is most satisfying and safe. Direct views of God—a solemn and holy intimacy with him—the study of him, such as the heart takes when he *communes with us from off the mercy-seat*, and breathes into the soul the spirit of adoption, are more secure and more blessed than any others. These satisfy the soul. They meet its immortal wants. God, a covenant God and Saviour, fill the mind, and satisfy its longings, as nothing but the knowledge and enjoyment of God ever can. Then, to have such a God is enough. His glories fill the eye. His love satisfies the heart. Human passions lie still; and a holy, calm, and solid peace possesses the tranquil and happy spirit.

My Christian brethren, if these things are so, how earnestly ought you to devote yourselves to *know the only true God and Jesus Christ whom he has sent.* This is your felicity, your usefulness, and your life. A field is open before you, on which the most precious fruits may be gathered, and fruits for *eternal life.* You ought to be ashamed and confounded, when you are satisfied with small measures of the knowledge of God, and are not aiming, with a longing intensity of desire, to know your God and Saviour better! In reading, in meditation, and hearing, and praying, and in the sacraments, you ought to aim at attaining a more deep, and clear, and thorough knowledge of God. By noticing his providences, and most of all, his gracious and wonderful providences respecting your souls, you ought to gain more clear and transforming views of his glorious attributes. The children of his adoption, if you are Christians, you ought to *live* in his family, and daily behold the face of your Father. You ought to see the glory of God, the beauty and desirableness of existing only to serve and enjoy him. You ought not to rest satisfied with only a trembling hope, and leave it to death, eternity, and heaven, to disclose to you the wonders and excellences of the Divine character. You ought to partake of the heavenly spirit. The grace and glories of redemption are revealed to you; and as you lift your eyes from the top of Calvary to the throne of the Majesty in heaven, your souls ought to become more and more like heaven; when you see how such a God can save such sinners, by the grace of redeeming love, and by the groans and blood of his Son!

Oh! it is not fit, it is shameful that a Christian should live in the world, under such a government of God, and have such chances to know him, and love him, and serve him better, and, after all, be satisfied to have his mind in ignorance, and the lights and comforts of his religion little! Such be not ye. Awake, and learn to know God as he is. Arouse yourself, and enter into the knowledge of God; and let this science drive out sin, and selfishness, and worldliness, from your happy and heavenly hearts.

But some of you, my beloved hearers, are still impenitent sinners! One of the dreadful descriptions of your condition contained in the Bible is this—*them that know not God*. And can you, will you rest thus? You are hasting to meet him. To you, that *great white throne* will soon be clothed in the majesty of redeeming attractions, or rocked with thunders! Prepare for that hour! Go not up to that throne an enemy of God! I beseech you by all that is sacred, learn to know God! By the terrors and mercies of that tribunal—by the songs of bliss and groans of despair beyond it—by all the desirableness of *eternal life* and the blood that bought it—I beseech you, my beloved, but unhappy friend, *awake,* and learn to *know God! acquaint now thyself with him, and be at peace.*

Wisdom of God in Mystery.

We speak the wisdom of God in a mystery.—1 Cor. ii. 7.

PAUL, the author of these words, here gives a characteristic mark of the gospel message. He is speaking of this message; and with appropriate and characteristic peculiarity, when he would depict it to us, and set before our mind a just delineation of its nature, he dips his pencil in colors of mingled glory and darkness. No man ever knew better than he, the depth of blasting and pollution which sin hath brought down upon all mankind; and no man ever understood better, the mingled mystery and brightness of the scheme of God which saves them that believe. And no man was ever more skillful and more truthful, in saying just what he ought to say—in carrying his explanations as far as to the just point and no further, making even every hint and every suggestion conducive to the true end of study, and leaving off at the true point of propriety—a point, beyond which curiosity and caviling may delight themselves with vain questions, but neither reason nor piety can be profited. This he does in the text. He calls the Gospel *the wisdom of God in a mystery*. It is both. Light and darkness are here mingled together. It is *wisdom*, but it is wisdom *in a mystery*. We may know from it enough to make us *wise unto salvation*, to guide us through the changeful and often trying scenes of a wildnerness-pilgrimage, and to

plant our footsteps firmly and safely on the happier soil
of our promised land. But we can not know every thing.
This wisdom *will be* a mystery. The most limited
genius might ask the Gospel a thousand questions, to
which it would deign to give him no reply. And he
would be wiser than unbelief generally is, if he would
never reiterate them again, if he would only use, for its
glorious purpose, the light that is given him, and be
cheered by it, and walk on in that grace-illuminated
track, where beams of brightness shine, and not turn
himself so foolishly to be bewildered in the dark way
which he ought never to tread, and which neither cheers
him nor saves him. The Gospel never proposes to give
answers to the catechism of curiosity. But it does profess to tell every sinner, that will heed it, all he needs to
know about God, about pardon, holiness, and every thing
else embraced in his being *wise unto salvation. Mystery*
though it be, it is the *wisdom of God.* It could not be
the wisdom of God, if it were not mystery.

This is the idea of this text, and this is the theme of this
sermon. We are going to show, that the Gospel is the
wisdom of God in a mystery—that it reveals a way of
salvation marked with the traits and unity of God's
wisdom, and comporting with the "clouds and darkness
that are round about him."

That this discussion may not become too long to be
definite, and, more especially, that we may have before
our mind the precise point which the Apostle had before
his, let us notice the matter on which he was speaking.
We can not mistake it. It was the mighty theme on
which he loved to expatiate. Here his thoughts centered.
Here his heart exulted. Here his hope soared and his
love sung. It was the *salvation* of men through the

sacrifice of the Son of God. Just before the text, in the second verse of the chapter, this is made manifest: *I determined not to know any thing among you save Jesus Christ and him crucified.* He is talking about the death of Christ. He wants faith to stand there—not in *the wisdom of men*, but in the *power of God.* And after the text, and in the very sentence of which it constitutes only a single clause, he brings out the same idea of the crucifixion. *We speak the wisdom of God in a mystery, even the hidden wisdom which God ordained before the world unto our glory; which none of the princes of this world knew; for had they known it, they would not have crucified the Lord of glory.* The Apostle speaks of the *death* of Christ for our salvation; and this, with him, is *the wisdom of God in a mystery.* This remark will limit our range of thought, while it comports with the duties of this day, and justifies the plan of this sermon.

I. Let us fix in our mind the matter of mysteriousness which the Apostle had in his.

II. Let us demonstrate, that this mysteriousness is wisdom especially in one respect, that is, that it is just so great as we ought to expect, and no greater, on the subject-matter and in the field of its operation, wherein it accords with all the other arrangements of the plan of redemption. We speak on the principle, that human reason expects God to be uniform, and consistent with himself—*like* himself—analogical every where—not by mere nature's analogies, but by his own. This is one mark of wisdom. The mystery of the expiation comports with the mystery of sin itself, and with the whole matchless procedure of that grace which conducts a sinner to heaven.

I. We remark the mystery which lies in the crucifixion of Jesus Christ as he was *slain for us.*

It would certainly be no evidence of either Christian wisdom or humility in any man, if he were to pretend, that to *him* there is nothing of mysterious aspect in the showing of the Gospel, when it speaks of the death of Christ, its necessity, and the benefits that grow out of it. We need not largely explain what we mean by mystery. We take the term in its every-day significance. It imports something inexplicable—something which at present we do not fully understand. In every affair of science or business, there is not a more distinct mark of a clear mind or a great one, than the discrimination which the mind makes between the matters of its knowledge and those of its ignorance. On the contrary, there is no more certain sign of a confused or contracted intellect, than for a man to imagine he knows every thing. That is the mark of a novice, a sciolist, a pretender. Invariably you may take it as a certain proof of an ignorant mind and a weak one, whenever you come in contact with a man never willing to say, "I do not know." And if you can find a Christian man or a Christian minister professing to see all things clearly, avowing that his mind finds no difficulties in any of the ideas that occur to it on the subject of religion—that he can explain every thing, decrees for example, just as easily as duties; you may be assured on the spot, both that he is a novice on the subject, and that his mental powers are of very limited comprehension. Up to a certain and a very intelligible point, every man may know and ought to know, on the subject-matters of religion. The point is this: he may know and ought to know just those clusters of facts which concern him, and which the

Gospel unfolds to him. Beyond these, inquisitiveness and curiosity may range, and imagination conjecture, and fancy dream, and hope inquire and long; but the mind can not have a single bright item of satisfying and substantial knowledge. And it ought to be enough to warn a man effectually off from the confines of that dark region which lies beyond the field of revelation,. when at every step he takes in that region, he is compelled to feel that his eyes are dim and fog-bound—that he has no firm foothold—that the ground is uncertain beneath him, and can not furnish to him the comforts of an unquestionable security. This ought to confine him effectually and gladly within the limits of that bright field, bathed in sunshine, over whose surface prophets and apostles and all the army of the faithful have delightfully walked before him. But, whether he will or not, he must stay there. He can not overstep the boundaries and gain the fruits of knowledge beyond. On the other side of the boundaries lie the fields of a Divine mystery; and he will be nothing better than a foolish dreamer, if he does not let them alone, till the coming of brighter and eternal day. Let him attend to duty, and leave the darkness. Let him use his conscience, and leave his conjecturing.

The *subject* on which the mystery of the text lies, is that of the atoning work of Christ accomplished in the crucifixion. Now, it is perfectly clear in the Gospel, that Christ was crucified—that he died for sinners—that the punishment due to us was laid on him—that Divine justice was satisfied by his death, the Divine Being rendered at least reconcilable—and that, by this august and amazing expiation, an everlasting righteousness is procured, through which believing sinners may be forgiven and entitled to the favor of God and all the bliss of a revealed immortality. Thus far, there is no mystery. All is open : all is clear and certain as the disclosure of words can make it.

But beyond this lies the region of an inaccessible mysteriousness. It is overhung with clouds, whose borders only are tinged with the glory that lies hidden behind them, and which no eye will see till the curtain of eternity is lifted.

To shorten the matter, let us name a few of the items.

It is entirely a mystery to us, how it could comport with the justice of God to lay the punishment of our sins on the head of an innocent Being, *holy, harmless, undefiled, and separate from sinners.* He has done it. There is no mystery about *that.* And those astounding accompaniments of the crucifixion seem to mark the deed with signals of amazement. The sun went out! Solid rocks were rent asunder! Graves opened! and buried saints walked from the door of their sepulchers back again into the holy city. Nature, as she hung a pall over the heavens, seemed to be astonished at the transaction, and well may we join in the solemnity of her wonder! We can do nothing but wonder, and love, and adore. We can not explain. No man can tell us, how justice, punitive justice, the justice of God, could ordain that transaction—a holy Being standing in the place of guilty ones, and receiving the strokes of an offended justice upon his devoted head. This is one mystery.

A second one is, how justice could be *satisfied* through such an infliction. We can not tell. We know nothing about it. All we know is, that Divine justice positively did receive there the very last item of her demands, when her heavy sword drank the blood willingly offered for the ransom of sinners. But it was innocent blood. And how justice could take it, and *be* justice— and how justice could be *satisfied* with it as justice, is all a mystery to us; and perhaps it will be a mystery for ever. This is a second mystery.

A third one is, how Jesus Christ *could render* satisfaction to Divine justice, while, at the same time, he was the Being to whom satisfaction was rendered, and the very Being who rendered it—the Avenger and the Sufferer under vengeance. He *was* so. There is one God, and God was the satisfied party; while we can not be ignorant of that inspired description of the Church, *the flock of God which he hath purchased with his own blood.*

It is a mystery to us, how it can come to pass, that, while the Divine nature is utterly unsusceptible of pain and death, nevertheless the sufferings and death of Jesus Christ have all their value and efficacy from the Divine nature of the Victim. We know it *is* so; but we know nothing further. We know that the *blood of bulls and goats can not take away sin;* we know that when the Father *bringeth his only begotten into the world, he saith, Let all the angels of God worship him.*

It is a mystery our reason can not explain, how there could be, in the "one person" of Christ upon the cross, such a wonderful union of grandeur and humiliation— of glory and ignominy—of complaining and omnipotence—in one word, such an inexplicable union of immortal Deity and expiring humanity! How do these things comport with one another? No tongue can tell! A prophet, an apostle never tried. They are truths, but they are mysteries. They are the Divine mysteries of Divine truth.

Our reason can not explain the mystery, how that Son

on the cross, in whom the *Father was well pleased*, and who at that very moment (with an obedience never equaled) was doing the very will of the Father in a most amazing transaction, could have been abandoned by him at such a moment, and left to that bitterest wailing, *My God, my God, why hast thou forsaken me?* Even an earthly kindness will pillow the head of a dying son. Profligate as he may have been, and now dying for his crimes, parental affection will take him up in that hour, and soothe him if it can, and catch his last breath, and speak words of tenderness to his death-struck bosom. But God did not treat Jesus Christ so! Not even a look of tenderness did he bend upon his dying Son! Jesus Christ was no *martyr;* and God forbid that herein he should be an *example* for us. We can not afford to die so. He died thus that we might be free. He wailed, that we might exult. He died in gloom, that we might die in glory.

It is a mystery beyond our reason to fathom, that the love of God should ever have brought Jesus Christ to the cross. There is a hell. It has victims in it. It has room for more. Sinners deserve it. Oh! how could God, so infinitely great and exalted, ever love sinners, beings so contemptible and mean, well enough to perform in their behalf all the wonders of the crucifixion? Bend, bend, proud reason, under the burden of these mysteries! Learn the narrow limits of thine empire! Take, as thou oughtest to take, at the hand of God, the testimony that he has given thee, *the wisdom of God in a mystery*. Redemption would be *un*reasonable, if there were not in its achievements something which reason can not fathom. What reason could calculate the price of an immortal soul? or gauge the depth of its bottomless abyss, its home, but for the high and mysterious ransom?

II. We turn to the *demonstration*, that all this mysteriousness is no greater than we ought to expect on the subject-matter before us. We are going to show that all this mysteriousness perfectly accords with all the facts and all the other arrangements of the plan of redemption. In this accordance beams out the *wisdom of God.*

Be not offended, if we beg your most definite attention. We desire you to fix precisely in mind the *exact point* with which we are dealing, and remark how it bears on the matter on hand. We maintain, that redemption for sinners by the death of the eternal Son of God has something about it of amazing mystery; but that the mystery in this case is a manifestation of the *wisdom of God;* and, so far from constituting any difficulty to a wise man, this mystery ought itself to incline him to accept the doctrines, and instantly venture his soul upon it as a reasonable duty. Faith, on this account, is the more reasonable; and that, especially, because the Deity *herein* accords with all the other mysteries connected with this subject. We select *five* items to illustrate this principle.

1. Sin was the great evil which brought our Saviour into the world and took him to the cross. And the *existence* of sin is just as mysterious a matter to us, as its expiation on that bloody tree. Sin is an exception to all that could be expected under God's attributes. It is infinitely hateful to his infinite holiness. It is just as hateful to his infinite goodness. It is the only thing which has ever dishonored him, or thrown a single look of contemptuous disregard upon his high and holy character.

It constitutes the only thing which has ever dared to impeach his wisdom; the only thing which, by marring felicity, and spoiling holiness, and building hell, seems to frustrate the great ends for which God's high attributes are all embarked. How *could* God permit its introduction? Where slept the arm of his omnipotence in that dark hour when sin first sprang into existence? Where was goodness, infinite goodness, that it did not wake the energies of Omnipotence, and prevent that awful act which dishonors God and dooms immortal spirits to the pains of hell for ever? How could such a God ever permit such a monstrous evil? Awful mystery! Human reason would have supposed it impossible that sin should come into existence, except by dashing into pieces the throne of Omnipotence!

Yet, here it is! Its effects are visible. Its history is written in tears, in hearts that bleed and break! It is written in the birth-cries and death-groans of a dying humanity, and spread out in the line of march over which every mortal travels from his cradle to his coffin! Well may the spectator, in such a world as this, ask, where is the goodness of God? The world, indeed, read by the light of Divine Revelation, may give numerous proofs of it, but it is very noticeable how the admirers of nature fail in one signal matter. In no instance that I recollect, has any one of those impassioned children, who revel so delightfully in the mere fields of nature and taste, ever looked only on one leaf of nature's volume. His ecstasy has been experienced, and his poetry has sung, and his taste reveled, only when reason has reeled—when he has turned away from the dark mysteries of a miserable world, and opened his eyes only on the few bright spots before him. He may have been happy

in the sunshine, but not in the dark and stormy day.
He may have been satisfied with nature's revelations and
tuition when he saw health, strength, and happiness, but
not when the life-blood stagnates at the bidding of inex-
orable death! Nature builds coffins! Nature digs
graves! Nature takes from us our dearest solaces—the
sweetest she ever gives; and, when we have deposited them
in the tomb, she settles down upon them the darkness of
an impenetrable midnight to brood over them for ever!

How *can* these things be? How can a *good* God permit them? In vain do I put these questions to all
Nature around me. She gives me no answer. Silence,
an awful silence, is her only reply! Something more,
therefore, is indispensable. And when God comes to
give me that something—when he tells me that these
dispensations shall receive the visitings of mercy—when
he assures me, that, though sin exists, and men die, and
death-struggles and deep graves are facts, yet still he is
good, and his goodness is yet going to be manifested
when a whole army of believers shall fling off their wind-
ing-sheets, and take their flight from the grave-yard upward to glory; can I not afford to have God just as
mysterious in the mode of recovery, as he *was* when sin
began, and *has* been all along the tearful line of its dreadful history? Is it not wisdom in God to accord with
himself? And if I can not stand before his attributes of
infinite goodness and power, and tell how he could permit sin and its evils, and if all nature can not tell me,
do I not need something *beyond* nature, and something
just as amazing and mysterious in *curing* sin and its
evils, as there is in its dark existence and dark miseries? as there is in its dark graves and deep hell? If
such a mystery as the existence of sin could be, and the

attempt to atone for it and undo its evil had no mystery about it, my faith never could fix, and my heart never could rest on that attempt. I should be afraid that there might be hidden somewhere, in the darknesses of sin, evils and dangers that the remedy could not reach. If sin is a mystery, the expiation of it *ought* to be a mystery also. And so it is : *Great is the mystery of godliness, God manifest in the flesh, seen of men, believed on in the world, received up into glory.* Yes,

2. He *was* manifest in the flesh, seen of men, believed on in THE WORLD. And why did the Son of God select this world as the theatre of his redeeming wonders? There had been sin in heaven. Spirits as precious as ours had fallen. Like us they were the creatures of God. Like us they were immortal. Like us they were capable of never-ending felicity and glory. Capable are they, too, of an awful misery, as they know full well, *reserved in chains under darkness unto the judgment of the great day.* As in our contemplations we mount up to the city of God, and gaze at those vacated seats whence angels fell, with "Lucifer, son of the morning," and then turn and look at the redeemed myriads of happy spirits taken home from this dark and miserable world, how can we solve the mystery, *why* the Son of God *took not on him the nature of angels, but took on him the seed of Abraham?* Why did God pass angels by when he rescued us? Why is not every one of us manacled in chains that weigh down devils in hell? It is all a mystery ! No answer to the question comes to us, except, *even so, Father, for so it seemed good in thy sight.* There we must leave it. And if it is all mystery to us, how God came to select this apostate world for the work of redeeming mercy, it accords with God that that work

itself should be a mystery also. The mystery of the
work assorts with the mystery of its field. The wonders
of the incarnation, of the " man of sorrows," of his death
of agony, of the efficacy of his great atonement for *our*
souls, are things which perfectly correspond with the
other mystery, why God dooms sinning angels to hell,
and invites sinning men to believe in the Saviour and go
to heaven.

And if any unbeliever among us will reject the doctrines that Christ bore the penalty *for us*, and made an
efficacious atonement, because there are mysteries in
these doctrines ; for the same reason he may just as well
reject Christianity altogether, cut himself off entirely from
the Gospel, and affirm that the angels sung a falsehood
in the anthem of the incarnation !   Our redemption is
all alike : *we speak the wisdom of God in a mystery.*

3. There is an entire correspondence between the doctrines of Christ's effectual expiation of sin, and satisfaction of justice by his death, and all the other information
we have about the Saviour himself. The incarnation of
Jesus Christ is just as mysterious to us as his atonement.
So is his person, that he should exist "in two distinct
natures and one person for ever." There is something
inexplicable in this. The fact is so ; but how it can *be*
a fact, no prophet or apostle has even undertaken to tell.

That Jesus Christ should be able to give strength to
the poor cripple's bones, and yet be himself weary and
way-worn, and sit down to rest—that he should feed
thousands of men, and yet be a man of hunger—that he
should control the stormy elements, and yet *have not
where to lay his head*—that he should soothe anguished
hearts, and yet himself breathe the bitterest prayer that
ever quivered on anguished lips—that he should control

death, and yet be its wailing victim—that he should
please the Father, and yet the Father be pleased *to bruise
him and put him to an open shame;* these are things before
which faith and love may wonder and adore, but which
reason can never explain! The great atonement, which
we remember to-day, corresponds, in mystery and grandeur, with all else that belongs to its wonderful Author.

4. There is something truly amazing in the *mode* of
the redemption of sinners. It is not less amazing than
the fact, whose mysteries we mentioned in the first part
of this sermon. If it were so, that justice *could* turn
aside from the guilty, that Jesus Christ were coming into
this world to ransom sinners, we should naturally have
expected that he would come in the chariots of his
omnipotence! We look for victories, for high and wonderful achievements, in something which comports with
their own magnificence. And if Jesus Christ were to
come out from heaven on a high embassy of government, and visit this rebellious world, and wipe out its sin,
and recover back to a heavenly allegiance its sinning
inhabitants, our reason, all the reason we can bring to
bear upon the matter, would have expected him to come
laden with the honors of his high commission. Not only
would our reason look for his honorable credentials, but
look to have his person held sacred, and guarded by all
the thunders of the throne he had left behind him.
Reason would expect him to stand here in the acknowledged majesty of a high and mighty deliverer. And
even if Revelation had taught her, that his life must be
given a ransom for the redeemed, she would still expect
to see him, in all the might and majesty of his Godhead,
grappling with the king of terrors! And, whatever might
befall him, she would expect the eternal Father, whose

name and government he came to honor, would never
forsake him. But, how different the facts! He was a
poor man! His mother was a poor woman! He was
born houseless, and fled defenceless from the sword,
whetted for his infant blood! He stood on the world he
came to rescue, an outcast, and almost unbefriended!
*The foxes have holes, and the birds of the air have nests, but
the Son of man hath not where to lay his head!* Approaching nearer to the end of his work, instead of receiving
any signals of triumph, he was dragged from court to
court as a culprit, insulted by a bantering Pilate and a
covetous Herod! He was mocked as an impostor—he
was spitted on as a man—he was scourged as a villain!
And when the last hour was come, he was not permitted
that poor boon, to die in peace! They insult his lips
with vinegar and gall! while the forsaking of his Father
forces from him the only complaint his tongue ever
uttered! This is the *mode* in which God treated his
Son! It is most mysterious, most amazing! It corresponds with the mysteries of its design—the satisfaction
of justice and the salvation of the guilty. It is *the wisdom
of God in a mystery.*

We can not stop till we have named one more article.

5. Through this Christ, some sinners are brought into
favor with God. They are believers. They are adopted
into God's family, and he loves them with an unequaled
tenderness and strength. But how does he treat them?
Does he free them from suffering, since Christ suffered
for them? Regenerated and made saints, does he never
suffer them to fall into sin? Must they weep, since
Christ wept for them? Will they die, since Christ died
for them? Along their track of life, and then in the
hour of their coming dissolution, will God's treatment of

his people be according to their character, so that the holiest of them shall have fewest griefs, and die the happiest deaths? We should expect it; but it is not so! The very pathway by which believers travel to the city of God is a matter corresponding in wonders with all the rest of their redemption! Sometimes they fall into sin! Sometimes, brethren though they be, they do not love one another! Sometimes they will be forced to writhe in anguish under the thought that their God has taken away from them the mercy which they could least of all spare! Some of them will bury their children, and some of them will die, leaving them behind in such circumstances that they could die happier if their children had died before them!—they must leave them, unbefriended, to a tempting, and cold, and comfortless world!

We ask you, if your very way into heaven, along the path of temptation and tears, and winding down rapidly into the darkness of the tomb, does not correspond in mysteriousness with that great work which shall beam brightness on that tomb in the day of a coming resurrection? Go on joyfully in that path. Lie down quietly in that tomb. The darkness of your allotments is no evidence against your adoption into the family of God. If you are a believer, your life, like your adorable Redeemer, will be the *wisdom of God in a mystery.*

This afternoon, some of you, my dear hearers, are going to pour dishonor on this wisdom of God! You will not be at the Lord's table! Most solemnly and most affectionately, I ask you, *why?* What do you wait for, before you will believe in Christ—before you will consent to trust your soul to his blood? What do you want the Almighty God to do for you, or to teach you more? He has done, and has taught, and has promised, and has called and invited, precisely as your situation, your sins, and your souls need! If any thing is reasonable and trustworthy, it is this blood-bought redemption. If you will not take up with this, a wise, unique, appropriate, consistent system—a system that reaches aid this moment to your guilty helplessness, and stretches on to your death-bed and eternity—it becomes a serious question to you how you will answer it at the bar of God. If you will not believe God, what will you believe? If you will not trust God, what are you going to trust? If you recoil from the mystery of the atonement, and fall back on Nature, you can find neither light nor hope there! Wherever the Bible is mystery, Nature is more so. If you will reject a redemption which accords with all we can know of God, and which corresponds to your sins, your consciousness of want, and your dying condition, then you must perish! You must perish! but when you perish, the justice and mercy of God will be faultless! Oh! that you were wise! You would then take God at his word. You would renounce sin and the world. You would be a miracle of grace, and an heir of bright and happy immortality.

My brethren, you are going to commemorate, this afternoon, the greatest wonder in the universe. Your exercises of adoring love and trust ought to have some correspondence to the love that has saved you. At the table of the Lord you will remember the adorable love which made Jesus Christ a victim, that you might be delivered from the depths of ignominy, and pain, and shame everlasting. Aim to have your faith, your filial confidence, your spirit of adoption, as freely draw you to take Christ as he has given himself to ransom you

from going down to the pit. Ye are the children of
God. Come and take, at your Father's table, the children's portion. Come with a child's confidence, a child's
heart. Come to assure your hearts. As you lift that
cup to your lips, say freely, *He that spared not his own
Son, but freely delivered him up for us all, how shall he not
with him also freely give us all things?* And then drink of it
in filial confidence, as a child of God. Let no fear dis-
quiet you. If he loved you to the death while you were
yet enemies, much more will he save you as friends.
He will perfect all his mysterious redemption. He will
attend you in your sometimes dark pathway, as you
tread onwards toward the tomb. He will not leave you
there. You have contemplated him mysteriously dying
in ignominy upon the cross—you shall yet see him coming in the clouds of heaven to *judge the quick and the
dead!* As your soul has sorrowed for sin, and your
heart sunk within you, you have heard him wonderfully
saying, *Be of good cheer, thy sins are forgiven thee.* You
shall yet hear from his lips that crowning wonder, *Come,
ye blessed of my Father, inherit the kingdom prepared for
you before the foundation of the world.* Christ on the cross,
and a ransomed sinner in heaven, are the two greatest
wonders in the universe—they both exhibit *the wisdom
of God in a mystery.*

7*

Election.

Blessed be the God and Father of our Lord Jesus Christ, who hath blessed us with all spiritual blessings in heavenly places in Christ, according as he hath chosen us in him, before the foundation of the world, that should we be holy and without blame before him in love.—EPHESIANS, i. 3, 4.

FOUR ideas are peculiarly prominent in these words: The first is, the ascription of praise and blessing to God, the *Father of our Lord Jesus Christ.* The Apostle, just commencing his Epistle to the Ephesian converts, has barely announced to them who it is that addresses them, and wished them grace, mercy and peace, before he breaks out into a kind of rapturous exclamation, *Blessed be the God and Father of our Lord Jesus Christ!* He could not proceed (it would seem) to impart to them those counsels and consolations of which his heart was so full, before he had lifted up his heart in holy and devout thanksgiving and praise to God. He loved the Ephesian converts. He rejoiced in all their spiritual good. He delighted to unfold to them the riches of the Redeemer's grace, and furnish them (through the inspiration of the Holy Spirit) with such principles, and promises, and timely admonitions and warnings as should aid their advancement in the Divine life. But all that *he* could do, or *they* anticipate, flowed from the wonders of grace. There was nothing in all his enrapturing theme,

Christ, and pardon, and heaven, which would let him, for a moment, forget that praise and blessing for it all was due to God. He seems to have felt that he could not enter into the consideration of Christian subjects— could not unfold or enjoy the rich provisions of Christian grace—without remembering at every step that it all came from the bounty of Heaven—the wonderful overflowings of the grace of God! The very first thought of the Gospel brought the Apostle directly to the grand, and the glorious and the delightful sovereignty of God: *Blessed be the God and Father of our Lord Jesus Christ.* Then follows the reason for this:

His *second* idea is that of the spiritual blessings which God has bestowed; *Who hath blessed us with all spiritual blessings in heavenly places in Christ.* The word *places* is not found in the original. Perhaps some other word would be as appropriate: *Blessed us with all spiritual blessings in heavenly* THINGS; that is, in grace, mercy and peace, pardon, redemption, and the fruits of the Spirit, may, perhaps, be the meaning of the passage. But I am of the opinion that *heavenly places* is a phrase that more perfectly presents to us the idea which was in the Apostle's mind. The *mode* in which his mind revolved the matters of the Gospel seems to me to have been this: he considered the whole as one connected, consistent, certain system, *well ordered in all things, and sure*, from the beginning to the end, established in the covenant, and resting on the faithfulness of God. He considers *heaven*, therefore, as already bestowed upon believers. It is theirs by promise, and theirs by the possession of something of that holiness which qualifies for it. And when he says, *blessed us with all spiritual blessings in heavenly places,* he means that all the privileges and

places of holiness are *already* bestowed upon believers—
they are given in the covenant—they are promised, and
believers have an invested *right* in them—they are
theirs. The same idea is found in the sixth verse of the
second chapter of this Epistle : *God, who is rich in mercy,*
. . . . hath raised us up together, and made us sit together
in heavenly PLACES *in Christ Jesus.* Where there is grace,
there is something of heaven. Spiritual blessings are
eternal blessings. Divine life is immortal life.

But we need remark, at present, only the *spiritual*
bestowments. It was on account of them that the Apostle makes such an ascription of blessing and praise to
God.

The *third* idea is that of the *rule* or arrangement by
which *God hath blessed us with all spiritual blessings.* It
is the rule of Divine, eternal election—the sovereign
choice of God; *blessed us . . . in Christ* ACCORDING *as he*
hath CHOSEN *us in him* BEFORE *the foundation of the*
world.

The *fourth* prominent idea is the *object* of the Divine
choice, or the explanation of *what* it is to which God
hath chosen us in Christ before the foundation of the world.
He chose us *that we should be holy and without blame before*
him in love. He elected believers that they SHOULD BE
holy—not because they were going to be holy and he
foresaw it, but to *cause* them to be holy. It was his
object in election to render them *holy and blameless before*
him in love—a company of holy men and holy women,
maintaining a careful and blameless walk, and growing
up in holiness and love, till they should be ripe for a
translation to heaven.

The amount, therefore, of what is prominent in these
words, may be briefly expressed in this way :

1. The Apostle blesses God (when he thinks of the Gospel).

2. He does it on account of bestowed spiritual blessings.

3. He tells how they came to be bestowed—we were *chosen.*

4. He tells the design of God's choice—*that we should be holy.*

The DOCTRINE, therefore, to which we invite your attention in this discourse is, that

The election of God effectually secures holiness in the elect, and thus, we may be assured, prepares them for heaven.

In substantiating this doctrine, our appeal is,

I. To the Law and to the testimony. The sacred Scriptures, in places too numerous to mention, teach us that God hath chosen saints, elected them in Christ Jesus, *before the foundation of the world.* Some of these passages we are going to recite. And you will notice, while you listen to them, how commonly election and sanctification are coupled together not only, but more particularly, how election is mentioned as the cause of sanctification; how the believer's holiness, all his holiness, originates in the election of God.

Our text is of this nature: *God hath blessed us with spiritual blessings;* why? *according as he hath chosen us.* It was his choice, his election, which secured *spiritual blessings.* It was not because we *were* spiritually blessed, or because he foresaw we should be, that he chose us; but we are spiritually blessed *according as he hath chosen us.* He hath blessed us with spiritual blessings *according* to election, and not elected us according to some foreseen spiritual character of good in us. This is one demonstration from the text itself.

There is another. *He hath chosen us in Christ before the foundation of the world, that we* SHOULD *be holy.* He chose us to holiness, therefore, if we are holy. God hath elected believers, that they should be holy, not because he saw they were going to be holy. Their holiness was embraced among the purposes of election. When God elected them, he elected them to be holy. It was his object in election, that they *should be holy, and without blame before him in love.* And either HE (all holy, and omnipotent, and changeless as he is) must fail to accomplish the purposes of his choice, or the elect will assuredly receive, at his hands, *all spiritual blessings,* and finally be made *holy and without blame before him.* He chose them for this; and his choice effectually secures it.

Rom. 8: 29. *Whom he did foreknow, he also did predestinate to be conformed to the image of his Son.* Conformity to the image of his Son consists in sanctification; and this sanctification, the Divine writer tells us, springs from predestination. God predestinated this conformity.

Rom. 8: 30. *Whom he did predestinate them he also called.* This calling is to holiness, and it comes from predestination. "Effectual calling" is one of the results of election.

2 Thess. 2: 13. *We are bound to give thanks always to God for you, brethren, beloved of the Lord, because God hath from the beginning chosen you to salvation, through sanctification of the Spirit and belief of the truth.* Salvation is included in election; but not merely freedom from punishment, and admission into the presence of God. There is something more. We have a very imperfect idea of salvation not only, but we have a very erroneous

one, when we conceive of it merely as pardon and a residence among the saints before the throne. Salva-tion includes holiness of nature. The sanctified alone can be saved, let pardon and the mansions of heaven be as they may. The sanctified alone are qualified to get good—to receive blessing, and glory, and joy from standing in the presence of God. And God *hath, from the beginning, chosen to salvation* THROUGH *sanctification of the Spirit*. The choice, the election of God, effect-ually secures sanctification of the Spirit.

1 Thess. 5: 9. *God hath not appointed us to wrath, but to obtain salvation.* Believers are saved by the *appointment* of God. In holy, sovereign wisdom he has ordained the end from the beginning; and the means for its accomplishment will not be unappropriate to the objects designed.

Eph. 2: 10. *We are his workmanship, created in Christ Jesus unto good works, which God hath before ordained that we should walk in them.* God hath foreordained the *good works* of his people, as the fruits of holiness, and not merely their new creation by the Holy Spirit.

1 Pet. 1: 2. *Elect according to the foreknowledge of God the Father, through sanctification of the Spirit unto obedience.* A sanctified mind leading to *obedience* is, therefore, the result of *election*.

But we need not multiply quotations. You are famil-iar with passages like these. Such ideas are scattered every where throughout the New Testament, and blind-ness alone can miss them.

The character of believers, their disposition, their quali-fication for the service and enjoyment of God, their obedience, their holiness—some one of these things is usually mentioned in the Scriptures in connection with their election, and as the result of it. Indeed, wherever the method in which election operates is brought to mind that method is sanctification. Believers are elected to salvation, it is true ; God is said to have *chosen them to salvation.* But when the medium of salvation is mentioned, the nature of it, the means of it in the creature ; then holiness, sanctification, the qualities of the believer are suggested to us. Men are sometimes fond of separating these things. God put them together. Men, who would fondly indulge the hope of salvation while neglecting the cultivation of a holy temper of mind and holy habits of living, often connect the election of God with the eternal felicity of the elect, but separate the idea of that felicity from the idea of the believer's separation from sin. Men, too, whose wicked hearts are opposed to the sovereignty of God, who hate the doctrine of election and desire to make it appear odious or absurd, often take the same course, and represent the doctrine of election as teaching that eternal life is secure to the elect, let their course and their character be what they will. But this is not the election of the Scriptures. They make no mention of such an election. They mention holiness as the result of election, and heaven as the consequence and reward of holiness. This is their universal sense, and in numerous passages it is fully and clearly expressed.

II. We make an appeal to the nature of the case, to show that election secures holiness in the elect.

The election of believers is no singular and isolated thing in the economy of God. It is only one item of a great and universal system—the system of predestina-

tion. " God, for his own glory, hath foreordained what-
soever comes to pass :"—not some things, but all things.
His predestination is just as extensive as his providence.
Predestination is God's eternal purpose to rule his universe just as he does rule it. (And if men are reconciled to the manner in which he does rule it, it seems to
me they need have no quarrel with his determining to
rule it so.) Election, then, is embraced in predestination.
It is only one item of the eternal purposes, the decrees
of God. Now, the purposes of God are wise. They are
reasonable, and consistent with the proprieties of things;
for God is not the author of confusion and absurdity.
And, therefore, when he determined any end to be accomplished, he must have determined the means for its
accomplishment: when he chose his people unto salvation, he must have chosen them unto holiness. A renewed soul, a soul conformed to the image of God, a
soul disposed to holiness and finding felicity in it, is indispensable to salvation. Without it, salvation is an
absurdity, an impossibility. When God elected saints,
therefore, he elected their sanctification. When he chose
them in Christ, he chose them *that they should be holy.*
His election effectually secures their sanctification, because, as the universal Lord, he determined HOW to rule
all things ; determined all means for all ends ; determined to maintain one reasonable, connected, consistent
system, wise in its purposes and wise in the method of
their accomplishment. The infinite wisdom of God
would be as much dishonored as his rectitude, by supposing that he resolved to save some of our fallen race,
without any regard to the means of their salvation, or
the qualities of those who should be admitted into
heaven, where *there is fullness of joy.* The nature of the

case, therefore, demonstrates the position, that election secures holiness in the elect, because,

First, election is a part of God's universal predestination;

Second, holiness is the means of which salvation is the end; and

Third, holiness is a quality aside from which no election could secure to the soul the felicities of heaven.

III. Let us now advert to the tendencies of this doctrine on the minds of men.

Before entering into the particulars of this article, we wish it to be noticed in what manner it applies to our subject. Our doctrine is, that election secures holiness in the elect; (*ye have not chosen me, but I have chosen you;*) and, consequently, we should expect that the knowledge and belief of this doctrine would have a sanctifying tendency: we should expect that its *effect* upon the minds of men, (as a means,) would be a happy effect. Or, to express the idea in another form, when we show that the doctrine of election preached to the people tends to make them holy, then we have presented a very strong kind of proof that election secures their holiness. We thus show the *practical influences* of the doctrine, its operations and tendencies. We do not attempt, indeed, to solve its difficulties. We pass by what is unknown and mysterious, to examine the plain facts which every body can see. We do not attempt to lift the veil which hides the mysterious agencies of the Divine hand; but we look on this side the veil, taking the place of an open spectator, beholding the effect wrought on human sensibilities and human character by the great doctrine we preach. That effect is holiness. The tendency of the doctrine of eternal election is to lead men to the attainment of *all spiritual blessings.* Listen to five items of illustration.

1. The first is taken from the history of holiness among men.

We wish, my hearers, that you were better acquainted with the history of the Church. We invite you to that branch of study. And we do not hesitate to affirm, that you will find the most holy, and firm, and devoted people, to have been those whose hearts embraced the doctrine of the sovereign election of God. This was one of those great principles which laid the foundation of that heroic and devoted piety, which achieved the wonders of the Reformation. Those great minds, whose energies, tempered by piety and guided by God, possessed power enough in holy science to fling abroad a light that chased darkness from nation after nation, were trained and tutored under the doctrine we preach. Those great hearts, devoted entirely to the truth, undaunted by terror and not discouraged by difficulty, and ready, if need be, to sprinkle with their life's-blood the pathway of discipleship, beat quick, and beat strong, and beat true to the doctrine we preach. This doctrine has always been dear to the most signal and devoted piety. Those churches have always been the most firm which have embraced it. The whole history of holiness among men will demonstrate to you (if you will examine) that this and kindred doctrines have always been among those fundamental principles, which have founded, and fostered, and guided the most pure and perfect holiness ever witnessed among human kind. Look over Christendom. Select those times, or those countries, wherein holiness, true holiness has been most manifest and pure, and you have selected the very times and places wherein this doctrine of election was most preached and most believed. Again, look over all Christendom. Select those times or places wherein the doctrine of election has been opposed, disbelieved, and stricken out of men's preaching and the creeds of the churches, and you have selected the very times and places wherein Christianity has been shorn of half her power! How England and Scotland contrast with one another at the present moment. In the established Church of England, it is well known that this doctrine and those kindred to it have been very commonly rejected for a series of years; and a system of Arminianism has usurped most of the pulpits of the establishment! And what is the result? At this moment, not a few of her ministers are more Popish than Protestant! In Scotland, in the established Church, the doctrine of election and its kindred truths were never rejected. And what do you see there? A purer virtue than the English Church ever had; hundreds of ministers and thousands of private Christians giving up all their churches, and all their church property at once, sooner than allow a corrupt civil government an opportunity to impose a corrupt ministry upon them. You will never see such a spirit of sacrificing and suffering for Christ and his truth, where such doctrines as we preach have been discarded. The Puritans, the Covenanters of Scotland, and the Independents of New England, have been trained, from the cradle, under the doctrine of election and its kindred truths; and among these men there has appeared, from age to age, the most active virtue, the purest holiness the world has ever seen. History proves that the doctrine we preach tends to holiness.

And so plain and indisputable is this, that an able writer of the Edinburgh Review, who seems to have no friendship for this doctrine, was compelled, by the force of a truth so plain in history, to make this remark: " Predestination, (says he,) or doctrines much inclining towards it, have, on the whole, prevailed in the Christian churches of the West, since the days of Augustine and Aquinas. Who were the most formidable opponents of these doctrines in the Church of Rome? The Jesuits—the contrivers of courtly casuistry and the founders of lax morality. Who, in the same church, inclined to the stern theology of Augustine? The Jansenists—the teachers and the models of austere morals. What are we to think of the morality of Calvinistic nations, especially of the most numerous classes of them, who seem, beyond all other men, to be most zealously attached to religion, and most deeply penetrated with its spirit? Here, if any where, we have a decisive test of the moral influence of a belief in necessarian opinions. In Protestant Switzerland, in Holland, in Scotland, among the English Non-conformists, and the Protestants of the North of Ireland, in the New England States—Calvinism was long the prevalent faith, and is probably still the faith of a considerable majority. Their moral character was, at least, completed, and their collective character formed, during the prevalence of Calvinistic opinions. Yet, where are communities to be found of a more pure and active virtue?"* Thus spake a mere political, literary writer. He knew from history, that such doctrines as we preach universally give rise to the most active virtue. They tend to holiness.

* *Edinburgh Review* for Oct. 1821.

2. This doctrine tends to holiness, because its proper and common effect is to make men humble.

There are few obstacles to holiness more powerful than human pride. Pride of heart is opposed to gospel grace. God often complains of it in men, and often enjoins the opposite graces of meekness and humility. The doctrine of election has a tendency to diminish it, and finally eradicate it from the hearts of his people. This doctrine admonishes them of their obstinate and wicked state by nature. It shows them that they were so deep in sin, and so attached to it, that they had not delivered themselves; that they are indebted to the electing love of God, (choosing them for himself in Christ Jesus,) for their present state and joy as Christians, and for all they hope ever to attain. They have not become Christians because they were any better than other people. They are Christians because they were *chosen in Christ before the foundation of the world that they should be holy;* and in his own time, and by his own Spirit, it pleased God to make them *willing in the day of his power* (Ps. cx. 3), and bring them to Christ. It has a very humbling effect upon the Christian's heart to reflect, that he must for ever owe it to the choice of God, and not to himself, that he has been saved. To account for his repentance, for his faith, for his love of holiness, for his prospect of heaven, he must go away from himself, from his merits, and his powers: he must go to the unmerited grace of God: he must go back to the eternal election which God made of him, a poor helpless sinner, before the world was. Thus pride is humbled; *not unto us, not unto us, but to thy name give glory.*—(Ps. cxv. 1.) And thus the believer, under view of this doctrine, becomes more and more meek and lowly of heart. He is subdued. The asperities of his character are softened. His loftiness is laid low; and he attains more and more of the child-like, meek, single-hearted, and holy temper of the man of God. Election strikes at the *root* of pride. It was not any thing in man —it was the sovereign election of God which first opened the least prospect that a sinner could be saved.

3. This doctrine tends to holiness, because it is eminently calculated to awaken feelings of gratitude towards God. What were we that we should have any expectations of good? What were we that God should look on us, and pity us, and love us, and choose us in Christ to be his? The believer is thankful, when he remembers the electing goodness of God. God did not pass him by, and leave him, as justly he might, to the darkness of his sinful condition, and finally to the sadness and despair of eternal death!

> " He saw him ruined by the fall,
> But loved him notwithstanding all;
> He saved him from his lost estate—
> His loving-kindness, oh! how great."

4. This doctrine tends to holiness, because it tends to show the evil nature of sin. We can not fully unfold this idea; we hope, however, to be understood. Sin is a thing so improper for the practice of moral beings, such a contradiction to the demands of their nature, such an *exception* among the things for which moral nature has any provision for resistance, that when it has once commenced, it requires the counsel and control of God to arrest its ravages. Were it not for this counsel, it would have gone on in the heart of every sinner for ever. His own counsel or power never would have arrested it. It is that one mighty evil, which required the action of the Eternal Mind; and is never arrested from working out

the damnation of the soul, but by the election of God. To recover from it, to save the sinner, occupied the thoughts, and fixed the choice of God, before the foundation of the world. God elected, and Christ covenanted to die, and the voice of mercy burst from the skies, *Deliver him from going down to the pit; I have found a ransom.* (Job, xxxiii. 24.) This doctrine wonderfully discloses the strange nature of sin, and thus leads the believer to shudder at its perpetration.

5. This doctrine tends to produce holiness, because it increases veneration and reverence for the Deity. The fact is not to be denied, that those who reject this doctrine and its kindred truths, do manifest a most sad want of solemn veneration and awe for the names, and the word, and the attributes of God. They have a lightness of manner, and an unbecoming familiarity when speaking of the Deity, and even when addressing him in prayer, which are often painfully unpleasant to many pious hearts! That awe, that solemnity, that solemn recollection of the distance between God and us, which ought ever to prevail, are wonderfully wanting! Ours is a doctrine which exalts God upon the throne. It shows him as the infinite, sovereign dispenser of bounty, by his own holy unchangeable will, accomplishing all the purposes of his eternal election—*restraining the wrath of man*, or causing it *to praise him*—bringing, by his own Spirit, to the feet of Jesus Christ, the objects of his love, and, at the same time, hindering no sinner from salvation, but offering it *without money and without price.* In this doctrine, God is like himself—sovereign, holy, mysterious, and good. Such views of the character of the Deity are just, and sober, and humbling, and holy in their influences.

Omitting further arguments, we mention, in conclusion, some of the lessons of instruction which the view we have taken of this subject furnishes :

1. This discussion shows us the error of those persons who pretend that the election of God is only a *national* election, or an election to the enjoyment of privileges, and not *personal*, relating to individuals.

We have seen that believers are elected, *that they should be holy*. God chose them for this. His choice, then, was no mere determination to furnish nations with privileges, but a choice of individuals, *that they should be without blame before him in love*. His choice related to *character*, and not barely to opportunities and privileges.

2. We see from the view we have taken of the doctrine of election, the great mistake of those who represent the doctrine as *fatalism*—a system fixing the eternal destinies of men, without regard to their character. We preach no such doctrine. This representation is a monstrous, and (I am afraid) a wicked misrepresentation of one of the doctrines of grace which we preach. Our doctrine is diametrically opposed to this. It represents the *character* of the Christian, his regeneration, his holiness, to be just as much a matter of God's eternal choice as the *salvation* of the Christian. It connects these two things together. Indeed, it makes the one stand as the constant and unvarying *cause* of the other: *chosen, that we* SHOULD *be holy*. There is no fatalism here.

3. Our subject shows us the monstrous error of those who tell us if the doctrine of election is true, it is no matter what they do, for if they are elected to be saved they shall be saved, and if not, all attempts would be in vain. The doctrine of election says no such thing! It tells us directly the contrary. So far from assuring us it

is no matter what we do, it assures us most definitely
that it has regard to those who are *holy and without
blame before God in love.* God does not hinder our
becoming such. On the contrary, he offers us every
motive and every aid. It is the election of God, and
that only, which effectually and for ever cuts off all hope
of salvation without holiness. Election excludes from
heaven the unholy. Were there *no* decision of God on
this matter, the wicked, in their darkness, might hope,
perhaps, in some way to be saved in their sins. But
election dashes down such hopes. It assures them that
the election of God, *before the foundation of the world,*
embraced holiness. Those who would be saved must
aim to be *without blame before him in love.* There never
was a more monstrous perversion than the pretense that
if election is true it is no matter what we do! It is for
this very reason that it *does* matter what we do. Election
is the very thing which calls on us to cultivate holiness
and love, because these are the qualities which election
will welcome into heaven. Hence,

4. We perceive the strange mistake of those who tell
us that this doctrine leaves them nothing to do in preparing for salvation. It gives them *every thing* to do.
They must learn to become holy, as God is holy. Election never saves men in sin. They must repent of it,
hate it, forsake it. They must *follow holiness* (Heb. 12 :
14). Their very *calling is to holiness* (1 Thess. 4 : 7).
They must cultivate the *fruits of the Spirit, love, joy,
peace, long-suffering, gentleness, goodness, faith, meekness,
temperance* (Gal. 5 : 22). They are to be *made free from
sin,* to *become servants to God,* to *have their fruit unto holiness,*
if their *end* shall be *everlasting life* (Rom 6 : 22). Election makes it certain, that without holiness no man shall

see the Lord. And fallen sinners like us have much to do, if we would mortify sin in our members, and become fit subjects of all *spiritual blessings in heavenly places in Christ.*

5. Finally: we learn, from this subject, the great mistake of those who represent the doctrine of election to be a very discouraging doctrine. It is not. It is the very foundation of hope. Had it not pleased God to choose some to be *holy and without blame*, what ground could you now have for entertaining the most feeble hope of eternal life? You could find none in your merits—none in your powers—and, if this doctrine were gone, none in the provisions, the securities of God! But since he has chosen some, there is reason to hope. All will not perish. Christ has not died in vain. Election hinders nobody from holiness; and every sinner on earth may have just as much evidence of his own election as he has of his own true holiness. Let him be holy, and he may know God has chosen *him*. God chooses men to holiness, and, therefore, in every effort they make to be holy, they may have the consolation of reflecting that the electing God beholds their efforts with an approving eye; and not only so, but every step they take in holiness is an evidence of their election of God. If this is not ground of encouragement, what is? Men may go on working out their salvation, making their CALLING and ELECTION SURE, and be cheered by the unequaled encouragement, that from eternity God had them and their salvation in his eye—that he who has begun a good work in them *will perform it until the day of Jesus Christ* (Phil. 1 : 6), because, if they are holy at all, God IS *blessing them with spiritual blessings in Christ*, ACCORDING *as he hath chosen them in him, before the foundation of*

the world, that they should BE *holy and without blame before him in love.*

We leave this subject to your reflection. It calls you, my dear hearers, to the most careful and blameless walk. Election and holiness go hand in hand. Never separate them. The Divine word puts them together. What God's election *is* you know not; it is hidden among those veiled mysteries which lie beyond the darkness that envelops his throne. But you do know you are called to holiness. Election calls you to it. It dashes down your pride. It tells you that GOD reigns, and will reign, and assures you that there is no election or calling of God but this, that ye SHOULD *be holy and without blame.*

Go, then, submit your soul to a SOVEREIGN GOD. Submit it to him *in Christ.* Go, *work out your salvation with fear and trembling.* Go, *make your calling and election sure.* Go, where God is calling you in the footsteps of Jesus Christ; and though you are *dead in sin,* you shall be *made alive* unto God; and, finally, you shall go to the full and eternal enjoyment of all spiritual blessings in heavenly places in Christ.

God grant it to you, through infinite grace in Jesus Christ our Lord. *Amen.*

Atonement.

Christ hath once suffered for sins, the Just for the unjust, that he might bring us to God.—1 Peter, iii. 18.

THE central point of Christianity is the Cross of the Redeemer of men. Around this point, the whole Divine system encircles itself; and whatever it is, in the principles of instruction, or in the sensibilities of experience, that does not feel the paramount and supreme attraction of the Cross, is something false, empty, delusive; and its erratic tendency must be corrected, or it will wander off, alike beyond the securities of truth, the mercies of God, and the felicities of man. The Cross— the sacrifice of the Son of God—the atonement made for sin, where *Christ suffered for sins, the Just for the unjust,* is the central and supreme idea in the system of salvation.

It ought to be enough to convince us of this, when we find the holy Scriptures constantly referring every general and every special subject to the sacrifice of the Saviour for its elucidation. They always do so. Things most unlike, most distant from one another, most opposite to one another, are referred to the Cross. For example, at once the attributes of the Deity and the malignities of sin; the justice and the mercy of God; the boundless majesty of the Eternal Throne, and the smallest, gentlest sympathies a dying sinner needs, are brought to the sacrifice of the Saviour, to teach us what they are, and give them their due influence over us. This is the style of the Holy Ghost speaking in the Scriptures. This is the method of Divine tuition.

The text is an example of this. It is not one of the most prominent and leading things in religion of which the apostle is speaking, but one of those unobtrusive and every-day duties which might find their enforcement and the principles of their exercise almost every where ; and yet he brings it to the primary idea of Christianity : *It is better, if the will of God be so, that ye suffer for well-doing than for evil-doing ;* and even this plain idea, to give it its proper shape in the mind of the Christian, and its proper impression upon his sensibilities, must be referred to the atonement of Jesus Christ : *For Christ hath once suffered for sins, the Just for the unjust, that he might bring us to God.* This is the method of Christianity. It baptizes every idea with the baptism of Christ.

It is because of this connection of a minor idea of religion with the Atonement, that I have chosen this text, and formed the plan of this sermon. The Atonement comes in every where. This is the remark I make upon this text, and the idea on which I found this discourse.

And hence, it is easy to see the necessity of having correct sensibilities of the nature of the Atonement itself. This is the life of the Christian system. It is the spirit which animates it ; and if our apprehensions and impressions about this are wrong, our religion will be wrong. In proportion to our error on this point will be our unhappiness in Christian experience. If we do not catch the true sprit of the doctrine of the Atonement, we shall not catch the true spirit of Christian life ; and if we live at all to Christ then, it will be a diseased and sickly life; and, instead of resembling those who breathe the pure atmosphere that quickens a heavenly existence, we shall resemble those who breathe the poisoned and pestilent vapors that sometimes float even over the green fields of the Zion of God. The Atonement is the believer's breath of life. He can not take a step, he can not speak a word, he can not feel an emotion in religion without it. It tempers all his hopes, his fears, his faith. It governs his humility, his peace, his love. It guides his gentleness, his goodness. It opens the fountain of his tears. It is the key-note of the song he sings. And, when he goes forth to do good, it turns him from the track of the *Levite and the Priest*, to the better path of the *good Samaritan*, who bears his oil and his wine. If this pervading principle, therefore, becomes corrupted, all else will partake of the taint. If the truth of the principle is all lost, grace will not exist in the soul, and the soul will not be saved.

As the plan of this discourse, therefore, I will mention and explain two different methods of apprehending the Atonement of Jesus Christ, and point out their distinctive characteristics. This shall be the first thing.

And, having thus shown their diversity, I will demonstrate which is the proper method of influencing a believer's sensibility. This shall be the second thing.

But the nature of this subject is such, that we need some caution in speaking and hearing. Allow me, by way of preface, therefore, to remark:

1. That in treating of this theme, I have no reference to that long-continued dispute in the Church, about the extent of the Atonement, whether it is universal or particular, general and unlimited, or special in its nature.

2. That the error at which I aim is found (for aught I know) as frequently among those who adopt one of these theological systems, as among those who adopt the other. It is an error compatible at once with the idea of general, and the idea of particular atonement.

3. That the evil of which I shall speak, and the opposite excellence which I shall aim to commend, are not so much matters of theology as of experience; that they are things affecting the sensibilities of a Christian's piety, far more than the principles of a believer's creed.

4. Final remark; that, so far as I am going to say any thing of principles, and views, and doctrines, as connected with Christian unhappiness or mistake in this matter, I do not mean to censure any principle, or view, or doctrine *by itself:* I do not complain of any one as false. The evil at which I aim is more subtle, more deep, more difficult of detection, more difficult to be spoken of in such a manner as to be understood. We must bespeak your attention. The evil in *principle* (if there is any except in mere *sensibility*) consists, not in false principle, necessarily, (mark this distinction,) but in giving to different TRUE principles an improper proportion of importance. It makes a secondary truth a primary one, and degrades a primary truth to a secondary station. This, if any, is all the *doctrinal* evil connected with the matter, which I would lead you to deplore and shun.

With these cautionary and explanatory remarks retained in the mind of the hearer, we shall not be likely to be misunderstood in the heart of the subject on which we now enter.

I. We are to mention and explain two different

methods of apprehending the atonement of Jesus Christ,
and point out their distinctive characteristics.

There are two very different methods of being *affected*—
(that is the word—I do not say, *opinionated*, or *indoctrin-
ated*—I say *affected*—every word has been carefully
studied;) there are two very different methods of being
affected by the idea of the sacrifice of the Saviour. Probably these methods arise from different methods of
apprehending the Scripture doctrines on this point.
Principles govern the believer. They must govern him.
They mould his sensibilities, they rule his heart, as he is
a child and disciple of the truth. In both these methods
the truth may be embraced; but one way of embracing
it is very different from another, and gives rise to a very
different habit of religious thoughts and impressions.
In one case, the *essence* of the atonement seems to be a
satisfaction rendered to Divine justice and authority for
the indignity done to them by sin: its *object* seems to be,
to sustain the honor of the Divine law; to vindicate the
rectitude and wisdom of the Divine legislation; and
maintain, in all its unimpaired vigor, the energies and
respect of the Divine government. Its *origin* seems to
be, that infinite and holy regard, which the infinite and
holy Ruler of the world has, and must always have, for
his own holy law, which sin has broken, and for that
whole system of moral control, by which he is pleased
to administer the government of the world. Sin (the
folly and the hardihood of man) has committed the
enormity of transgressing the law. In doing so, it has
trampled an infinite authority, called in question the
infinite wisdom of God's legislative requirements, and
dared to break in on the order, and beauty, and harmony of that system of Divine rule in which the

8*

Deity delights. Hence, God is offended! His system of wisdom has been set at nought! His broken laws are scattered around him! Disorder has marred his plan! And if something is not done to maintain the respect due to his authority, and to preserve the integrity of his government, the Deity will be for ever dishonored, and the sinner for ever undone. To pardon will not do, for the law has a penalty and will not relax—for the veracity of the Deity must be true to the threatening—for government must be maintained; and, if one guilty race of the rebellious shall be acquitted and go free, no fear, no respect, no effective motive will be found, to influence other races, in perhaps other worlds, and other ages of time or eternity, to abstain from sin. Hence, Jesus Christ must die, or the sinner can not live. Law, order, the Divine government, demand the death of the Saviour. God's own love of holiness and hatred of sin demand it. His regard for his own honor and the preservation of that moral system, by which he rejoices to rule his moral creatures, demand it. On *this* ground many a believer apprehends that the Atonement for sin was made ; and its essence, its leading idea seems to him to be an offering to Divine justice, or a plan to sustain Divine law and government, while a guilty creature is forgiven and saved.

This is one method of apprehending the doctrine of atonement. The ideas of one, who apprehends it in this way, will recur naturally to the law, the justice, the government of the Deity, whenever the expiation made by Christ is considered. The sensibilities, the emotions, the habitudes of pious feeling with such a one, will all be connected with the proprieties of holiness, the Divine government and honor. These things will be *first.*

They will take *the lead*. They will temper the grateful piety of the heart; and, when the blood of Atonement comes into view, one who views it in this way will see that the *law is magnified and made honorable*, and a door of hope opened to the guilty. This is one method of apprehending the Atonement. And all these ideas, taken separately, are just. God does love his Law; his government and authority must be maintained; and it did enter into the reasons for the Saviour's death, that God *might be just and the justifier of him* who believes in his Son.

But there is another style of apprehending the Atonement. It makes the illustrious sacrifice of Jesus Christ less public, but more personal in its aims. In this case the sensibilities of the believer, his habits of feeling as he resorts to Christ and his cross, are *not primarily* affected by any ideas of a public nature or governmental transaction. With such a one, the *essence* of the atonement seems to be, a satisfaction rendered to the Deity for the offence of the sinner, (I do not say for the offence of *sin*, but the *sinner*,) so that the sinner can be saved: its *object* seems to be to make peace for the sinner with his offended Father, so that the alienated may be reconciled, and God, in the fullness of his tenderness, may throw the arms of his fatherly embrace around his guilty, but forgiven child: its *origin* seems to be, that tender and wonderful love which God has for even poor, guilty sinners; so that, even when justice demands it, and the throne of God would be for ever spotless, if they should all sink to perdition, God will not give them up. But while justice is offended, authority outraged, law and government dishonored, and the sinner himself is as ungrateful, as rebellious, as undesirous to be reconciled as he is guilty, the kindness of God still pursues him and pours on his deafened ear that flood of persuasion, *God so loved the world, that he gave his only begotten Son, that whosoever believeth in him should not perish but have everlasting life.* In this case, sin is regarded as having ruined the sinner, and Christ as having died out of love to save him; and the sensibilities of a believer's piety, instead of being affected, as in the other case we mentioned, by a great governmental transaction, are far sooner affected by such ideas as that—

> " This was compassion like a God,
> That, when the Saviour knew
> The price of pardon was his blood,
> His pity ne'er withdrew."

In this case, it is not the *government* of God but the *compassion* of God—not the honoring of law, but the pardoning of the sinner, that seems to come most naturally and sweetly over the heart of the believer. This is his method of Christian affection; this is the way in which the believer is accustomed to have his impressions regulated, his faith, his hope, his love, his sacred confidence quickened by the ideas of the Atonement of Christ. His sensibilities, his habitudes of pious feeling, are all connected, *first*, with that paternal but infinite love which followed hard after him in his prodigal wanderings, and would sooner give up the Son to bathe, with his blood, the sword of Divine justice, than leave even such a guilty sinner to his deserved doom. In this case, whenever the Atonement comes to mind, the love, the kindness, the compassion of God come with it. These things are first. They will take the lead. They will temper the grateful piety of the heart. And as believers, who apprehend the Atonement in this method, indulge the hopes and tenderness of their piety, they learn to say : *We love him, because he first loved us—he is our peace— he hath reconciled us to God*, not merely to his government, but *to God, by his cross*.

And all these ideas, like those we have mentioned in the other case, are true. The difference between these two methods of apprehending the Atonement does not consist in the fact, that either of them embraces falsehoods; or in the fact that any particular ideas of the one method are, *in themselves*, incompatible with any particular ideas of the other method. The difference consists rather in the order, the arrangement of truths, in the shape in which they lie in the mind, and the method in which they influence the feelings of piety. The same believer may, at times, employ both, without changing one of the principles of his creed. The difference is more a matter of sentiment than of doctrine. It belongs to the heart, not to the head.

But it is certain there *is* a difference. These methods are not the same. Perhaps I shall be more clearly understood, if I place in immediate contrast some of their distinctive characteristics. Let us see.

One method of apprehending the Atonement makes it governmental, the other individual. In the one case, the believer sees first, that law must be honored, Divine government maintained : in the other, he sees first, that the love of God yearns over the poor sinner.

One method makes the Atonement honor law : the other makes it save the sinner.

One method makes it a public thing : the other makes it one of the actings of special love.

One makes it great : the other makes it affectionate.

One represents God as glorifying himself in the whole: the other, as endearing and glorifying himself in a single *sinner that repenteth.*

One method exalts his authority as king: the other, while it exalts, endears his authority as a Father.

The one makes God a contriver of matchless wisdom: the other makes him a friend of matchless tenderness.

The one method makes individual sinners happily subordinate to a plan of infinite wisdom which (while it saves sinners) is going to manage a universe, and, by the mighty vastness and harmony of its great redeeming transactions, give lustre to the diadem that crowns the brow of *the King of kings and Lord of lords:* the other makes the great plans of eternal and infinite love subordinate to the felicitous interests of the least of God's moral creatures, and gives the brightest glory to the diadem of God, when it writes upon it, for the sinner's view—*Father of mercies, King of saints.*

The one method would lead the sinner to stand by the cross, as the centurion stood; and, while *the rocks were rent* and the heavens grew dark as the Saviour groaned, would lead him to exclaim, *Surely this was the Son of God:* the other would lead him to stand there, as John and Mary stood—silent, subdued, and satisfied, not a word to say, but every thing to feel, as the august but dying Victim exclaims, *It is finished—and gives up the ghost.*

These, as near as I am able to express them, are some of the distinctive traits of these two methods of being affected by the sacrifice of the Saviour. They both embrace the same truths, but they yield to them different degrees of proportionate regard.

II. I am to demonstrate which of these two is the proper method of Christian sensibility. I name to you six or seven proofs, to show that our hearts ought to apprehend the Saviour's atonement, not so much as a plan to prepare the way to save sinners—not so much as a public governmental transaction due to law, to holiness and the authority of the Deity—as a more personal and special sacrifice to meet the sins, and sorrows, and wants of the soul itself.

1. The first proof is taken from the manner in which the origin of the redemption purchased by Christ is usually spoken of in the Scriptures. It originated in the kindness of God for ruined man—*God so loved the world.* Here is the fountain of it. It flows from the depths of the compassion of God. It originates in the love of a Father's heart over the misery, and profligacy, and rebelliousness of a ruined child. He has wandered from home. He has abandoned his best interests, while he has rebelled against the most kind and holy authority. He has lost every thing. He merits nothing. And the true method of appreciating the Atonement—the Scripture representation of its origin, is this: that God feels toward the sinner just as a father would feel toward a prodigal son. What is it that makes such a father's heart bleed? What is it that fills his eyes with tears, as the recollection of the ruined child presses upon his bosom? It is not the disregard of his authority—it is not the dishonor of his family and his name—it is not the dreadful ingratitude of his ruined child. All these he could have borne. But that his child himself should be miserable and guilty—his son, his beloved son, over whose infancy he watched, and prayed, and poured out his tears—over whose youth his heart beat such unutter-

able emotions, as he hoped that son would be useful, and honorable, and happy—would stay up the trembling steps of his age—would smooth his dying pillow, and lay him in his grave—that *this son* should be miserable and guilty, is more than the father can bear! This is his anguish! This is his wormwood and gall! And this is the *primary* feeling which would influence him to do any thing for the recovery of the wanderer: almost the *only* feeling. It overshadows all others. Make *that son happy,* and the father would be willing that his own gray hairs should descend dishonored into the grave. It is thus that the Scriptures represent the origin of the Atonement. It comes *from the* LOVE *of God* toward sinners, not from his mere attachment to a holy moral government: *The kindness and love of God our Saviour toward man hath appeared, not by works of righteousness which we have done, but according to his mercy he saved us . . . that being justified by his grace, we should be made heirs according to the hope of eternal life.*

This is the Scripture representation. The Atonement originates, not in the love of God for a holy system, which sin has broken and dishonored, but in the love of God for a precious being whom sin has ruined. His holy system might have been honored, his justice honored, his government honored, without it. They *were* honored when Sodom burnt and when Satan fell. The spirits in prison, reserved in chains unto the judgment of the great day, demonstrate that the Deity has a method of maintaining his authority aside from the cross of his Son.

2. The second proof is found in the style of the Scripture expression respecting the *object* of the Atonement.

I am not aware that that object, in a single passage of

Divine writ, is said to be to honor the Divine law, or sustain the authority of justice and the Divine government. These things are often spoken of, indeed, as being done by the sacrifice of Christ—he *magnified the law, and made it honorable.* But if you will particularly notice the manner in which they are spoken of, you will perceive these are merely *incidental,* or secondary, while the primary *object* of the Saviour's sacrifice was another thing. It is the persons that are first had in view to be saved—not the great plan of holy and universal government to be honored. *He was wounded.* For the honor of a broken law? How dreadfully that would change the sentiment of the Scriptures! I perceive, while I utter it, the very idea makes your heart sink within you! No, no! He *was wounded for* OUR *transgressions,* he *was bruised for* OUR *iniquities, the chastisement of* OUR PEACE *was upon him, and by his stripes* WE *are healed.* This is the style of the Holy Spirit. The sacrifice of the Son of God was no mere exhibition—no mere public opening of the way of mercy. He was *slain for us, the Just for the unjust, that he might bring us to God.*

3. The third proof is taken from the proper and most distressful feelings that we experience about sin. What are these feelings? Not that the Divine government has been dishonored—not that the proprieties of a system of righteous conduct have been disregarded—not even that the thunders of Heaven are aroused and ready to burst upon the sinner's devoted head. All this he can feel in his *impenitence,* and before the Holy Spirit has made on his heart the most proper and distressful impressions of the evil of sin. These impressions are different. They contain the deep sadness of the conviction, that God's

love is forfeited—that the anger of God (the most distressful of all ideas) is righteously incurred—that of ourselves, we are so undone, and guilty, and unworthy, we cannot attain peace. Sin itself is then a burden to us! Our Father's heart is estranged from us! Our own heart is void, and blank, and bleeding! It wants something—something to lean upon! not *a plan*, but *a friend*. Conviction of sin is the dreadful desolation of a robbed soul; guilty, unworthy, helpless, fatherless! it is cut off from God!

Now, if such is the essence of conviction, what is the essence of the sensibility which the heart experiences, as it closes with the Saviour?   Does it close with a *a plan?* or with *a friend?*   Does it close with a governmental contrivance? or close with a precious Christ?   You have often sung its experience:

> " That blest moment I received him
> Filled my soul with joy and peace,
> Love I much, I 've much forgiven;
> I 'm a miracle of grace."

The believer through Christ is something more than reconciled to righteous authority; he is restored to a Father's heart.

4. We take a fourth proof from the method in which believers, all those of the most sweet and marked piety, have rejoiced. They have rejoiced exactly like young converts—in the sweetness and simplicity of a blessed confidence—in what God calls *the kindness of their youth, the love of their espousals*. When piety has been pure, when they have had grace enough not only to be religious, but to be happy in religion, all their joy, their peace, their triumph, has been intimately connected with

a personal reception of Jesus Christ as their own Saviour, their friend, their *elder brother*. They take his righteousness: they are sprinkled with his blood: they enter into all such arguments as breathe in that passage, *because I live, ye shall live also.*

Notice this, when, by the power of Divine grace, they can tread the world under foot: *God forbid that I should glory, save in the cross of our Lord Jesus Christ, by whom the world is crucified unto me, and I unto the world.*

Notice this, when the confidence of faith challenges the claims of righteousness: *Who shall lay any thing to the charge of God's elect? It is God that justifieth: Who is he that condemneth? It is Christ that died, yea rather that is risen again, who is even at the right hand of God, who also maketh intercession for us.* It is *for* US. Christ hath been delivered up *for us.* This is the idea; not for *a plan*, but for *his people:* this is the leading and the sweetest impression.

Notice this, when the power of religion transports a believer beyond himself, in his desires to serve God and win souls to Christ: *The love of Christ constraineth us, because we thus judge that if one died for all, then were all dead; and that he died for all, that they which live should not henceforth live unto themselves, but unto him who died for them and rose again. Henceforth, know we no man after the flesh: if any man be in Christ, he is a new creature; old things are passed away, all things are become new, and all things are of God, who hath reconciled* US *to* HIMSELF *by Jesus Christ. We are embassadors for Christ. As though God did beseech you by us, we pray you in Christ's stead, be ye reconciled to God. For he hath made him to be sin for* US, *that we might be made the righteousness of God in* HIM. FOR US—IN HIM: The Apostle can not speak without indicating in which method *he* apprehends the Atonement of Christ. This is the style of feeling in which all happy and triumphing believers speak; and this comes from the very nature of spiritual life.

> " Jesus, I my cross have taken,
>   All to leave, and follow thee ;
> Naked, poor, despised, forsaken,
>   THOU from hence my all shall be.
>
> Farewell, every fond ambition,
>   All I 've sought, or loved, or known ;
> Yet, how blest is my condition,—
>   Christ and heaven are still my own."

5. We bring a fifth proof from the nature of that faith that saves. What is its nature? what does it do? It is the gracious and indissoluble bond of union that connects—what? the soul to an economy?—to a contrivance?—no, nothing like it; but, the sinner to Jesus Christ. *I am the vine; ye are the branches.* Faith receives him and rests on him. *He* is the offer that God makes to a sinner. *My beloved is mine, and I am his*, are the two exultations of faith.

6. You may find a sixth proof in the best frames of heart which ever cheer and comfort the people of God. Their frames are not all alike. The believer's heart does not always *burn within him*, but only while he talks with a risen Christ. In the times of your coldness you still feel that Christ honors law; in your best frames you feel that Christ is your friend; this is the sensibility of your sweetest and tenderest moments :

> " He saw me ruined in the fall,
>   But loved me notwithstanding all ;
> He saved me from my low estate,—
>   His loving-kindness, O how great !"

Such is the strain of the songs that the Christian loves to sing in times of revival; and with which he loves to indulge his heart when alone in the sweet solemnity of his closet he communes with God. Plan, government, is forgotten; but Christ has come into his *banqueting-house*, and *his banner over you is love.*

7. I find a final proof in the necessities of my own nature. Man is in the world but a little while. Through distressful changes he is hurrying on to another. His experiences often convince him that he knows but little of what it is that can make him happy; and, whether in this world or in another, his nature is such that, among his vicissitudes and his trials, he needs *a friend.* As he looks forward to the uncertainties before him— to his death—to his eternity—he cannot be satisfied with any *plan* for his felicity, with any profusion, or promise of bounty, without something more. The heart demands more. It has a want, a void, that no mere arrangement, or economy, or plan can fill. The child would not be satisfied, and could not long be happy, without something more. His parents may supply all his outward wants, may protect, defend, and teach him; but if he is a virtuous and affectionate child, all this can not make him happy. He needs their LOVE. This is the want of his heart and he can not, if he would, dispense with it. The wife could never be satisfied (and ought not to be) with all the attention and care, and all the protection and supply that the most vigilant husband could furnish. Amid all this, she would pine and languish—grief would. consume her heart, if she knew all this attention and arrangement were dictated by no affection for her, but only by a cold sense of propriety. Give her the confidence of requited

love, and she will bear any thing without a murmur, side by side with him round whom her heart clings. She will share his crust, and his cabin or his cave, if he can do no better for her. It is *nature* that works thus. The heart demands something to repose upon. Plans, arrangements, contrivances will not do. Affection would spurn them when substituted in the place of the communion, the tenderness, the sympathies of love. Profusion, bounty, promise will not do. There is one thing, and there is but one, that can fill up the void and pour happiness into the aching bosom.

Just so, only a thousand-fold greater in degree, are the sinner's wants for eternity. He can see but a little way. Death will soon remove him into a state of untried being. He is going to leave all the sympathy and fellowship that have cheered him here. He must take a final leave of his family. He is bound to eternity, and can not tarry. And he is going there, a poor, helpless, and unworthy sinner. He is going to be judged. All his sins shall come to light. He who sits upon the judgment-seat is holy and just, and holds all the destinies of a dreadful eternity in his hand.

Now, the Atonement of Christ is enough to meet all this. It perfectly answers to the sinner's wants, and perfectly satisfies his heart, and many a dying believer has longed to *depart and be with Christ*. But it could not do these things, if Divine grace only taught him to repose upon the abstractions of wisdom, and left him without *a friend*. But it has not. It has taught him that there is One whose love will not fail him. He needs not only to be provided for, to be pardoned, but to *be loved*. He needs to have God love him—the holy Judge and Father of Eternity. And all his want is supplied, when, in the true method of apprehending the Atonement, he says of the Saviour, *Who loved* ME, *and gave himself a ransom* FOR ME: *Christ hath once suffered, the Just for the unjust, that he might bring us to God:* HE *will come again and receive us to himself, that where he is there we may be also:*

> " He near my soul has always stood,
> His loving-kindness, oh! how good."

This subject needs not a word of application to believers. They have made the application as we have gone along. I should be ashamed to insult you with any other.

But, in view of this subject, ought we not to wonder and exclaim, over the senseless hearts of these sinners, who will not be drawn by the love of Christ? and who, on the next Lord's day, when Christ will meet his loved ones at his sacramental table, and pour the balm of comfort upon their wounded hearts, will turn away from the banqueting-house of God's eternal love! I would not do it for a thousand worlds. How can you treat so one who has loved you as Christ has loved you, and done for you what no other being could? Be astonished, oh heavens! Here, on this sin-cursed world, which has drunk the blood of the Son of God, a sinner turns his back upon him! If there is compassion in the universe, it is God's! If there is kindness, tenderness any where, it is found in that Saviour, whose blood you are trampling under foot! If you have got a friend in the universe, it is Christ; and yet, " You treat no other friend so ill."

Mystery Appropriate in Redemption.

For I would that ye knew what great conflict I have for you, and for them
at Laodicea, and for as many as have not seen my face in the flesh;
that their hearts might be comforted, being knit together in love, and
unto all riches of the full assurance of understanding, to the acknowledgment of the mystery of God, and of the Father, and of Christ; in whom
are hid all the treasures of wisdom and knowledge.—COLOSSIANS, ii. 1–3.

IN few words, we desire to give the briefest possible
exposition of this passage. Five points will suffice.

1. You will notice the apostle speaks of his own Christian desire, of the *great conflict* in his own mind, as he expresses it, in behalf of other Christians, some of whom he
had never seen. As is common with him, he speaks out
of the fullness of his heart as a believer and a Christian
minister, and, therefore, you need not expect him to be
confined to the intellectual mode of a mere human reasoning. He will reason like a child of God—as if he had
a heart, and an immortal soul.

2. You will notice that his desire for these Christians
was, that they *might be comforted.*

3. You will notice that the *mode* in which he expected
them to be comforted, embraced two things, LOVE, *that
their hearts might be knit together in love*, and, UNDERSTAND-
ING, *i. e.* knowledge, the desirableness or value of which
he expresses by speaking of *all riches of the full assurance
of understanding.* By this *love*, and this assured and rich

knowledge of the Christian system, he desired that believers should be *comforted*. He supposed they had some comfort; and, by growth in affection and knowledge, he desired they should have more.

4. If they *had* it, he supposed it would lead them to the *acknowledgment* of, *i. e.* to the avowed confession and glorying in, *the mystery of God, even of the Father and of Christ*. And then,

5. You will notice, that, having mentioned *Christ and mystery*, he adds, in respect to Christ, *in whom are hid all the treasures of wisdom and knowledge*. Of the Christian system he speaks as a *mystery*, and yet he speaks not only of an *acknowledgment* of it, but of the *riches of a full assurance of understanding*, just as if there were some way of coming into the mystery, and he speaks of our Lord Jesus Christ as being that way—the grand treasury of the wisdom of God. This is a brief exposition of the text.

There are other texts much like it. In 1 Cor. iv. 1, he speaks of ministers of the gospel as *stewards of the mysteries of God;* because they are to unfold his mysteries to men, teaching them Christianity. In 1 Tim. iii. 16, this same Apostle affirms: *Great is the mystery of godliness; God was manifest in the flesh, justified in the Spirit, seen of angels, preached unto the Gentiles, believed on in the world, received up into glory.*

It is very evident that the redeeming work of Christ is the special matter which the Apostle has in his mind, when he mentions *the mystery of God*, and that he expects believers to have the *comfort* which he so much desired for them, just by a *full assurance of understanding* respecting it, or by an established and intelligent faith. It would be easy to demonstrate, were it necessary, that just Christian *comfort* is to be attained in no other way.

It is faith which both establishes and purifies the heart. Thus it saves.

When the Apostle mentions the *mystery of God*, I suppose he employs the word *mystery* in its general New Testament sense, to signify that which is wonderful, or something beyond the ordinary manifestations of God, and therefore something beyond all the discoveries of an unaided reason, and yet (when once revealed and understood by faith) of such a nature, as to be capable of an *assurance of understanding*, so that a believer may justly and reasonably make an *acknowledgment* of this mystery of God, or, in other words, *glory in the cross of our Lord Jesus Christ.*

We propose to attempt this subject. We propose to show that the *mysteries of God*, the wonders of redemption by Christ, have their excellency, and their appropriateness, and their *comforting* nature, just because they have this character of mystery, of marvelousness, of something beyond all the range of nature and all the powers of an unaided human reasoning.

I have often been struck with the idea that the difficulties and objections that some men find in the system of our religion, and on account of which they tell us they find it hard to embrace our doctrines, are all founded on the very same things which make true believers adhere to the system with most confidence and most comfort. The very things which have been objected to, as unreasonable, or as hard to believe, or as having no analogy in all other works and ways of God, are the very things which, to the believer, make Christianity most valuable. The atonement made for sinners by the death of Christ, is perhaps the most signal instance of difficulty. Men have said, and are still saying, that this is a hard matter for human reason to believe. That God should inflict misery and death upon an innocent Christ, and on that account deliver from punishment a race of sinners— that the guiltless should be put into the place of the guilty—that the justice which condemned some should be satisfied with a substitute whom no justice could condemn—that an unchangeable law should turn aside its penalty from its manifest violators, and should pour out its dreadfulness upon Him who never violated it; such things have constituted a difficulty and a ground of objection to Christianity with thousands of human reasoners. They cannot see the justice of this transaction. They cannot conceive how law is thus satisfied, or God thus honored. They tell us that this is a transaction which certainly seems contrary to all human notions of retributive justice, and certainly finds no analogy in any thing else which the Lord God is known to do—no analogy in nature.

Perhaps it is not unnatural, and ought to be expected, that these men should bring up these objections, and be staggered at such formidable difficulties. Two causes contribute to lead to this—their principles, and their perceptions.

First: The principles of these men are all principles gathered on other subjects, on other fields, relate to other matters, are *after the rudiments of the world*—as the eighth verse has it—*philosophy and vain deceit*, and therefore ought not to be introduced here, as fit principles of judgment and reasoning. They appeal to nature; and they ask us, where in nature do you find any analogy to the atonement? They appeal to human justice; and ask, where among all the decisions of a respectable jurisprudence, or among all the sane ideas of men in respect to

retributive justice, can you point to any thing which resembles the atonement of Christ and its claimed consequences? *Nowhere*, we rejoice to answer, *nowhere*.
And we remind men who find this difficulty in their way,
that when they come up to the subject of religion,
they enter upon a matter infinitely higher than any
mere matter of nature, of human jurisprudence, or
man's injustice to man, and, therefore, their *principles*—their mere philosophical *principles*—which may
do very well for the little fields of this world, and
its life, will not answer for them on the higher and
wider fields of religion.   But they are all the principles
they have got, and we may expect them to use them.

Secondly: The perceptions of these men contribute to
their embarrassment.   There is a wide difference betwixt
a convicted and an unconvicted sinner.   With one who
justly sees his sins, there are perceptions about character,
and condition, and unworthiness, which enter much
further into the matter than any perceptions of a mere
reasoner.   There are things about God, about his holiness,
and the dreadfulness of his indignation, perceived very
clearly by men when conscience is alarmed, and the Holy
Spirit brings the light of truth into the deep recesses of
the soul, which unconcerned men know very little about.
Till they have more just perceptions, and those more
appropriate to the great subject-matter of religion, it is
no wonder if they object to the very things in which a
believer most rejoices.

If you will attend to a few of the particulars which
we are going to name, you may perceive, by even an
ordinary reason, as I think, at least something of the proprieties of those strange wonders for which nature has
no analogy, and which do not come within the scope of

mere human reasonings. These particulars may at once be comforting to the Christian, and a reproof to an unbeliever.

Men are staggered by the mysteries of God; such things as the incarnation, the atonement, the justice of God satisfied for sinners by the death of Christ.

I. Let them consider, that this salvation is itself a high and peculiar matter. There is nothing else like it. The affair has respect, too, to the *high and awful awards of eternity*. An immortal soul is to be saved or lost. Heaven is built for it. Hell is dug for it. The celestial inhabitants of another world are bending over the battlements of heaven, to take cognizance of the mortal beings who are soon to leave this world, and ready to rejoice *over one sinner that repenteth*. *The devil and his angels* wait amid their glooms and the *fire prepared* for them, to hail with a hellish malignity the addition to their companionship, to be made when a sinner dies unforgiven. Such is the matter in question.

Now, what shall we say in respect to the fit modes of meeting its high and awful exigences? Will any ordinary procedure do? Will it be reasonable in such a case? Will it suit the occasion? Will it be trustworthy? An immortality is periled! An eternity is at stake! And I appeal to all that is sense, and all that is sensibility, if it is not wrong to bring up the ordinary proceedings of this little world, and ordinary principles and practices of this little race of mortal creatures, and this little inch of time to meet the high exigences of the case. I appeal to all that is sense and sensibility, if, in such a case, there is not occasion for some new machinery or movement, some grand, and peculiar, and unparalleled work of God, which shall cope with the nature of the matter in question—which shall cope with all the grandeur of God, and the grandeur of eternity, and throw the strength of its security around all the majesty and magnificence of immortality. We *want* the atonement—we want the incarnation—want the wonders of the crucifixion, the resurrection, all the miracles, from the manger of Bethlehem to the ascension from Mount Olivet. We want something which goes beyond all analogy, and all nature, and all human reason ; else the mode of our salvation cannot correspond with the salvation itself, and by such a correspondence confirm our reason, and comfort our hearts with the confidence that God himself has undertaken for us.

You may take your ordinary principles, and analogies, and reasonings to guide you, in all other matters, as you will. We have no quarrel with you about that. But when we come to a matter of eternity, of immortal life for a sinner, or everlasting death ; both our understanding for its *full assurance*, and our heart for its *comfort*, demand that you fling your analogies to the winds, and let us have something coming out of the *mystery of God, even of the Father and of Christ*, which shall assort with the *thing to be done* for a sinner—with all the deep importance and high splendors of immortality. The salvation of a sinner is not a temporal matter to be provided for—not any earthly exigency to be met; and, therefore, the plan that shall save him ought to rise infinitely above the principles of mere nature, and the analogies of this world, and be peculiar, august, and grand, as his hoped-for *glory, and honor, and immortality.*

II. In this matter of a sinner's salvation, the *eternal God himself* forms a special part of the question. His demands are to be met. He is angry with sinners, and his anger is to be pacified. We should, indeed, have a very erroneous idea of his anger, and an idea derogatory to his character, if we were to conceive of him as having an anger similar to the anger of men. His anger is not passionate, not hasty, and agitating, and unseasonable; it ruffles no composure; there is no perturbation about it. It is cool, calm, determined, reasonable, and therefore the more dreadful. It moves to the performance of its purposes with a holy and settled decision, just, inflexibly just. The quarrel which a sinner has with God is, therefore, very unlike his quarrel with any other antagonist. God cautions him of this, when he says to him, *I will not meet thee as a man.* The most awful of all ideas, that I know any thing about, is the idea of the anger of God. With a reasonable creature, every hope dies, and every joy sinks in that abyss of horror—God his enemy! The very character and person of God are involved in this matter of a sinner's prospects.

What, then, shall be done for such a sinner? Will you resort for an answer to this question, to those systems of justice which prevail betwixt man and his equals, and thence determine a matter which lies betwixt man and his God? Will you demand that this high and awful business shall be settled on principles which find some analogy among the little interests, and on the little fields, of an earthly existence? Impossible! Absurd! perfectly absurd! You can find no analogy for God—no analogy for the anger of God. You can not fathom the offence against sin which lies in the depths of the Divine mind, and your puny reason can not touch the question, what shall pacify it. You can only know, that the magnitude of the recovery must assort with the magnitude of God; and, therefore, a sinner needs for his salvation some mighty achievement, some untold wonder which shall be able to cope with the difficulty—the anger of God. Who can tell what this shall be? God only can tell. Not a created being in the universe could answer the question, or reason about it. Christ could answer it, because he was God. He did answer it: *a body hast thou prepared me. Lo, I come to do thy will, oh God;* and now the august and adorable wonder of the sacrifice just assorts with the magnitude of the difficulty, and thus opens a highway for the sinner up to the very favor of God. The Divinity of the atonement is the foundation of its efficacy. Its mystery, its adorable wonder, its being something beyond all the analogies of nature, and all the explanations of human reason, is the very thing which carries its efficacy where sinners need it, to quench that anger of God which he has told us *burns to the lowest hell.*

III. This matter of salvation has most, if not the whole of its nature, from the *matter of sin.* It must save sinners. Sin is the strangest thing, save one, in the universe. Nothing but the Christ who died for it equals its wonder. It is an infinite marvel how a holy and almighty God could ever have permitted it to come into existence. It seems to be an exception in the universe—a dark exception to all God's other permissions. Its existence is an infinite wonder. Why did not God prevent it, if he could; and if he could not, where was his omnipotence? If he did not choose to prevent it, where was his benevolence? If he is good, where slept his goodness, when he permitted a creature of his own formation to ruin himself by becoming his enemy? Strange questions! Who can answer them? What finite mind can grapple with the dark grandeur of such interrogatories, which have respect to the very wonders of God? But sin is here: strange thing as it is, it is here. Powerful, holy, and benevolent as God is, sin is here. Here it has begun its mischiefs, loading our air with its sighs, and making our world a grave-yard!

Now, in the nature of the case, on an occasion like this, what shall be done? Sin is to be met, and sin is an infinite mystery, whose very existence you can not explain. And in such a case, to meet the demands of such an embarrassment, to come in upon this field of eternal wonder, would your heart be satisfied, your reason be satisfied, to have God Almighty do nothing more than he does in his ordinary government over the world? Must there not be a *proportion* betwixt the thing to be done, and the means for its performance? Would you send an infant to lift a mountain? would you expect the dew to extinguish a volcano? would you raise your puny arm to stop a hurricane? If God had not gone beyond his other performances in this matter of sin, this eternal wonder, you could not trust him, for you would not believe him to be in earnest, or that his means met the demands of the occasion. The human mind seeks a proportion betwixt means and ends; and, if the wonders of redemption do not assort with the wonders of sin's existence, they are insufficient to grapple with the difficulties of the case. The means of salvation for sinners must be able to carry their wonders as far as sin carries its wonders, and, among graves and the bones of the dead, show that they *are* means adequate to what is expected of them! Yea, they must be such as to be able to carry their wonders up to the very character of God, and wipe out that stain upon his benevolence, which the existence and miseries of sin seem to have placed there! Oh, Deist! oh, materialist! oh, thou fond child of nature, striving to pick up among the analogies of this world a religion which shall suit you and save you, remember you are a sinner: look on a corpse, cast your eye down to a grave's depth, and tell if you do not need all the wonders of God in an atoning redemption, in order to see light in that grave's depth, and see life coming back into the cold marble of that corpse! Give me the Gospel, its Christ and its crucifixion, and I can see that, after all sin's strangeness and evils, there is a power at work which shall yet show that sin and the benevolence of the Deity are not at war with one another; or, if they are, that the benevolence of the Deity is, after all sin's doings, unstained and infinite, and shall come off victorious. Give me the wonders of the Gospel, and I can see that, when I stand by my pious friend in the strugglings of his death-hour, and then bear his corpse to the land of silence, nothing has happened to him which shall not be good for him, and was not ordered by the benevolence of God. He shall be happier in heaven eternally, than if he had never been a sinner, and had never died and been buried. The wonders of sin are surpassed by the wonders of Christ. Blessed be God.

IV. Sin is the transgression of *God's Law*. God has *acted* as an infinite moral Legislator, and thus committed himself in the sight of a universe of intelligent creatures. Law is a matter of inconceivable moment. Obedience to it among men is the grand means for securing earthly interests; and Law is the security of heaven. "Its seat is the bosom of God." Every one of its enactments proceeds from his infinite benevolence. His government is just one of the workings of his infinite good-will towards his creatures. But sin has violated his law, and on his veracity, as the guardian of his universe, he is committed to sustain it.

What, then, shall be done? This sin is not a mere matter of acting contrary to human enactments and human relationships—it is a matter of acting against the relationship which a sinner sustains to God, and against the duties which bear on the destiny of his whole eternity. No mind can gauge the dimensions of importance which belong to this violated law. And, therefore, does it belong to human reason to contrive any means which shall save the sinner and not tarnish the law? Since all the stretch of human reason can not measure the importance of the law of God which sin violates, does not reason itself demand that something shall be done (if a sinner is to be saved) which reason itself can not comprehend ; something which shall be able to reach as far as law reaches, and carry its influences as far as sin could carry its consequences, and thus cope with all the magnitude of that difficulty in which a sinner is floundering, when the thunder of God's law is out against him, to guard God's rights, and the eternal weal of God's creatures ? I declare to you, if I have an item of understanding, a single ray of reason, I can not conceive how any reasonable being could rest his hope of escape from the eternal penalty (if he is a sinner) on *any thing* which should not stretch itself beyond his comprehension, and put on the character of an eternal wonder, *a mystery of God*. If I could explain the atonement, I should spoil it ! I want it to be an inexplicable wonder. I want it to reach sin's evil. I want it to satisfy God's

law. I want it to silence God's thunders not only, but
turn them all in my favor, and let every one of my
enemies know, that, if he touches me, he touches the
apple of God's eye. My reason demands miracles in this
awfully grand matter. It welcomes, it hails the miracle
of the Incarnation, of Gethsemane, of the Crucifixion, of
the announced Atonement, of a Law honored by a Substitute, and a sinner saved by the blood of another. My
God here is *like* God, an infinite and eternal wonder, inconceivably great and inconceivably good! Praise him!
oh my soul, praise him! Earth, a world of sinners,
praise him! His redemption copes with the grandeur
of his government, and brings the aids of its security to
a sinner who deserves eternal wrath!

V. This business of a sinner's salvation stands connected with God's *honor and glory as a moral governor:*
sin is against his moral government, and therefore comes
into conflict with the highest department of his glory.
The essential glory of God, indeed, remains ever the
same, and nothing can ever conflict with it. But his
declarative glory, or that excellency and honor which
his intelligent creatures can perceive to belong to him
on account of his works, has different degrees belonging
to it, and may be greater or less according to the nature
of his operations intelligently perceived and contemplated. In the works of nature, as we call them, we
have some of these different things which honor him in
different degrees. He himself often appeals to them. The
*mountains which he weigheth in scales and the hills in a bal-
ance,* and the *isles which he taketh up as a very little thing,* are
manifestations and claims of an honor which belongs to
him. A still higher honor is his due, when he gives life to

matter, clothes the *grass of the field* with its green, paints the *lilies of the field*, and animates the wild-bird that carols on the wing. His honor rises still higher when he gifts with intelligence and reason, *maketh his angels spirits*, and man capable of studying his works. But his highest glory lies in none of these. He is a moral governor. He is a holy God. There, on that field, in that department, above mere matter, mountains and seas— above the high kingdom of intelligence, and in the department of right and wrong, of moral beauty and excellency, there lies the most valuable of God's declarative glory. Nature is but a subordinate system. Nature must give way to moral purposes. The Red Sea must give way : Sinai must tremble : the sun must stand still : the widow's *cruise of oil and barrel of meal* must forget to diminish, and dead men must leap into life, if the moral purposes of God demand it. Scholars would do well to remember this, and remember how, in all God's moral dealings with men, he has steadily shown that even the ways and laws of Nature shall stop, if a moral purpose require it. God puts all such things subordinate to something higher, and scholars have no right to reason on what they may find in nature, as if nothing but natural laws, in common operation, had any thing to do with it—as if Chemistry, and Botany, and crystallization, and air, and fire, and water, were of such station that they must act only on their own common laws. They shall all act for God's moral purposes. Let geologists remember it.

And now, when sin is a matter which comes in upon this moral department of God's empire, where lies the highest glory of God ; when a sinner is to be saved whose sin has dishonored God on this high ground, is there not a demand for something high above all the analogies of nature, and fully coördinate with the high majesty of God?　Give me only something which shall assort with nature to save me, or something which shall assort with the kingdom of mind; and, however grand it may be, you have not touched even the borders of that field, that moral field, on which sin does its dishonor to the Deity.　There is a seen and felt necessity of something beyond—something which shall bear a proportion to the wonder of sin's malignity, and, by its inconceivable greatness, carry relief to God's honor, and fling the grandeur of its security around the sinner who hath touched that awful thing.　Come, wonder—come, *mystery of God*—come, *Immanuel God with us*—welcome, Christ, Calvary, the crucifixion, the vinegar and the gall, the death-groans of the Son of God: your wonders, miracles, every one, are needed to show that *God can be just* and yet justify the sinner who has dishonored the highest matter of his majesty !

VI. I have only one point more.　It relates to *affection*—human affection.　You know that in affection lies the very essence of religion.　Men must love God.　Sin has estranged their affections from him, and, if they can not be won back to him, the sinner can not be saved.　What shall win them back?　On what ground can a sinner ever be led to repose such confidence in God, that his heart shall yield him its love?　What shall the Lord God do which shall avail to convince a sinner that God still loves him, especially when here he has so many miseries to suffer which he knows can not cease, till he sleeps in his winding sheet?　Examine affection for a moment: think of the nature of love.　There is nothing so tender as affection, nothing so delicate, nothing so de-manding. It looks on its object with a scrutiny which nothing escapes; no little thing—no trifle. It wants the heart, the whole heart. It wants evidence that the heart requites love, or love can not be satisfied. An affection-ate wife wants this evidence in her husband. It is not what he *shall do* for her; she does not care so much about that, if he only does the best he can, and requites her love. If she is sure of his heart, that is enough. With happy heart she will share his cabin, his cave, his scanty morsel, without a murmur, if she only knows he loves her. But she must have his *heart:* it is at once her right and her necessity. Without it she can not con-fide in him and be happy. Such is the nature of affec-tion.

And now, when a sinner's affections are estranged from God, and need to be attracted back to him—when sin makes him suspicious, and an accusing conscience makes him distrustful of God—when the affections, the most sensitive and tender of all things, and which can not bear a single item of doubting, are to be influenced—what shall be done, what shall God do to convince a sinner that he loves him?—to lay a foundation of confidence for a heart whose delicacy and hesitancy are such that a single item of doubt or difficulty would be an eternal barrier, and would fling a sinner into despair, instead of attracting his faith and his love? Something must be done, of more than ordinary character. Some demonstration of God's *kindness and love* must be made, which shall defy doubt, and meet the timid delicacy of an indescribable fearfulness. Well, God has done the best he could!— just what love wants—the best he could! He has surpassed herein all his other wonders. He has put his own Son into human flesh—into the law-place of sinners; he has held him to the penalty of death on their account; and if, in order to be convinced of God's love, your heart demands the most precious of God's things, you have had it—he has withholden nothing. If you could possibly conceive of any thing which God could possibly do for you more—if you saw God staggered at any thing, holding back any thing, refusing any thing, you might feel that something was wanting in your ground of confidence, when your poor soul would rise to peace and love with God, and enter into the high sacredness of his eternal fellowship as a loved child, your home the bosom of God. But you have no occasion to feel so now. Demanding as your love may be, it has got all that it can demand. God has done what he could. He has held back nothing. The matchless wonders of redemption have unfolded to you his heart, and to-day claim your own. These ideas ought to be sufficient for the *full assurance of understanding, to the acknowledgment of the mystery of God, even of the Father, and of Christ, in whom are hid all the treasures of wisdom and knowledge.*

Communicants, you have high and adorable reason to have your hearts *comforted.* God has done wonders for you which surpass all his other wonders. Be of good courage. What have you to fear? What shall make you hesitate to open your heart to God when God opens his heart to you? What shall make you afraid to come to him, as friend meets friend, and brother meets brother, and enter with all sweet and blessed confidence into the sacred intimacy of his fellowship? Stir up all your faith. Call all your sweetest, tenderest and most confiding love into exercise. Come near to your soliciting God, who, with the amazing wonders of his love, aims to win your own. Tax your heart to make itself large enough to take in the overflowing kindness of God. Consent to be his child, his humble, happy child. This is what he wants of you. Shall he not have it? Will you not love him? Will you not confide in him? Will you not consent to dismiss every doubt, hush every fear, and be as happy as God wants you to be, on the high ground of your glorious redemption? Be assured you honor God most, you please him best, when you take his Divine comforts most fully to your soul, sprinkled, and guarded, and sealed by the blood of the great atonement. I know that there is something terrible in being a sinner, but all that terror is most triumphantly met by what God has done for you. I know that some fearful things are before you which may well make nature shudder—death, the grave, the judgment, to all which you must come, are solemn and awful realities. But you will not come to them alone. Christ will come with you. He will take you out of the arms of your friends, to bear you to the house provided for you. He will set his seal upon your grave, and claim your reanimated dust in the day of the general resurrection. He will claim you when *the books are opened*, and crown you with immortality. Be not afraid. Eat that bread, and drink that cup with holy, solemn, happy love.

But who are these that turn their backs upon the table of the Lord? Why do they thus? If God has wrought such wonders to redeem sinners—if herein he has embarked all his love—what shall become of those whose cold hearts this love can not win? Oh! sinner, if the demonstrations of the appropriateness of this redemption to the wants of your immortal soul can not convince your understanding—if the adorable love which prompted it can not affect your heart—I do not know what you can expect. Nature can furnish you no aid, and God has nothing more to offer you! Dark and dismal are your prospects! Dreadful is the cloud that hangs over all your eternity! It need not be so with you. I beseech you by all that is sacred—by the wonders of God, and all the solemnities of eternity—let the recollection of that seat which you leave vacant at the communion table to-day follow you; and, if you live till another such season, come and occupy it, a penitent and believing sinner, a happy child of God, and an heir of immortal life.

May the God of mercy bring you to this. *Amen.*

Legal and Evangelical Justification Distinguished.

That no man is justified by the law in the sight of God, it is evident, for the just shall live by faith.—GALATIANS, iii. 11.

THERE is something strange in that principle of human nature which leads us to be most ignorant of things most easily known. But this is common. We often wonder at the want of knowledge discoverable in those who have the best means for attaining it. This is true not only in religion, but in every thing else. The man who has the daily opportunity of learning, and knows he can learn whenever he desires to do it, rests contented in his ignorance. He satisfies himself with the reflection that he is not debarred from knowledge— he can attain it whenever he will. The man who lives in the neighborhood of the most wonderful curiosities, the most towering mountains, lifting their granite battle-ments into the region of eternal frost, the most stupen-dous cataracts or deepest caverns, lives on from year to year with little desire to visit them. He can do it with ease, and is therefore indifferent. Place some obstacle in his way, render it difficult for him to gratify his curi-osity, and his indifference vanishes; his desires are excited by the very obstacles to their gratification.

This is a very common principle of human nature, and is often remarked. And it is this which does much to keep men in ignorance on the plainest topics of Christianity, and consequently renders it necessary for the preacher to guard against presuming too much on the knowledge of his hearers. It is this which often forces him to define and explain, when definition and explanation seem almost unnecessary, and are pretty sure to be regarded as uninteresting and dry.

There is another reason for this humble procedure in teaching the truth. We are ignorant of many things we ought to know, merely from the supposition that we know them well. We have had them taught and explained to us from our childhood. We have ourselves learnt to talk of them, and perhaps begun to practice upon them, and therefore suppose we are not ignorant and in any danger of error. The truth is, we have a *general* notion, but not a particular one, of many subjects about which we converse, and with which we suppose ourselves well acquainted. Our *general* idea may be correct, while, at the same time, it is too general to be secure—we may not be able to give it a just *particular* application. Often this is the case in religion. We have heard of faith, hope and love all our days, of the just and the unjust, of repentance, and holy zeal, and charity—we have learnt to use these words and converse about these things, and therefore we are led to suppose we understand them well, while in reality our knowledge of them is extremely small. And *because* we suppose we understand them, we are impatient in listening to them—we think our preachers insult our understandings, and treat us as novices.

The great evil that arises from this is, that when we come to give our principles an *application*, we err. This is inevitable. For our knowledge is only general, and is not, therefore, fitted for particular application; and we have neglected to make our knowledge more special under the influence of the impression that we did not need it.

This limitation of our real knowledge, and the evils naturally arising from it, render it necessary to define, and specify, and apply, when treating of even the most common subjects. Hence the plan of this discourse.

We will explain the *terms* of the text, and its *propositions*, in their general significance. And we will connect with these explanations those particular ideas and specific applications necessary to render our knowledge secure; and will attempt to show how, for the *want* of these particulars, we are exposed to run into dangerous errors and delusions. This is the plan we shall pursue.

No man is justified by the law. . . . The just shall live by faith. Here two kinds of justification are spoken of: justification by the *Law* (which the Apostle rejects), and justification by *Faith* (which he espouses, or adopts), through which he tells us *the just shall live.*

What are we to understand by Justification by the *Law?*

. The man who seeks justification in this method, approaches God *directly;* he relies on his own character; he puts himself on trial, and claims to receive salvation as a merited reward. According to the character of the law of God, he consents to be judged. Perhaps he confesses some sin—perhaps he acknowledges he has in many points violated the law; but he brings up arguments from the other side; he counts over his good works, and presents *them* as an offset to compensate for his transgressions. He places his *goodness* in a balance against his *iniquities*, and fancies that it weighs them down. He keeps a book of debt and credit with his Maker; and when he strikes the balance claims salvation as his pay.

This is the *general* principle on which he proceeds who is seeking justification by the law.

There are several *particulars* into which this general principle enters, and the individual sometimes proceeds on one of these particulars, and sometimes on another.

At one time he relies upon the *good* he has done. He may be sensible that he has done some evil, but, on the whole, he thinks he has done more good than hurt, and therefore must be saved.

At another time his *repentance* is placed in the scale against his sins, and he claims salvation because he has been so good as to repent and be sorry for his iniquities. When he is doing this, he is often entirely insensible that he is claiming justification by the law. He thinks himself a sinner and acknowledges it, and therefore supposes he is not pretending to be just with God. But he is. All this while he is relying upon his repentance to be a compensation for his sins, and is claiming to be, on the whole, more worthy of life than of death.

At another time his *humility and self-abasement* are brought in to be an off-set for his sins. He humbles himself, as he imagines, to a most holy degree. He places himself, as more low, and mean, and worthless, than the least of God's creatures; and *because* he is so self-abased and dependent, thinks God is under obligation to save him. He has placed himself in the dust, and asks, what can he do more? All this time he knows not that it is his *pride* which has placed him there, and never imagines that he is claiming justification by the law, because he confesses he has broken it. But all this time he is relying upon his confessions and humility to make satisfaction for sins, and claiming to be, on the whole, more worthy of life than of death.

In these, and a thousand other methods, men are left to seek justification by the law without suspecting their error. They not only throw in their good works, but throw in their graces, to bring their Maker in debt to them.

It matters not what PARTICULARS men present in their own behalf. They may plead their good works, or they may plead their graces; it is all the same. They may talk of their being full of love and zeal; they may boast of being altogether spiritual, and ardent, and engaged in religion; they may tell of their orthodoxy; they may tell how they live nigh to God, and how bright and strong are the graces that burn in their bosom; and all this only shows them to be deceived, and blinded, and in danger. They are keeping an *account-current* with their Maker; they are self-confident, and proud of their graces; they are really seeking to be *justified by the Law in the sight of God. Whenever* men approach God *directly*, and put their whole character, their sins, their good purposes, and good works, and graces *on trial*, to stand or fall, according as the balance shall be for or against them—then they are seeking *justification by Law.*

And now, in order to bring the principle and its application side by side, let us ask ourselves if there is not reason to fear that many do this who little suspect it? We speak not of those who put in their innocence, their good works, their common morals, as their claim for salvation; we speak not of those who deny the Deity

of Christ, and consequently destroy the whole of his
atonement, taking him only as an example in godliness,
and claiming salvation because they pretend to follow it,
and to be fit for heaven.   These are *manifestly* expecting
justification in that way in which the Apostle tells us
no man shall be *justified in the sight of God.*   But we now
speak of those whose error is more secret and obscure ;
of those who do not pretend to be just before God ; of
those who confess their sins, and think themselves penitent and humble, and having no thought of being justified
by law.   And have we not reason to fear that too many,
even of these, have mistaken the foundation on which they
are building ? and too many of those who are Christians
indeed have mistaken the nature of Christianity so much,
as to be ignorantly running into the same error in some
of their practices and some of their feelings?   If this is
not the case, I ask, whence comes it, that we hear of professing Christians rejoicing so much in their own graces?
Why are they sometimes so happy in thinking of their
own zeal, and ardor, and love, and thus gathering their
joy from their own hearts?   Will not the rejoicing of
the individual arise from that source whence he expects
his justification?   I wish you to contemplate this question ; will not the rejoicing of the individual arise from
the same source whence he expects his justification?
Does not the proud moralist, who expects salvation by
his own merits, derive his satisfaction from contemplating
his morality?   Does he not dwell upon it, and rejoice
over it as his title to heaven?   Does not the deluded
heathen, who expects to propitiate his gods by the offerings and sacrifices he presents, derive his satisfaction
from the idea of those sacrifices?   Does he not rejoice
over them as the foundation of his hopes ? (if, indeed,

he can be sufficiently deluded to rejoice at all.) And is it not universally the case, that the joy and satisfaction of the individual will arise from the contemplation of that source whence he expects his justification?

What shall we say, then, of those people who rejoice in their *mere feelings?* who look into their hearts, (with an Arminian eye,) and tell us how full they are of the fruits of the Spirit? whose rejoicing arises from contemplating the mere feelings of their heart? who boast of being wholly in the Spirit, and full of grace? Since their rejoicing is *in themselves,* I can not see why they are not expecting *justification* in themselves. Probably they do not know it. Probably they have never once suspected it. But since their joy rises from the contemplation of their *graces,* I can not understand why they are not as much expecting justification from their graces, as the moralist is from his morals, or the heathen from his offerings! I see not but they are presenting their graces in which they rejoice, their love, zeal, and prayers, as the offset for their sins, and their title to heaven? It is to be feared, that there is very much of this bribing heaven in the world! We know that many are seeking justification by the law, who confess themselves sinners; but who plead, that, on the whole, there is more good than bad about them. And there is reason to fear that others, who confess themselves sinners, are expecting justification by law, when they are rejoicing in their hearts merely, and thinking how evangelical, how zealous, and prayerful they are. Surely there is no impossibility in this. We may as easily offer our penitence, our faith, our zeal, and our prayers, as a compensation for our sins, as we can offer our morality or our sacrifices. And when we gather our joy from these

10

acts of penitence, and faith, and zeal, thinking how good they are ; when we take our comfort from the idea that we have a great deal of *religion*, I can not understand why we are not relying upon these things to be just before God : *God, I thank thee that I am not as other men.*

If people look into their own hearts and examine their experiences, only to prove whether they are Christians or not, only *to examine themselves whether they be in the faith*, they are doing only as they ought to do, they are acting wisely. But when they are looking into their hearts to find how good they are—to live upon their experiences—(as the old Divines used to say, " to feed upon experience ")—to find their religious rejoicing in the excellence of their graces, they are acting unwisely, they are deluded, and in danger.

And we have heard of those who found abundant joy in themselves; who were so deceived in this matter, that they imagined they were full of grace, and piety, and spiritual life, and felt entirely happy *in themselves!* Sink, sink thyself in the dust, deluded sinner ! Lift up thy voice in lamentations, and cry for mercy ! Grace never yet made a child of God to rejoice in the perfection of his graces ; and thou couldst present no stronger proof that thou hast little grace, than the confidence that thou hast so much. If thou wert near to God in the exercise of spiritual affection, thou wouldst see thy deficiencies ; thine unholy heart would be the burden of thy *complaint*, instead of the source of thy rejoicing ; and thy graces (however much thou hast) would seem in the midst of thy heart, like a feeble spark flung loose amidst the heaving surges of the ocean, to be preserved only by a constant miracle of God ! Thou wouldst cry, *God be merciful to me a sinner ! If thou, Lord, shouldst be strict to mark iniquities, oh Lord, who could stand! Oh! wretched man that I am, who shall deliver me from the body of this death!*

The more near any individual lives to God the more humble he will be; the more he will behold his deficiencies and in-dwelling corruptions; the more he will see of the extreme littleness of his graces. God is a being of spotless holiness, and the more near we come to him, the more striking will be the contrast between his awful holiness and our own base pollutions and sins. We never seem so vile in our own eyes as when we are admitted to close communion with God. Our graces never seem so little as when we rise to try them in heaven. We never realize our *want* of grace, our deficiency in love, and penitence, and holiness, and zeal, so much as, when in the exercise of them, we have come nearest to God. Where, then, should this boasting of being full of grace, this self-confidence, this rejoicing in one's self, be ranked? Surely, we must place it among those *strong delusions;* too strong to be corrected by proofs, and too obstinate to feel the power of the clearest demonstrations. And we leave it for you to judge, whether there is not some reason to fear, that those who are so self-satisfied, and think themselves so perfect, or so near perfection, are really (though unconsciously) seeking justification by the law. We leave it for you to judge, whether they are not rejoicing in their imagined religion, their love, zeal, ardor, prayerfulness, *only* because they are expecting justification from them, and claiming heaven because they are so well entitled to enter into its rest.

The Apostle speaks of another method of justification. *The just shall live by faith.*

We have seen what it is to seek Justification by Law, and have pointed out some instances in which men may be doing it, when they are far from knowing what they do, and when their self-confidence renders it vain to attempt to correct them. Let us now see what it is to seek Justification by Faith.

The man who expects to be justified by faith, acknowledges himself guilty of sins which deserve the utmost rigor of punishment. *He* dare not approach God directly, and put himself on trial. He confesses that he deserves to wear eternally those chains of darkness that weigh down the damned, and dwell eternally amid the flames of that fire that is never quenched! But he is not afraid of these punishments. He hopes to be justified of God, and live for ever in heaven, because he believes God will deal with him, not according to his own character but according to the relation he bears to Jesus Christ. It is through the medium of JESUS CHRIST, and not through the medium of his RELIGION, that he approaches God. He trusts Jesus Christ to save *him*, a poor sinner. He does not yield to that gloomy despair, to which the sense of his sins would hurry him; but he hopes to be saved from his sins and from their punishment through the medium and mercy of our Lord Jesus Christ. Consequently, he *counts all things but loss for the excellency of the knowledge of Christ.* Why? *that he may be found* IN HIM, *not having his own righteousness,* WHICH IS OF THE LAW, *but that which is through the faith of Christ, the righteousness which is of God, by faith* (Phil. iii. 8, 9). He sees that pardon is by no mere act of *amnesty* from God. He sees iniquity lifted off from him and laid upon another. In that OTHER alone he trusts to be just with God. There he rests: there he hopes: there he hides. This is the general idea of Justification by *Faith.*

But this is too general for entire security; and, consequently, we find the Divine writers defining it more particularly. They not only present Jesus Christ as the great and supreme object of Faith; but they trace out the *exercises* of that Faith, and secure us from error by particular illustrations. Jesus Christ dying for sinners—offering himself a sacrifice to the justice of the Father, is the SOLE OBJECT on which the mind of him fastens who shall be justified by his faith. But as this idea is still general, as it is not specific and particular, men are liable to think themselves seeking to live (like the just) by faith; when, in reality, they have none of the faith that saves. Let us examine the matter.

Faith is a term of very indefinite signification; and the indefiniteness of the word is the source of danger. Sometimes faith is put for mere historical belief: *through faith we understand that the worlds were made* (Heb. xi. 3). Sometimes it is put for those special acts of confidence with which the working of miracles was connected: *if ye have faith as a grain of mustard-seed, ye shall say unto this mountain remove hence to yonder place, and it shall remove* (Matt. xvii. 20). Sometimes it is put for the credence exercised by devils: *the devils also* believe and tremble (James, ii. 19). This word, therefore, is of vague significance; and, therefore, the Christian should heed well what is the *object* of saving faith, and what are the particulars of its *exercise*, lest he should suppose himself to have faith when he has none.

Jesus Christ offering himself a sacrifice to satisfy Divine Justice for sinners, is the object of saving Faith. Now, men are exposed to think themselves living in the exercise of this faith when in reality they are not. There are numerous methods in which they err, and

usually they err because all their ideas are too general—
not clearly definite enough and particular.

1. There are those who make their *faith itself* the
meritorious ground of their justification. They know
how much efficacy the Scriptures ascribe to it: they
delight to dwell upon the commendations bestowed upon
it in the Word of God. And when they imagine they
have this faith, they rejoice in it and hope in it, as that
which *lays the foundation* of their expected eternal life.
Their joy, their hope, is vain. It is not the FAITH of the
believer which constitutes the meritorious cause of his
justification, and he has no right to rejoice in it or hope
in it as such. The meritorious cause of our justification
is Jesus Christ alone ; and all our hope and joy should
be *in him*, as our foundation-rock. It is he who justifies us, and not we ourselves, not our faith. Had not he
left heaven on his high mission of mercy to tabernacle
in the flesh—had not he borne for us the wrath of God
—had not he stood in our law-place and been *wounded
for our transgressions and bruised for our iniquities*—had
not he died for us that we might live ; all our repentance
and faith in God, (if such things could have been,) and
all our efforts for eternal life, would have been of no
avail. It is not *faith* that merits eternal life. Other
*foundation can no man lay than that is laid, which is Jesus
Christ.* (1 Cor. iii. 11.) Faith is not the *foundation*, it is
only the *instrument* of justification. What is faith?
"Faith in our Lord Jesus Christ is a saving grace, whereby
we receive and rest upon him alone for salvation as he is
offered to us in the gospel." Faith is that act of the believer, which God has made it necessary that he should
exercise, in order to be interested in the salvation which
Jesus Christ has procured for him, and without which

act, Jesus Christ *becomes of none effect* unto us. Jesus Christ is the foundation and cause, and faith in him is the instrument of justification. Jesus Christ is the meritorious and efficient cause of our justification, and faith is that act by which we are made partakers of his benefits. Now, when men are hoping IN THEIR FAITH, instead of hoping in Jesus Christ, they are evidently building upon a wrong foundation; they are taking credit to themselves; they are claiming merit for their faith. It is true, *the just shall live* BY *faith;* but it is not said the just shall live UPON it.

Let us learn to discriminate. Let us not rely upon our faith to justify us, insteading of relying *by faith* upon Jesus Christ. Let us not create a fictitious zeal, a false hope, a blind reliance, a vain *self*-confidence, by mistaking the means for the end, and trusting in our faith instead of trusting in the Lord that bought us. Let us build on the sure foundation, and be cautious that we build there alone. Let us always take our places in the dust as sinners, confessing that all our graces, our faith, repentance, and zeal, and love, are far too feeble. Let our rejoicing and our hoping be in Jesus Christ, and not in our graces; and *then*, let us not fear that we shall ever rejoice or hope too much; let hope brighten and zeal burn in our hearts; let our prayers be fervent as our desires for heaven; let all the feelings of our soul kindle into a sacred ardor, as we love God, and live, and labor, and pray for the cause of our Redeemer and Lord. We need not fear any excess of hope, and zeal, and happiness in religion, when we have secured the right kind. But let us beware how we forsake Jesus Christ and build upon our faith. Let us beware how we hope, and trust, and rejoice in *ourselves*, instead of rejoicing, and trusting,

and hoping in *him*. Let us beware how we have more
FAITH IN OUR FAITH, than we have in the merits and
words of our Saviour.

2. We have said that Jesus Christ, suffering and dying
for a sinful world, is the great object of saving faith, the
meritorious cause of our justification. We have said
that saving faith is that act of the believer which unites
him to Jesus Christ and makes him a partaker of the
benefits of his death. Now, there are others, who, on the
point of faith, run into error, and a very different error
from the one we have been considering. They err, like
the former, for want of discrimination and particular
knowledge.

They have asked themselves, and perhaps others have
asked them, if they DESIRE to be saved by Jesus Christ?
if they are willing to be wholly indebted to his grace for
the pardon of sin and all the benefits of salvation?
These questions they can answer in the affirmative. It
is their desire to be saved by Christ, and they seek no
heaven but that offered through his blood. And BE-
CAUSE they *desire* to be saved in this method, they conclude they have faith, and are in a state of salvation.
This is all the foundation of their hope.

This hope is vain. The *mere desire* to be interested in
the salvation of Jesus Christ is no proof that we are
Christians. It *is* proof that we are welcome to his mercy,
and that we may come at once to him to save us. But
to have a mere desire for his benefits, without taking into
the account the *method* in which we may have them, is
no good proof that we are Christians. On this point
I desire you to treasure in your memory the four following considerations:

(1) There may be a desire to be saved without any

desire to be sanctified. There may be a kind of faith which may rely upon Christ for salvation, and yet not trust his *rules* to guide the soul to heaven. That faith is not only imperfect but spurious which does not as much to confide in Jesus Christ to *qualify* for heaven as to *entitle* to it. The Gospel does not merely propose to us the pardon of our sins but the subduing of them. And, therefore, one may desire salvation by the mercy of Christ, and still *not* desire it in the way it is offered ; *not* desire it in the way of holiness, and by a heartfelt submission to the *rules* which promote the growth of holiness in the soul. Yet, if any one, who possesses only this presuming and fictitious faith, is led to suppose himself a child of God and an heir of heaven, may he not *rejoice and be exceeding glad,* though still in carnal security, not a sinner subdued ?

(2) A mere desire to be interested in the merits of Christ, may be, at best, no better than a *dead faith.* It may be inoperative. It may not *purify the heart,* or *work by love.* It may be as much dissevered from holy affection as it is from humble obedience. Still, if one with an unmoved heart imagines that Christ will save him merely because he has a desire he should, will he not rest in hope, and rejoice in hope, though possessing only a *dead faith ?* a heart cold towards God ?

(3) True faith *unites* us to Jesus Christ, makes us one with him, *crucifies* us with him. It animates us with desires to be partakers of his redemption, notwithstanding all the self-denial required of us. But the mere desire for his benefits is not a willingness to bear the cross, and how can it be a proof of faith ? It may be only a faith that presumes in hope, but not a faith in following. Yet, if any one, on account of his mere desire, believes

10*

Jesus Christ will save him, he will hope, and may rejoice and exult, though never united to Christ and crucified with him.

(4) The mere desire of salvation by Jesus Christ does not include in itself a single principle of faith—has nothing of the nature of faith. This desire does not necessarily give up the *mind* in faith, to be taught by his instructions; the *heart* in faith, to rest upon his sacrifice; the *will* in faith, to trust and obey his rules. Therefore, it does not even *resemble* faith at all.

These considerations may convince us that, to have a mere barren recourse to the satisfaction of Christ for sin, and to entertain an indolent desire to be saved by him, are no good evidences of faith, and no good reason for peace of mind. And yet, is there not reason to believe that some are resting on this rotten foundation; and then taking credit to themselves because their faith is so unshaken? And is there not reason, also, to fear that some true believers, when they *would build themselves up on their most holy faith, praying in the Holy Ghost,* (Jude 20,) often cultivate this fictitious faith, and rejoice that they have so much? joy in their *religion,* instead of having joy in God?

It were easy to point out other methods in which souls are liable to err on this subject. This is a fertile source of danger and delusion. But we leave the whole matter to your reflection. You see there is a heaven-wide difference between aiming after Justification by Law, and after Justification by Faith. Bear it in mind, in every part of your religion, that that faith by which *the just shall live,* has one great OBJECT, *Jesus Christ, and him crucified.* To him it yields up the *mind* to be taught in religion—it receives his word—it believes the whole

Bible. To him it yields up the *heart*, to rest *in hope of the glory of God* upon his sacrifice, and to love Christ, and love that kind of felicity (viz., holiness) which Jesus Christ proposes to the soul : it trusts him solely—embraces him gladly—and expects salvation through his unmerited mercy. To him it yields up the *will*, in delighted obedience to follow the supreme authority of Jesus Christ : it trusts his rules to fit the immortal spirit for heaven : it loves his laws, as well as his mercy ; and seeks holiness with the same ardor it seeks heaven. Thus it embraces the whole man—mind, heart, and will—and makes him feel that he *is dead, and his life is hid with Christ in God.*

REMARKS.

1. No wonder the Scriptures are so much taken up in setting forth Christ, and his crucifixion. Christ is the sole foundation—Christ is all in all to a sinner.

2. No wonder the Scriptures insist so much upon self-examination. Christ must be in us the hope of glory, or we can not be saved. There are many ways of missing him.

3. No wonder that the Scriptures steadily insist upon the necessity of *faith*. It is the *one* requisite which can never be spared. Without it all that is done on God's part, and all that can be done on the sinner's, must for ever be vain. Faith is that one link that unites us to Christ, and shelters us from the deserved curse of God's law.

4. There is a vital difference between a legal and an evangelical spirit. An eye on Law is one thing—an eye on Christ is quite another thing. The first is the attitude of Nature, the second the attitude of Grace.

5. Hence we see .the justness of the Bible descriptions of the first step in religion. They speak of it as *conversion: Turn ye, turn ye.* The sinner must turn. Over his *legal* path lightnings flash, and thunders peal! He must turn him to that track sprinkled with redeeming blood, and over-arched with the bow of a promising God! While he stands between Sinai and Calvary, by nature and disposition, his face is directed only toward the mount of thunders: no hope for him is *there!* only *blackness, and darkness, and tempest!* Let him turn to the hill of crucifixion : the light of Heaven's love for sinners beams on its top ; and, while it throws a new glory over the Godhead, it invites and sanctions the hope of the darkest sinner that lives !

6. Finally : That convicted sinner whose eye is directed only to the evil of his own heart, and who expects to find cheering from something within him, is greatly mistaken. It is not by looking to the darkness there is within him, but to the truth there is without him, that he may find peace. It is not by contemplating what he will do for himself, but by trusting to what God has done for him, that he will find his obstinacy give way, his suspicions of God take their departure, and his heart move towards God as one that loves him. Let him turn off his eye from the darkness of that abyss within him, and lift its cheered vision to the light that shines above him, and he will see that God is his best Friend, and is holding out signals of relief, and hope, and love, to his dark and troubled soul. Only let him BELIEVE, and he shall see the salvation of God.

Vanity of Man if not Immortal.

Remember how short my time is : wherefore hast thou made all men in vain ?—Psalm, lxxxix. 47.

THE vanity of human life is a theme much dwelt upon in the Word of God. The sacred writers seem disposed to impress upon the mind of their readers such a sense of the utter worthlessness of the world, to a being who is so soon to leave it, that the mind shall be constrained to turn to the world to come. *Vanity of vanities* is the inscription they write upon the world. They have such an impression of the frailty and brevity of human life, that they borrow their imagery to describe it from the most tender, and fragile, and fleeting things that meet the human eye. It is *the flower of the grass;* just the little fragile blossom, that dies, even beneath the tenderness that touches it! It is the *tale that is told;* just the little story, to which even the child can lend its attention, and then it is done! It is the *vapor, that appeareth for a little time, and then vanisheth away:* the eye sees it—and it departs on the breath of the feeblest wind that moves!

There are probably different reasons why human life is spoken of as a thing so very vain. Its brevity; the smallness of its pleasures; the frequency of its disappointments; the number and severity of its pains, are all of them evidences that man, in his earthly state, is little else than *vanity*.

The occasion of the expression in the text was probably some of the calamities which befell the kingdom of Israel. In the reign of Rehoboam, ten tribes of Israel had revolted. Their king was the powerful adversary of the king of Judah. The honor and power of the family of David seemed to be almost extinguished. While the kingdom was rent by internal dissensions, foreign foes were watching for its ruin. Egypt poured forth her legions to bring the shock of war against the throne of Jerusalem. The Psalmist had probably witnessed the glory and felicity of the nation, in former years; and now, when he beholds that felicity and glory no more, the bitterness of his feelings appear to be too much for expression. Even in prayer to God, he exclaims: *Thou hast made void the covenant of thy servant: thou hast profaned his crown by casting it to the ground. Thou hast broken down all his hedges: thou hast brought his strongholds to ruin. All that pass by the way spoil him: he is a reproach to his neighbors. Thou hast set up the right hand of his adversaries; thou hast made all his enemies to rejoice. Thou hast also turned the edge of his sword, and hast not made him to stand in battle. Thou hast made his glory to cease, and cast his throne down to the ground. The days of his youth hast thou shortened: thou hast covered him with shame. How long, Lord, will thou hide thyself, for ever? Shall thy wrath burn like fire? Remember how short my time is: wherefore hast thou made all men in vain?* Seeing the vanity of life in the mournful example he was contemplating, the Psalmist is led on to the vanity of all human existence, and utters the distressful interrogation, *Wherefore hast thou made all men in vain?*

It is manifest, that the Psalmist utters these words while his thought is confined to this world; and not in reference to that eternal existence which awaits man beyond the grave. And, in speaking from them, we propose to show, that,

Man, considered merely as a creature of this world, and without respect to his eternal existence in another world, may be said, without extravagance, to have been made in vain.

This is our theme. In pursuing it, we propose,

I. To present some direct proofs of the vanity of human life;

II. To continue the illustration, by examining into the real value of those things which seem to render our existence of most worth; and

III. To make the same conclusion more plain, if possible, by closing with such reflections as the subject suggests.

1. *How short my time is*, is the lamentation of the text. The brevity of our mortal existence can not fail to have affected every contemplative mind. We look around us, and the oldest persons we see have lived but a little while. They are passing away, and another generation is pressing upon their heels! We look back upon the past, and we find it dressed in sadness; those aged people, whom we used to know and reverence when we were children, are numbered among the dead. Our mothers, young as we are, we have many of us buried them! Our fathers, where are they? Sweet be their memory—but they are gone! And even many of those who entered upon life when we did, have passed away. So soon do we pass off the stage of life, that our business here seems to be little else than to be born and die. All

human kind seem to be engaged in one united *rush* toward the end of our present existence. To make up for the deficiencies which death causes, we are obliged to be perpetually forming new acquaintances. Without this, we should very soon be almost strangers in the world. How vastly few of those whom we knew twenty, or even ten years ago, are now in the land of the living! There is no extravagance in the expressions of the Scriptures: *My days are swifter than a post; they are passed away as a shadow; thou hast made my days as an handbreadth, and mine age is as nothing before thee; as for man, his days are as grass: in the morning it flourisheth and groweth up; in the evening it is cut down and withered.*

The brevity of human existence demonstrates the unutterable littleness of man—the utter worthlessness of his being—if he exists only in time.

But, transient as human existence appears to any casual observer, it is, on the whole, far more transient than even a careful observer would be apt to imagine. One fourth part of all that are born into the world die before they have lived one year! Another fourth does not survive to see twenty-one! Thus one half of mankind are swept into the grave before they have scarcely reached the years of maturity. The average length of human life is by no means so great as as we should suppose, when we look around upon a promiscuous assembly, and behold clusters of the young among a multitude in middle life, and the whole assemblage graced with not a few whose locks are silvered with the frosts of age. Those youth, those children, have been spared from among as many more that have died. Young as they are, they have buried half their cotemporaries. Those middle-aged people (little as they think of it) have out-

lived almost three-fourths of their generation.   And
those venerable in age are but a little fraction of a generation that will soon be entirely extinct.   On an average, the lives of mankind do not amount to more than
about twenty-three years.   In the city of New-York,
the average length of life is less than twenty years.
Only one tenth of mankind ever sees fifty years.
Surely, aside from his immortality, man was *made in
vain*.   The little time that is allotted to him is scarcely
sufficient to learn how to enjoy what good the world
does contain and offer to his enjoyment.

But this is not all.   Short as life is, there are some
large deductions to be made from its hours when we are
counting up its value.   Let us see what they are :

There are hours in human life which seem to be (for
their own sake) not worthy of being reckoned valuable.
They are hours (so to speak) of *indifference*, in which we
are sensible of neither joy nor grief; in which we do
neither good nor hurt; and, therefore, during their continuance, our existence can be little more than a mere
matter of indifference to us.

Such are those seasons of musing thoughtlessness,
when we are destitute of mental movement—when the
mind roves over every thing, and fixes on nothing—
when thought has no object, and, therefore, neither in
its exercise nor in its attainments, can be of any value—
when we are so lost to consciousness and to sensibility
that we seem scarcely to be thinking beings.   These are
hours of a kind of indifference, and surely these are not
worth living for.   In them we gain nothing, we enjoy
nothing, we do nothing.

Such, too, are those seasons which we spend in *sleep*.
Whether our business is to do or to suffer; whether

grief or pleasure is our portion; whether virtue or vice occupies our waking moments, we must have some repose. Sleep locks up our senses, and consigns us to a state of uselessness and indifference—a state, surely, scarcely worthy of being coveted for its own sake. If we could do nothing but sleep, our existence would be valueless. And yet, so worthless, or worse than worthless, are our waking moments, how often are we glad to escape from trouble by consigning ourselves to an oblivious repose by sinking into a state of indifference, in which we are alike incapable of vice and virtue, and scarcely sensible of either good or evil? And in this valueless state of existence, we are forced, by the infirmity of our nature, to spend nearly one fourth part of the transient life we have to live.

But this is not all. We must add to these all those portions of time which we regard as a kind of necessary evil: in which we are not living in enjoyment, but only in hope, and which are regarded by us as valuable, not for their own sake, but only because they help us onward toward what we expect to attain. I mean such seasons as we are constantly wishing to annihilate. It can not have escaped you that there are many of them. We find them when we are just entering upon life, and they are seldom corrected by the wisdom of maturer years. For instance, the *child* would be, at once, a youth; he would willingly annihilate the years that separate him from the age and the companionship of those who are older, and, he thinks, happier than himself. The *youth* longs for manhood. The years that he must pass away before reaching it, are a burden to him. He would gladly give speed to the flight of time, and rush, in a single moment, over a period of years. And even the wiser *man* often

finds himself not much wiser; and is so dissatisfied with
the present that, in order to arrive at some future and
expected good, he would most willingly

"Lash the lingering moments into speed."

Thus we are perpetually wishing away different portions of our existence. They are portions which we do
not esteem worth having for their own sake, but regard
them as a kind of necessary evil.

Now, if we take away these seasons of indifference,
these seasons of sleep, and these seasons of expectation,
which we are constantly wishing at an end; if we take
them from the length of our very short life, how much
will there be left that can wisely be regarded of any
value? Surely, the hours of *enjoyment* in human life are
extremely few. All the real felicity that we attain here
is of small amount. If this life is all, there is no extravagance in the idea that *all men are made in vain*. The
shortness of human life furnishes, at best, but a little time
for any thing desirable; and even that shortness, in order
to find what is valuable, must be diminished by many
hours of indifference, many hours of rest, and many
hours regarded by us as an evil, or at least as worthless
in themselves. The extreme shortness of human life, and
the still shorter period of happy human sensibility, stamp
an unutterable worthlessness upon man, if there is no
immortality beyond the grave.

2. Let us now consider some of the positive evils that
are in the world, and see if we shall not be furnished
with another proof of the vanity of our existence, considered aside from another world.

But, before entering upon this point, pardon us for
detaining you to listen to three remarks in relation to it.

One remark is this : that when we are speaking of evils, of the miseries which afflict our race, we do not pretend to decide whether pain or pleasure weighs heaviest in the great scale of human destiny. Some have thought that the world contained more happiness than misery. Others have maintained the contrary. It is not easy for us to decide the question. And it is probable, that those who have given their opinion on this point have been much influenced in their decision by the temper of their own mind. Those of easy, contented temper, disposed to make the best of every thing, have examined the brightest side of the question, and concluded that the happiness of the world outweighed its miseries. Those of fearful and desponding temper, ever on the look-out for some calamity, have examined the darkest side, and concluded that the miseries of the world are greater than its joys. It is probable, that in the most favored regions, and in the most happy periods, there is more of enjoyment than of suffering; while in regions and periods less favored, suffering outweighs enjoyment. What the truth, on the whole, is, we know not. When we mention the evils of life, we do not mean to affirm that they excel its joys.

The second remark is, that when our thought is turned to consider the misery of the world, we should be on our guard lest we become dissatisfied with the allotments of Divine Providence, or acquire a diminished idea of the goodness of God. There *is* affliction in the world, but still God is good. This life is not our time of blessedness : this world is not our heaven. The blessings our Saviour intends for us are to be found in those *many mansions,* where death never dissolves friendships— where tears never embitter joy—where God pours the full tide of his love upon souls ransomed for immortality. So short is this life, that if our Maker, during its whole continuance, were to bestow upon us all the felicities we are capable of receiving, it would be a mere trifle, a bestowment scarcely worthy of God to give, or worthy of us to receive. Not that we are to despise the enjoyments God gives us here; but that we ought not so to overvalue them, as to have a low or limited idea of the goodness of God, when we find them few.

The third remark is, these very evils that we experience, though they do prove to us the vanity of this life merely, yet, considered in reference to the life to come, may be some of the most beneficial bestowments that God ever makes. There are virtues that we could never exercise in prosperity. Adversity is needful to give exercise to fortitude and patience, if not to faith. It is suffering over which Pity sheds her tears, and there is pain in that wound into which the good *Samaritan pours* his *oil* and his *wine*. Let us not think that, to the *Christian*, the evils of life are useless, although we may be forced to conclude that, if there were no hereafter, our multitude of ills would demonstrate that we *were made in vain*.

What are they? Let us take a hasty view of them. Our plan compels us to be general. We are looking at the worth of all human existence on earth.

(1) It is scarcely possible for us to be happy, when tortured with sickness and pain. And it is no small portion of our time that a disordered body is our lot. Disease stalks over the world, assuming every shape of terror and affliction. What multitudes of our race are, every moment, tossed and racked with pain! Thousands, this moment, are in the agonies of death! It

furnishes us a striking view of the disorders and maladies of life, when we behold more men employing their time and talents, throughout the country, in the practice of medicine, than in any other of what are called the learned professions. Indeed, the great aim of the human sciences seems to be, to learn how to escape disease, want, and other "ills which flesh is heir to." And after all, the world is full of sickness. Its pains and its maladies would make man's existence vain, if he were only a mortal.

(2) Wars and fightings are a source of misery. (We are obliged to name these. Our subject calls us to view the world and its history.) War is a giant evil. As if disease were not enough—as if the *pestilence, that walketh in darkness,* did not sweep away his race fast enough to satisfy him—man rushes to the field of battle, breathing that *destruction that wasteth at noonday.* The first man that died, died by violence. And ever since that time the history of the world has been written in blood. In the wars of Napoleon, for example, from 1802 to 1812, there perished more than five millions eight hundred thousand men. This is a world of blood. Nation is armed against nation. Towns are sacked. Cities are plundered. Villages are burned. And, when the din of battle is hushed, and the thunder of the battle-field dies away in the distance—what do you see? David mourning for Absalom! Rachel weeping for her children! Ah! yonder is a host of trembling fugitives, helpless women and children, hurrying from the scene of desolation, and scarcely daring to turn a single glance backward to the spot where lies the husband and the father in his blood! It is no over-wrought picture. Open almost any Nation's History, and you will find the burden of that history consists in accounts of warfare.

There is an inconceivable amount of misery from this source. Attractive as is the laurel of victory, it is colored with blood; and grows only on the soil which has drunk the tears of the widow and the orphan !

(3) Famine often follows in the track of war. No matter what causes it, the miseries it produces can be calculated by no arithmetic, nor expressed in the language of man. And this is no unfrequent calamity. Even in enlightened and Christianized nations, and in this improved age of the world, many men die for want of food. And in less favored nations, the evil is a thousand-fold more appalling. It would make a most fearful amount, if we were able to reckon up the whole number of our race that have perished by famine.

(4) And, finally, time would fail us to tell of the miseries produced by earthquakes, shaking down cities and burying their inhabitants beneath their ruins; by volcanoes, pouring their liquid fire over hamlet after hamlet, and sometimes burying whole cities beneath ashes and burning lava, not a soul left to tell the tale; by swelling floods; by stormy wind; by lightning, hail and tempest; by southern heat and northern cold, and the thousand causes which seem to sport themselves with human life, and delight in the miseries of man.

The positive evils of life are not to be numbered. They are so many, that we are forced to the conviction, that, apart from their immortality, *all men have been made in vain.*

But you will say, there are, at least, some things of value in the world; some sources of felicity open to us, so full, so flowing, that it is no vain thing to enjoy them. This would seem to be true; and to examine them, con- stitutes the

II. Part of the train of thought we proposed to

you. As we enter into it, let us not forget our limited time of enjoyment—let us not forget our positive miseries.

There are things in the world which we value highly : we will not now say too highly. But, after all the good we• can derive from them, it may fairly be questioned, whether a reasonable man would say they were worth living for, and would not the sooner say, if there be no immortality, *all men are made in vain.* What are they ? We name four, the 'most distinguished that we can think of—possessions, intellect, friends, religion. From all these we derive, indeed, no little present good. But still let us examine them.

1. Those who have extensive worldly possessions, a superficial observer might conclude to be in so happy a condition, that, if this life were all, they would not live in vain. They seem to possess all they can use—they gratify every desire—they bask in the sunshine of prosperity—and therefore their present life, short as it is, being filled up with happiness, is no vain existence. Thus a casual observer might think, and thus, perhaps, most men do believe. But, my hearers, I am persuaded this is a delusion. Let us see.

Worldly possessions are mostly employed for two purposes ; for the gratification of pride and vanity, and for the gratification of the senses.

(1) It may be gratifying to vanity and pride, to be in distinguished condition—to be surrounded with splendor—to be able to command the homage of those around us, and flatter ourselves that we are better than other people. But is, this gratification of much value ? Is it a worthy end of our existence ? Is it as extensive or as real as we are prone to think ? By

no means. It consists only in a vain elation of mind, an imaginary, dreaming felicity. There is nothing substantial in it. It is mere fancy. The child of imagination, building his castles in the air, is just as really and as permanently blessed. One idea of the reality breaks both alike. If wealth brings the pleasure of pride, it brings the pain of envy; and the ostentatious and proud have more misery by envying those above them, than they have felicity in ostentation and pride before those they deem below them. At least, it is usually so. Moreover, those who value the outward respect they receive on account of wealth and splendor, have often the extreme mortification to know—(and if they but knew men's hearts they would have it oftener,) they have the extreme mortification to know, that this respect is rendered to them most insincerely, and by those who, at the very time, despise them in their heart. *This also is vanity.*

(2) The gratification that worldly possessions furnish to the senses is very much qualified.

That gratification, pursued beyond a very limited extent, destroys itself, and often the life of him who pursues it. Excess disqualifies, and soon ruins. And the rapidity with which it hastens to ruin, may be intimated in the history of him, who said, *Soul, thou hast much goods laid up for many years, take thine ease. God said, thou fool, this night shall thy soul be required of thee!*

And if there is no excess, the pleasures of sense can scarcely be worth living for, because of the care necessary to restrain from improper indulgence; because, after all sensual enjoyment, the soul is not satisfied with that; because, it is not to be supposed that man's existence is of much value, if he must find his enjoyments merely where the brutes find theirs, in animal gratifications.

11

After all the failure, and fiction, and insincerity, and
envy, that attend worldly possessions, we cannot surely
suppose them of much real value. They may cheer
human life, but, ordinarily, they do not make the rich
man any happier than the poor man ; and, if we had only
what they afford, we should be compelled to confess we
were *made in vain*.

2. But *intellect*, it may be said, is no vain thing. To
acquire knowledge, to discover truth, to exercise those
faculties that lift man above the brute, is a dignified and
noble employment: it is a source of high felicity ; and
the existence that is employed in this way, short as life
is, ought not to be stigmatized as *in vain*.

My hearers, I suppose I have as high an idea of the
dignity and felicity of intellectual employ, as any one
that hears me. But still, let us see how this source of
good is qualified.

Knowledge is not necessarily happiness. We are not
going to say, that increase of knowledge is *always* increase of sorrow (putting an extravagant interpretation
upon the words of the wise man—Eccl. i. 18); but we
believe most of the happiness that we find in knowledge,
in exercising intellect, in discovering truth, springs from
the hope we entertain of making our knowledge subserve
our happiness in other respects. If our only felicity consisted in *knowing*, we believe it would be extremely
small. And how little, even men called learned, succeed in making their acquisitions advance human felicity,
the whole history of cultured intellect too sadly tells.
As man improves in knowledge, it is true, he invents
and discovers many things tending to make him happy ;
and it is just as true, that he strikes upon many things
to make him miserable. If he invents printing, he in-

vents fire-arms, and gunpowder, and implements of death! If he discovers medicines that do him good, he discovers also what does him hurt; and the fiery deluge of intemperance may illustrate the idea, as it rolls misery over the world, and wafts thousands down to the drunkard's final doom. So that neither knowledge, nor the results of it, forbid the exclamation, *man was made in vain!* But this is not all.

It is only a small part of the human family that have the opportunity of cultivating mind. It is so here. It is so every where. It always was. Even in the most enlightened countries, there is an immense mass of our race whose whole intellectual improvement does not extend beyond the skill necessary to manufacture a button or a pin. Poverty is too pressing for mental culture. Hunger has more powerful arguments than science can present. Valuable, therefore, as intellectual action and acquisitions may be, they are valuable to only a few; and if man were made for these, he was *made in vain.* But this is not all.

Examine the lives of the most distinguished proficients in knowledge, of those most eminent in all that pertains to cultivated mind, and you will find their intellectual felicity extremely small. Disordered passions, disappointed hopes, defeated designs, make them very much like other men. Intellect is neither virtue nor felicity. As man is here, power of mind may be only power for misfortune. The fact is before us, the trained intellect of men does not make them happy men; they have much the same woes as others. Were there no life but this, in the halls of the Academy, and on the temples of Philosophy, we would write the inscription, *this also is vanity!*

3. We mentioned friends as a *third* valuable item.

We thought some one might say to us, the joys of friendly attachment are neither few nor small ; they are pure ; they are peaceful ; they are noble. What excellence in that affection which binds families together, and makes home an image of heaven! Is there nothing good in that love which binds the heart of the mother to her children ? which fastens the whole soul of the father upon his sons ? which calls into action all that is tender in sentiment and all that is dignified in virtue? Short as life is, is that life vain in whose circles such joys are clustering? My hearers, this is an enchanting picture. It seems like malice to ruin it. But let us remember there are regions where the husband and the father is the tyrant ; where the mother murders her offspring ; where the wife is the slave ; and where the widow burns on the funeral pile of her husband! Let us remember, too, how often friendships give place to enmity ; how often the tenderest affection, the fondest, the purest, receives a most sad requital in coldness and indifference, in the disobedience or profligacy of some abandoned child! Let us remember how often we are miserable because we can not make our loved ones happy. And, if all this is not enough, let us hear the lamentation that love utters in its bereavement: *Oh my son Absalom! my son, my son Absalom! would God I had died for thee, oh Absalom, my son, my son!* When half the world is dressed in mourning, its friendships can scarcely convince us that, apart from another world, *all men have not been made in vain.*

4. We mentioned religion as a *fourth* item, seeming to qualify, if not contradict, the sentiment of the text.

There are those who make religion the great object of their life ; who serve God and love to serve him ; who disregard *things seen and temporal* in comparison with

things unseen and eternal; who hope in God, and believe
that he has pardoned their sins, sanctified their hearts,
accepted their persons, and will finally take them to
heaven through the mediation and redemption of Jesus
Christ.   They have joys the world knows not of; peace
the world meddles not with.   Sometimes troubled and
dark as their hearts may be, still they find seasons of
rest, and never would they give up their hope in God for
ten thousand worlds.   They love communion with their
God and Father.   They count it joy to *deny themselves,*
to *bring every thought into captivity,* and look forward to
the final appearing of Jesus Christ to come and receive
them to himself.

Now, what is all this religion good for, if there is no
future life?   If this life is all, even these people of God
have been *made in vain!   If in this life only we have hope
in Christ we are of all men most miserable,* (1 Cor. xv. 19.)
Religion is vain, if the world is all.   Its votaries are
miserably deluded.   They have renounced the world, but
gained nothing.   *Verily, they have cleansed their hearts in
vain, and washed their hands in innocency,* (Psalm lxxiii. 13.)
They are going to be utterly disappointed, if there is no
immortality.   They live, they labor, they pray in vain!
For a mere fiction—a dream—a lie—they sacrifice their
best interests and devote their best powers!   They give
up the world and devote their life for a falsehood!   All
their joys and hopes are only imaginary!   Their labor
is lost, and their hopes perish for ever!   Thus, on the
suppostion of no future life, we confess the worthlessness
of even the Christian's existence, and write upon his
altars the vanity of his being!

But no : *now is Christ risen from the dead, and become
the first fruits* of them that slept; and all them that *sleep*

in Jesus will God bring with him. Religion is as reasonable as it is consoling.

III. Some of the conclusions we draw from this subject ought to give depth to its general impression.

1. We learn from this subject the amazing difficulties of that species of infidelity, which denies a future state. On that system, all the world—man—body—soul—virtue—vice, are vanity! On that system, we see no reason why man should have been created! why the world should exist! Man is vain; the universe is vain; the Creator himself has been guilty of the most arrant folly! On that system, *every thing* is involved in perplexing mystery, in confusion, darkness, and uncertainty! How true it is, that Christianity is the best philosophy.

2. This subject teaches us that the doctrine of immortality, the truths of religion, are very needful to us, in order to make us happy even here. Remove these—and what is the *universe?* a vain show, a worthless bubble! Remove immortality—and what is *man?* a distressful dream! a throb—a wish—a sigh—then, NOTHING! But, blessed be God, *life and immortality are brought to light.* Yes,

3. This subject teaches us, that the true Christian is the happiest man. He is not perplexed with a thousand doubts and difficulties that trouble the unbeliever. He knows *what* it is, that has produced the miseries of the universe; and *why* it is, that the world is full of evils. He knows man has revolted, rebelled against his Maker, and *therefore* the curse is on the world. He knows that Chance does not rule; that Accident does not make hearts bleed and make men die. He knows that, after

all, God is good, and man was *not made in vain.* He knows that God *hath reconciled* believers *to himself*—that *God is in Christ reconciling the world to himself, not imputing to them their trespasses.* His religion, therefore, teaches him the reason of the ills of life, and furnishes him with motives and grace to bear them. He sees IMMORTALITY before him. True, he must suffer—must pass through many fiery trials; but—hear him, as he enters into the furnace: What is he saying? *This light affliction, which is but for a moment, worketh for me a far more exceeding and eternal weight of glory.* True, he must part with many that are dear to him; he must commit his fathers, his children to the grave! But—hear him, as he stands by the earth just lifted over his friend by the spade of the grave-digger: *Lazarus sleepeth !* Jesus Christ is *the resurrection and the life !* True, he must lie down and die ! But—hear his broken accents, amid the crumblings of nature: *This corruptible shall put on incorruption, this mortal shall put on immortality—death is swallowed up in victory !*

4. This subject teaches us the powerful urgency of religion. Religion is every thing to man. Without it, man is nothing: his value, is a song; his life, a sigh; his property, a grave !

5. And, finally, we can not but think that this subject should be peculiarly impressive to the young.

Many of my young friends here are thinking much about the world. Your hearts are warm: your bosoms beat high with hope. You are looking forward to much joy, to many days of happiness. The world seems pleasant to you. Your sun is rising brightly in the heavens, and your prospects promise much good.

My young friends, believe me, I would not stand over

your youth to prophesy evil. I would not poison your
bliss, nor say one word to make you unhappy. But I
must tell you, you are going to be disappointed! The
world is not what you think it! If your hopes and
heart center upon it, you will gain but very little; and
even that little mingled and imbittered with much that
is sad! As you pass on in life, your expectations will
often be frustrated, your plans deranged, your prospects
darkened! the buoyancy of your spirits will cease, pain
will press upon your bosom, and tears be sprinkled along
your path! This life, merely, *is* a vain thing; the
world is not worth your having! There is but one way
in which you can be happy. Be Christians—love God—
and trust in his Son, and set your heart on heaven. At
most, you can get but little good out of this world, and
you can live to enjoy it but a little while. Religion will
deprive you of none of that good, not an item, and you
will be the more happy by becoming Christians.

Let me warn you not to be tempted by what the
world offers, to neglect eternal life. The world will
never satisfy your heart; and if it did, it will soon be
burnt up, and your spirits will be in Eternity! I beseech you, think often, think deeply, where *you* will be,
when this short life is done! Remember your IMMOR-
TALITY! Yea, remember NOW *your Creator in the days
of your youth, while the evil days come not, nor the years
draw nigh when you shall say, I have no pleasure in them.*

The Mercy of God.

The Lord is merciful and gracious, slow to anger, and plenteous in mercy.—
PSALM ciii. 8.

WE invite your attention, to-day, to a wonderful subject. It is the mercy of God. If we are able to
understand this subject rightly, we shall be furnished with
an attractive argument to draw us toward salvation. If
we shall understand it rightly, there will be no gloom of
guilt, no trembling of fear, no despondency, no dread,
no darkness, no sense of unworthiness, no horrors of
judgment, that can prevent our being drawn toward
our God and Father, as *with the cords of love, and the
bands of a man.*

David celebrates the mercy of God in the Psalm
before us. In the beautiful poetry of an Eastern fancy,
and, what is more to our consolation, in the poetry of an
inspired and sanctified mind, he contemplates this mercy
of God, diffusing itself over both worlds. While it
reaches down to the minutest wants of a single sinner,
*forgiving his iniquities, healing his diseases, satisfying his
mouth with good things,* it reaches abroad over the
extended world, encompassing the whole family of man,
executing judgment for the oppressed, and *not rewarding
according to iniquity.* And while it does not forget this
temporary world, and the little interests which figure in

11*

it, between the time of its rise and the time when it shall be devoted to ruin, the inspired writer sees this mercy lying back in the remoteness of a past eternity, and extending onward to the remoteness of an eternity to come—encompassing the very period of the Divine existence.

There is something very beautiful in this. It meets *nature*. It satisfies us amid the tearfulness and tenderness of our experience. Read from the eleventh verse, onward: *As the heaven is high above the earth, so great is his mercy toward them that fear him.* Till you can measure the distance to his throne in the third heavens, you can not tell the magnitude of his mercy: *As far as the east is from the west, so far hath he removed our transgressions from us. Like as a father pitieth his children* (you see he passes beyond mere *thought*, and speaks to the experience of those human *sensibilities* which no language can paint)—*like as a father pitieth his children, so the Lord pitieth them that fear him.* This is the *heart* of the Lord God. *For he knoweth our frame and remembereth that we are dust. As for man, his days are as grass ; as a flower of the field, so he flourisheth ; for the wind passeth over it, and it is gone, and the place thereof shall know it no more. But the* MERCY *of the Lord is from everlasting to everlasting upon them that fear him.* The mournfulness, therefore, that weeps over a dying race, may dry up its tears, as it turns to the *everlasting mercy* of God. It is *from everlasting to everlasting*—

> " Yes, spring shall revisit the moldering urn,
> And day shall yet dawn on the night of the grave."

For the Lord hath prepared his throne in the heavens, and his kingdom ruleth over all. How delightful the idea!

Man fadeth like the flower of the field, but God's mercy is *from everlasting to everlasting*, after all! Well may the cheered author finish his song: *Bless the Lord, ye his angels; bless the Lord, all ye his hosts . . . bless the Lord, all his works . . . bless the Lord, O my soul.*

The mercy of God is the theme of the Psalm. The Psalm is designed to set forth, as the text itself does, THE PREËMINENCE OF THE DIVINE MERCY.

This, then, is our theme for to-day. We commence it this morning, we propose to finish it this afternoon.

This subject is not without its difficulties. It has some difficulties for the hearer, and it has more for the preacher. *Yours* we intend to remove; *ours* we are constrained to weep over. You know we are not accustomed to complain and to draw on your partiality or indulgence for any undue sympathies in our trials; and we would not now mention this, only we wish you to remember more carefully the need of prayer, and the impropriety of reliances upon a ministry of imperfection and sin—a ministry of dust and ashes! *Brethren, pray for us.* Our trial is this, and it is one of no minor sort. There are texts and themes, there are subjects in the Gospel, which seem, more than others, to lie in the very depths of redemption, and to embody in themselves the very essence of all that a sinner's soul needs to experience in order to fit it for heaven. To be able, at all, to enter into such subjects, regeneration, repentance, faith, love, are not enough! The minister needs something more—he needs the *full* of these; he needs to *walk with God*, like Enoch; he needs the resting-place of John (when he rests), on the bosom of Jesus; he needs to have his delight when he culls the flowers that bloom in the garden of Arimathea; he needs to have his *heart burn within him,* like the disciples conversing with the unknown but risen Christ. And the conviction of this— the sad and sinking conviction of it—has often compelled us to turn away from those august themes of the wonders of redemption, to which any strength, and light, and faith, and piety in us were manifestly unequal. One of our heaviest trials is, that there are texts in the Bible we can not preach from. But this is one of those difficult themes. And we mention this for the double purpose of cautioning you *not* to estimate the mercy of God by our explanation of it, and of eliciting prayer from your hearts that the God of mercy will not allow his truth to become *like water spilled upon the ground, which can not be gathered up again.*

The Lord is merciful and gracious, slow to anger, and plenteous in mercy. The idea is, the preëminence of the Divine Mercy. This idea is repeated in different forms, according to the custom of the inspired author, when aiming to express his own strong and vivid emotions.

In attempting to understand this subject as well as we may, let us,

I. Define the idea of mercy, and give as much precision and exactness to our notions of it as we can.

II. Let us guard against an error to which we are exposed in relation to it.

III. Let us explain how it comes to pass that the mercy of God, which ought to affect our hearts so much, really does affect them, while unconverted, so little. And

IV. Let us enter more fully into the wonderful subject, and endeavor to gain some just ideas of the mercy of God.

The first three of these things occupy us this morning;

and we hope may prepare us for the more interesting one in the afternoon.

I. The definition of Divine Mercy need not detain us long.

Mercy is the exercise of benevolence, of good-will, toward those who do not deserve it; and, in especial manner, toward those who have merited anger and punishment. Mercy is favor to the guilty and undeserving. As God exercises mercy, he extends forgiveness to those who have broken his law, provoked his anger, and forfeited all claim to his favor. Unworthiness and criminality in the recipient, and good-will in the other party, are essential to the exercise of mercy. As the Deity exercises it toward us, it is a modification and a part of his infinite benevolence. It respects us as utterly unworthy of his kindness, and by our own deservings eternally undone. Without it, our guilt would ruin us; a broken law would be against us with all the weight of its penalty; and hope and happiness would finally expire together, under the frowns of an angry God.

It is important for us to have some precision in our ideas of this. Divine Mercy is not mere Divine goodness: That is, there are a thousand expressions of Divine goodness, which have no mercy in them. And it lies among the common errors of unconverted men, that they confound the ideas of goodness and mercy, and solace themselves with a hope that rises out of the confusion. Goodness is exercised toward the innocent sometimes: mercy, only toward the guilty. Goodness is shown toward angels that never sinned. It was shown toward Adam before he fell. God's goodness pervades every part of his universe, *save one;* and carries felicity, more or less, to every order of sensitive beings, *save one.* Hell only, and those miserable reprobates who inhabit its eternal abodes of despair, experience nothing of it. God's goodness fills the earth. It extends to man everywhere. It extends to beasts, happy in their sunny fields, or roaming the forests amid the wilds and richness of smiling nature. It extends to the birds of the air, singing their songs of joy, and warbling out the expressions of their felicity from melodious throats, as they mount, buoyant and happy, on the wings that God has feathered for them. The Divine goodness reaches all sensitive being. It reaches down to the worm beneath your feet, and the insect decked with its gilded colorings, to make them happy according to their measure. And the order of irrational creatures would be more happy, were it not for man's sin. They suffer, and they die as they would not have done, had not *sin entered into the world.* The world groans under the disorders sin has brought; and the inferior order of beings would have enjoyed more than they do from the goodness of God, if sin had not introduced irregularity, and mischief, and perversion.

Mercy is something more, therefore, than mere common goodness. Divine Mercy is what no man can claim from God. It is the exercise of a Divine benevolence in respect to a guilty being, and *such* an exercise, that if it had been wholly wanting, if the God of heaven had stood unmoved over the miseries of man, and seen this guilty world sink down to eternal ruin, no reason, no just judgment could ever have impeached the benevolence of God. Mercy is the intervention of gratuitous goodness. It is benevolence, bending in pity and compassion over the very creature, whose guiltiness has deserved the frown, and the everlasting abandonment of Heaven. Aside from it, no attribute of the Godhead would have been dishonored—no injustice done to man—no ground of complaint could have been found in the depths of his miseries and the dark eternity of his despair.

This is sufficient explanation of what is meant by the mercy of God.

II. Let us guard against an error to which we are exposed in relation to it.

We are in danger of misconception at the very outset. When we speak of the preëminence of the Divine Mercy, we are in danger of conveying the idea, that the mercy of God infringes upon his other attributes, or overshadows them, and flings them into the shade. It is vital to the accuracy and truth of our ideas, that we avoid this. The error we wish you to avoid consists precisely in this—precisely in the difference there is between the notions of Divine Mercy entertained by an intelligent and humble Christian, and those entertained (commonly, if not always) by unconverted sinners at ease in their sins. If you who are believers, therefore, will cast back your thoughts to that unhappy period of your lives, when you lived (as multitudes now live around you) unalarmed and fearless, though still the *enemies* of God—if you will recollect your ideas of Divine Mercy *then*, and compare them with those you have *now*, you will see precisely the error against which we would caution you. We need not describe it. Your hearts feel it. You have often prayed God to forgive you for the offense of your former thoughts of his mercy and grace.

But you who are *not* Christians can not be cautioned thus. You have never experienced that transition from

darkness to light—from error to accuracy—from alienation to adoption. Your hearts are no guide to truth.
And we can only tell you, that, when we speak of the
preëminence of Divine Mercy, we are speaking of that
thing which we, as Christians, feel to be of all things
most calculated to make us fear and hate sin. We love
the Divine Mercy. We love to take shelter under it.
We have higher ideas of it than we can give you. But
we see clearly that it does not countenance impiety and
sin. We see clearly that it does not encourage us to live
prayerless lives. We see it does not render the Deity
indifferent to his laws; it does not infringe upon his
justice, or make him less terrible, but more terrible, to
all who will indulge themselves in sin. But still the
Divine Mercy is preëminent. By this attribute God
peculiarly shows himself. And while his justice is infinite, his purity infinite, his wisdom, his holiness, his
faithfulness infinite ; and while his mercy, as infinite as
any of these, is in perfect and unbroken harmony with
them all, at the same time there is something in the
Mercy of God which stands up in solitary magnificence
and grandeur. And if you knew how much you are indebted to it ; if your unconverted souls but realized how
wonderful it is that God has borne with you ; if your delusions in sin did not diminish your ideas of your unworthiness, and thus diminish your ideas of the mercy
of God, we should have no fear that this text or this sermon would aid your indifference, and make you more
ready to continue in an unconverted state. If you did
not pervert the Divine Mercy, you would feel it as an infinite attraction ; you would hear its voice whispering
comfort into your ears; you would find its solace reaching the deepest woes that ever trouble your agonized

spirit; on the everlasting arms it extends to you, you would lie down soothed and satisfied—God a friend, and hope stretching to immortality! And it is with the hope of being able, by Divine grace, to affect your hearts, that we ask you to consider the mercy of God to-day. Ye indifferent sinners—ye hard-hearted and far from righteousness—ye prayerless, rebellious, hardened, guilty, yet unconcerned, our message is to you! Hear it. Heed it. We stand up in the face of all your sins, your fears, your guilt; ah! in the face of all your hardness of heart, and tell you you need not die! You may be saved! Your magnitude of sin weighs nothing before the magnitude of mercy! Will you give ear to the message? Will you allow yourselves to be attracted by it towards God's forgiveness and a glorious immortality? You reluctate! You are not more than half ready to allow Heaven to win you. Therefore,

III. Let us explain how it comes to pass that the Mercy of God, which ought to affect sinners like us so much, really does affect us (especially in an unconverted condition) so little. This explanation ought to prepare us better to attend to the truth which we have assigned to a fourth head, and which we reserve for a separate sermon.

You can not be insensible to the very remarkable fact that the human heart is naturally very slow to be affected by any idea of the mercy of God. No doubt the sinfulness of human nature renders us less sensible to *any* of the Divine perfections. And it is noticeable in every believer's experience, that his religion not only gives him more sensibility to the attributes of God, and gives the idea of these attributes more influence over him, but his religion, his very experience, consists very much in this. The existence of God, the omniscience of God, the omnipresence of God, his power, his faithfulness, his holiness and mercy, all that God is, becomes more influential to a believing heart, and in that influence experimental religion very much consists. The believer *walks with God* and lives in Christ. The believer has his *conversation in heaven.* He sees God in all things, and all things in God. He knows what it means when he sings, and loves to sing,

> " Within thy circling power I stand,
> Upheld and guarded by thy hand ;
> Awake, asleep, at home, abroad,
> I am surrounded still with God."

The influence, and a sweet and sensible influence of the perfections of God, all his perfections, comes over the renewed heart. An unregenerated heart fails in this. And it fails in a very remarkable manner to be affected by the Divine Mercy. The very child, who trembles when it thunders, as if syllables of anger were uttered from the lips of a just God, is unaffected by the mercy that sends the lightning harmless over his head; or he can go out under the brilliancy of the cloudless heavens, and never see any thing of the goodness of God

> " In those bright skies that bend above
> His childhood like a dream of love."

The man, who, in his sickness, is ready to fear the justice of his Maker, in his returning health forgets the mercy that has made him well. The man of adversity realizes that God is dealing with him then ; but in his prosperity he did not look up to God, and say, THOU *crownest my life with loving-kindness and tender mercy.*

And he can see then, when it is too late to remedy the evil, that in his prosperity he did not use his gifts as bestowments coming from the goodness and mercy of God. The world is full of such examples. Human nature is more reluctant to be properly influenced by the Divine Mercy than by any other perfection of God. · And this is especially the case in respect to that mercy in the highest sense—the forgiveness of sin and eternal life through the redemption of Christ.

There are several things which conspire together to cause this.

The *first* is found in the nature of mercy itself. Sin in the human heart tends always and uniformly (when the heart is unaffected by the Divine Spirit) to put God out of mind. That is a graphic description of its tendency, *not willing to retain God in their knowledge.* And there is no possibility of presenting the Divine Mercy to the mind of a heedless sinner, in that bold and commanding method in which other perfections come up before him, and compel him to feel their influence. The very nature of mercy forbids this. What is its nature? It is gentleness, clemency, forbearance, kindness. It is a tenderness which scarcely probes the wound it would heal. It would not drive, but win the sinner. It would not alarm him willingly; and not at all, if alarm were needless. Its delight is in soothing every affliction; in making the sinner happy; in putting out of his heart the miseries which afflict him; and causing him, in the fullness of his enjoyed felicity, to forget (as far he can either safely or happily forget) that he ever had an affliction to weep over. All this is un-terrible and mild. It is the tenderness of Heaven. It is the clemency, the gentleness of God. In this, therefore, there is nothing to challenge and arrest

the atheistical tendencies of sin ; there is nothing to command and compel the reluctant heart into sensibility to
this attribute of God. Justice has her sword, and shows
it, whetted and bathed in heaven ! Judgment has her
scales, and hangs them up, balanced on the throne of
God ! Omnipotence has its thunders, and at the voice
of its bidding, worlds leap into existence, and worlds are
blotted out ! But Mercy comes to sinners with the still-
ness and gentleness of the dews of the night. It comes
down to the deep and hidden miseries of the human
heart. It comes to whisper peace in a *still, small voice,*
and draw us to the God of mercy by cords as gentle as
they are strong—by cords, whose strength itself consists
in their gentleness. This is one cause of the little influence of this attribute of God upon us. Its nature is such
that it does not challenge and force the tendencies of sin.
This fact is no compliment to the human heart—a heart
unfit for every thing but the strokes of severity.

The *second* cause is connected with this. It is found in
the fact that sin, in the human heart, has made its most
perfect triumph over those very sensibilities which mercy
aims to affect. Mercy aims to affect our sense of kindness and good-will in God—our sensibility to clemency
and compassion—our filial affections—those feelings
which would lead us to say unto God, *Abba, Father,* in
which the exercise of a holy faith and happy faith so
much consists. Sin hath left us the power of fear—the
power of ambition—the passion for glory ; and it hath
done its worst work in the human heart, by making it
most of all insensible to the love and mercy of God. It
is the office of faith to embrace this mercy, to believe in
it, to rejoice in it, to love it, and lean upon it. It is the
effect of unbelief to spread insensibility toward God, in

an especial manner, over those sensibilities which mercy solicits. Go round these seats, and look into the hearts of these unconverted sinners, and you will find more sensibility toward God in any other respect, than in respect to his kindness. The reason is, that the operation of sin on the human affections tends to perpetuate its own dark empire, and works worst of all, on those views and feelings necessary to be exercised in a believing return to God.

Convicted sinners often err on this point. They are sensible of their hardness of heart. They mourn over it, and wish it would break. They strive to render their terrors of God more dreadful, their sense of guilt more oppressive, their fears of hell more distressful. They suppose they must. By this, they suppose their hearts must be made to yield. But they err. It is not so. The fires of hell convert nobody. The torments of horror and despair tend to confirm unbelief, but they never awaken faith. Let such sinners cast aside their dark, and gloomy, and unjust suspicions of God; let them know that they fail, most of all, to be duly affected by his kindness, love, and mercy; let them yield their hearts to his free grace, and requite him with love for love, and tenderness for tenderness; let them turn from their prodigal starving to rush into the arms of their forgiving Father; and then, and not till then, their hearts will meet, when they hear him saying, *This my son was dead, and is alive again; was lost, and is found.*

A *third* reason is found in the sufferings that fill the world; *i. e.,* the ideas of irreligious people about these miseries give them a wrong idea of the Mercy of God. The world is full of affliction. It is little more to us than a place of tears, and then, a place of burial! unless,

in the vanity of our mind, we make it a place of vision-
ary dreaming! As a sober mind contemplates the
miseries that fill it, and remembers its own sad experience of ills; such a mind, while without religion, is very
apt to have erroneons ideas of the Mercy of God. If
God *is* merciful—is so merciful—is merciful like a God—
why are such tears of bitterness streaming, such griefs,
such fears, such disappointments, such mountains of
sorrow, resting on so many thousands of hearts? And
especially, why do immortal souls experience such perplexity and anguish, in relation to the attainment of that
very salvation, to bestow which is the very office of God's
highest mercy? Such thoughts will come up. A sinner cannot always avoid them. And we dare not say
that they are always to be reckoned among the worst,
though, surely, they are among the most unhappy of his
sins. Such ideas are wrong. They do not invite faith.
They rather drive toward despair. They are wrong.
They are superficial. They are false. *Three* errors,
especially, enter into them.

The *first* is, they forget that these very miseries are
mercies. Heaven means them as such. They are such.
The mercy of God has made this world so full of evil, in
order that a wise man looking on it, and gauging the
dimensions of its miseries, if you forbid his faith to anticipate an immortality, will be obliged to look up to the
Infinite Creator of all things, and ask that question,
Wherefore hast thou made all men in vain? These miseries,
therefore, compel us to take in futurity. Without that
futurity, the world is useless—our existence useless—and
this fabric, soon to be fuel for the last conflagration, had
better never have risen out of its primitive non-existence!
If an atheist is a fool, a murmurer is a fool also!

The *second* error, in those impressions against the
mercy of God which are derived from the miseries of
the world, is this : these persons do not reflect that sin
maintains its empire over the human heart by putting
the world in the place of God. Religion says to man,
Love not the world, neither the things that are in the world.
And mercy, Divine Mercy, flings poison into our earthly
cups of bliss, flings pestilence upon our winds, and plants
thorns in our path, in order to drive us off from this
world, and lead us to give God our hearts.   When we
have hewed out our cisterns, laboriously chiseled from
an earthly marble, mercy, Divine Mercy, does us the
kindness to dash them into pieces, and show us that they
are *broken cisterns, which can hold no water*, in order to
turn our parched lips to the *living fountains* of God.

And if sinners, still charmed with the world, would
but see this—would but understand that the world is
that which *satisfieth not*, and Mercy has made it so ; they
would begin to cluster around our altars ; they would
say to us—

> " People of the living God,
>   I have sought the world around,
> Paths of sin and sorrow trod,
>   Peace and comfort never found !
> Now to you my spirit turns,
>   Turns, a fugitive unblest ;
> Brethren, where your altar burns,
>   Oh, receive me into rest !

> " Lonely I no longer roam,
>   Like the cloud, the wind, the wave ;
> Where you dwell shall be my home,
>   Where you die shall be my grave !
> Mine the God whom you adore,
>   Your Redeemer shall be mine ;
> Earth can fill my soul no more,
>   For God, for heaven, I all resign."

The *third* error in these impressions is, that when earthly miseries seem to us to limit the mercy of God, or constitute an argument to qualify its significance, we ourselves do limit the range that is due to our thinking capacities ; and limit, too, the very mercy whose narrowness afflicts us. Truth, grace, spreads out this mercy to overshadow an eternity. This is its main object. It cares very little about time. God cares very little, comparatively, what we enjoy or what we suffer here. Let us not be Deists. Let us be Christians. Let us not be materialists, to weigh nothing but dust and ashes, and the earthly felicity that springs out of them. Let us think as immortals—feel, hope, and fear, as immortals. Let us go out in our contemplations, and plant our feet on the borders of that unbounded field, as wide as eternity, and, by the Mercy of God, as blissful as heaven ; and then we shall not be tempted to think God's Mercy little and unworthy to be trusted, though he should give us but few joys here. He *intends* to give us but few. He *means* to show us that he cares very little about the dying bliss of this dying world. And if we understand his Word rightly, we *shall* understand that he mentions his earthly mercies to us, not on account of any value he puts upon them, but only as tokens and attractions to that infinite Mercy which would save, eternally save, our sinful and immortal souls. God cares every thing for these. Divine Mercy brought Christ from heaven to save them ; and not a want, no, not a single want that takes hold on eternity, is now denied to a sinner's soul. Mercy stretches over his immortality ! From his bed of death, she stoops from heaven, to lift him to his home, his Christ, his God ! This is Divine Mercy. And this only is worthy of God to provide, and worthy of you to prize and to receive.

On next Lord's day, the table of mercy will be spread here. The covenant of mercy will be rehearsed, and some will enter into it. How happens it that some of you will turn your backs upon *the table of the Lord?* Is there no mercy for you? I know some of you think so; but, my dear friends, your unbelief *makes God a liar!* It is, therefore, a great sin—a horrid sin! It is bad enough that you have broken God's law. It is still worse that your unbelief rejects God's offered Mercy! Christ, forgiveness, heaven, is offered to you in all the sincerity of God! All that poor, guilty, helpless sinners need, is offered to you *without money, and without price.* This is certain. Will you believe it? Will you open your eyes and behold God's infinite readiness to receive you, love you, save you? There will be room for you at the Lord's table on next Lord's day; and if you are not there, the reason must lie in your unbelief, and not in God's Mercy. I call on the sacred emblems, on the covenant, Christ, on heaven and earth, to witness, that if you perish, your blood will be upon your own head, *for the Lord is gracious and merciful, slow to anger, and plenteous in mercy.*

12

The Mercy of God.

[CONTINUED.]

The Lord is merciful and gracious, slow to anger, and plenteous in mercy.—
PSALM ciii. 8.

THE existence of God is that great truth which lies at
the foundation of all true religion. The attributes
of God give true religion its character. True religion,
with man, is what it is because the attributes of God are
such as they are.

The text speaks of one of these attributes, and would
affect us by it.

In this Psalm, David celebrates the *Mercy* of God.
The text is only a declaration of a fact which gave rise
to all the expressions contained in it: *The Lord is gracious and merciful, slow to anger and plenteous in mercy.*
Mercy is good-will to the undeserving. It is the exercise of good-will toward those deserving of anger and
punishment. It is a modification, therefore, of benevolence or love.

We have not time now to recapitulate even an outline
of what we advanced this morning on this wonderful
subject, the Mercy of God. We need not. It is one of
the happinesses of this ministry we exercise so unwor-
thily, and with so much anxiety and pain (and it is a

happiness for which we ought to be deeply affected), that the attention of this congregation, as we preach to them, furnishes reason to hope that they retain some knowledge of what they hear.

IV. Leaving, therefore, the ideas of this morning to the fidelity of your recollection, we enter upon the fourth head of discourse that we announced—to endeavor to gain just ideas of the preëminence of the Mercy of God.

This is the precise sentiment of the text. David's mind lingers around the idea. He will not let it go. He repeats it in different forms: *The Lord is merciful . . . and gracious . . . slow to anger . . . and plenteous in mercy.* His sentiments of piety and praise give an eminence, an exaltation to the Mercy of God. There is something singular in this. Divine Mercy has a Divine preëminence. While God is infinite in every perfection, in his wisdom, power, holiness, justice, truth; and while his mercy, infinite also, stands in harmonious combination with all these; at the same time, there is something in the Mercy of God which rises up to the wonderfulness of an amazing and solitary magnificence! It is not easy to give you a clear explanation of what we mean. You will know before we have done. But as the basis of our meaning, it will be sufficient here to name to you two ideas of explanation. The one is direct, the other is taken from the application of the subject.

The *first* is, that while they are all infinite, still, all the perfections of God do not hold the same rank in the Divine character. One perfection may be more glorious than another. That omnipotence which *weigheth the mountains in scales, and the hills in a balance,* may yield to the gloriousness of the eternity, and the infinite truthfulness of God. That omniscience which embraces, every moment, all the very thoughts of all the creatures in the universe, possesses not such eminence in the Divine character as belongs to that infinite wisdom that infallibly produces the best of all possible results, by the best of all possible means. There is no error nor irreverence in saying that in the Deity, infinite every where, one perfection has not the same eminence as another. On this ground it is that we are speaking, when we mention the preëminence of the Mercy of God. This is the direct idea in the explanation.

The other is taken from the application of the subject. The Deity manifests something of his perfections to his creatures. On earth, and in time, they are visible, even to eyes like ours, so soon to be dimmed and extinguished in death ; and in that brighter world to which faith invites us, they will be more gloriously visible, as the saints of the most high God enjoy the vision of *the Lamb in the midst of the throne,* and have thoughts and sentiments worthy of God, and worthy of eternity. But as the attributes of God *apply* to his creatures, they do not all apply alike : they do not all produce the same wondrous views, and the same elevation of sentiments. The preëminence in this respect belongs, and will ever belong, to the *Mercy* of God.

Let us, then, enter into the theme as well as we may. We have seven sources of argument, taken from,

1. The peculiar delight of the Deity ;
2. The nature of the Divine Revelation ;
3. The method by which Divine Mercy operates ;
4. Its unlimited extent ;
5. Its equal readiness for all sinners ;
6. The smallness of its requirements ; and

7. The greatness of the sin of neglecting it.

These are our topics. Let us consider them as well as our time will allow.

1. Mercy is that attribute, in which the Deity peculiarly delights. It has been styled, "the darling attribute of God." We do not like the expression. To many minds, it seems to imply that some of the perfections of God are no favorites with him, and must be made to yield and give way before this. Nothing could be more untrue. Entire harmony reigns among the attributes of the Deity. But after all, though there may be an error in this phrase, there is a truth in it, too. It is a truth, that the Infinite One peculiarly delights in the exercise of his Mercy. You may apprehend the meaning of this idea by what takes place in your own mind.

You are a citizen of this commonwealth. As such, and as a good citizen and subject of the laws, you owe various duties which you delight to discharge. But they are not equally delightful. Some of them fall in with your own preferences more than others. You lend your influence and labor to render property secure, law dominant, and to prevent violence and disorder : you delight in this. But, as a wise citizen, you have more delight in aiming to secure the same benefits in another way ; you have more delight in giving your influence and labor to render all classes of society industrious, intelligent, contented and happy ; so virtuous, so conscientious, that they shall be a *law unto themselves*, and have no need of legal sanctions to keep them in order.

As a member of society, you delight to render even justice to every one, in all your various intercourse— intercourse of trade—intercourse of science, of literature, of society, of religion. But you have more delight, as a good member of society, in being able to go beyond the mere measure of justice, and, even at some personal sacrifices, in doing something to dry up the streams of human misery; your kindness wipes away the orphan's tear, and carries gladness to the heart beating such unequaled throbs under the weeds of the widow. In all these duties you may be equally perfect, but you are not equaly happy. This illustrates what we mean by the peculiar preferences of God. His delight is in the exercise of his Mercy. He delights, indeed, in justice, holiness, faithfulness; and he has an infinite delight in them; that is, his delight accords with the infinity of his nature, and is perfect in relation to the importance of the attribute he exercises. But in Mercy he peculiarly delights. This is his own repeated testimony. He is *not willing* that any should perish. He affirms that he has *no pleasure at all in the death of him that dieth.* All that he has seen fit to teach us in his Word, respecting his own infinite and holy feelings, gives preëminence to his Mercy. Mercy, indeed, has its methods—its way of wisdom—its rules: if it had not, it would lose its nature and become something else. The poet failed in that so much admired conception,

"A God all mercy is a God unjust."

That is truth, but it is not all the truth—it is too feeble for the fact. Such a God would be something more than unjust; and the licentiousness of the attribute among a world of sinners would turn the mercy into unkindness itself. Still, the Divine Being has peculiar delight in the exercise of his Mercy. God loves to forgive sinners. He loves to save them. He loves to adopt them into his family. He loves to cheer them with his promises. And never did a saint on earth have so much delight in receiving the grace of God, as the infinitely gracious God has in bestowing it. Much as you may find in the Bible to teach the infinitude of all the attributes of the Deity, and their preciousness to him, you can not fail to see the justice of the idea that he speaks in most singular style of his Mercy. The delight which he has in it, the singular and peculiar delight, demonstrates that kind of preëminence which we have affirmed belongs to it. It is Mercy that unfolds to us the heart of the God of heaven ! It is Mercy which he most of all things delights to exercise. His glory, his infinite and eternal blessedness, stand in peculiar connection with this. Justice, judgment, the vengeance he takes upon the wicked, even he himself denominates his *strange work* (Isaiah, xxviii. 21). It is not what God likes. Mercy is more natural to him. It is more like God. Even when Mercy is refused—rejected—spurned; and judgment is compelled to act on the wicked, Mercy goes out upon the Mount of Olives to shed her tears over the devoted city ! He wept over it : *Oh, Jerusalem, Jerusalem, how often would I have gathered your children together, even as a hen gathereth her chickens under her wings, and ye would not!*

2. A second argument is found in the nature of the Divine Revelation.

The great purpose of this Revelation is to disclose to us the Mercy of God, and lead us to accept it. Other things which we need to know about God, are more disclosed to us in his works than this. The light of nature teaches them, we mean, they are taught *by* nature; we do *not* mean, that man *understands* the teaching, unless the Bible aids him to understand it. With that aid, the exercise of sober reason acting upon the things seen in creation and providence, leads us to quite a tolerable knowledge of the attributes of God; only with this singular exception. The Mercy of God toward us guilty and unworthy sinners is of such a nature, that the magnitude, the wonders, the grandeur and combination of all that is contained in creation and in the common providences of God, could not disclose it to us. This wonderful creation (we will not dispute the Psalm), fitted up with so much wisdom and magnificence, is full of lessons about God. We may read them in the vast worlds hung out, like gems, above us, in the midnight skies, as if to deck the pathway for the footsteps of the Deity. We may read them in the dews of the night, in the wild-flower's beauty, and in the wild-bird's song. The power, the intelligence, the wisdom, the goodness, the justice of the Deity—these are to be learnt, and pretty well learnt, as we look out on Nature, investigate her laws, and study the various orders of beings and the changes which we behold. But the *Mercy* of God creation can not tell us. The declaration must come from his own lips. It is something which lies so deep in the depths of the Divine nature, that this material universe, with all its magnificence, and variety, and order, and wisdom, cannot tell it to us! Aside from direct revelation, indeed, we may learn something by the power of our own reason. We may find proofs that God is merciful; but there we must stop. We can find no proof, perhaps not a hint, that that merciful God will ever forgive a sinner! The human understanding can not see this. It can only see a little way. By three different considerations, indeed, it may properly be led to conclude, that God is merciful; but none of these will furnish a single item of assurance that

Divine Mercy will ever forgive a sinner. Let us see—let us learn to understand how dumb all Nature is, and how deep in the perfections of God lies the Mercy which can pardon us.

The *first* consideration is, that our Creator has formed us with such minds and hearts, that we esteem Mercy an excellence. This is a decision of human nature. We can not do otherwise. Singular enormity of wickedness and vice may furnish some exceptions, perhaps, but they are few. You must descend to the very worst classes of human kind, before you can find a single individual who does not regard mercy as an excellence of character. God has so constituted the human understanding, as to compel it to do so. But it is unreasonable to suppose that God would form his intelligent creatures with understandings compelling them to dis-esteem himself. He must, therefore, be merciful. It is unreasonable to suppose that he would have made our souls such as to deem mercy an excellence, if he were destitute of it. Mercy is indispensable to a character of perfection, according to the decision of the human understanding.

But here reason must stop. She can not go a step farther. Nature can not lead her a step. In all her conclusions, there is no assurance of the forgiveness of a single sin! Human reason can only discern a general mercifulness in God. She can not demonstrate from man's mental formation—from the esteem he has for a character of mercy—that Divine Mercy will ever reach, or can reach the worst wants of the world, and grant the pardon of even the smallest transgression! Human reason can not tell us, but our guiltiness, as sinners, surpasses all the mercy there is in God! She can not decide by any indication, much less by any proof, that it would not be an imperfection in the Deity to forgive sin. One of the most masterly minds among the Grecian philosophers doubted whether it were possible for the Deity to pardon a sinner. He was a heathen, without the Bible ; and this shows us at what point the human mind will stop, must stop, unaided by the revelation of God. It may deem God merciful, and that is all! What it will be proper for a perfect God to do unto such rebellious and guilty creatures as we are, the human understanding has no means of determining! It casts not a single ray of light on the abodes of guilt ; it flings not a hope into our coming eternity. It can not tell us but our own minds, formed as they are to esteem mercy an excellence, when they come to understand, in eternity, what a perfect God ought to do, will see that it is indispensable to his perfections to punish us eternally !

A *second* consideration is the treatment that we receive. We experience mercies every day. We are guilty of sinning, as all men well know, even without any Divine Revelation. Strict justice would punish us at once. But it does not. We are spared, and not only spared, but loaded with providential favors. This is mercy. God positively does exercise it towards us. And, therefore, by our own reason we may know that he is merciful.

But here again we are limited. Reason can not tell us that this Mercy shall ever reach beyond outward goodness—reach a sin and blot it out. It can not assure us of favor for eternity. It conveys no hint of any Mercy beyond our earthly allotments ; but, on the contrary, all the mercy there is in *them* seems to be more and more forsaking us as we draw nearer the tomb. Pained limbs, dimmed eyes, hearts incapable, in age, of enjoying the delights they once relished, the distresses of our last illness, and the pangs of death, seem, and must ever seem, to unaided reason, as indications that God's Mercy is fast forsaking us, and as cause for a *fearful looking-for of judgment* in another world; a world not reached by the Mercy of God!

A *third* consideration is the goodness of God. All his works contain proofs of his goodness. The Deity is infinitely benevolent. Mercy is a part of benevolence—a modification of it. Human reason can discover this, and properly conclude, therefore, that Mercy belongs to the Divine character.

But here again it must stop. Human reason can not discover that propriety and justice will ever permit the Mercy of God to extend to the forgiveness of iniquity, and the communication of future happiness to the sinner. Whatever is best to be done in time and in eternity, reason teaches us that God will do. But what *is* best— whether final forgiveness can ever be granted to the sinner—is something which Reason can not tell; she knows nothing on this point. As Reason looks out upon this strange and tearful world, she sees God doing things contrary to all that she could expect. He fills every chapter of the world's history with wonders. He sends famines! he shakes down Lisbons with earthquakes! he buries Herculaneums with lava! he drowns Limas with the waves of the sea! Pestilences do his bidding; and even without their death-march, one fourth part of our race goes down to an infant's grave! These things are beyond our understanding. Reason, therefore, can never decide for God, and know that the Divine Mercy is so great as to reach the pardon of sin.

Besides, as she turns from the manifestations which God makes of himself in such things, to consider the extent of his kingdom and all its vast and eternal concerns, Reason can not but see that the interests of that kingdom demand things which she can not at all understand. She is forced, therefore, to be silent—dumb! She can demonstrate no Mercy for sinners beyond the tomb! The patience of God exercised towards the unworthy here, and the blessings his goodness pours out on guilty heads, manifest a disposition and a degree of mercifulness, and lay the foundation of that habit of prayer which the heathen exercise in their miseries and fears. But this is all! The world—the whole world—all the goodness sprinkled over it, all the forbearance exercised towards it by God himself, furnish no evidence that a just and holy God is still merciful enough to restore a sinner to his heart's favor and final salvation. The Mercy of God has such an eminence that material worlds can not disclose it. Their order, their beauty, their ranks of beings, their laws, are unable to whisper a single syllable of comfort into the ears of a dying man! As this clay tabernacle is crumbling, they never teach him to say, *this dead body shall rise.* As the spirit is torn from this temple, human reason never promises it wings of angels to bear it to the bosom of God! God has trusted his world to demonstrate his other attributes, but *not* to demonstrate his Mercy. His mountains and his seas—his winds, his lightnings, and his thunders—his worlds wheeling in infinite space around his throne—suns, stars, and comets in their order—the existence and nature of this material universe, God has trusted to unfold to us his wisdom, his omnipotence, his justice. But the Mercy of God can not be told by matter. It has such a pre-

eminence that he himself must speak it out to us from
his hiding-place in eternity! The purpose of THIS BOOK
is to disclose to us the Mercy of God. It tells more in a
single page than all the universe tells. This is the
second demonstration of the preëminence of the Divine
Mercy.

3. We pass to a third. We find it in the plan by
which Divine Mercy operates. This plan is evidently
singular, and an infinite remove from all the possible discoveries of reason, and, be it remembered, from all the
analogies of the universe! Other attributes can operate
in the other plans of God, and it is an exercise of filial
piety, we admit, to be attracted to the Deity by the road
of creation and providence. But there is a better road.
The way of redemption is the way of sufficient mercy.
Divine Mercy is of such preëminence, that its method of
operation is entirely singular, and unlike any thing else
which God Almighty does. It operates by the incarnation, life, and death of the eternal Son of God. He *who
thought it not robbery to be equal with God, for our sakes
became poor, that we, through his poverty, might be made
rich.* He connected himself, in a manner miraculous,
intimate, and eternal, with flesh and blood. He became
allied to sinners, and *was not ashamed to call them his
brethren.* He was born in a stable and laid in a manger.
His mother was a poor virgin, and her betrothed husband
a poor man. Destitute of protection, his parents fled
with him by night from those who sought his life; and
destitute of wealth, he laboriously wrought in the business of a common carpenter to earn *his bread by the sweat
of his face.* He suffered fatigue, hunger, and weariness.
He was tempted of the Devil. He preached the Gospel
to the poor. He healed their sick. He wept in their

sorrows. He raised their dead. He went about doing good. He *had not where to lay his head.* He died the death of a malefactor, most humiliating and distressing. Other good men have died in triumph, but he died in the bitterest agony. The foresight of his sufferings in the garden of Gethsemane forced him, with all his un-equaled submission and iron fortitude, to *sweat great drops of blood falling down to the ground.* Lifted up on the cross, God his Father removed the light of his counte-nance from him at the very moment when we should have expected something else, and extorted from his dying lips the bitterest of all wailings, *My God, my God, why hast thou forsaken me ?*

This was Jesus Christ! This was the Son of God! This was he who had power to raise the dead, and could easily have changed the sneers of his murderers to confu-sion, and *come down from the cross.* But then there would have been no sufficient Mercy for sinners. Mercy, to reach the forgiveness of sin, and secure us the favor of God in another world, requires all this. It asks the heart's-blood of the Son of God! It demands the wonderful singularity, that the eternal Son shall leave the bosom of the Father—shall be allied to sinners, worms of the dust—shall be tempted—shall suffer—shall die under the wrath of God, endured for us, and go down in tears, and ignominy, and blood to the tomb! This is Mercy's operation, and surely it is singular. There is nothing else like it. God himself never did any thing else like it! Infinite power, infinite intelligence, infinite holiness, have no such exercises as infinite Mercy. Mercy, then, has a Divine preëminence. It makes God act as nothing else makes God act! The angels knew what they were doing, when, over the plains of Bethlehem, they came,

" where the infant Redeemer was laid," to sing, *Glory to God in the* HIGHEST, because, on earth, on this wicked and sinful earth, there could be *peace* from God, and *good-will* could reach and save—eternally save—guilty, unworthy, rebellious man. The Apostle knew what he was doing, when he puts the very creation of God under the feet of Divine Mercy : *Who created all things by Jesus Christ to* THE INTENT, *that now unto principalities and powers in heavenly places, might be known by the* CHURCH—a body of forgiven sinners—*the manifold wisdom of God*.

4. We pass to a fourth consideration. And would to God it could reach every hard heart in this assembly! It ought to do so! And especially, there are some of us grown gray in sin—and others of us, whose hardihood has greatly enhanced our offences—whose hearts ought to entertain this consideration. It is this : the promises. of Mercy in the Gospel are absolutely unlimited by human guilt. They furnish refuge for every penitent from the demands of Divine justice. There is no exception. There is no crime so odious, no circumstances of sinning amidst light and warnings, and the strivings of the resisted Spirit, so aggravating, no gray head so guilty, as not to be pitiable and pardonable, when the sinner affectionately and sincerely turns him to Jesus Christ. This is singular. This is wonderful! Human reason could never have conjectured this. Human sentiments, without grace, never have any thing like it. Let us see.

You can presume more on a mother's affection than on any thing else I can think of. Alas! filial ingratitude and disobedience have often tried it; and an unkind and reckless son has given woes to a mother's heart surpassing all others that spring from mere earthly affliction. But that mother's heart still hangs round her cruel child! It will bear with him, and hope in him, longer than any thing else! It will forgive him, and pour out midnight prayers for him, to the merciful and forgiving God! But if you remove from it the sentiments of Christianity, and leave it to the mere sentiments of nature, you can never be assured that that cruel son can not sin beyond the extent of her forgiveness. There *is* a point where even maternal affection will die, (especially if not sanctified affection,)—killed, crucified, and blasted by filial ingratitude and cruelty! But God's Mercy is not so. It has no limits on this side the tomb! The greatness of sin, the enormity of sin, the aggravations of sin, the multitude of sins, *any,* yea, *all* of these put together never exclude a penitent from the blessed forgiveness of God! Who can limit the Divine Mercy? To which of you, in your old age of guilt, or in the sturdiness of your younger rebellion, do not its offers extend? What sinner did the Mercy of God ever repel? what wounded heart did it ever fail to heal? If you will turn to it, you may leave all your fears behind you. Mercy, God's Mercy, will never ask how you have sinned—how long you have sinned—or through how many Divine influences you have gone on hardening your heart! *The Lord is plenteous in mercy.* The extent of Mercy has forgiven Nebuchadnezzar and Manasseh. It has forgiven Paul, who persecuted the Church, and Peter, who denied his Master. It has forgiven David, his conscience polluted with lust and blood, and the woman taken in adultery! This extent demonstrates its preëminence. God is merciful, beyond all that human hope could conjecture. He is willing to forgive any sinner. If obstinate perseverance in evil, if the *sin against the Holy Ghost, which hath never forgiveness,* forms an exception, it is not because Mercy is insufficient, but simply, solely, because there is no disposition to seek it. But this is not all. Take a

5th Argument; for its *readiness* ought to affect you. There is something singular in this. There is something wonderful. It surpasses the measure of human sentiments, and sometimes staggers even a Divine faith. What we mean is this, that the extent of the sinner's guilt makes no difference about the readiness of his forgiveness—that the Mercy of God will forgive him if he repents at any stage of his sin on this side of hell, with precisely the same facility and readiness! This is pre-eminence in Mercy. God pardons all the penitent with equal readiness—the greatest and least offenders. This doctrine may seem strange to those whose sentiments have not drunk deep at the Gospel fountain, and been formed amid contemplations of the infinite atonement of the Son of God. But we dare affirm it. We challenge your examination of the whole Gospel, to detect any difference in the readiness with which God forgives penitent sinners. *You* would make a difference; but *God's thoughts are not your thoughts. You* would find it a more difficult thing to forgive the enemy, who had loaded you with insult, and abuse, and injury, all your days—who had wantonly destroyed your happiness, marred your peace, insulted your kindness, and done all in his power to make you contemptible and miserable; you would find it a more difficult thing to forgive such a one, at the last, than at the first of his offences. You would *do it,* if you are a Christian; you would do it, when he said, *I repent,* even to *seventy times seven.* But you would find

it a trial of your Christian temper; and probably, if you
are *not* a Christian, all your feelings would refuse it. But
it is not so with God. He forgives the greatest offender,
when he repents, as readily as he forgives the least.
Not a hint in the Gospel opposes this idea. Not a single
hint or suggestion flings any difficulty in the way of the
most free and ready forgiveness of the most guilty sinner that ever lived. That guilt makes no difference
about the readiness of his forgiveness. It *does* make a
difference about the probability of his repentance, and
his seeking forgiveness; but it makes no difference
about the readiness with which the God of mercy will
throw around the penitent the arms of a forgiving and
fatherly embrace. It makes no difference about the
readiness with which your *heavenly Father will give the
Holy Spirit to them that ask him.* Mercy, Divine Mercy,
is preëminent. It surpasses all .the extent of human
reason, human expectation, human sentiments and hopes.
It not only reaches the greatest offences, but the greatest
as readily as the least.

We had marked two other aguments. One was, the
small requirements that Mercy makes of us—only to repent and fall into the arms of God for eternal favor and
eternal life. The other was the most bitter dreg in the
cup of a sinner's condemnation—that he rejected Mercy,
while mercy might be had, and will find the preëminence of his woes in the remembrance of the preëminent
Mercy that offered to save him from the anger of God
and his bed in hell—that the rejection of Christ digs his
pit deeper! We must leave these two ideas to your
own contemplation.

But, my dear friends, this eminence of Mercy ought
not to be in vain to you. It is this which solicits your

faith. God, the infinite God, has done more to convince you of his boundless Mercy to sinners, than to convince you of any thing else. The tendency of sin is to make your hearts insensible to the powerful attractions of God, and suspicious of his kindness towards you. In the revelations of his mercy, he is striving to affect your hearts. You mistake your own nature, if you think the terrors of judgment and the fears of hell are ever going to bring you to God in faith. They never will. They may bring you to despondency—to a life of gloom, and to a death-bed of despair! But they will never bring you to a happy faith.

We know there is reason to fear God—but there is more reason to love him. He has done this most wonderful of all his works, out of love to us, poor, guilty and dying sinners; and if we would only believe God, and turn ourselves to his compassion, there is no depth of sin—no extent of it—no gray-haired iniquity, his Mercy would not forgive! Revealed Mercy is the very burden of the Gospel. Ye, impenitent and unbelieving sinners, ought to be melted by it. Ye, fearful and suspicious of God, ought to bear the message of Mercy home to your own souls. You ought to say to yourselves, each one of you: I see how it is; I see God is of such mercy, that all the magnificence and goodness of the material world could not reveal it; I see how it operates; I trace it from the manger-cradle to the marble tomb of the Son of God; I see where it extends; I stand on the outskirts of an opening eternity, and, glancing my eyes upward to the throne of the Almighty God, I perceive its thunders are hushed, and an innumerable company of happy spirits, once sinful and unworthy as I, now forgiven and loved of God, bathed in the light and glories of immortality: I see (ye ought to say it), I see, there is mercy *for me:* the Gospel takes me up, where Reason and the Light of Nature forsook me, and tells me what the infinite God can do, about the sins of this guilty soul, and its deathless destinies in eternity. *I will arise and go to my Father.* Yes, God is my Father still; I will say unto him, *Father, I have sinned against heaven, I am no more worthy to be called thy son !* Well, Go! go in welcome! go, and live! go NOW! go, *to fall into the hands of the Lord, for his mercies are great !* Go, and guilt can not ruin you—hell can not claim you! He that sitteth upon the throne, will say, *This my son was dead and is alive again, was lost, and is found.*

> " *Saved !* the deed shall spread new glory
> Through the courts, the crowds above !
> Angels tell the blissful story,
> *A sinner saved*—for God is love !"

What will you do? Put the question to your own soul—thou, my immortal spirit, bound to eternity and cannot tarry, my own soul, what will you do? Will you have this mercy, this heaven for your own?

> " Say, will you to Mount Zion go ?
> Say, will you have this Christ or no ?"

When God shall make up his jewels, it shall be known in heaven whether you spurned his Mercy to-day !

God no Pleasure in the Death of the Wicked.

(SHOWN FROM THE PURPOSES OF GOD.)

As I live, saith the Lord God, I have no pleasure in the death of the wicked.—EZEKIEL, xxxiii. 11.

IN these words, God affirms something about himself. It is no new idea to the minds of this congregation, that the character of God is the leading idea in religion.

Scarcely any theme of instruction is more difficult than the regard of the Deity for a sinner. To give to the revolted subject of God's righteous government a correct apprehension of the feelings with which his God regards him, is an attempt attended with peculiar embarrassments. These arise, not so much from the obscurity of the subject itself, as from the strong tendency to misapprehend it. There is something in the nature of the case which contributes a great obstacle to correct apprehension. When we speak of the Deity as righteous, and man as under his rule, there is something of accusation immediately conceived. Conscience goes to work. The hearer at once feels that there is a design to reprove him; and the consequence of this feeling is, he puts himself on the defence. And even if we avoid all accusing terms—if the Bible avoids them—if we do not say that man is unrighteous—if we take pains to avoid all methods of expression which bring his own character to mind, and strive to present the subject in such a manner that he may examine it without the excitements of prejudice, and as an unbiased spectator, we are not able, after all, to accomplish the designs—the failure always shows our deficiency of skill in persuasion, and should humble us as preachers. The truth is, if we present the subject in the abstract, it will not be received so by the hearer. If we do not bring him into the question, he will bring himself in; neither our art nor eloquence can avoid it. And he usually comes prepared to defend himself, in some manner or in some degree, from the imputation which his own consciousness has suggested. Guilt is suspicious: *This is John the Baptist risen from the dead.* We can not speak of those attributes of the Deity necessarily associated with his being reconciled to an offender, without awakening something of the self-love and pride, if not something of the prejudice of him who still needs reconciliation. The nature of the case, therefore, renders it hard to give the proper impression to such a one. The Deity will be regarded, by those who have never been taught by the Spirit, in some measure as an enemy; and in such a case, surely, it would be the hight of human candor to examine his character and his offers with unprejudiced fairness.

We are far from believing that most men *design* to run into this abuse. However self-love or self-respect might lead them to plead their cause strongly if they were to speak upon it, we are far from supposing they soberly intend to be uncandid when only called upon to think. To deceive and willingly ruin themselves is a thing distant from their designs. No man is willing to deceive and destroy himself.

But men desire to avoid the present unhappiness which the truth might create. Their hearts are opposed to it. And for these reasons they hazard the unhappy consequences of the future. In this sense they are guilty of willing self-deception and its wretched results. For these reasons they are not apt to look impartially at the character of God.

But this matter is no less important than difficult. An error here is particularly unfortunate and hazardous. All our ideas of religion are intimately connected with the character of God. That character lays the foundation of all that man can hope, and of what man must be. And if we have a false notion of that character, we shall have false notions of religion; the God we worship will be an imaginary God; the homage we render will be agreeable to our misconceptions; our religion, begun in error, will end in wretchedness, and we ourselves shall become those of whom it is said, *deceiving and being deceived.*

It becomes us, therefore, to examine such a subject in all its connections and with the utmost candor. To shield ourselves from the truth can be of no lasting benefit, and may be, in the end, of most awful disadvantage.

And, perhaps, there are few points where we need this caution more than we do when God tells us of his mercy. The text we have just read to you is one of those passages in which God condescends to meet one of those complaints which our hearts are apt to make against him. He here exonerates himself. He declares what is his disposition in regard to sinners, and thus removes one of those vain excuses which men sometimes weave to themselves for continuing in their wickedness. *As I live, saith the Lord God, I have no pleasure in the death of the wicked.* The design of this expression seems to be, to correct our ideas of the feelings of God, when we have run so far into error as to think him capable of pleasure in our destruction. Human hearts do often meet the peculiar emphasis of this declaration. There are those who have no religion, and who are prevented from making any determined efforts to attain it, because they are unhappily persuaded into the opinion that the pleasure of God is opposed to their salvation. This passage was designed to correct them. There are those who allege the controlling power of God, their dependence upon him, and his designs and dispositions, as a kind of apology for their irreligion. This passage was designed to rebuke them. There are those (and would to God there were more of them) who are desirous of securing eternal life, but, sensible of their sins, are afraid to approach God, lest there be something in his character unfavorable to their salvation. This passage was designed to encourage them, to remove that despondency which prohibits action, and animate with that vigor which hope alone inspires.

The text is in itself an unqualified declaration of God, that he does not take pleasure in the destruction of the wicked. The declaration is needed. The wicked sometimes half believe he does. Such a belief is an injury to them. God would have them abandon it. He here condescends to exculpate himself, and, consequently, his conduct in relation to sinners, and thus would bring them to take courage in seeking God, or take the blame of their ruin upon themselves.

Now, the sentiment which this declaration opposes takes its rise, and is sustained in the mind of the wicked, by considerations drawn especially from three sources :

The Purposes of God;

The Nature of Religion ; and

The Condition of the Wicked.

Could we give men just impressions about God, they would need no other instruction on these points. If we could throw the blaze of purity across these springs of error, it would dry up the fountains of falsehood, and stop the flow of those streams that waft so many down to the abysses of the damned. A just impression about God would teach man that the Divine purposes do not oppose his salvation. A just impression about God would teach man that the religion enjoined upon him is not so severe as to compel him to be lost. A just impression about God would teach the wicked that God has not placed him in such a condition in this world that his ruin is unavoidable.

But to meet definitely the sentiment to which this text is opposed, let us consider its three sources separately, and endeavor to justify the declaration of the text.

I. The Purposes of God. This will occupy us in the present discourse. The others will occupy us in two other discourses, to come afterward.

The perfections which enlightened reason always concedes to the Deity, oblige us to believe that he has created nothing which he did not want—nothing which has frustrated his expectations. Before he exercised one act of creating power, he saw all the consequences of his creation, knowing then, as perfectly as now, and as perfectly as he ever will know, all the results of felicity and wretchedness that would ever be realized in heaven, earth, and hell. And with all these before him, as the certain consequences of that constitution of things he was

13

about to establish, and that creative energy he was about to exert, still he resolved, that under such a constitution, such a creation should rise. He spake and it was done. Having acted with previous knowledge of all the results of his actions, nothing that occurs can be contrary to his expectations.

So far, enlightened Reason coincides with the Word of God, and is satisfied with it. But *here* they separate. Not that they are contrary to each other; but that reason has reached her limits, beyond which she can never pass, except under the guidance of revelation, and she must trust that revelation henceforth at every step, or wander in darkness and error. Because God is the author of all creatures that exist, and knew, before their existence, all the results of it, we are sometimes apt to conceive of him as the sole author of all the miseries of his creatures. And as his power is sufficient to accomplish all his purposes, we draw the conclusion, that if we perish, it must be because he is pleased with our destruction.

Now, I wish,

1. To convince you that we have no right to draw any such conclusion.

2. To show you where such a principle of reasoning and drawing inferences would lead.

3. To name to you the considerations which should correct us.

1. We have no right to conclude that the Almighty is the sole cause of the miseries of his creatures, from the fact that he is the Author of their existence, that he knew, before he created, all the consequences of his creating, and that none of his expectations and purposes are frustrated.

The error of this method of reasoning lies *in the inferring of consequences from principles that are unknown.* What are the principles? The purposes of God. What are the consequences? God's pleasure in the sinner's destruction, and the sinner's unhappiness that he is subject to the purposes of God. But who is acquainted with these principles? Who has fathomed the eternal purposes of Jehovah? *Who has known the mind of the Lord, or, being his counsellor, has taught him?* The purposes of God are beyond our reach. We know he *has* his purposes and will accomplish them, because he has told us so, and because they are necessary to the perfection of his character. But who knows what they are? Who has plunged into their depths? Who has traced their arrangements, their combination, their extent? Who will undertake to spread them out before us, and tell us how they affect us? They are placed beyond our reach. They are deep in themselves, and obscurely taught in the Scriptures, and no man can boast of understanding their nature, their combination, the mode of their application. How, then, can any man presume to draw conclusions from them. (We never do. Our hearers should not.) They are premises which a man does not know. He knows only in the general. He is ignorant of their nature, their power, their combination, and he can tell of no instance of their application, except those which God has taught him. What kind of logic then, must he use who will draw inferences from such unknown premises? Tell me in what *method* the Purposes of God apply to the ruin of a sinner, and I will consent, for ever afterwards, that you make the application. Unfold to me the Divine Purposes—tear away the *clouds and darkness* that are *round about* the Deity—unseal the secret book of God, never yet read by the highest seraphim in glory; and then I will confess your right to reason from the purposes of God.

All that we know of the purposes of God is general. There is nothing special or particular in our knowledge. Our conclusions, therefore, must not run beyond our premises. Our knowledge of God's purposes is not so particular that we can tell *how* they affect any action or any result. God has not told us; and when men have attempted to tell, they have always become bewildered. We have no right, therefore, to attempt to determine particular questions by all that we know of these obscure general principles. When we attempt it, we are wielding an instrument too heavy for us, whose edge and temper are unknown. It was made, not for an arm like ours, but for the arm of the Omnipotent One.

Before we can apply the purposes of God to particular things—to our conduct, our destiny, or the pleasure of the Deity—we must know the method of application; we must know the particular character of the purposes; we must be able to understand *how* they affect the particulars. Before I can draw safe conclusions from the principles of science, I must know what these principles are; I must understand the manner in which they apply to the subject; and, therefore, I must understand their nature and their combinations. But *no man* has such knowledge of the purposes of God. And, consequently, no man has any right to make such an application of them as implies this knowledge. No man has any right to conclude that God has any pleasure in the death of the wicked, on the ground that his purposes are at all opposed to their salvation. This is the first thing we proposed to show.

2. The second was to show *to what results* the principle of reasonings against which we contend would inevitably conduct us. If it is lawful for us to infer, from the purposes of God, that he has pleasure in the destruction of the wicked, then it is lawful for us, on the same principle, to infer that he has pleasure in that wickedness itself, which leads to destruction. For what is the principle on which the first inference is made? It is simply this—that because God is the author of every being that exists, and every thing that results from that existence, he must be the sole cause of all the *miseries* of his creatures, and, consequently (as he has every thing in his own way), must have pleasure in the destruction of the wicked. But the *wickedness* which ends in misery is as much a result of his having formed his creatures, as is the misery itself. And, consequently, if he is pleased with all the results of his creating power, he is pleased with the *wickedness* of men. The principle will apply here as well as to their destruction; and you may say, therefore, that because God is the author of every being that exists, and every thing that results from that existence, he must be the sole cause of all the WICKEDNESS of his creatures, and, consequently (as he has every thing in his own way), must have pleasure in the *wickedness* of the wicked! There is no avoiding this argument. If God must have pleasure in the death of the wicked, because he foresaw it, and yet determined to create them, he must, for the same reason, have pleasure in their *iniquity!* We may conclude, therefore, on this principle of reasoning, that God is pleased with sin! This is the result of attempting to reason from the secret purposes of God.

Again. The design of the argument we are combatting, is to prove that men do not destroy themselves. The argument itself is, that such destruction is agreeable to God's purposes, and, therefore, is unavoidable—it was predestinated. But if such destruction is agreeable to God's purposes, and is, therefore, unavoidable, then, on the very same principle of reasoning, the *guilt* which incurs it is agreeable to God's purposes, and is, therefore, unavoidable. We may conclude, therefore, on this principle, that there is no such thing as *accountability*—all the conduct of men being the result of an unavoidable necessity. Yea, therefore, we may conclude also, that there is no such thing as *sin*, all the conduct of men being the result of an unavoidable necessity! We may call, therefore, the incendiary with his torch, the drunkard with his bowl, and the assassin with his steel, as innocent and pure as the spirits that never fell! These are other results of attempting to reason from the secret purposes of God.

The inevitable consequence, therefore, of this method of reasoning would be to destroy all idea of moral character among men; and, consequently, to prove him as pure, who is suffering for his crimes, as he who is honored for his virtues. That man who excuses his irreligion by the argument of God's purposes, has no right to resent an insult or resist an injury, to the inconvenience of its perpetrators. How could they avoid it? This is another result to which this style of argument would lead. It would overthrow all human law, and all common sense.

3. The consideration which should correct this error is, the narrow limits of our understandings. We ought to bear in mind, that there are depths into which it is dangerous to plunge ourselves. The purposes of God

he has never unfolded to us.   He has nowhere shown us how far they extend *specifically*—how they apply, nor traced for us their combinations.   He has not told us to receive them as our rule of action, to employ them to justify our conduct, or to measure our innocence or our criminality.   The connection which these purposes of the Deity have with what he is constantly bringing to pass, is a connection wholly unknown to us: God has not told us what it is, nor given us sagacity sufficient to discover it.   And here is the primary error of attempting to draw conclusions from the Divine purposes.   We are pretending to employ in our reasoning a connection of which we are utterly ignorant.   We have not *the least* knowledge of the nature of the connection which exists between the purposes of Jehovah and the actions of his creatures.   And yet, we are apt to think and talk about this connection as if it were a thing we well understood— as if it were just the common link which joins causes and effects.   Let the recollection of our incapacities—our limited understandings—our small degree of knowledge, correct our error.

And what, as ministers, we say to other people, we are willing to apply to ourselves.   If it is wrong for the hearer to argue his innocence from the purposes of God, we confess it is no less erroneous for the preacher to attempt, *from* these purposes, to prove that his argument is false.   The attempt has been made a thousand times, and a thousand times it has failed.   Should any assert that his impiety is not his fault, and that his condemnation would be not from any fault of his own, because it would be the consequence of the purposes of the Deity, and so connected with these purposes, that he could not avoid it; we confess our inability to show directly from those purposes that he is mistaken. We have other ways of showing his mistake; but we confess our inability to show it in this way. We could show, in this way, that his argument was *not* conclusive, and that is all; we could not prove from these purposes the opposite doctrine. We shall see pretty soon in what manner this error might be corrected, when we show, from other sources, that the pleasure or purposes of the Almighty are not the reason of the sinner's ruin. But we know so little of the eternal counsels of God, that we are unable, from that kind of knowledge, to affirm what *is* or what is not their influence. To have the power to make such an affirmation, we must attain a perfect knowledge of the purposes of God; we must know all their combinations; we must unfold to ourselves the manner of their influence; and then we must place them side by side with the dispositions of the sinner, and compare them with those dispositions so exactly as to prove by that comparison the precise nature and extent of their influence. But if we should attempt to do this, we should be running into the same error in reasoning of which those are guilty who reason from the purposes of God to show *their* innocence, and the pleasure of God in their ruin. This error consists, as we have just seen, in reasoning from unknown premises.

We will take, therefore, to ourselves the caution we gave to them. We will confess we can not fathom the purposes of God. Standing by the darkness that girds the throne of the Eternal, we will confess our eye is too dim to penetrate the cloud, and pass onward to the glories that lie beyond. Contemplating the infinity of the Divine Mind, we will receive the rebuke of our littleness: *It is as high as heaven, what canst thou do? deeper than hell, what canst thou know?* But we will *never* mourn the darkness of the cloud that pavilions the habitation of God, as long as the bow of promise sweetly rests upon its bosom, and, spanning heaven, extends its covenant arch down to earth to embrace it.

But though we are incapable of unfolding the Divine Purposes, and proving thereby, that the Deity has no pleasure in the destruction of the wicked, and that these purposes do not render sin and death unavoidable, yet we have other methods of showing this. He who alone knows perfectly those purposes and the dispositions of the wicked, has told us, and we have, therefore, the strongest of all possible evidence. If he had *not* told us, we confess our utter inability to have ever proved, from all we know of these purposes, that they do not violate our liberty, and render sin and its eternal punishment unavoidable. But he has told us they do not; and if we will not credit his testimony, what will we credit?

1. He has told us, in the language of the text: *As I live, saith the Lord God, I have no pleasure in the death of the wicked.* If the purposes of God were of such a nature as to compel the wicked to his wickedness, and thus bring him to eternal death unavoidably, this declaration could not be true.

2. He has told us so in those explicit declarations which charge our destruction upon ourselves: *Oh, Israel, thou hast destroyed thyself.* Now, if the Divine purposes forced men to sin, or placed insurmountable obstacles in the way of their salvation, I can conceive of no sense in which this declaration could be true.

3. He has told us so in those numerous passages which expressly declare, (what our text implies,) that is, he is *not willing that any should perish, but that all should come*

13*

to repentance. Now, if the purposes of God were of such a nature as to prove the pleasure of God in the destruction of the wicked, we might change this declaration of Holy Writ; we might affirm, he *would not* that all men should be saved; he *is* willing that some should perish, but not that *all should come to repentance.* But who dare thus trifle with the Bible? *Let God be true, but every man a liar.*

4. He has told us so in those tender expostulations and earnest entreaties, which he employs to win sinners to himself. *Turn ye, turn ye, for why will ye die?* is only one among a thousand passages which express the same tender sentiment. Now, did the purposes of the Deity *force* the sinner—did they confine him in the bondage of corruption—did they prohibit success in attaining the favor of God, (as some of you sometimes affirm;) where would be the *sincerity* of God in calling him to *turn,* while he himself had rendered it an impossible thing?

5. He has told us the same thing in those lamentations which he utters over the doom of the wicked. *Oh that my people had hearkened unto me! Oh, Jerusalem, Jerusalem!* Now, how unworthy of the Deity would such utterances be, if he *had* pleasure in the fact that they had *not* hearkened unto him, so much as to have rendered it impossible by his immutable purposes that they should?

6. He has told us the same thing when he calls us to contemplate those attributes with which he clothes himself—attributes of mercy, forbearance, long-suffering and tender compassion. Take one of them, his *long-suffering,* as an example. He exalts his mercy, by naming the long-suffering which continues the offer of it: *The Lord God, gracious, merciful, long-suffering.* So he speaks of himself. But now, if the purposes of God prohibit re-

pentance, how can he be any more merciful by exercising *long-suffering* with a sinner, and giving him year after year to repent in, than if he exercised no such forbearance, but cut him off the moment he began to sin? More: if the predestination of God prohibits repentance, then the long-suffering of God seems to be directly the *opposite* to mercy; for surely, by granting a wicked man three-score years and ten, while all the time he prohibits his repentance, he is only forcing him to enhance his wickedness, and ripen for a deeper condemnation. Were this the case, long-suffering would be the most dreadful attribute of God; and you ought to pray God—Smite me now! Wake thy thunderbolts of vengeance! Execute now on my devoted head the penalty of my guilt, before my unavoidable sins have prepared me for a deeper hell!

Now, in all these ways (and we could name a thousand others), God has told us that his purposes do not violate our liberty, and never can show that he *has any pleasure at all* in the death of the wicked. Let us believe, my hearers, what he has told us. Let us not pretend to *reason* from the secret purposes of God. Those purposes are not the rule of our conduct or the measure of our innocence. They rest with God. They are the rules which he has been pleased to establish for his own conduct, not for ours. They are only his determination to govern his universe, just *as* he does govern it. With God let us leave them. He has not so definitely taught us what they are, and how they affect us, that we have any security at all when we take them as the basis of our reasonings. We have *other* premises, from which we may reason securely, because they are definitely known. But when we plunge ourselves into those obscurities where the Bible sheds no light, our way is darkness, and commonly its end is error. Let us confine ourselves within the limits that God has assigned to us. Let us believe that God *has* his purposes, because he has told us so, and because they are necessary to the perfection of his existence; and let us be willing to preach, and willing to hear of these purposes all that the sacred Scriptures contain. But let us not pretend to understand the connection of these purposes with our conduct or our destiny; for this God has *not* told us. We are left in ignorance of many points respecting these purposes. Their combinations, their efficiency upon the universe, the mode of their application, are all beyond us. Let not the preacher, therefore, vainly imagine that he can so unfold them as to silence every objection, or satisfy every honest difficulty; and let not the hearer, with the same audacious vanity, suppose that he knows enough about the purposes of God to prove that the wicked must unavoidably perish as they do, because God has *pleasure in their death.* Let the preacher silence objection and solve difficulty by employing other truths—truths more fully revealed and more accurately understood; by pronouncing the language of this text: *As I live, saith the Lord God, I have no pleasure in the death of the wicked;* by saying to the sinner, *Thou hast destroyed thyself.* And let the hearer believe it. It is the direct testimony of Him who can not lie. How much more worthy of credit than those foolish conclusions which men foolishly gather from premises unknown.

This text is a vindication of God's character. He comes down to meet the prejudices and difficulties of sinful men, to teach them that their ideas about the pleasure of God in purposing their eternal death, are altogether false. He announces their falsehood in the most emphatic manner: *As I live, saith the Lord God, I have no pleasure in the death of the wicked.* *As I live:* he knew what difficulties would perplex our minds; he knew how often the idea would intrude itself into the heart of a sinner, that the benevolence of God toward him is very questionable. He knew what a gloomy use Satan would make of it to bind the captive in his chains. He, therefore, utters the declaration in the most solemn style: *As I live, saith the Lord God, I have no pleasure in the death of the wicked.* He would convince every wicked man that he has *not*, in any way, on any account, the least pleasure in his death. He would drive that gloomy opinion from every mind that ever dares to entertain it. He would break that bond of Satan, and let the captive go free.

Of this whole subject, then, you may make specific applications.

There are those who have such ideas of God as to keep them from repentance. Through the devices of Satan and the deceitfulness of sin, they are led to think of God's purposes as an apology for their course; they say, if they *are* on the road to ruin, it is God's pleasure. But what daring impiety is this! They give to the Deity the most unlovely of all characters! They turn his benevolence into malignity, and his long-suffering into a trap and snare! They dare to lift up the voice of a worm of the dust, and contradict the very oath of God; they say he *has* pleasure in the death of the wicked! Let this affirmation of God rebuke them!

There are those who have sometimes struggled against the power of sin within them, impelled by fears of the wrath to come, but whose attempts, few, perhaps, and feeble, have not been successful. Hence they conclude there is something in the purposes of God which hinders their deliverance. They are not (like the others we just mentioned) accustomed to make the purposes of God their apology for sin, and the cause of their feared condemnation. But still, the purposes of God are their stumbling-block. They imagine that they should long since have been Christians had not God's purposes opposed them.

It would be barbarous, inhuman, to utter a harsh word to such persons. We pity them. We could weep over them. We know the deep misery of their situation, for we have been in it; and may the God of all mercy deliver every such soul from the bitterness of its bitter bondage ! And if there is one such in this assembly, let me tell you the idea which afflicts you is all delusion; it is a device of the Devil to keep you in your sins. God has no pleasure in your destruction. His purposes are *not* opposed to your salvation. They offer no violence to your liberty. They constitute no obstacle to your religion and your eternal life.

Let me expostulate with you. Tell me, my dear fellow-sinner, my immortal companion, hastening with me to the tomb, how do you know that the purposes of God oppose you? Show me in what manner they affect you? Point me to the connection between one single design of Deity and one single instance of your unhappiness? Prove to me that the purposes of God *have*, in any instance, *so applied* to you as to become the least obstacle to your salvation? Do this, and I will weep tears of blood over you, and blot for ever from my creed the article that seals your doom! But no—you can do none of these things. Such an opposition, such a manner, such a connection, such an application, can never be shown.

Then why will you believe it? It is unsustained by the least evidence. It is opposed to the very oath of God. Let this oath correct you. God knows better than you do, and his word assures you you are mistaken. Cast aside, then, this gloomy delusion. *Watch and pray.* Seek, and struggle, and agonize. Be assured the purposes of God do not oppose you in your attempts, for he has no pleasure in your being lost, but in your being saved.

There are those who are sensible of their sins, but who fear to approach the Lord God, lest there should be something in his purposes opposed to their acceptance and salvation. This is a fear which the great deceiver would foster, to keep such a sinner at a distance from God. And this is a fear which the declaration of the text ought for ever to dispel. No sinner, who desires to be reconciled to God in Christ, ever *finds* the purposes of God opposed to him. Great and long-continued as may be his sins, God is ready to forgive. Let him not despair on account of their number or their enormity. Let him count them all over—let him weigh their aggravation—let him tell against how many monitions he has offended, how many cautions he has abused, how many warnings he has slighted, how many sermons have been lost upon him; let him swell the catalogue till memory has reached her limits, and weigh his crimes till thought is lost in the wilderness-account; and, after all, it will be true that the purposes of God are no obstacle to salvation—he has *no pleasure in the death of the wicked.*

Perish who will, the character of God will be for ever untarnished and lovely. He desires the happiness, but not the damnation of sinners. He does not say to the wretch delighting in his iniquity, It is my purpose that impels you to it. He does not say to the once inquiring, but now careless or lingering sinner, You failed, because my purpose must be accomplished. He does not say to the anxious, trembling mortal, now asking what must I do to be saved?—You must perish, because your sins are so great, and my purpose is fixed. No. On the contrary, he opens the gates of heaven; he offers the blood of Christ; he sends the Holy Spirit; he tells of mercy, forgiveness, and free grace; and, to take out of the mouth of the lingering sinner his last apology, he records here his oath, *As I live, I have no pleasure in the death of the wicked.*

It is not his decree that fastens you in sin, and prohibits your repentance. It is not his decree that bars heaven, and denies grace. It was not his decree that dug hell, and kindled the *fire that is never quenched. No,* sinner, *no, no !* The chains that bind you are of your own forging. The grace you need is freely offered. And the hell into which you are plunging is kindled up only by the cherished wickedness which God entreats you to abandon ! Hear—hear this declaration of the Lord God ! He has *no pleasure* in your *death.* Let neither earth nor hell persuade you that the merciful God would have you perish ! Cast aside your irrational conclusions ! *Believe* the testimony of the Eternal ! Break the enchantment of your gloomy conclusions, and anchor your eternal hope in the ocean of God's mercy. You may be saved—you can be saved. For *the Lord God has no pleasure in the death of the wicked.* Do not *destroy thyself.*

God no Pleasure in the Death of the Wicked.

(SHOWN FROM THE NATURE OF RELIGION.)

As I live, saith the Lord God, I have no pleasure in. the death
of the wicked.—Ezekiel, xxxiii. 11.

WE said, on a former occasion, when we addressed
you from these words, that there were, with some
people, three matters of difficulty in religion, against
which this text is uttered :—

I. The Purposes of the Deity.
II. The Nature of Religion.
III. The Condition of Man.

From all these sources an unbeliever is sometimes
accustomed to draw conclusions unfavorable to his salvation. The partial view he takes, as well as the
erroneous opinions he entertains, is apt to sustain the
misfortune of his conclusions. He beholds, in the purposes of the Deity, as he believes or half-believes, an
insuperable obstacle to his salvation. In the Nature of
Religion—that religion which the Bible teaches him is
necessary to his salvation—he finds difficulties which he
is unable, as he imagines, to overcome. The condition
in which he finds himself, as a sinner, is made to plead

his excuse for neglect of salvation, and speaks to him a comfortable solace, even while he continues in his sins. These are his difficulties—these the sources of his objection—these his errors.

To the first of these, the Purposes of God, we have already attended. The second, the Nature of Religion, occupies us in the present hour.

Those whose minds have surmounted one difficulty in religion often meet with another. Driven from one stronghold of error, we are apt to betake ourselves to another. Such creatures we are. One mistake is corrected, but we are not safe. One delusion is dispelled, but another delusion rises before us. Thus we are beset with hinderances. When we have learnt that the Purposes of the Deity do not infringe upon our liberty, and oblige us to be lost, the Nature of Religion comes up to lend to our mistake a lame apology.

Nor can we be surprised at these frequent difficulties, when we find them in our own mind, or in the minds of other people. What is there that is valuable, whose acquisition is not attended with some trouble? The riches you covet cost you many a day of laborious diligence, and many a weary pain. The learning you value has been acquired only by laborious study, careful attention, diligence, and self-denial. There is scarcely any thing of value, whose acquisition is perfectly easy and unattended with difficulty. Difficulties will arise, either from the nature of the object sought, or the imperfection of the creature that seeks.

It is in the latter method that the difficulties of our salvation assail us. Our obstacles lie in our own nature—in that inherent wickedness which we love to foster, and are unwilling to eradicate.

But, if we are inclined, after all, to murmur that *Religion*—a thing so indispensable—is beset with so many difficulties, let us hush the murmur with two reflec- tions—the one humbling to our pride, the other com- plimentary to our nature.

The first one is, that the difficulties which beset us in our attempts after religion are mostly, if not altogether, placed there by ourselves, through our own wickedness and folly. The other is, that that very characteristic of our nature which renders us capable of religion, or of sensibility to its difficulties, is the very characteristic which distinguishes us from the lower order of creatures. Our Creator, in forming us such as we are, has given us an exaltation. We are not created merely *capable* of enjoyment; we are created for *attaining* it. We are not formed to be the mere passive recipients of good; but formed with a far more exalted nature; formed with capabilities for seeking and attaining good. And when we complain that all needful religion is not bestowed upon us as a free gift, without any efforts or attention of our own, we are, in reality, complaining of our high station in the scale of existence. God requires of us a religion suitable to our nature; and by it he would lead us to excellences of duty and of enjoyment, of which that nature is capable. Had 'he enjoined upon us no such religion, we should not have in prospect any higher kind of felicity than that of which the brute is suscepti- ble. And if we still complain that we have so much *to do* in the religion that God requires, let us remember that this activity is absolutely to the enjoyment of that felicity which religion proposes. We are moral beings, and religion treats us as such. We are moral beings, and religion rewards us as such. In the nature of things, it is wholly impossible (as I apprehend) that one should be the mere passive recipient of the enjoyment that religion proposes to man. And if you complain of this state in which you are placed, then envy the brute—covet the enjoyment of the reptile in his dust—take from the beast his stall—and envy the stupidity of the ox or the oyster.

Still, men are accustomed to render a sort of apology for continuing in their unbelief, by alleging the difficulties of religion. And we are not surprised to find it so. It is the very nature of criminality to excuse itself; and you know the religion of the Bible supposes all men to be criminal—guilty before God. You can charge iniquity upon scarcely any being deserving the charge, who will not strive to invent some apology for it. And though the apology may not be expected fully to *justify*, yet it is relied upon at least partially to *excuse*. There is but one exception—that is, when the transgressor is either reclaimed, or so powerfully convinced of his need of reformation that he fears to add to that necessity by denying it. Always, when the evil of sin is *not* deeply felt, there is a secret, if not a manifest disposition to palliate it and apologize for it. And I am persuaded that if we should thoroughly examine our own hearts, we should find this disposition often influencing us when we little suspect it. We are not to be surprised, therefore, if we find men alleging the difficulties of the religion that God enjoins upon us as a kind of excuse for the neglect of it. If they do not suppose these difficulties will *justify* them, they have a sort of secret hope that they will render them more excusable, and relieve them from any punishment. Here, then, is one reason why such apologies are uttered—to soothe fear by pacifying con-

science. There always is, and must be, a kind of tormenting fear attending known and acknowledged sin. And
the sin is palliated to diminish the torment of the fear.

Another reason is found in the power of pride. There
is something humiliating in the feeling of guilt. Guilt
is degrading; and every guilty creature feels that moral
beings look upon him as more unworthy and mean by
reason of being criminal. He can not bear the contempt
(and perhaps can not bear the pity) of those who behold
him. Hence the unconscious blush of even the uncon-
trite culprit at the bar; and hence even innocence, suspected of evil, is compelled to wear the burning blush of
shame. And, therefore, both are disposed to plead some
apology.

Another reason is found in the disquietudes of conscious sin. Sin is a great tormentor of our peace. When
we *feel* ourselves guilty, it is not in our nature to be un-
disturbed by it. The Author of our existence has
stamped upon our soul itself this testimony to his own
holiness, and his abhorrence of sin. We may turn away
from it—we may forget it—we may obscure it and
cover it over; still it is *there*, living in the hand-writing
of the Creator and can not be blotted out. Conscience is
as immortal as the soul. And though for a time she
may sleep, yet she never dies; and when in the light of
eternity she shall unroll her scroll, the record of even her
slumbering moments will be found to wear a most fearful accuracy. But, to avoid the torment of her present
reproaches, men are accustomed to make some apology
for their present wickedness. This apology may comfort for a moment, and we render it instinctively. But
when it is torn away from the heart, our unhappiness
returns. And I suppose in this consists much of the

supreme infelicity of devils and lost spirits. They are unable to quiet conscience with an excuse. Their guilt, in burning lines, is drawn upon the spirit! Nothing can hide it from their view. No sophistry can conceal it, and no apology excuse! How much better to feel it now, than vainly lament it then.

These are some of the reasons which lead men to excuse themselves. And when, by false reasonings, they can not force the Purposes of God to plead for them, they bring in the Nature of Religion to perform this office, and pretend that the religion which the Bible imposes is so difficult that they can not attain it and be saved. They will not, perhaps, boldly contradict this text, but they will speak in such a manner of the religion of the Bible, of the obscurity of its instructions, of the multitude of its mysteries, the absurdity of its doctrines, the difficulty of its duties, the rigidity of its morals, that they almost persuade themselves to believe that, although the decree of the Deity may not have bound them over to destruction, his religion has.

But now, in the face of all these prejudices, let us vindicate the religion of the Gospel. Let us show that it contains nothing to contradict our text, and by its difficulty to prove that men do not destroy themselves.

We are far from saying there is no difficulty in religion. We only contend there is nothing insuperable. Some have sadly erred on this point, when they have tried to vindicate religion from the aspersions of unbelief. They have made it more easy than the Gospel makes it; and while they supposed they were smoothing the path to heaven, were really widening the road to hell! There *are* difficulties in religion. We would have you all believe it. We would not persuade you it is so easy a

matter, that a few moments' attention will be abundantly
sufficient. We dare not tell you that you need devote
to this subject only the last energies of an exhausted
body, and the last sighs of an expiring life. But there
are no difficulties which are insurmountable. There are
no obstacles which may not be overcome. There is
nothing in the nature of religion to justify your gloomy
opinion that you can not be saved—that, somehow, religion lies beyond your reach.

What is there, then, in the religion which God proposes—(not in his anger to bind you over to hell, but in
his compassion to guide you to heaven)—what is there
in it, that makes it an impossible thing that you should
attain it and be saved?

Take any item you will.

I. Do you allege its mysteries? Do you say it contains and claims to contain many things mysterious, of
which you know not what to think? Then let us examine this.

Its mysteries perplex you. But what have you to do
with its mysteries? Are you required to understand
them? No, not at all—you have simply to believe
them; that is, to believe what is recorded concerning
them. Are you required to regulate your practices by
them? Not an item, not a single item, any further than
they are plainly revealed, and have thereby lost (so far)
the character of mysteries.

But you say you would have no mysteries in religion—
you would have every thing plainly revealed—and you
are doubtful of a religion which contains any thing high
and mysterious. Before replying to this objection, I
will only say it *deserves* no reply. It contains the im-

piety of pointing out to God what kind of a religion he ought to have given to man! This is impudent daring! But we are vindicating religion, and will therefore answer,

1. If a religion required of me to practice upon its mysteries, the meaning of which I did not understand so far as my practice must extend, I should be doubtful of its truth. My mind is so constituted, that I always require to understand what is the meaning of the conduct which I am commanded to pursue. And I could receive no religion as coming from my Creator which did not agree with this original principle which my Creator has implanted in the soul. The *reasons* for that conduct I can dispense with. If God speaks, I confess I ought to obey, whether he tells me reasons or not. The highest of all possible reasons for believing any thing or doing any thing, is simply this—God has said so.

2. I confess the mysteries of a religion would render me doubtful of its truth, if they were contradictory to reason. I never could believe *that true* which contradicted the reason which God has given to me. I avow my readiness to receive a religion which contains many things wholly superior to the highest efforts of unaided reason—wholly above it, beyond—but I can receive nothing which I know to contradict it, and hence, nothing which contradicts my senses. I require my religion to agree so far with my nature as *not* to show that it can not proceed from Him who is the Author of my nature. And if it contained that which I could prove to be contrary to reason, I could not but reject it. At the same time my religion might contain many things so mysterious, that I could not prove them agreeable to reason, though nothing which I could prove contrary to it.

3. I confess that mysteries would render me doubtful of a religion, if its mysteries were favorable to immorality and vice. Nothing could convince me that the Author of my existence looked with approbation upon vice, especially when I behold his standing testimony against it, written out in that wretchedness to which I see it leads. Vice is ruinous and degrading. The attributes with which my mind is compelled to clothe the Deity, oblige me to believe that he would enjoin no religion productive necessarily of such effects : on the contrary, that a religion coming from him would have a tendency to reform and exalt. If, therefore, the mysteries of a religion were favorable to immorality, I could not receive it.

Here, then, are three classes of mysteries, any one of which (to say the least) would render me doubtful of the truth of a religion, and constitute an insurmountable difficulty to my receiving it. In compliment to skepticism and infidelity we will add a

4th. I confess, then, I should doubt the divinity of that religion which contained such mysteries that I could *reject* the religion and not involve myself in still greater difficulties. Prove to me that the difficulties of infidelity are not still greater than the difficulties of Christianity, with all its mysteries, and I promise to you never will I attempt again to persuade you to be Christians. For, by the constitution of my mind, I must believe that the *Deity* could never propose to man a religion, the reception of which would involve him in greater difficulties and uncertainties than the rejection of it; and if the religion is not from God, of course I could not receive it.

In all these four cases of mystery, I confess I should

14

not be able to become a believer. But there is *nothing like* any one of these cases in the religion of the Bible.

Still, you would have a religion that contained no mystery. Let me tell you, then, it would be a religion which *you could never receive.* Could you receive a religion as coming from God, which was manifestly discordant with the works of Creation and Providence? Must you not have the God of your religion and the God of Creation correspond? You allow it, and so will every man of any respectable intelligence and candor. But the works of Creation and Providence embody many mysterious things. Every where we are meeting with things we can not unfold—depths we can not fathom. Tell me why is that young man cut down in the vigor of life, while the aged is spared? Why is the house of the widow burnt up, while that of the strong man (able to erect another) stands safe by the side of it? Not to trouble you with examples, let me say to you, that if your religion contained nothing mysterious, you would reject it : you would say it did not agree with the aspect of Providence and Creation. You would say, that when God speaks to you in creation, his language brings up that which is mysterious : looking at your own frame you would exclaim, *I am fearfully and wonderfully made.* You would say that when God speaks to you in Providence, his language brings up that which is mysterious : looking at the bereaved, (for example,) you would exclaim, why should the mother weep for her darling daughter, and the father live to build the sepulcher of his sons? You would demand, therefore, that when God speaks to you in religion, his language shall sometimes bring up that which is mysterious—that it must sound like the same voice which speaks to you in nature, and have at least a general correspondence with the language of Creation and Providence. And if it did not so correspond you would be obliged to reject it; you could not worship one God in nature and another in religion. For immortality, for the great and amazing matters of an eternity to come, for the unseen spirit that tabernacles within you, soon to be out on the fields of a spirit's existence, you can not only afford to have God more high and mysterious, but your mind demands to have him more mysterious and high above you, than he is on these fields of matter, and for the little lapse of your *three-score years and ten*. Religion is a deeper system than nature, reaches further, lasts longer. You *need* to have him here more grand, mysterious and amazing.

True reason, therefore, instead of being staggered at a religion containing mysterious things, is compelled to reject a religion which contains none.

And, after all, what are these mysteries? They are not things needful for us to understand—desirable to be known—perhaps not things which, from our limited minds, we could understand if they were unfolded before us. Who can understand God to perfection?

There is nothing, then, in the darknesses of our religion, which ought to trouble you; nothing that excuses you from embracing it; or proves by its difficulties that God has any *pleasure in your death*.

II. You are troubled with the obscurity of its doctrines. You can not embrace them. There are *some things hard to be understood*, which you are required to believe; and some things, you say, apparently inconsistent with one another; and this renders Christianity so perplexing to you, that to require you to accept it, you think is little less than to delight in your ruin.   Let me answer this.

I grant that the Bible contains *some things hard to be understood, which they that are unlearned and unstable do wrest, as they do also the other Scriptures, unto their own destruction.* But every thing necessary for us to know is fully revealed, as far as it is necessary that we should know it. There is an *extent*, indeed, to most, if not to all the doctrines of Christianity, which we are unable to measure; for there are connections, and combinations, and applications too numerous for our limited powers of mind.   But the *fact* which we are to receive is fully set before us; the doctrine itself is clearly taught; and we are, therefore, acquainted with it as far as necessary for us.

The object of the instructions of our Bible is our sanctification ; and in giving us instruction, God has pursued that mode best adapted to promote our sanctification. It might gratify our curiosity, and perhaps our pride, to have the deep things of God more fully unfolded to us. But it would not advance our holiness.   Indeed, we should find ourselves *injured* by having these deep things presented as objects of study and necessary knowledge. Suppose the Word of God contained a full illustration of all those abstruse points which so often trouble you ; suppose it revealed to you the reason of every act of God—unfolded to you the whole counsels of the Godhead respecting our world—gave you the rule by which you could trace out every thing mysterious—and left out nothing for you to ask ; what an immense volume your Bible would become!   You could not lift it !   Your life would be too short to read it ! much less would your life suffice to understand it !   Even now, though our Revelation records nothing useless, how extremely imperfect is

that understanding of it which the best of us ever attain !
Were we to enter upon the study of those deep things
of God which he has mercifully concealed from us, and
were it needful for us to comprehend them in order to
be saved, we should at once sit down in despair ! How
much time, and attention, and careful study it requires
for us to attain any considerable knowledge of an earthly
science ; even with all the assistance which the best books
and the best teachers can give us ! We are forced to
labor year after year, and yet how small is the portion
of knowledge that we attain. And where is the perfect
master of even the simplest science ? Where is the pro-
fessor who will pledge himself to solve any problem in
his favorite department that I will propose to him?
pledge himself to clear up any obscurity that I will
name, and satisfy the longings of my utmost curiosity?
Should any one avow himself adequate to such a task,
you would smile at his conceit, and say that his pre-
sumption was equaled by nothing but the stupidity
which allowed it. It takes much time and study to understand things intricate and perplexed. And if we are
unable, in the few days we have to spend, to attain a perfect knowledge of earthly science ; how should we be
able, in the few years we stay on earth, to attain a perfect knowledge of those eternal truths which God has
wisely and mercifully concealed from us ? This, probably, will be a work for eternity. Here it may be commenced. God has furnished us the means for knowing
all we need to know here, in order to secure our salvation. The rest he has wisely concealed. Had he called
us to plunge into the deep things of God—to study the
infinite combinations and dependencies of things, and lose
ourselves in intricacies which it may take us age after

age of our eternity to comprehend, what time should we have left for the common duties of life ? what moment could we spare for the duties of charity to the poor, for the consolations we owe to the sick, and for the relief our religion sends us to carry to the distressed ? Indeed, what hour could we devote to our own hearts, to study their dispositions and eradicate their evil propensities ?

It is of God's goodness that he has called us to study only those things which tend to promote our holiness and comfort, and thus prepare us to study more deeply the world to come. If he has taught us any doctrine, he has told us all in relation to it that would be of any avail for us to know. The *fact* we are taught. The *manner* of the fact would do us no good. Hence, God has concealed it. Every thing necessary to our present duty is placed before us. More might flatter our pride, but could not promote our piety.

There is nothing, therefore, in the obscurity of our doctrines which conflicts with our text. Our Revelation on the darkest side wears the light of that glorious truth, that *the Lord God has no pleasure in the death of the wicked.*

III. It is worthy of remark, that *Christian morality* is extremely plain. All those things which concern our present and immediate conduct are not difficult to be understood. It is only those things, the knowledge of which could do us no good, and the study of which (as it would draw us off from more important matters) would probably do us much hurt—it is only such things that are concealed from us. What we ought now to do, and how we ought now to feel toward God and toward man, are things too plain to be misunderstood. And if we still complain that our Revelation does not lead us further, let us hush the complaint with one reflection. It is this: that the religion of the Gospel is so practical and progressive, that the further we advance in it, the more perfect will the guidance of our revelation appear. The Bible will scatter the doubts of that man who will reduce the Bible to practice. It will unfold itself more and more to him. If he will not be a *forgetful hearer, but a doer of the word,* he will find it will lead him much further than at first he anticipated. The novice in Christianity may not be able to decide in advance those questions which concern one only who has been going on year after year in the growth of *grace and knowledge of his Lord and Saviour.* But let the novice in Christianity pass beyond his novitiate: following the light he now has, and performing the duties which now concern him, let him grow up to such an age and such a stature that those questions shall concern *himself,* and he will find little difficulty in deciding them; he will find the Bible a more perfect guide than he supposed. The cloud so dark at a distance will brighten as he approaches it. The light that tinged its edge will grow broader and bolder, till, all luminous with Deity, it pours a flood of light upon the path once so dimly seen.

Let no man, then, complain of the obscurity of our doctrines. Let him put duty before curiosity or captiousness, and reduce the doctrines to practice so far as they now concern him; and, as he advances in religion, their obscurity will be done away as fast as his necessities require it—and his pathway, like that of the just, will *shine brighter and brighter unto the perfect day.*

The manner, therefore, in which all Christian morality

is taught, bears its full testimony that *God has no pleasure in the death of the wicked.*

IV. There is *self-denial* in religion. Men often think it too severe. An idea of blended folly and sin floats around their mind, that if God had been sincerely desirous of their salvation, he would have made the way into heaven more easy, and sinners might have walked in it without finding it to cross their inclinations at every step. But whence does the necessity of this self-denial arise? It arises wholly and in every part of it from sin. It is benevolence, therefore, which imposes it. I grant it is severe, (if you choose to employ such a word to describe it.) It is the *plucking out of a right eye,* and cutting off of a *right hand.* But for what purpose? To preserve the *whole man from hell.* The necessity of it arises from corruption alone. We are required to deny ourselves in that which is sinful, and God requires this self-denial in love. He would lead us from sin, and thereby lead us from misery. Sin is the great destroyer of happiness, and God would have us forsake it. He would not have us forfeit heaven for *the pleasures of sin for a season.* He does not require us absolutely to hate ourselves, but, in reality, directly the contrary. He would have us love ourselves, and by a wise mortification, for a little time, of those appetites which plunge us into misery, he would have us secure to ourselves *pleasures for evermore.*

This is the reason for the self-denial of religion. And what less would you have? Would you have a religion proposed to you which should leave you at liberty to sin? a religion which should impose no restraint? a religion which should plunge you into immorality and vice? a religion which would multiply your crimes thick

upon you, and promise to take you to heaven at last?
You would reject such a religion. You would say it
was an absurdity—an impossibility. You would declare
that a religion which left you to delight in sin here
could not prepare you to delight in holiness hereafter;
you would affirm that such a religion could not make
you *relish* heaven, and it would be no heaven to you.
You would say it was unworthy of God and unworthy
of yourself. You would say it was contrary to the constitution of things, for you could every where behold the
proof, that the tendency of sin is to lead to misery. And
much sooner would you accept the self-denial of the
Gospel, and by a few acts of transient mortification prepare yourself for a superior felicity.

V. But perhaps you are troubled with the *humility* of
our religion. But why should this trouble you? Does
the requiring of this prove to you that the Deity would
confine you in sin, taking pleasure in your destruction?
Then, what is humility? Is it a thing degrading to
your nature? Is it shocking, revolting to reason? Is
it any thing more than justice? Not at all. It only
demands of us to be just and reasonable; to estimate
ourselves according to truth—not to *think of ourselves
more highly than we ought to think.* More than this. The
very aim of this humility is to exalt us. It would have
us put together the knowledge of what we are and the
knowledge of what we are capable of being, and, by the
comparison of the two, teach us to think meanly of what
we are, and learn to aim at being more exalted, more useful, and more happy. God would have us humble, because
he would have us just, and wise, and happy. Pride is
not just. Pride is not wise. Pride is not happy. It is

not just, because it leads us to exalt our present worth
beyond its value. It is not wise, because it leads us to
rest in what we are, instead of aiming at something
better. It is not happy, because it feels its claims dis-
puted, or fears they will be; and because its aims are so
often defeated. And God, in requiring us to be humble,
only requires us to be just and reasonable, and aim at
the highest good. There is nothing, then, in this feature
of our religion which goes to show that God would not
have us accept it and be saved. But,

VI. Repentance. Men must repent; and this troubles
you. You ask, if God had not been *willing* that I
should *perish*, would he not have dispensed with such
difficult thing as my repentance? What, then, is repentance. It is sorrow for sin—hatred, abhorrence of it, and
forsaking of it. Very well: if you *have* sinned, erred,
done wrong, should you *not* be sorry for it? If your sin
has already destroyed much of your felicity, and threat-
ens to destroy it all, ought you not to abhor it? If, by
transgression, you have offended the best and wisest of
Beings, ought you not to confess it, and forsake it?
What less could justice, propriety, truth, order, demand?
What less would you yourself be satisfied to render? A
religion that did *not* require repentance, you would not
hesitate to reject. You would say it was not consistent
with justice, propriety, truth. But,

VII. You are troubled because God requires you to
trust in his *mercy*—to believe in Jesus Christ. But if
you can not trust in Jesus Christ for salvation, where can
you trust? Can you rely on your own righteousness?
Can you lift up your voice to heaven, and say, *I am*

pure, oh, Lord thou knowest?   You shudder at the idea.
What, then, can you trust?   Would you have religion
propose to you a more precious and exalted Saviour?
You dare not pretend it.   And does the free gift of such
a Saviour—the free offer of pardon and eternal life,
peace and heaven, through his blood, prove to you that
God has *pleasure* in your death?   And,

VIII. Finally.   Do not the motives of religion compel
you to believe that God has *no pleasure in your death?*
What can you soberly and really desire, that religion
does not offer to you?   Do you pant for exaltation?
Religion offers it to you : not the exaltation of a moment
of life, but that of eternal ages.   Do you love pleasure?
Religion proposes it to you : not that which you drink
from a poisoned bowl, and imagine felicity in the deadly
delirium which drinks up your spirit, but that which is
worthy of a human soul—that which is gathered from
converse with the Deity—*joy unspeakable and full of glory.*
Do you pant for riches?   Religion proposes to you the
acquisition of such riches as no earthly charter can secure—*durable riches*, laid up in heaven, safe from the
vicissitudes of time, and secured by the promise and the
pledge of Jehovah.

Such are some of the articles of that religion which
the Lord proposes to you.   We have spoken only of
those from which the unbelieving are apt to recoil; we
have taken only those items which they imagine unin-
viting.   And now let me ask, is there any thing in all
this which makes you look upon the religion required
of you as a thing so difficult that you can not be saved—
so difficult as to contain any indication that God, while

he enjoins such a religion, is not sincerely willing that
you should be saved? Indeed, I put it to your own
reason and conscience, what less could God have required, and what less would you be willing to receive?
I do not believe there is one ingenuous mind in this assembly that does not confess that nothing but wickedness
can reject such a religion.

The most difficult features of our religion, and those
of which we are most apt to complain, prove to us, most
conclusively, that God has *no pleasure in the death of the
wicked.* And if we are lost, we are *not* lost because the
conditions of our deliverance are hard. The mysteries,
the doctrines, the morality, the mortification, the humility, the repentance, the faith, the motives of Christianity, will all bear the examination of the most
difficult mind. There is not one appearance of severity
or rigor in all the religion of the Bible, which is not
absolutely indispensable in the nature of the case, and
which is not proposed in love, and to exalt our felicity.
In conclusion, then, I have but this one question to propose to you : What degree of misery will he deserve
who will reject such a religion, in order to lose his own
soul?

God no Pleasure in the Death of the Wicked.

(SHOWN FROM THE CONDITION OF MAN.)

As I live, saith the Lord God, I have no pleasure in the death of the wicked.—EZEKIEL, xxxiii. 11.

IT is the first perfect achievement that truth makes over the heart of the sinner, when it brings him to confess his guilt, his obstinacy, and his wretchedness, and cast himself upon the unmerited aids of Divine grace. This is the *triumph* of the truth—the victory over obstinacy hitherto unrelenting, and depravity hitherto unsubdued. Till this period, corruption reigns; her dominion is not broken down, and even is but partially restrained. After this, grace reigns; her dominion is established in the soul; and though much of corruption, and obstinacy, and sin is still lingering there, the dominion does not belong to them. They are vanquished foes, having already experienced that defeat which is the certain prelude of their final extinction. Before this period, the heart itself, with its firmest feelings, is the standing opponent of the truth. After this, the heart is enlisted on the side of the truth, and its better feelings all unite to destroy the last vestiges of sin.

But there are usually many refuges of lies to be swept away before the heart of a sinful man is open for the reception of the truth. There may be, indeed, not a little candor (I wish there were more) among those who have no true faith; many of them, perhaps, sincerely intend to be ingenuous. But the *heart is deceitful above all things and desperately wicked*, and such persons are often ignorant of their own purposes. With an intent to be honest, their hearts deceive them; and they have some long-cherished excuse for not being Christians indeed—some long-harbored apology which influences their practice, intrenched strongly in the heart, though perhaps never suffered to become vocal on their lips—concealing itself so closely in the darkness of its retreat, that it remains unknown and unsuspected. And hence we find those who have opened their hearts to the truth, wondering at themselves—astonished that they have been so long ignorant of what they were, of what errors they were in, of what inclinations controlled them. They marvel at their blindness, their folly, their weakness, their con-trolling corruption, hidden year after year from their own knowledge. *Once I was blind, now I see*, is the graphic description of their experience.

We are not to be astonished, therefore, if many of those whose understandings have received no spiritual light should not believe their spiritual or mental condition to be as the Scriptures affirm. It is not strange if they feel themselves abused when Divine truth carries its torch into their hearts to show them to themselves, to their amazement and shame. And hence, too, as truth troubles them, when they feel the *dividing* kindness of the *two-edged sword*, it is nothing wonderful if they flee from its flash, and seek quietude and ease where weapons are employed less perilous to their peace and pride. This is common. Many a sinner has fled from the truth, and, so doing, has ruined his own soul. To hear smooth things—to be complimented and caressed—to have his pride flattered—to have his wickedness unrebuked, his corruptions unassailed, his carnal pleasures undiminished, is the great desire of an unrenewed sinner; and he wishes to be away where truth will not trouble him, and so he will put on the form of godliness, or run into any error or any infidelity.

But we are not to flatter his pride or favor his prejudices to the ruin of his soul. His errors must be exposed—his *refuges of lies* destroyed—his deceptions dissipated, or he will never be led to the knowledge of himself and the knowledge of Christ.

God would convince every sinner that he may be saved. He invites, and warns, and cautions, and expostulates, and commands, to enforce this conviction. He corrects mistakes, he detects deception, he instructs ignorance, he entreats obstinacy.

One of the most fatal delusions of unsanctified men is attacked in the text: *As I live, saith the Lord God, I have no pleasure in the death of the wicked.* Satan persuades many a sinner that the pleasure of God is opposed to his salvation—that he fails of being a Christian, not because he will have it so, but because God will have it so. This notion, as we told you on two former occasions, is sustained (through error) by considerations drawn especially from three sources; the purposes of God; the nature of religion; and the condition of man.

The first two of these we have already considered.

We have shown that the Purposes of God offer no violence to our liberty, and do not oblige us to be lost. We detected the foundation of the error, which consists in supposing that they *do*, and showed that this is an unfounded conclusion, because it is drawn, in all its parts, and as a whole, from premises unknown.

Then we took up the next error. We vindicated the character of our religion. We showed that those features of it which corruption and error consider most severe, really wear no aspect of severity—that there is nothing in our religion which reason and justice do not sanction not only, but nothing which reason and justice and common sense could content to dispense with: and that, therefore, the religion required of us is not so difficult as to show that God has any pleasure at all in our being lost.

Still there is another refuge to which sin flies—the condition of man. When the Divine purposes and our Divine religion can not be forced to excuse a sinful man for his irreligion—when the decrees of God are cleared from the slanders which wickedness utters against them, and the religion of the Gospel is proved so reasonable and appropriate that nothing but sin and stupidity can reject it—then, the *condition of man* is called in as an excuse or plea for irreligion. This condition is alleged to be of such a nature that the individual can not extricate himself from it, and attain salvation. True, he says, the decrees of God may not confine me in sin and bind me over to perdition—true, religion itself may not be so severe as to forbid the attainment of eternal life, while it offers all I can ask and delivers from all I ought to fear. But still, my own condition is in my way. I have always been a sinner. Sin is natural to me. I am inclined to evil. The dispositions of my very nature confine me, if the decrees of God and the requirements of religion do not. Suppose it is corruption, stupidity, folly to reject religion. So much the worse for me: stupidity, folly, corruption are natural to me. The nature which God has given me—the condition in which I am placed, renders my case hopeless. So he talks—so he half thinks. He says repentance may be reasonable enough, but he has no heart to repent: religion may have its attractions for some people, but he cannot feel interested in the matter.

This is the last apology which our text opposes. *As I live, saith the Lord God, I have no pleasure in the death of the wicked.* God here exonerates himself. He has not placed a sinner in such a condition as forces him to sink down into hell. He has not given him a nature incapable of deliverance, and thus being a proof that he has *any pleasure at all* in his ruin.

Now, there are six characteristics of this apology (an apology drawn from the nature of man) which ought carefully to be noticed. Let us look at them. If, after after examining them, we find this apology for our irreligion a good one, let us live upon it—let us die upon it—let us carry it on our lips to the bar of the final judgment. From truth we have nothing to fear. And if it is true that our condition obliges us to be lost, let us take that idea along with us to annihilate half the pains of perdition.

I. The first characteristic of this apology for irreligion is, that it is *altogether hasty*. How does this irreligious man know that his depravity is invincible? What right has he to conclude that his condition is such, that he can not accept religion, repent, and be saved? Has the Almighty told him so, who alone knows perfectly his nature, and perfectly knows the religion that he enjoins as adapted to it? The Almighty has told him no such thing. He commands him to repent, to believe in Christ, to turn to God and live. How then does he know that his nature forbids his salvation? He does *not* know it; and the supposition is only a hasty conclusion which has no foundation in truth.

If he had tried—if he had made a full experiment in the matter, and, after doing all he could do (as sinners sometimes say they have,) had found all his efforts unavailing, then there would be some ground for his conclusion. But he has *not* tried. (Men do err when they say so.) Some little, feeble, unfrequent attempts perhaps he may have made. But he has not done all he could. There are three proofs of his hasty conclusion gathered from the experiment itself which he affirms he has made. 1. It was an unwise one. 2. It was a feeble one. 3. It was a short one. Glance at these items.

1. It was an *unwise* one. For where, upon this whole footstool of God, is there a man still irreligious, who has ever *informed* himself, so perfectly as he might have done, about what God requires of him, and what, therefore, he must do to be saved? Lay your finger on the man still without religion, who, though he has sometimes made some attempts to be religious, has done all he could to be *wise unto salvation*, and learn the *method* he must take to get into the kingdom of heaven. You can not do it. Among all the multitude of unbelievers around us, where is one whose Bible does not cry out to him, Thou hast greatly neglected me? Whose closet does not exclaim, Thou art greatly a stranger here? Whose studies, prompted by the pride of learning, or devoted to the wealth and honors of this world, do not bear testimony that the will of God and the way of salvation have lain much in the background, as things

to be thought of only occasionally, or in some little shred of time, when there was nothing else to do? And if the attempt to be religious has been made very much in this hap-hazard manner, without striving for that wisdom necessary to make it as it should be, surely the conclusion that the nature of man renders it an impossibility, is *altogether hasty.*

And if the experiment was unwise, so,

2. It was feeble. Call to mind, unconverted man, the energy you exerted. Compare the efforts you made for salvation (efforts which you now complain were unavailing)—compare them with the efforts you are accustomed to make for other things. Ask your honors, if they have not cost you more toil and time, more study and solicitude, than you have ever devoted to your salvation. Ask your science, gathered with days of diligence and nights of sleeplessness, if it did not cost you more effort than you have ever given to religion. Ask your wealth, if it has been hoarded by no more care and caution, and toil and trembling, than you have devoted to the *one thing needful.* What will these things answer? What is the testimony of any thing you have got—your learning—your merchandise—your skill—your houses—or herds? Will they tell you, that you have devoted no more energy to their acquisition than you have devoted to attain salvation? Far otherwise. Their testimony is all against you. It proves that your attempts after religion were feeble attempts. Then call up your passions. Ask *them* to testify of your religious endeavors. Ask your pride, if you have done as much to subdue it to the rules of religion as you have done to foster, gratify, and sustain it, in opposition to them. Ask ambition, if you have directed her eager eye to-

ward the high places in Christ Jesus as often as toward some seat of honor among men. Ask covetousness, if you have guided its aim to the *durable riches of everlasting life* as often or as fondly, as to the *gold that perisheth.* Both your possessions and your passions give a terrible testimony on such a trial. They plainly affirm that such energy has been devoted to them, as has never been devoted to religion. In the one case you have done much, and done it vigorously; in the other, you have done little, and done it feebly. And if your attempt to be religious has been made so *feebly,* surely the conclusion that the condition you are in by nature prohibits your being religious is altogether *hasty.* There is not an unconverted sinner here who has done all he could to be saved. If you were to die to-night—if to-night, at the moment the clock strikes twelve, you knew you were to be taken out of the world, and have your eternal destiny sealed—you would do what you have never done, and your cry of anguish would go up into heaven, loaded with pleadings for mercy.

And even if your trial to obtain salvation has not been feeble and unwise—if you have studied all in your power to know what you ought to do, and aimed with all your energy to do it, remember,

3. The experiment was *short.* A few months—perhaps a few weeks—perhaps even only a few days, were sincerely devoted to it—yea, perhaps only a few *occasional* attempts, made when some fearful alarm compelled you to do it. And after so short an experiment, such transient attempts, are you prepared to conclude that your nature is such that you can not be a Christian and be saved? What if you had reasoned thus in science? what if you had come to the conclusion that you were

incapable of any science you may have mastered, when you had tried no longer than you have ever tried in religion? What if you had reasoned thus as a merchant? what if you had concluded that you were incapable of pursuing the mercantile profession, when you had only made an entrance upon your apprenticeship, and had tried the matter no longer than you have ever tried in religion? What if you had reasoned thus as a mechanic? what if you had concluded, at the first blunders you made with your tools, that you were by nature incapable of learning to use them skillfully, when you had tried no longer than you have at any time tried in religion? What if you had reasoned thus about getting rich? what if you had concluded that you were incapable of any success the very next month after you entered upon your enterprise, when you had tried with no more patience than you have ever tried in religion? Had you reasoned so, science, intelligence as a merchant, skill as a mechanic, art, wealth, honor would never have been attained, or whatever else you may have acquired in spite of the obstacles or inaptitudes of your nature.

You believed, perhaps, that you need only devote a little time to your salvation, and you would be safe—you would come to repentance, be a new creature, a disciple of Christ. But where did you get this opinion? God has not told you so, and does not your entertaining so low an opinion of religion go far to prove that you have taken little pains to be *wise?* The religion that God enjoins upon us is not an affair to be done up in a moment, and ever afterwards neglected: it is not a matter of mere occasional concernment, but one of constant interest, and demands constant attention till the day we die. And if your attempt to be a Christian has been so limited as to extend only to a few years—if you have not continued it till the last day of life is spent, and the last breath of life has departed from your nostrils, you have no right to come to the conclusion that you have made a perfect trial. But how different from this have been your attempts! few, short, and far between! And perhaps you ceased from them just as you were on the point of success. It may be that one effort more, one prayer more, would have gained you the victory, and made you a child of God. You ceased to fight when the battle was almost won, and became more of a slave than before! And if the attempt to attain salvation has been so short, surely the conclusion that your condition prohibits your being a Christian is *altogether hasty.* Your trial in the matter has been unwise, feeble, short—therefore no fair trial at all.

II. The second characteristic of the apology drawn from the condition of human nature, is its *illegitimate application.* When the depravity of nature is alleged by the irreligious as an obstacle to the practice of evangelical virtues, and allowed to have some claim to consideration, the irreligious are accustomed to make it into an apology for running into vice : they construe their inability to good into a necessity of evil—their negation of power to be altogether holy into a positive power and positive necessity to sin worse and worse, in vanity, thoughtlessness, and lack of prayer. Their insufficiency for evangelical virtue, aside from the aids of Divine grace, they torture into a necessity of committing whatever wickedness they know themselves to be guilty of.

This is an application of the depravity of human nature which I should be sorry to make. Impotent as the unrenewed man may be for bearing the *fruits of the Spirit*, he is under no necessity, from that impotence, of running into those courses, or those vices and crimes, which so rapidly sear his conscience, and degrade his nature, or those vanities which take off his mind from every thing good. Let him affirm he can do nothing in religion without grace, and we will agree with him. But when he affirms his insufficiency, without special grace, to abstain from those practices which so rapidly render him incapable of religion, by blinding mind and blunting conscience, we disagree with him. And this is the misapplication he makes of the condition of human nature. He does not distinguish between the insufficiency for religion, and the necessity of thoughtlessness and vanity and vice. When the Bible teaches him that he can not be a Christian without the aids of the Divine Spirit, he misinterprets it, pretending it has taught him that he can not avoid the wickedness of which he is guilty. But there is a vast difference betwixt our insufficiency without grace for the practice of evangelical religion, and the necessity of rendering ourselves, by negligence and prayerlessness, still more insufficient. We may be unable to break our bondage, but we are not forced to forge its chains. Our incapacity to burst our fetters is not a necessity to make them stronger, and rivet them on. There is a wide difference betwixt being confined to a bed of sickness, unable to rise to the strong exercises of life, and being obliged to employ the deadly drug or dagger to take away whatever of strength and life we have. But these two things are confounded by those who plead their depravity as an apology for their irreligion. They make no distinction between their unassisted incapacity for being Christians, and the unavoidable necessity of plunging themselves into courses of negligence, forgetfulness, and further departure from God.

This error in reasoning would be of less consequence, were it not the cause of much ruinous practice. But the results of it are most deplorable. By an abuse of the Scriptures, a sinful man persuades himself that he can not (without special, converting grace) avoid the inattention to religion, the carelessness and dissipation of mind of which he is guilty; and, consequently, he excuses himself while he indulges. He is guilty of that inattention to Divine truth, which he might avoid without grace. He runs into those excesses from which his own powers might save him. And by this course of carelessness and dissipation of mind, he renders himself still less capable of turning from sin and securing salvation. He resembles a prisoner furnished with a key to unlock his prison, who, instead of using it, flings it away. He resembles a man in a gulf, from which he is unable to extricate himself, and who, instead of availing himself of the aid proffered for his deliverance, turns from the hand that would lift him out, and plunges still deeper down the chasm that stretches its unfathomable abysses beneath. And if by such madness he places himself beyond the reach of assistance, let him not imagine that God has pleasure in his ruin—that his condition demonstrates it. For if he had used the powers he had, and accepted the aid he might have had, deliverance instead of death would have been his portion. Verily, *God* has *no pleasure in the death of the wicked. O Israel, thou has destroyed thyself.*

III. The third characteristic of this apology drawn from the natural condition of man—(a condition which is taken to go far to prove that the pleasure of God is opposed to a sinner's salvation), is the tendency of this apology to excuse from moral virtues. These are virtues which those practice who have not been renewed by the Spirit of God. This fact shows them capable of being practiced without the aids of supernatural grace. Other motives than the love of God, and other aims than holiness have influence upon human conduct. But when the power of human depravity is alleged as an apology for not being Christians, men make it into an apology also for neglecting the moral virtues. How often, how very often, does the idea come across the mind of a sinful man, that his inattention to moral duties is more excusable, because he has never professed to be a Christian! If he were a child of God, he says he should feel himself obligated to all good conduct; but he is under the control of a fallen nature—of an unrenewed heart. This is the reason that he does not feel bound by the laws of outward conduct, which he says bind a believer. But God has not made him an exception. He has given him these laws, and commanded him to obey them. And if he has refused to cultivate evangelical graces under the sought guidance of the Holy Spirit, certainly he has the more fearful reason, on that account, for an external obedience—for sobriety—for thought—for practicing all the moral virtues. But what does he do? He alleges his native disposition, his heart, while he casts off fear and restrains prayer, and indulges *the lust of the flesh, the lust of the eye, and the pride of life,* and, by doing so, he is burying in the earth the *one talent* committed to him, *unfaithful over a few things,* simply because he has not *many things.* He forfeits confidence and claim to more.

15

Because external conduct is not internal grace, because the moral virtues have not necessarily the nature
of evangelical religion, (though such religion invariably
leads to them ;) sinful men often mistake the bearing of
these virtues. The man who lives in the neglect of them
(virtues of which by nature he *is* capable) is taking the
most direct course to render himself insensible and inaccessible to the motives and means of an evangelical religion. Those who have broken over one restraint, have
acquired strength, and courage, and tendency to attack
another. Those who neglect the outward duties of religion, have taken the surest means to shut out from the
heart the inward spirit of religion. Those who have
learnt to be shameless before man, have taken one step
toward being fearless before God.

The apology of native condition, therefore, as it leads
so naturally and commonly to some neglect of moral
virtue and some carelessness in the outward actions
which have respect to religion, has a tendency to unfit
the soul for evangelical graces. The condition of man
by nature does not *force* him to all this. Let him not,
then, allege his condition as an apology for the want of
those virtues and that conduct, of which by nature he *is*
capable—and which, for aught he knows, may be the
necessary and surest means for his becoming a child of
God. Let him take the blame to himself, and confess that
God has no pleasure in the death of the wicked. Morals, the
very morals he neglects—habits of thought and prayer,
habits he never forms, might be to him as stepping-stones
and scaffoldings to help him him up to the height he
never reaches—the heavenly places in Christ Jesus—the
spiritual temper of a child of God.

IV. The fourth characteristic of this apology, (taken from the condition of man,) is its direct *irreligious* tendency : it is taken as an excuse for the neglect of those religious duties which every irreligious man is capable of performing. There are such duties. The perfect and acceptable performance of them in sincerity, *in spirit and in truth*, may not lie within such a man's power; but there is an action, an endeavor which such a man may put forth, if he will. But how often does such a man neglect prayer, because, as he alleges, he is incapable of the true performance of the duty! How often, for the same reason, does his Bible lie neglected—his seat in church become vacated—his thoughts of God unfrequent, and every external religious duty remain unattempted! But all this is not from any necessity of nature. It is willing disobedience. There is nothing in his native condition which compels to this. However the power of his will may be inefficacious over his heart,·it has full efficacy over his habits. If he can not manage his spirit, he can manage his manners. The external duties of religion lie quite within the scope of his ability, and if these are neglected, what shall show that it would not be the same with all spiritual duties if they lay as much within the range of his power? And if he is unable, while not *born of the Spirit*, to render spiritual worship and service, surely there is the more urgent reason for coming as near to it as he can. The bones in Ezekiel's valley did not lie still under the words of his prophesy. *Bone came to his bone.* They took the shape of a living humanity. *Sinews, and flesh, and skin* came upon them; else, how *could* the spirit of life enter into his tabernacle? If, therefore, a man fails of salvation, because he neglects the religious conduct of which he is capable, let him not charge his failure upon the *pleasure* of God manifested in his native condition; let him confess, as he sinks into hell, that God *has no pleasure in the death of the wicked.*

V. The fifth characteristic of this apology is the idleness attending it. Hope is an active principle. Despondency is an inactive one. The Gospel of God addresses hope. Temptations are addressed either to worldliness or to despair. The man who gets the idea fixed in his mind, that God has no pleasure in his salvation, is thereby prevented from striving to attain it. He says all his efforts will be unavailing—his condition, as a sinner by nature, will mock all his endeavors. But God has not said so. The text says the contrary. Where has God told us that we can accomplish nothing in working out our salvation? Where has he told us to rest contented, or rest discouraged, till *he* converts us? Where has he said, that *striving to enter in at the strait gate* will be of no avail? What passage of his word assures us, that the Holy Ghost is going to convert us in our idleness—that all the attempts, and prayers, and cries of the unsanctified are unnoticed in Heaven? Still, because a sinful man is dependent upon the aids of grace, he excuses himself for attempting nothing. He does not exert the powers he *has*, and which God requires him to exert. He charges upon the *condition* in which his Maker has placed him in the world, what does not belong to his condition, and what he has capacity to avoid. He *can* avoid his negligence, his idleness, his inattention, his prayerless habits, *without* converting grace—yea, and he will avoid them, if he is ever saved. For where is the Christian who ever became a Christian in his idleness? Who was ever delivered from the bondage of sin, without effort at deliverance? Ask any child of grace, if his experience will testify that personal effort is an unnecessary thing. More: ask him, if sincere, determined effort, hope and heart embarked in it, was ever unavailing. God does require unconverted sinners to seek him —to deny themselves—to pray for mercy; and *strive* to enter in at the strait gate. And what ground or right has any sinner on this side of the *smoke of the torment*, to say or to believe, that his nature is such, that all these will be of no avail—as if God were mocking his miseries?

Man, indeed, does not convert himself. Nor is he converted by the mere force of the motives before him. Yet an unrenewed sinner has no exuse for his idleness. He ought to unite what God has united in his Word— the duties of the sinner, and the agency of God. *Work out your own salvation with fear and trembling:* here is the duty of the sinner. *For it is God that worketh in you both to will and to do:* here is the agency of God. *Behold I stand at the door and knock:* here is the agency of God. *If any man will hear my voice and open the door:* here is the duty of the sinner. *Make you a new heart and a new spirit, for why will ye die:* this is the duty of man. *I will take away the stony heart out of your flesh, I will put my spirit within you, I will make you my sons and daughters:* this is the agency of God. And where upon all the earth is the sinner who can say he has done what he could, and still has gained nothing—his efforts not seconded by the agency of God? Let him not charge upon his native condition what does not belong to it. Let him not lay down the fruits of his idleness at the door of the Holy Ghost. Let him confess, as he sinks to perdition, *the Lord God hath no pleasure in the death of the wicked.*

VI. Finally. The most strange perversion of all, is the argument from the depravity of nature, for *not* seeking the aids of grace—the saving efficiency of the Holy Spirit. This is the use which a sinful man, in his obstinacy, hardness, and wickedness, often makes of his insufficiency to save himself. Because, just because he is insufficient *without* the Spirit of God, he neglects to ask for the Spirit of God. The very reason which ought to fill his mouth with arguments and send up his cries thick into Heaven, is made to silence his prayers, and to excuse that cherished alienation from God which refuses to pray. He says he can not be saved, or attain any thing embraced in salvation, by any power of his own. All that is true. Aside from the Holy Spirit, his case is just as hopeless as if judgment had already proceeded upon him. And this is the great reason why he should besiege the throne of grace, as standing upon the very borders of the pit, that God would save him from going down to eternal death ! This he can do. His condition does not prohibit it. This he ought to do. His condition demands it.

We know how much has been said about the irresistibleness of converting grace. But God has not said it. His Word holds a different language. Indeed it very much sounds like an opposite language when it says : *Quench not the Spirit: grieve not the Holy Spirit of God whereby ye are sealed.* And how often does the Divine Word promise gracious assistance to human endeavors : *If ye will seek me as silver, and search for me as for hid treasures.* How often, too, does it account for religious failures : *Because ye have forsaken me, therefore I have forsaken you.* And even then, how often does it enjoin upon us to seek after efficacious grace : *In me is thy help, return unto me, and I will return unto you.* After all this, therefore, while a sinful man refuses to *seek the Lord,* to call upon him who is so ready to *give the Holy Spirit to them that ask him,* let him not complain of the condition in which he finds himself. That condition is not incompatible with his seeking and obtaining help from God. Let him take the blame of his ruin, if he will perish, upon himself. Let him say, as he sinks into hell, *The Lord God hath no pleasure in the death of the wicked.*

Bad as the condition of man may be, that condition does not oblige him to be lost. God has not pronounced his doom in the act of his creation. Let him make of his native dispositions and his dependence what he may, he can not draw from such sources an argument for his exculpation, if he continues an irreligious man. There is nothing to be found in the purposes of God, in the nature of required religion, or in the condition of a sinner as he is born into the world, which proves that the pleasure of God is opposed to the salvation of sinners.

The economy of grace far more than compensates for the difficulties which beset us. Be our condition what it may, God accommodates his aids to meet all its exigences. He offers to save. He would break every chain, guide in every perplexity, cast down every foe, light up every midnight, and lead his own child by the hand, till his feet stand on the pavements of the New Jerusalem. He comes to-day to say unto you: *As I live, I have no pleasure in the death of the wicked.*

Who ought to despair? What sad heart should limit the Holy One of Israel? Where is the discouraging circumstance, the difficulty or the devil, that should be allowed to damp my heart, when I would put forth my feeble strength to *lay hold on eternal life?* Fear not, trembler. Greater *is he that is in you than he that is in the world.* You shall come off victorious, if you do not falter and give back.

Who ought to neglect? Where is the doomed sinner that may not seek salvation and find it? Who is shut out from grace and heaven by any thing there is in God? It is not his decree that violates your liberty and binds you in fetters of sin. It is not his religion that, by its difficulty, mocks your misery. It is not your condition in sin that shuts up heaven and kindles the devouring flame! The soul that is lost will feel the tormenting truth that it has carried out its own destiny; that salvation was once within its reach, but it neglected and spurned the mercy which offered to deliver! Amid the miseries of the lost—amid those chains of darkness that weigh down the damned—the wail of the lost soul will be, *I have destroyed myself, for the Lord God has no pleasure in the death of the wicked.*

My dear friends, let us believe in God's mercy. Let us seek his grace *now,* and seek it all our days. Let us bear our burden of guilt or difficulties, our hard hearts, up to the top of Calvary; and where the blood of the Victim streams upon the rock, let us plead: Deliver— oh deliver me from going down to eternal death, for thou, *Lord God, hast no pleasure in the death of the wicked.*

Help in God for Sinners.

In me is thy help.—HOSEA, xiii. 9.

WHEN sinners are seeking salvation, it is very important that they should know where to find it. This world is full of errors and follies. Men have not much wisdom at best; and there is no subject on which they are so likely to err as the subject of salvation. Nowhere else does the heart exert such an influence over the mind. On no other subject are the conclusions to which God would lead men so much at variance with the conclusions at which they naturally desire to arrive. God teaches us in his Word that the hearts of men are not right toward him; that men have *carnal minds which are at enmity with God;* and, therefore, we might expect that what God likes men would not like, what God desires men would not desire, and what God requires of them they would be very unwilling to perform. And when we look abroad in the world we find it *is* so. They do not *seek first the kingdom of God,* putting eternity before time. Unregenerated men do not usually live in any good degree as God would have them live. For the most part, they are not men of prayer. They meet their families in the morning, and part with them in the evening, without asking God's blessing. It is not so with all

15*

unconverted men, but with the most of them. And just
so in respect to other things that God requires of them.
They are not pleased with the requirements of God, and,
therefore, though they are driven by fear to obey some
of them, yet they are not pleased with them, and their
attempted obedience is very limited.

Now, since unregenerated men are so apt to be dissatisfied with the rules of God every where else, we might
expect them to be dissatisfied with the plan of salvation,
and make many mistakes when they are seeking to be
saved. Not that God will suffer them to err and to be
lost if they sincerely seek him with an honest heart, open
to the truth; no, let them do this, and they will not err
to their destruction. But the evil is, that they are not
willing to yield their hearts to God; and while they are
under the unbroken influence of a carnal heart, they are
apt to run into errors, even though in some measure
seeking to be saved.

And I do not know of any essential truth necessary to
be known, and felt, and practiced upon, that awakened
sinners are so apt to lose sight of, as the one in this text.
God says, *In me is thy help.* The meaning of this is unlimited. The sinner's only help is in God. He can not
help himself. He can not take one step toward heaven
without the aid of the Almighty. He is lost—he is
ruined—his case is just as hopeless, without Divine aid,
as if he had gone down to the blackness of darkness, and
the doors of his eternal prison-house had closed upon
him! There is no respect in which he can help himself.
He is often willing to admit and willing to feel, that he
can not blot out his own sins; but at the same time he is
not willing to feel that he possesses such a heart, that without an immediate act of God upon it, he will never turn

from his wickedness, hate sin and be fitted for heaven. But though he is unwilling to feel this, it is true. The sinner is as much dependent upon God to make him ready for heaven, as he is to open heaven for his entrance. He possesses such a heart that, without Divine influence, he will never love God, love holiness, and accept salvation in Jesus Christ.

This is the thought to which I propose to direct your attention. In God, awakened sinner, is your help. Without this help you will never have a heart that is right with him, you will never be reconciled to him, you will never be a new creature in Jesus Christ, nor enjoy the happiness of heaven.

1. The first proof of this is found in the language of your Bible. God here speaks of those who are in a state of salvation, *as born of God—born of the Spirit.* Surely, this language must mean that God has helped them— that it is an immediate act of the Holy Spirit which has made them new creatures.

2. The second proof is found in the nature of the unrenewed heart. It is a heart that is *desperately wicked.* Its wickedness is hopeless. There is no hope in it. It is a heart that is opposed to God and holiness, and in love with wickedness, the world and sin. Now it is easy to see that such a heart will not turn to God, and love God, and desire holiness, without some influence different from its own natural desires. Its desires are not one of them holy, and it has no pleasure in holiness. It is a contradiction to say that an unholy feeling desires holiness A desire for holiness *is* holiness, because it is a holy desire ; but the unsanctified heart has no holiness, and therefore no real desire for it. And it can not, therefore, be the desire of an unholy heart to turn to

God and be holy, because its love of sin forbids this. And if God leaves such a heart to itself, there is no hope for it : wickedness will reign and rankle in it, till destruction comes and there is no remedy !

3. The third proof of the necessity of Divine influence is found in the inefficiency of all other influence. Here are unconverted sinners, whose parents and friends have exerted their endeavors in vain to persuade them to *set their affections upon things above, where Jesus Christ sitteth on the right hand of God.* All their lives they have been surrounded with the strong influence of Christianity and Christian friends ; and all their lives they have been able and willing to resist that influence, because their hearts loved sin. They have been proud, and obstinate, and unyielding. They have heard many strong, and tender, and affecting persuasions. But all this has not saved them, and never will. An angel might preach to them, and his words would not turn them from sin without Divine influence. It is not all that earth or Heaven can do, that will turn one sinner to Jesus Christ, if God denies him his Spirit. His help is in God—not in the influence, the persuasions, the entreaties, or the eloquence of men.

4. The fourth proof is found in the inefficacy of all motives. God has placed before you, my dear friends, all the motives that can have any tendency to influence you to repent and give your hearts to God, and you have resisted them all. Every unconverted sinner here has been told, time after time, of the infinite love of God— of his eternal wrath—of the unceasing torments of the lost—of the unlimited mercy of Jesus Christ, and the endless felicities that the penitent shall have in heaven. But these motives are not effectual. Many of you can

hear of heaven and hell as unmoved as if you had no souls. And you go on, year after year, pressing your way in thoughtlessness to eternity, in spite of the songs of the blest and the groans of the lost! Your hearts are so much in love with sin, that eternity may roll before you—Jesus Christ may tell you of his love—God may threaten—heaven invite, and hell may blaze, still onward you go, the same unregenerated sinner! All these motives do not turn you to God, because your wicked hearts refuse them, resist them all. Such hearts would resist any thing. All Heaven might come down, and it would not move such a heart to repentance. All Hell might come up, and it would not be motive enough to make you love God!   .

I am willing to admit that you are not always *sensible* of your resistance ; but the reason is, that you consider these things so little, and examine your own hearts and lives so little, that you remain in almost entire ignorance of yourselves. If you would look into this matter, there is not one of you who would not soon find that you are resisting the strongest motives to penitence and piety, that even God can present before your minds. Where is a more endless motive than your immortality? Where a more blessed one than heaven? or a more awful one than hell? Surely, if your hearts would yield to motives, you have enough.

Still, many of you are waiting for stronger motives. You are somewhat awake to this subject, and you vainly imagine that some more powerful motive would bring you to God. But you will have none. If you will not yield to those before you, you will die. Heaven will not become more happy to win you, nor hell more miserable to warn. God is as merciful now as he ever will be, and Jesus Christ is as able and willing to save, and the Holy Spirit is as ready. It is wickedness and pride of heart, and not want of motives, that keeps you in your sins.

Sinners do persuade themselves, and they are able to persuade themselves, that some stronger, more powerful motives would influence them to turn to God. And I remember one who carried this idea along with him into eternity, and when his own soul was lost, he thought if one were sent from the dead to preach to his unconverted brethren on earth, *they would repent.* But he was told, that if *they believed not Moses and the Prophets, they would not believe though one were sent unto them from the dead.* Motives do not convert men. They have been tried, and you have resisted them; and many of you are resisting them still. Your help is in God, not in motives. Aside from Divine influence, you will never yield to the motives of the Gospel; and if you ever know your own hearts, you will know that nothing but the power of God can make them yield to the motives before you. You will have no other. If you do not yield to these, through Divine assistance, you can not be saved.

These proofs ought to convince you that *in God is your help.* Aside from his agency, you can not be saved. This is one of the leading truths of the Gospel we preach to you—one of the essential principles of that religion which must lead you to heaven, if you are ever saved.

But remember, your helplessness is your guilt. You are so helpless, just because you are so sinful. Your sin is voluntary, and that is the worst feature of your case. If no redemption had been made for you, and if you were not *willingly* continuing in your sin, then your criminality would not be so great, though your condition were deplorable. But your helplessness is your sinfulness. Your attachment to sin is what makes you so helpless.

II. Let us now see, in the next place, if we can not gather some practical improvement and profitable directions from this doctrine.

1. We learn from this subject the folly of those who seek salvation in themselves. There are not a few who do this and think themselves safe. They reform their morals; they attempt to restrain and regulate their own hearts; they have much resolution on this subject, and imagine if they keep on a little while, they will soon be very good Christians. And, no doubt, multitudes of poor, deluded sinners rest just here. They think they have done much, and expect they shall do still more, and finally shall get at salvation. But, all this time, the true nature of their own hearts, the real extent of their wickedness, has not been discovered. If they had opened their hearts before God—if they had seen themselves in the light of his holy character—if they had entered into the real science of their sinfulness, and known what they are, they would have had no more hope of putting their own hearts right without immediate help from God, than they would of raising the dead; they would as soon expect to make a world as to save themselves.

It is all very true that the sinner who seeks salvation must strive against sin, must shun temptation, must deny himself, must guard well his heart, or he will not be saved. But when he relies upon himself and not on God, when he seeks to help himself instead of seeking help from God, he is leaning on a broken reed! Without Divine aid he will die. He can not help himself. And if he only seeks to do this, without trusting to God to help him, he may seek for ever; he will not be saved. Those are false conversions, spurious and useless, which are made by the mere *will of the flesh* and without the Divine Spirit.

But man must work *while* he depends. Divine grace and creature effort go hand in hand. *Work out your salvation with fear and trembling, for it is God who worketh in you both to will and to do.* Man must work just as diligently as if he had no Divine assistance to pray for and rely upon; at the same time, he must trust just as implicitly as if he had done nothing at all. Hence,

2. We learn from this subject the reason why so many of those who are awakened to a sense of Divine things, and begin to seek salvation, never attain it. It is simply because they try to save themselves. They wish to take themselves out of the hands of God. They rely on their own strength, their own purposes, and power, and wisdom simply. They will not throw themselves without reserve into the hands of Divine Mercy, and let God do with them as he will. They hold back their hearts from God, just as many in this house are now doing, vainly imagining that they can regulate their own hearts and put them right. It is in self, not in God, that they are seeking help. No sinner ever yet failed of salvation, or ever will, who cast himself upon the mercy and power of God; and no sinner ever attained salvation, or ever will, who seeks only to take care of himself, to manage his own heart. He might as well attempt to chain the lightning or tame the heaving surges of the sea. Try how you will, continue it as long as you will, if you only depend upon yourself, you will not be saved. It is God

alone that can save you, and if you will not depend on
him to control and help you, you will die in your sins.

3. We learn why it is that sinners who are making
some attempts to be saved, sometimes continue so long
in affliction and trouble before they find peace with God.
It is simply because they do not seek *help in God*. At
one time they are relying on the advice of friends—at
another on the prayers of Christian people—at another
on some winning or alarming sermon. Indeed, they are
very apt to fly to any thing but God. And they give
themselves a great deal of unnecessary trouble, and linger
long in bondage, because they will not come to God to
help them; will not *turn unto the Lord that he may have
mercy upon them, and unto our God who will abundantly
pardon.* This is the case with many of you who hear
me. You are relying upon yourselves, your friends, or
opportunities to save you. You flatter yourself that the
use of means will save you. You have hopes that your
conversations with one another will by-and-bye put your
heart right, not remembering that the wicked are always
strengthening one another in sin. And thus, day after
day, you are lingering on the soil of death, while you
might be saved if you would seek *help in God*. Hence,

4. We learn what is the great struggle of the sinner
in coming to salvation. It is simply to give his wicked
heart to God. This is what God commands him to do ;
this is what the Holy Spirit is now striving to have him
do ; this is what you must do, or you must die in sin !
And you whose minds are awake on this matter of
eternal life, will find no other great difficulty in being
saved, but that which you find in your own hearts. It
is not want of willingness and power in God to save
you—it is not want of light or want of motives—it is

your own obstinate and hard heart that keeps you from salvation. Sometimes you trouble yourselves with one thing, and sometimes with another, which have nothing to do with your salvation, and not only so, but they are things which take off your mind from your own present and pressing duty—repentance and submission to God in the faith of Christ. Sometimes you are attempting to make yourselves feel this subject more deeply, and you excuse yourselves from coming at once to God for salvation, with the vain plea that you can not repent till you are more troubled than you are now. But God does not tell you to be searching after more strong impressions, he tells you to *repent now;* and he is striving by his Spirit to bring you to repentance *now.* And suppose you were more distressed and afflicted about yourself, what good do you suppose that would do you, while you hold yourself unmoved in sin ? There are multitudes of sinners whose hearts are overwhelmed with distressing convictions, and still it does them no good, and never will. Hell contains hosts of them ; but their convictions do not change their hearts, and they would not change yours. And your expressions about want of more anxiety and feeling on this subject are only designed by your deceitful wickedness, to keep you from a present duty—giving your hearts to God, denying self and following Christ. Do you not see that while you allege your want of feeling, as a reason for your impenitence, your heart takes it as an excuse for not repenting, and, therefore, keeps you half at ease, as if you were under no obligation to be a Christian now ? God has shown you enough to convince you of your necessity of seeking help from him ; and still you will not come to him for help. And if you do not struggle harder against

the influence of your wicked hearts than you have yet
done, I have no hope that you will be saved. Your
strife is not with God, it is with yourself. God is willing to save you. He is striving to bring you to himself,
and you are resisting his Spirit while you continue to
excuse yourself. Instead of contending against yourself
as you ought to be, you are alleging reasons why you
are still in your impenitence; and thus hardening yourself in sin and resisting Divine influence. Not that you
mean to do it—but such is your unhappy mistake. You
ought to yield your heart to God to love him supremely—
you ought to cry out to him for help—to cast yourself
upon his aid. This you must do, or you must perish.
And this is the only obstacle in the way of your salvation; I mean your unwillingness to yield to God's Spirit—
to seek your help from his mercy—to give your wicked,
wayward heart to Jesus Christ, and let him save you
from yourself. Hence,

5. We learn that awakened sinners are often doing, or
attempting to do, something directly contrary to what
they suppose. They imagine that they are trying to
yield themselves to God in faith and submission, while,
in fact, they are striving to avoid it. The God of all
love and grace would have them come to him, as poor,
unworthy sinners, guilty and helpless, and trust him to
save them: this would be faith. They are attempting
to manage themselves, instead of relying upon God.
The Lord Jesus Christ would have every burdened
sinner come to him and find rest for his soul. The
sinner wishes to find rest first, and then he intends to
come. And while he is attending to this subject with
anxiety, and prayers, and tears, he is attempting to
accomplish for himself the very thing which he ought

to know that God must perform for him, if he is ever saved. But he is, on the one hand, too proud and too self-righteous to feel that he needs the unmerited help of God, and, on the other, he has such an unbelief and such an aversion to his God, that he is unwilling to seek and to rely upon the aid that God alone can give him. And thus many an awakened sinner, instead of striving to do what God commands him to do, is really striving to avoid it. He hates to trust God—hates to hear of his helplessness and dependence—hates to feel that he is a guilty sinner deserving the eternal frowns of his God, and *as* such a sinner to give himself to Jesus Christ to be *saved from wrath through him.* And, therefore, he is attempting to save himself. He strives to find something or *make* something in his own heart, on account of which he will be accepted of God. It is pride—wicked and unhumbled pride—and he is fostering it! He is willing to think of himself as wretched, but not as guilty! He is willing to weep over his condition as a misfortune, but not as a crime! He is seeking for God to pity him, but not to pardon him! It is unhappiness, not sin, from which he is seeking deliverance, and he is willing to be indebted to the power of God to deliver him from his calamity, but he is too proud to cast himself upon the *mercy* of God to pardon his sins and renew his heart. And, therefore, all his *striving* is only an attempt of an unhumbled heart to justify itself. He is, unconsciously, resisting God. He is attempting to do something directly contrary to what he himself supposes. Hence,

6. We learn that awakened sinners are often guilty of *resisting* the Holy Spirit, while they are vainly flattering themselves that they are doing well. The Holy Spirit

would lead them to Jesus Christ—would have them trust
his mercy to save them—would have them come to him,
just as they are, poor, vile, lost sinners, and beg for
mercy. They are not ready and willing to do so. They
imagine they *shall* be, but they are not ready *now*: they
have not yet brought their hearts to a right state, but
they mean to do it. Thus, they are resisting the Holy
One *by delay*, and refusing the mercy of Jesus Christ *in
pride*, and relying on themselves to put their own hearts
right instead of seeking help in God, giving him their
hearts that he may change them. They wish to save
themselves; at least to do *something* in the matter, enough
to save their pride. But the Holy Spirit condemns their
delay, their self-reliance, their pride. And in a little
time, they may be left of God! If they will not have
his help, if they will resist his influence, if they will love
sin and rely upon themselves, they can have no help
from God! Hence,

7. Finally, we learn that sinners are their own destroyers. God has done for them all that is needful to
open heaven, and block up the road to hell. It is true
they can not save themselves; but if they would allow it,
God would save them. Look and see: The counsels
of Eternal Love embraced the sacrifice of Jesus Christ—
in the fullness of time that sacrifice was offered up—the
justice of God was satisfied, his law honored, and the
whole way into heaven opened before the guilty, lost
sinner. And not only so, but, after the invitation is sent
out—*Come, for all things are now ready*—the Holy Ghost
himself comes down to strive with sinners to bring them
to our Lord Jesus Christ. He has come here. And
here are sinners who are resisting him! God the Father
loves them, and is *not willing that they should perish;*

God the Son is waiting to receive them; and God the Holy Ghost is making the last effort in the economy of grace to bring them to repentance and salvation, to have them yield their hearts to God and trust in the blood of his Son. All this God has done to help them, to save them, and they have refused it all! Verily, their destruction is of themselves! They refuse the aid of Heaven! And this is what I mean when I say if they would allow it, God would save them! Salvation is free. No man perishes because he must. No man goes down to hell, but he goes there willingly, of his own will turning a deaf ear to the voice of imploring Mercy, which follows him to the very door, *Turn ye, turn ye, for why will ye die!* No man goes down to hell, but he goes there wading in the blood of an offered atonement enough for his soul! No man goes down to hell, but he goes there resisting the Spirit of all grace admonishing him kindly in the inside of his own heart, *Prepare to meet thy God!* All Heaven is ready to save him, if he will consent to be saved. Guilt can not damn him—hell can not claim him—the Devil can not thwart him, if he will consent to be saved! Surely, if sinners perish, they are their own destroyers! If they continue to reject such grace, as they are now doing, they must perish, but Heaven, and all the help of heaven will be clear of their blood!

Awakened sinner, remember that you are guilty, not only of rejecting Jesus Christ, and refusing the love of God, but you are guilty of doing *despite to the Spirit of all grace.* Your error is not all of the past. It belongs to the present. Now, God is striving to save you. He has given you already all the help you need, if you would but receive it and not reject it. It is not for want of

Divine influence that you are not a Christian; it is because you resist Divine influence. It is true your only help is in God; and it is true, too, that you are guilty of refusing it in your unbelief. This hour, my dear friend, you may be saved, if you will: and in this hour, if you refuse the help of God, you are guilty! All heaven is ready for your salvation : and all the wickedness of earth and hell can not destroy you if you will cease to resist the Almighty, and will cast yourself upon the unbounded, unmerited mercy of your God.

Then, be wise and live. *Turn ye, for why will ye die?* God is love. Heaven is merciful. Angels will rejoice over you. Jesus Christ will save you; and peace will come over your soul, when you can look to heaven, and say, *God is my helper, I will not fear.*

Forgiveness.

Forgiving one another, if any man have a quarrel against any: even as Christ forgave you, so also do ye.—COLOSSIANS, iii. 13.

THE forgiveness enjoined here (which constitutes the theme of this sermon) is mentioned as a specification, or as a particular duty, coming in as one of the things embraced under a general principle. The general principle is mentioned just before, and relates to general disposition : *Put on, therefore, bowels of mercies, kindness, humbleness of mind, meekness, long-suffering.* These are general dispositions to be cherished. Then, as growing out of this state of mind, or as forming one of the applications of this general disposition, the Divine writer mentions the duty of forgiveness—*forgiving one another, if any man have a quarrel against any.* We propose,

I. To explain this duty.

II. To present some considerations to enforce it.

III. To make some remarks upon the general subject. This is our plan.

I. The explanation of forgiveness is not so simple a thing as one might at first imagine. Like all other moral duties which go beyond external action and relate to the internal disposition, it has an extent, and therefore, an importance and obscurity about it, which render it liable to be misunderstood.

There would be no foundation or call for its exercise, were it not for sin. In a universe or world never visited by moral evil, and wherein the affections and intercourse of all the inhabitants were uniformly regulated by holiness, there would never occur a single one of those injuries or offenses, real or imaginary, which so often in this disordered world provoke to resentment. All would be harmony and peace. All intercourse would be happy—without a jar and without suspicion. All duty would be done, and the doing of it would be universally satisfactory. On the one hand, there would be no disposition to infringe an item upon the rights or injure the feelings of others; and on the other hand, there would be no disposition to suspect any such evil. But in a sinful world it is not so. It is different on both sides. Offenses here will come: they must come, on account of the injustice of sin. And the evil is rendered still worse, because of the readiness to suspect them; which is also one of the results of sin, in a great measure, and can not be altogether attributed to the lessons of an unhappy experience. Experience, no doubt, (so unjust the world is,) would give rise to a degree of suspicion, and put a wise man on his guard against injury or injustice from a quarter whence he had often received it. But his suspicion, as a sinner, is very different from what it would be, if he were *not* a sinner: it is more ready, and more bitter, and vengeful. So that the forgiveness he is to exercise becomes not only a more difficult duty to perform, but a more difficult one to understand. It will not be easy for him always to discriminate betwixt the abhorrence of injustice which he may righteously feel, and the enmity, malice or hate, which he can not feel without sin.

Offense, some real or supposed injury or injustice, is the subject-matter of forgiveness. Against an offense, such as an injury or an insult, such as some injustice to our interests, name or feelings, we are so constituted that our mind naturally rises in the attitude of resistance. If our feelings would stop *there*, only to resist injustice and resist it fitly, our danger would be comparatively small, and our duty comparatively easy. But natural feeling prompts us further: it does not stop with mere self-defense: it is greatly prone to anger and vengeance. And under the idea that the offender *deserves* punishment, we are very much exposed to justify ourselves for inflicting it upon him, if not in act at least in the feelings with which we regard him. The duty of forgiveness relates to these feelings. The duty does not stop with our mere *forbearance* from any injury in return, or mere forbearance from the infliction of a punishment supposed to be deserved. It goes further. It reaches the inmost feelings with which we regard such an offender. To lay up his fault or offense in mind—to cherish the memory of it—to entertain an unfriendly feeling on account of it, is just the opposite of forgiveness. When the mind finds the offense still rankling within it, and the heart is less disposed to good-will on account of it, there is a manifest lacking in the spirit of forgiveness. True forgiveness is opposed to any remaining dissatisfaction with the offending individual. It may be judged of just by this rule, to wit: whether our feelings of personal kindness and good-will toward the offender have become just the same as if he had never offended us at all. If they have, that is forgiveness: nothing short of this is.

It may not be easy for us to discriminate between the offense and the offender always, but duty requires it. The offense, that is, any injustice, is to be abhorred; while the offender is to be forgiven. A regard for our own rights, interests, character, and feelings is not to be sacrificed; we are gifted with the power of resentment as one of the means of self-protection against the unjust. And such resentment, in fit kind and degree, is one of the securities of a virtuous society, which the world will never be able to dispense with as long as sin is in it. Crime *ought* to be abhorred, and the abhorrence manifested. Resentment *ought* to be felt, and the feeling ought to be shown when crime has injured us. It is a wild and silly dream to think that we shall do the world the most good by smiling as blandly on vice as on virtue. Vice has never been cured in that way, and never will be. But hatred of vice is one thing, and enmity toward the offender is quite another. Forgiveness has respect to this enmity, in all its shades and varieties. It would annihilate it, and all that springs from it. It would do this in every instance of offense wherein the offender evinces his repentance. And not only so, but it is a general spirit of forbearance and kindness not ready to *think evil*, but on the contrary, ready to forgive, and pass over and forget a thousand instances of offense and injury without any explanation at all. The true spirit of forgiveness will not be apt to stick on the point of restitution, or repentance, or of amendment of injury, especially where the offense was only personal, and has not done to society a general injury. It will ordinarily ask little more than that the offender shall cease to offend; and will often go beyond this, and itself cease *to be* offended with the same things.

But, wherever the specifications of its duty may lie, it is opposed, in general, to all anger, revenge, retaliation; to all enmity, bitterness and ill-will. It bears with injuries, and bears long. It is more inclined to apologize for them than to hunt up aggravations of them. It would return blessing for cursing, and good for evil, and kindness for injury and hate.

II. Now the arguments to enforce this duty are worthy of the most serious consideration. We name a few of them:

1. It may be enough for any true believer's conscience that this duty is so often and so emphatically *enjoined in the sacred Scriptures.* They have laid an impressive stress upon it, which has often astonished and revolted the minds of mere men of the world. (Luke, vi. 37:) *Forgive and ye shall be forgiven.* (Eph. iv. 32:) *Be ye kind to one another, tender-hearted, forgiving one another, even as God, for Christ's sake, hath forgiven you.* (Matt. xviii. 35:) *So likewise shall my heavenly Father do also unto you, if ye from your hearts forgive not every one his brother their trespasses.* (Matt. xviii. 21, 22:) *How often shall my brother sin against me and I forgive him? till seven times? Jesus saith unto him, I say not unto thee, until seven times, but until seventy times seven.* (Matt. xi. 25:) *And when ye stand praying, forgive, if ye have aught against any, that your Father also which is in heaven may forgive you your trespasses.* (Matt. vi. 12:) *Forgive us our debts, as we forgive our debtors.* There is unquestionably a sense in which this forgiveness is peculiarly a duty of Christians toward their Christian brethren; just as *to do good especially to them who are of the household of faith* (Gal. vi. 10) is peculiarly a duty. But the duty is not confined to them

(Luke, vi. 27, 37). In his sermon on the mount, Jesus Christ, in laying down the great general principles of moral duty, applicable every where, and obligatory upon every body, has made the duty universal: *Love your enemies; do good to them which hate you; condemn not, and ye shall not be condemned; forgive, and ye shall be forgiven.*

If it constitutes a matter of difficulty or embarrassment to any mind, that our forgiveness by God is made to hinge on our forgiveness of men that offend us, as if this were an easy way to attain God's forgiveness, or as if this were an unreasonable ground on which he should dispense it; the embarrassment may be removed by a little reflection. This is *not* an easy way to attain forgiveness of God, in the sense that men would attach to it: that is, it is no more easy than it is to become a true Christian indeed. Aside from true religion, there is no true forgiveness. Irreligious men no more forgive those who offend them, than they love God. What they call forgiveness is not such. It lacks the very essence of the matter—the heart, the life, the whole thing. It commonly consists in merely consenting not to hunt an offender and punish—not to take vengeance upon him—not, perhaps, to notice him enough, or dignify him enough to show him any resentment; while, at the same time, the heart has a distance and coldness, an indifference toward him, which gratifies itself with sentiments of scorn and contempt. This is about the measure of the world's forgiveness; at best, it is only an acquittal from vengeance, or coldness, scorn, and indifference—just the sentiment of selfishness and pride. Far different is a Christian's true forgiveness. It is more apt to sorrow over an offender than scorn him. There is no indifference about it. It is full of interest. It mourns the offender's offence, even if *he* does not mourn it. It mourns it for the offender's sake. And while it forgives him, it does it, not in coldness, but in warmth, and prays God to forgive him also. He that forgives shall be forgiven of God, because he that forgives is a true follower of Christ—a regenerated man. And if men, without faith, will but get a true and clear idea of what forgiveness is, there are few things which they will find it more difficult to perform. The outward action they may indeed put forth. They may restrain themselves from revenge. They may stand aloof from all injury and resentment. But it is only standing aloof, too selfish to bend, and too proud to scorn, and too indifferent to mourn another's unhappiness and sin. The natural heart never had, and never will have the genuine spirit of forgiveness in its full sense. It may smother rage, and may scorn to requite an injury; but both the scorn and the rage are proofs of an unforgiving spirit. The commands of Christ reach the heart.

2. The general amiability of human character or disposition depends very much upon the nature of those feelings which are habitually entertained. The heart has its habits of sensibility, as well as the mind its association of ideas. The harboring of sentiments of resentment, suspicion, or ill-will, is a vice among the affections which tends very powerfully to form an unamiable and unenviable character. On the contrary, a forgiving disposition, or any of those exercises which come nearest to it—the restraint of anger, the checking of the first risings of resentment, the putting away from the mind all thoughts of the offense, aiming to think *as well* of the offender as possible, instead of thinking of him, in dark and distrustful disposition, as *ill* as possible—will tend,

and tend strongly to cultivate an amiableness of disposition, alike commendable and comfortable. It is not safe for any human being to indulge much, and habitually, a resentful and unforgiving temper. No man can do it without misleading his own mind, misguiding his heart, and forming to himself a character repulsive and odious. Faults grow upon the mind that contemplates them with angry and resentful emotions; and often owe their deemed magnitude *more* to the brooding and moody contemplation, than to their own nature; so that the judgment, misled and deceived, is more prepared to be deceived and misled again. At the same time, the feelings of a heart that will not forgive, become more and more fixed not only, but prepare the heart for other feelings, which *resemble* resentment and suspicion. Jealousy and petulance become natural and easy. Indeed, there are few things which tend more to the formation of an undesirable character all around, than the indulgence of an unforgiving disposition. Hence,

3. Such a disposition is a constant source of personal unhappiness. It trains one to constant uneasiness. It magnifies offenses, and puts out peace of mind, as it broods over them. It creates a general inclination to think worse of human nature than is just, and prepares its possessor to *expect* injury or offense every where. And, consequently, the man who can not forgive becomes unfit, in fact, for the common scenes and relations of a society in which *offenses must come*, and unfit in disposition to find enjoyment therein. He can find little felicity where he finds so much to resent, and while he treasures up every offense to brood over as if he were surrounded with foes. A man far from a forgiving temper must be, in a world like this, far from such per-

sonal felicities as he needs, and ought to find, amid the intercourse of life.

4. It is equally unhappy with him in respect to his *adding any thing to the common stock of enjoyment.* He can add little. Man here is so imperfect, errors are so common, and misunderstandings so unavoidable, that, for the sake of all that species of felicity which springs from the exercise of the social affections, and is enhanced by the confidence, and endearments, and intercourse of social life, there is a necessity for bearing some injuries not only with patience, but with humility and kindness. Out of an unforgiving temper spring contentions, bitterness, and wrath, divisions, strifes, quarrels, and war. The peace of neighborhoods is broken up, kindly relations are exchanged for hostile ones, and human society loses much of its designed power of communicating an additional felicity to its members. In all ordinary civilized life, every individual is and must be indebted to society for no small part of the happiness he enjoys. Society is necessary to him. He can not be happy without it, except by being more than half *un*manned. In the exercises of the social affections, in loving and esteeming others, and in being loved and esteemed by them in return, and in the mutual offices of kindness, confidence, and good-will, is to be found one of the great sources of human enjoyment. A being who receives so much from society may well afford to bear something from it in return. He must form a very strange exception, indeed, if his fellows, on the whole, do not increase his enjoyments more than they diminish them; and probably a strange exception if they do not contribute to his felicity as much as he contributes to the common stock. To *that* he may contribute by a forgiving temper, if by no-

thing else—every living man may. And without something of such a temper, he can not avoid diminishing often and much the common happiness of life around him.

5. No man can live in a world like this without being himself sometimes an offender. Wittingly or unwittingly, he will offend. *In many things we offend all.* The man does not live who does not himself *need* forgiveness from his fellows. If his injustice has *not* offended, his pride may have done it; his coldness, his indifference, his haughtiness, his vanity, his lack of pity or sympathy, his distance and reserve, may have done it. And the wound he has in some such way given, may be worse than if he had injured the property or violated the external rights of his fellow. It may sink deeper into the heart, and lie among those tender and cherished feelings whose bleeding is most easy and most severe. And how inconsistent and inconsiderate it must be for one who may have offended so much and so deeply, and who must have offended sometimes not a little, to cherish offenses instead of forgetting them! *Himself* an offender and needing to be forgiven, how unfit it is that he should refuse to extend to others the very forgiveness he himself needs! To set himself up as superior to any such necessity, and, by indifference to the feelings of his fellows, or by reliance of heart upon his other resources of possession, power, or name, to be led to say or feel that he does not care for their forgiveness, is itself an offense; it is an insult and an injury of the worst kind. He *ought* to care. Duty, manliness, humanity, demands it of him. He *would* care if he were not at once supremely selfish and supremely vain ; yea, and supremely *mean.*

If men were duly sensible of their own errors and

16*

offenses, they would find strong reason to extend forgiveness to the offenses of others. But,

6. The duty of forgiveness has an enforcement that draws deeper still. We are offenders against God. As such we are indebted for all that we enjoy in time, and all that we can hope for in eternity, to the forgiving disposition of that Infinite Being whom we have all offended. Had he no disposition to forgive, the pall of an eternal midnight of despair had already settled down upon our prospects! He bears with us now, to furnish us with a space for repentance, because he is infinitely ready to forgive the very last of our offenses. If we *are* forgiven, and ever enter into heaven in peace with God, we shall owe it all to the sovereign mercy of his forgiving disposition. We have offended God more and oftener than our bitterest foe can have offended us. The offense against ourselves is from an equal, a fellow, a common mortal like ourselves; while our own offense, being against God, rises immeasurably higher. And shall that very offender who, this moment, is out of hell by forbearance, and who expects heaven eternally only as a gracious boon to an offender, and who could not even have had the *offer* of pardon had not the kindness that seeks to save him gone infinitely beyond all that *he* is required to do toward an offender, and taken upon itself the burden of his guilt, and, bearing it upon the accursed tree, brought out from dying lips the prayer, *Father, forgive them, for they know not what they do*—shall that very offender (himself out of the pit, and hoping for heaven on such grounds) turn round to his offending fellow with vengeance or angry resentment in his heart? Hide, hide thyself in the dust, thou shameless mortal! Cover thy-

self with the pall of an eternal midnight! Aim to be
forgotten and unknown for ever, if, such a debtor to forgiveness yourself, you can not forgive an offending fellow! Surely there is no man who fitly feels what a sinner he is, what a miserable offender, who can find it in
his heart to deal hardly or *feel* hardly toward an offending fellow. Your fellow, indeed, may owe you much of
apology or of restitution; but you owe *there* ten thousand
talents, and you have nothing to pay! Gone, gone for
ever would be your last hope, if God should feel toward
you the unforgiving temper which *you* exercise toward
your unpardoned fellow!

7. We have already said that a resentment which
aims at self-protection, and which manifests an abhorrence of crime, is due to the cause of virtue itself. But
in defending our rights, the spirit of forgiveness must be
mingled with such a resentment, to temper and control
it. If it is not, if we go *beyond* this, and would take
vengeance into our own hands, or, by hostile, cold, and
indifferent feeling toward an offender, would punish
him—let it be borne in mind that we are then coming
very near to an interference with the high prerogatives
of God. *Vengeance is mine; I will repay, saith the Lord.*
The injustice which has offended us has offended him
more; and till we can be certain that we know what it
deserves, it were better to leave the retribution to Him
who can not err. And when we remember that the
offender is in *his* hands—that he can not escape—that he
must repent and become all we could ask of him, or fall
under the final retribution of God, how can we bear to
pursue such a periled mortal with a single emotion of
animosity? Could we bear to make keener the sword
of the executioner? Could we bear to mingle our taunts

with the groans of a convict dying in the hands of human justice? Certainly nature feels that that justice is enough; and much more may we leave an offender to his God and our God. Our unforgiving resentment amounts just about to a declaration that we can not trust God to protect *us* or punish *him*. Let us beware lest our anger toward our fellow becomes impudence toward God. And let us be ashamed and confounded if, instead of trusting God *to punish* according to his holy wisdom, we want the pleasure of doing it ourselves, to gratify our heart!

8. It may not be altogether an avoidable result of sin, but it is a fact that our present felicities and interests often assume an importance that does not belong to them. This is especially the case with the whole generation of unbelievers. It would contribute much toward a readiness to forgive, if we were to be duly sensible how small are the injuries (after all) of the most careless or hostile offender. Our anger and resentment would guard only very trivial interests—mere trifles—the bursting bubbles of a speeding moment! The offender whom we will not forgive has not touched one of our dearest interests. He has injured us only in minor matters. No man thinks of being offended with his fellow because that fellow has injured his piety, or has made it more difficult for him to walk with God. No man thinks his eternal interests have been injured, or allows his unforgiving feelings to burn here on account of injury to meet him beyond the tomb. Anger and animosity sink down together into the peaceful bosom of the grave. And hence, in that honest hour when a man is taking the last look of all things earthly, and earth has put on, in the sight of his dying eyes, its true aspect, he finds con-

straint to forgiveness, which he never found before. His enemy, whom he leaves behind him, has not touched one of the interests that are now before him: he has not made the judgment more terrible, or God less forgiving, or heaven less sweet and holy. If men would let the just estimates of that honest hour come back now upon the interests and sentiments of life, they would be more ready to forgive. They would see that their offender has offended only in trifles—the veriest trifles of a vanishing moment and a passing world. Out beyond it, on the wide bosom of eternity, his offense has not touched an item. God is just as good—heaven just as happy, and its songs of eternal melody roll on just as sweetly. Oh! how inconsistent and uncalled for is an unforgiving disposition, since the offense of the offender has done so little harm! Harm to us, indeed, it may be, if we will *not* forgive him; but nothing, if we will. *Forgive and ye shall be forgiven.*

9. One thing more: for the littleness of the offender should stand side by side with the interests his offense has affected. This creature, whom we hesitate to forgive, is only a frail, mortal man. His face is set toward the tomb, and every step he takes in this wilderness-world brings him nearer to its deep and lasting silence. As he travels on, few joys meet him, and those that do only smile and sparkle for a little moment, and then are extinguished for ever! He has many woes and many burdens to bear; his heart will often bleed, and grief-tears often course down his blistered cheeks! Nowhere can he lay down his burden, till he lays it at the grave's mouth! You shall see him descend into it! The dust shall be piled upon him—the cold sod shall press upon his now stilled bosom! There he lies, and you stand by

and look upon the spot! Ah! are you not ashamed—deeply ashamed, and more deeply sorry that, in his life, your feelings of hostility pursued him for some little offense, which, perhaps, he never intended; or even for some great one which he did? Can you avoid being sad, that your hostile resentment ever burned for a moment against a creature of such littleness, such griefs, and such an end? and that you let him go down into the land of silence, unsoothed with a kind word, and unsolaced by your forgiveness? You are yourself as little and as mortal as he; you shall soon sleep beside him—your head as low, and the turf as unbroken and green that covers you! Is it *not* fit that you should *forgive one another, if any man have a quarrel against any,* even as you hope that CHRIST WILL FORGIVE YOU?

The Depths of Salvation.

(SACRAMENTAL.)

Oh, the depth of the riches both of the wisdom and knowledge of God!
How unsearchable are his judgments, and his ways past finding out.—
ROMANS, xi. 33.

WE blend together, to-day, what may well confound
an infidel, and what may well comfort a Christian. If Christianity is true, and founded on credible
evidences, or even if its direct evidences are not deemed
satisfactory, but if its nature and all its procedure are
seen to harmonize with the severest reason and all the
high attributes of God, an infidel may well be filled with
confusion. And if Christianity is true—and the more
profoundly a believer contemplates it, the more he finds
all its nature and all its proceedings to grow in wonder
and adorable magnificence upon him—such a believer,
seeing his religion to harmonize with God, may well be
comforted. Christianity is a wonderful system; it is full
of wonders. It is an extensive and connected system, one
truth linked with another in the manner of the severest
reason. And if, amid the logic of its connections, or
amid the high wonders of its revelations, an infidel can
discover no flaw and no failure, his infidelity may well
blush to maintain that men—mere men—men like the
poor prophets of Judea and the poor fishermen of Gali-
lee, have coined a system pure beyond comparison, and

sublime beyond conception. Mere wonder in an idea is no proof of its truth, indeed; but when a believer finds, as he contemplates Christianity, that its wonders all assort with God, and give him a more majestic idea of God, that its wonders all lie just where Reason wants them to lie, and are, therefore, just as light as they are magnificent—that its very darknesses are the very brightest of its light—he will not be an unreasonable man, if he shall allow his soul to rejoice and exult, just when he most wonders and adores.

The text is an expression of wonder and amazement: *Oh, the depth of the riches both of the wisdom and knowledge of God! How unsearchable are his judgments, and his ways past finding out.* What excited this wonder was the contemplation of the sovereign mercy of God in the salvation of sinners. The Apostle had discussed the whole subject of redemption. He had explained the atonement made for sinners by the sufferings of Christ, and when, in the application of that redemption, he comes to a sovereignty as adorable as he had found in the provision of it, he has no words to explain and unfold any longer; he can only pause, and wonder, and adore: *Oh, the depth, the depth!* Amazement takes the place of explanation; he has reached the end of reasoning and stops to wonder. We propose,

I. To show that this merciful and sovereign salvation for sinners is truly a wonderful salvation; that while it neither contradicts, nor utterly confounds human reason, it goes entirely beyond it, and thus becomes a matter of adorable wonder, such that the more deeply we study it, the more will our amazement grow upon us.

II. To show that this wonderful character of Christianity, while it exalts God, perfectly assorts with the severest reason, and ought to induce a reasonable man to embrace it.

I. Christianity is a system of wonders. No wise man can contemplate it far without exclaiming, *Oh, the depth of the riches both of the wisdom and knowledge of God.*

We mention to you *four* different considerations, taken from the election of God, the nature of Christ, his sufferings, and his satisfaction for sinners.

1. The very proposal of salvation for sinners is a matter of wonder. We can not, indeed, reason very well about God, and we are never safe in our reasonings a single step we attempt to take beyond where the light of Revelation shines upon our path. But after all that Divine Revelation has taught us, there is much ground for amazement in the fact that God should ever have conceived the idea of saving a sinner. His election was a wonder. He was not obliged to save him. His character and judgment would have for ever appeared spotless and perfect, if he had suffered that holy law, whose penalty is everlasting death, to take its dreadful course upon him. Sinners *had* perished under the law. The fallen angels had become devils, and their being *reserved in chains of darkness unto the judgment of that great day,* had brought no dishonor upon God. The law, which would have sent sinners of the earth to be their companions in torment, was a just law, a holy law, a good law; it was necessary; it stood, and still stands, as the friend of the good, as a terror to deter from evil, as the guardian for all the felicity there is in the universe (unless the felicity of God himself forms an exception); and if the death-penalty of the law, *the soul that sinneth it shall die,* had been carried into execution, and every sinner upon the

earth had become its eternal victim, not only the justice, but even the goodness of God would have been manifested in the judicial transaction; it would have demonstrated to the beholding universe, that the good God would not suffer sinners to be at large to break in upon the felicity of the good by their unrighteousness, and to spread contamination and destruction around them. Why then should God propose to save sinners? Why did he not annihilate them? He could have filled their vacated places in an instant with better beings, and held them, at his will, holy and unstained for ever. Moreover, sin is an infinite offense against him. It kindles his anger, and ought to kindle it. Reason could have but little respect for God, if he should have no displeasure against the guilty. And more still, there is a most noticeable singularity in this salvation. God does not appear thus on any other field of his own august wonders: when sin broke out in heaven, he did not appear so; he hurled the thunderbolt of a just vengeance. If, on the earth, any creature goes against the established laws of the natural world, God does not interpose by any new act, or any new agency, to prevent the misery or disaster of the violation. Why, then, save sinners? What ground for it could the severest reasoning ever discover? No man can answer. All we can say is, *Oh, the depth of the riches both of the wisdom and knowledge of God.*

Certainly here is ground for wonder and amazement. God appears, in this salvation, not only to have gone beyond all human reason, but beyond himself. He never did any thing else like it.

2. Another matter of wonder lies in the incarnation of Christ. His birth was miraculous not only, but a sort

of miracle beyond any other miracle of God.   His mother
was a poor virgin.   That which was conceived in her
was by the Holy Ghost.   Deity took upon himself the
form and nature of humanity.   He who was *in the begin-*
ning with God and was God, who thought it not robbery to be
equal with God, took upon him the form of a servant, and
being found in fashion as a man, he humbled himself, and
became subject to all the sinless degradation of human
nature.   This fact stands alone in the universe—in the
history of all existence, created or uncreated.   Jesus
Christ, the Son of God, became man.   He was one person.   That one person embraced in his high and mysterious personage, at once all the august attributes of
Deity, and all the littleness, and limitations, and capabilities of pain and death, which belong to the humblest of
mankind.   Among all God's wonders, you can find no
analogy for the person of Christ.   Reason, all human
reason stands abashed and staggered when it attempts
even the conception of a person, one person, the same
person, uniting in himself the extremes of glory and degradation—one person, who could make the winds and
the sea obey him, the dead obey him, devils obey him,
and at the same time be harassed and tormented with the
temptations of Satan ; be weary and hungry, be pained
and weep, just as any poor mortal man.   Mysterious
Being! peculiar, unlike any other, having no analogy in
heaven or earth.   *Oh, the depth of the riches both of the*
wisdom and knowledge of God.

3. Our ordinary idea of the proceedings of justice is
confounded, by the sufferings of Jesus Christ.   We are
accustomed, in our contemplation, to connect together the
ideas of sin and suffering.   At least we are wont to consider that an innocent and sinless being—one who has

given no offense, broken no law, come short in no duty, cannot *justly* be treated as a malefactor. Our reason seems to decide in a moment, that true justice can never allow such a being to be miserable, much less make him a direct subject and victim of penal inflictions. Yet, here stood the sinless Son of God. He *had not where to lay his head.* He was a *man of sorrows and acquainted with grief.* Men sneered at him, railed at him, scourged him as a culprit, hung him up with the wicked, and mocked at the agonies of his death. What has become of God's justice? how could it permit all this?—men and devils let loose upon an innocent and spotless being? And more than all, if there is one particle of righteousness in God the Father, how could he himself, always delighting in a Son who always obeyed him, abandon him at the very moment of death, and force from dying lips the agonizing complaint, *My God, my God, why hast thou forsaken me?* No human reason can answer these questions. Reason must stand aghast and exclaim, *Oh, the depth!*

4. If possible, amazement will rise still higher, when this suffering transaction is explained, even by the Bible itself. He suffered *the just for the unjust,* that he might *bring us to God.* And how could penal justice be satisfied or honored by the penal sufferings of an innocent One? If sin had been merely a commercial delinquency, a debt, so much due, and the debtor could not pay it—and if the law had been a mere heartless treasury, so much wanted and not caring where it came from, it not would be so much of a wonder that a friend should be allowed to step in, and, from the abundance of his treasures, make up the deficiency of the delinquent. But here is a delinquency that treasures can not meet. There

is no analogy betwixt the nature of debt and the nature of sin. Sin is not a mere borrower who has failed to pay. God is not a mere lender, claiming back his own that he has lent. If it were so, the pay might as well come from another. And when our Lord Jesus Christ suffers to satisfy Divine justice for sinners, the question is propounded, *How* his suffering *could* be any satisfaction at all to such a justice; or how it could consist with the very nature of such a justice to accept it in the sinner's stead; or how a just God could retain his character of justice, and at the same time exclaim, *Awake, O sword, against the shepherd and against the man that is my fellow,* and then bathe the sword of his justice in the blood of his spotless Son? The question confounds all human reason—no man can answer it—the only response is wonder and amazement. *Oh, the depth! the depth!* We can believe, and adore, and wonder, but all the world can not *explain* how it *can* be a just thing that the sufferings of Christ should be accepted as *a propitiation for our sins.* God has taught us the fact, and hence we believe it. The fact is a wonder.

These are only examples. Things of the same marvelous nature run all through the history of the system of Redemption. The more we study it, the more we see of them. The more we study it and understand it too, the more it rises upon us, not only in the wonders of its magnificence, but in the wonders of its mysteries. This is one of the things which confound infidelity. Infidelity can not grasp the matter. Infidelity attempts to proceed on the ground of reasoning, but Christianity, though it presents all credible proofs of its own truth, so that a just reasoner can not reject it, and so as to leave, therefore, every unbeliever *without excuse;* yet, Christianity soon plunges into those deep things of God, where Reason grows weak, and her light dim, and her mere disciple must grope and stagger in darkness. Infidelity is confounded by these depths. She can not fathom them. She can not weave any argument to disprove them, and therefore she is confounded again. So far as she can bring any of the principles of a just reasoning to apply to the things of our faith, just so far she finds Christianity to be just what reason wants her to be, and, therefore, she is again confounded. Infidelity is proud; as proud as she is foolish. She puts confidence in the power of her reason, but when she attempts to apply her principles to the economy of salvation, the nature of that economy stretches off into measureless distances beyond them, and therefore she is confounded again.

But what confounds an infidel comforts a Christian.

II. As the second part of this sermon, we propose to show that those deep and unfathomable wonders of which our religion is so full, are reasons for our accepting it and being comforted by it. We name to you but three arguments to prove this.

1. These deep things (some of which we have mentioned) constitute a feature of our religion which comports with our experience on all other subjects.

The *facts* which we have mentioned about atonement, incarnation, God's plan of mercy, the innocent suffering in the room of the guilty, and so on, are all *plainly revealed facts*. There is no darkness or depth in *them*. The depth and darkness meet us only as we proceed to philosophize and reason upon the facts, and ask such questions as a man can be a very good Christian without asking or hearing answered. Our reasonings and ex-

planations lead us into the deep things of God, where we
can not reason further, and can not answer a captious
man's inquiries.

Now, we maintain that this experience precisely
assorts with our experience upon other fields of knowledge and ignorance. The principle is this : the further
we proceed in our knowledge of the things of God, the
more deep and wonderful they become. The astronomer
finds it so, and, standing in his contemplation upon the
very last star his glass has reached, he can not have an
item of certainty that there is not more beyond him,
than all he has traveled over. His wonder grew as he
passed the moon, the sun, the planets, and trod along
the milky way; and now, as he casts his keen eye out
upon the illimitable space beyond him, God is beyond
him, his works are beyond him, his system stretches off
and off further, and he is compelled to feel that he has
not yet passed the porch of the temple of God. All he
can do is to wonder ; all he can say is, *Oh the depth, the
depth !*

In the opposite direction of experience, it is the same
thing. In the ever-descending field of a microscopic
study, the philosopher finds God growing more and more
marvelous as he descends. Matter teems with life, with
new forms of life. Millions of living beings inhabit a single
drop of the water, and sport themselves in all the vivacity
of life and enjoyment, with a sprightliness, a beauty of
form, and a perfection of muscular formation and movement, not surpassed by any thing he ever beheld before.
And where that descending life shall stop, how minute
shall be the utmost minuteness of it, in what conceivable
littleness he shall find the least creature that God ever
made, is something on which he dare not venture even a

conjecture. All he can do is to wonder; all he can say is, *Oh the depth, the depth !*

The providences of God afford another example. They are full of wonders. What a marvel is all human history ! How dark the track of the centuries which swept over the world ! They are digging up Nineveh ! They are reading the history of Sennacherib ! An earthquake is a wonder ! A pestilence is a wonder ! What does God mean ? Who can explain him ? Widows and orphans weep upon his earth, fears fill it, graves disfigure its broken surface, and the lean figure of Famine stalks over it and looks up to heaven, and then sinks down and dies in despair. And am I to stand upon the cursed surface of such an earth, and, amid graves and coffins and bones, amid bursting hearts and weaving shrouds and my dying kindred, must I look up into heaven and say, *The whole earth is full of the goodness of the Lord?* How *càn* I say it? An infidel can not ! I defy his tongue—he can not ! God goes beyond our reason. We can understand him a little way, but we soon reach our limits and are compelled to exchange understanding for admiration, *Oh the depth of the riches both of the wisdom and knowledge of God: his ways are past finding out, unsearchable are his judgments !*

2. There are many things of importance, but they are not all of equal value. There is a gradation of worth. The Bible acknowledges and employs this principle. Senseless and unorganized matter lies below the organisms of life. Life itself, as it exists in brutes, is of a lower rank than when it exists in man. The mental kingdom, while superior to the vegetable and animal kingdom, is inferior to the moral. There is, or may be and ought to be, a dignity and felicity in moral existence

surpassing any other. Even God himself is more glorious by being a holy God, than by being an almighty or omniscient God. That he is love is something more than that he is light.

Now, we are very limited creatures, and therefore we can not reasonably expect to have an equal understanding of all subjects; but we must expect to meet with the highest wonders in the highest things and highest departments. An infidel tells us he meets with the most wonders in Christianity. Very well. So he does. For that reason he rejects it, and for that reason we glory in it. For that reason he ought to glory in it too. Consider two arguments here, one taken from the glory of God, and the other from the value of the soul.

(1) God is glorious in every thing, but not in every thing of equal glory. The glory he gains from his universe is various, but his highest glory lies in his saving sinners. It does not lie in his mere holy justice; it does not lie in his building hell; it does not lie in his creating and keeping in heaven such beings as holy angels and holy cherubim and seraphim, exalted and mighty and happy for ever, *thrones and principalities and powers*. The angels who followed Jesus Christ to earth and sung his natal song over Bethlehem, knew this very well: *Glory to God in the highest*, because *on earth peace, good will toward men*.

What then shall we say? On that high field of wonders where God Almighty is more glorious than any where else, shall we demand of him nothing to assort with the magnitude of his own glory? Shall we not expect of him in the most glorious procedure to be more amazing and wonderful than any where else? Shall not our reason, our most cautious reason, our

17

severest reason, *expect* to find more deep and unfathomable things in that transaction which gives him his highest glory, than in any of the other workings of his eternal might and infinite mind? He is wonderful every where, adorable every where—but must be most wonderful, most adorable, where he is most glorious. He extends beyond us every where, but must extend most beyond us just where he is most glorious. Reason, therefore, sheer reason, common sense, ought to teach any man better than to reject Christianity, because of such wonders as lie in the person of Christ, his incarnation, his sufferings and death, and thereby a rendering of satisfaction to Divine justice for sinners. Reason approves the whole when we cease to explain and understand, when we are compelled to pause and adore, *Oh the depth !*

(2) Consider the soul. It is immortal. Perhaps its capacities will expand and enlarge for ever. Blest, its felicity may yet more than equal the joy that exists in heaven ; lost, its woes may yet sink it to a wretchedness that has never been equaled in hell. It is to be saved or lost. But it is a guilty, sinful soul. And to save it, to pluck it out of the jaws of ruin, to pardon its guilt, to still the anger of God, to satisfy and silence the law, and save such an immortal and precious thing from the dreadful doom of eternal death, shall God do nothing more than he would do for a beast of the field or the fowls of the air ? When a *soul* is periled—an immortal soul—when its hell is dug, the flames kindled, and fiends waiting to torment it—shall God for its salvation embark no more wisdom, no more wonders, and manifest no more earnestness than he does about the petty interests of a world of matter and beasts, *and threescore years and*

ten ? Shall God's wisdom and might and earnestness in managing the sun and moon and stars, be the measure or the similitude of the wisdom, might and earnestness which he shall embark to save my periled and immortal soul? God forbid! I declare to you, I could not believe God was in earnest to save me, I could not trust him, I could not credit my Bible, if I did *not* find in it the very mysteries and wonders—those surpassings of reason and those overleapings of analogy—which an infidel complains of. An infidel?—he is a fool! he is no reasoner! he thinks of a soul as he would think of a beast or a mountain; he thinks of sin as he would think of a trifle; he thinks of God's highest glory as if all its wonders must come as much within his comprehension as a problem in arithmetic! *God forbid that I should glory save in the cross of our Lord Jesus Christ, by whom the world is crucified unto me, and I unto the world.* Our doctrines contain all the amazement the infidels have ever attributed to them. This is their glory. This is an evidence of their truth. This is a perfect demonstration of their appropriateness. This is the thing aside from which no truly reasonable man would ever believe them. Reason could not accept a religion which did not compel her to exclaim in adoring wonder, *Oh the depth of . . . of God.*

3. We have not time to expand the argument which might be drawn from the wants of our nature—wants of which we have the testimony of our own consciousness, to more or less extent. Our idea is this: it is in these deep things of God, and these only, that we find any appropriate provision for our deepest and most urgent necessities. Reason can not hope except before the amazing depths of God's wisdom and mercy. As sin-

ners, as dying sinners, we need God to do for us just the wonders he has wrought. Had he *not* done them, we must have despaired. It appears to me that *I know*, just as fully and clearly as I know any thing, that I need to have my God interpose for me, and do for me, as a sinner hasting to the bar of the eternal judgment, such things as he has done nowhere else, and such as have no resemblances in the management of this world.

The wonders of this redemption, the great facts of our religion, all assort with the majesty and mercy of God, the woes of time, the mysteries of the world, and an eternity to come. And yet some of you in this house have never embraced this religion. I have no pleasure in adverting to your state. It is with inconceivable pain that I behold you, year after year, rejecting a religion which would save you, and pursuing a course which must finally land you in everlasting despair. Do you not see, do you not fully understand, that you need just such a Christ, just such an atonement, just such an infinite interposition of God as the Gospel proclaims? Ask your conscience, ask your coffin—put the question any where to your own soul, your fears, your world, your God, or your grave—whether our gospel-redemption in all its wonders is not precisely appropriate to such a sinner as you—such a mortal—such an immortal. And yet what do you mean? You contemn and reject God's most majestic and most appropriate work! You tread under foot the blood of his Son. This afternoon you will turn your back upon the table as an unbeliever. Oh, sinners, pause! Think! You are doing the worst work you could do. Your obstinacy sets at naught that most wonderful work your God ever accomplished! If you perish—if you will perish—the most amazing thing in your perdition—the deepest woe of your hell will come up just in this, that where God did his most wonderful work of mingled and adorable wisdom and mercy, you committed your most wonderful sin, and plucked down ruin from the very hand of infinite grace! Save me from that! Save me from spurning the depths of God. Grace calls you. Listen to the call. Fly to Christ while you may, and you shall be an eternal miracle of grace, an eternal trophy of an interposing God! *Come, for all things are now ready.*

The wonderful redemption of God's people ought to wean them from the world. At his table, this afternoon, I hope they will humbly and adoringly remember where he has done the most for them, and what they ought most to prize. Little as the world must be to you, you have enough of heaven. Let your hearts assort with the grace that secures it to you. Where God is deepest, adore him most, love him most, praise him most, and see that you labor most for that world for which he has done the most for you.

It may very well comfort a Christian that there are such adorable depths in the wonders of redemption. There are depths in sin. Its very existence under the government of a God who hates it is an infinite mystery, and it has whetted the sword of an infinite justice. But at the table of the Lord you are going to handle the emblems of a crucifixion whose august wonders assort with all the depths of guilt. You will take the cup, and in the face of guilt, and law, and justice, and hell, you will exclaim: *The blood of Jesus Christ his Son cleanseth us from all sin: Oh, the depth of the riches both of the wisdom and knowledge of God!*

It may not be an easy thing for a believer to wake up

in his heart the faith of fellowship with God. He is a creature, a very little creature, an unworthy creature—a sinner and a child of the dust. How shall he overstep the distance betwixt him and God, and venture to believe that God will ever condescend to commune with him? Let him say, *Oh, the depth!* and realize that the wonders of redemption accord with all the wonders of his wants.

God has done amazing things for you. He has done them like himself. He has done them in a manner to accord with your condition. He will carry them out to the end. Nothing remains to be done for you more wonderful than he has done already. In a little while you will be done with earth. If you believe, you shall see the salvation of God, you shall exchange the communion of earth for the communion of heaven. When you are stretched upon the bed of death, Jesus Christ shall come to you as he hath promised. He will destroy your *last enemy*. He will bear your released and redeemed spirit up to the *house of many mansions.* As your eyes open upon the splendors of immortality, and your soul laves itself in the ocean of glory, your lips will exclaim, *Oh, the depth! Oh, the depth!*

Sketch of the Plan of Salvation.

[SACRAMENTAL.]

God, who is rich in mercy, for his great love wherewith he loved us, even when we were dead in sins, hath quickened us together with Christ (by grace are ye saved), and hath raised us up together, and made us sit together in heavenly places, in Christ Jesus, that in the ages to come he might show the exceeding riches of his grace in his kindness toward us through Jesus Christ.—EPHESIANS, ii. 4—7.

MY brethren, it is a most oppressive idea which has led us to make choice of these words to aid your devotions this morning. Strange as it may seem that sentiments of grief should have thrown us upon such a passage as this, it is, nevertheless, but too true!

You know little about the trials of a minister. You never realized the difficulty of his studies and the dreadful perplexity of his plans, in those seasons of indifference, barrenness, and backsliding, when, to use the figure of the Apostle, *the Word of God is bound!* At such seasons, it is not easy to preach. It is most difficult. It is most burdensome! When religion prospers —when the beauty and richness of its fruits appear in the lives of its professors—when the unconverted are seeking the Lord—when the members of the Church— pious, prayerful, devoted, happy—are manifestly rising superior to the world and self, and are more anxious about following Christ and becoming like him, than about any thing else; then a minister finds but little difficulty. Whatever subject he chooses it becomes *a word in season;* whatever chord of the heart he would touch he finds it ready to vibrate, strung and tuned as it is to all the influences of religion. Then he may choose subjects, and form plans of sermons, without the burden of the idea to crush him, that these subjects and these plans will all be useless; that in presenting them, he must *sow to the wind and reap the whirlwind!* An uninterested and barren Church is a very different thing to preach to! A congregation of careless unbelievers is a most disheartening audience! To such a people what can a minister say? His words will seem to them *like idle tales!* What subjects shall he choose? What plans shall he form? What trains of thought shall he aim, with all his power, to put into the minds of his hearers, when he knows that the first influences of sin will scatter them all to the winds, and not unlikely the very hearers whom his hard labors strove to bless, will turn and make *him* the butt of their complainings! These are hard times! Their trials strike deep! They make a minister feel as Isaiah did when, forsaken by those who ought to have sustained him, he retires from his toils for man, to indulge his tears with God, and, seated on the lone crag of the mountain rock, he wraps his face in his mantle: *Lord, who hath believed our report?* They make a minister feel as Jeremiah did when, his message rejected by so many, he seems to wish he had never been born: *Woe is me, my mother! thou hast borne me a man of strife and contention to the whole earth!* Or when he seems resolved to renounce a useless ministry which made him so miserable: *The word of the Lord is made a reproach unto me and a derision daily; then I said I will not make mention of him, nor speak any more in his name*—he resolved never to preach another sermon.

This oppressive, this miserable idea, drove me upon this text. It had two influences upon me. One was, I dared not form a plan of a sermon—I dared not select any theme from the wide field of the Gospel, and attempt to explain, divide, demonstrate, and apply it under the ordinary rules of composition. The other was, I hoped— yes I did hope, and I bless God that I *can* hope—that a passage like this, just the ideas of the Holy Ghost, without any plan or arrangement of mine, and a passage so full of the mercy of God, might still find some access to your hearts, and draw you to the Lord's table to-day, under the power of sentiments which shall make this more than a common communion. I hope so still. After you have attended to this preaching of the Holy Ghost, I hope you will be constrained to say : *His word is in my heart as a burning fire shut up in my bones ; I am weary with forbearing and can not stay. Oh Lord ! thou hast drawn me and I was drawn ; thou art stronger than I, and hast prevailed ; draw me and I will run after thee.*

In the text we read to you, the Holy Spirit furnishes a *sketch of the great salvation.* He seems to call the mind to a flight from one eternity to another. He calls it back to the eternity of God, and onward to the eternity of saints. And he fills up the space between the two with all the grace-wrought achievements of the Son of God, and the privileges which belong to the believer. Hear him : *God, who is rich in mercy, for his great love where- with he loved us, even when we were dead in sins, hath quickened us together with Christ, and hath raised us up to- gether, and made us sit together in heavenly places in Christ Jesus ; that in the ages to come he might show the exceeding riches of his grace in his kindness toward us through Jesus Christ.* What a sketch! What a wonderful sketch of the *great salvation!* It goes from eternity to eternity. It shows the whole redeeming operations of God for poor sinners like us, *dead and alive again.* It contains a condensation of the Gospel; what a sinner was, and what grace makes him. So the Holy Ghost preaches to us. God grant it may not be in vain to our hearts.

In this Sketch of our salvation there are *seven* leading ideas :—

Its Author, *God.*

Its origin, *rich mercy.*

Its motive, *great love wherewith he loved us.*

The condition in which it finds its subjects, *dead in sin.*

Its operation, *hath quickened us together with Christ.*

Its exaltation, *hath raised us up together and made us sit together in heavenly places in Christ.*

Its glorious and everlasting purpose, *that in the ages to come he might show the exceeding riches of his grace in his kindness toward us through Jesus Christ.*

These are the ideas and this the order of the Holy Spirit. We will not go beyond them. Let us take these as the sermonizing of the Spirit, and if we are not moved by it, let *our* hearts not *his* method bear the blame.

Truth, you know, is in order to holiness. Light, knowledge, is the sanctifying instrumentality of God. The Author of our being deals with us according to the nature he has given us. Having formed us with minds and hearts capable of understanding and being affected by the truth, he does not approach us to affect us, to do us good, to offer us the blessings of his grace, or confer them upon us, as if we were to have no active and willing agency in receiving them. He expects us to conspire

with him. When he unfolds truth, he expects us to see
it. When he impresses it, he expects us to feel it.
When he points out its end and aim, he expects us to
put shoes on our feet, take *staff in our hand*, turn our face
toward *the wilderness*, and travel through its deserts by
faith, if we would ever reach the green fields of our
promised land. And when he preaches such sermons as
the text, it is for no mere exhibit of great principles, but
to have us *use* the principles—to have our faith, our
hearts, and our habits helped by them, if we would ever
expect to be saved. These ideas about our salvation are
full of meaning. They ought not to leave us barren of
either Christian improvements or Christian comforts.
Let us enter upon them.

1. In this sketch the *Author* of salvation is mentioned:
It is God.

My dear friends, your salvation would have been a
very different matter if this article had been different.
Had its authorship been any where else; had it been in
nature; had this system been nothing more than one of
the common operations of Deity on those principles which
we denominate natural principles, that fact would have
changed the whole system; and the human mind and
human heart *ought* then to have been affected by it in a
very different manner. A miracle is one thing, and the
common operation of God in his providence is quite another thing. The comparison is just. There is no extravagance in it. Salvation is a miracle—an infinite
miracle. In the whole, God is the Author. God, just as
much distinguished in the moral means and moral
achievements of salvation from all his other moral
achievements and means, as he is distinguished in a
miracle from his ordinary works. The man who walks

abroad in all the strength and agility of his feet, does so by the power of God, and he ought to realize it. When he goes into the contest in which his fleetness or strength gives him hope, he ought to remember that, without God, *the race is not to the swift nor the battle to the strong.* But far different ought to be the emotions of one, a *cripple from his birth,* now gifted with the ordinary powers of a man. He ought to be in the TEMPLE, *walking, and leaping, and praising God.* God is as emphatically and singularly the author of salvation as he is the author of that strength which has come to the cripple's bones. This salvation is a new work of God. It is as much out of the way of the ordinary operations of God as the healing of a man *lame from his mother's womb.* It is something of which God is the author by as direct an interposition, and an interposition as much removed from his common operations, as a miracle is from any ordinary fact. All the powers and principles of human nature, impelled by all the motives of a contemplated immortality, and aided by all the light of the universe, and all the sympathies and strength of it, too, from among angels and men, could never have saved the soul of one poor sinner. Man might have sighed and angels might have sympathized with him and lent him all their aid; he might have taxed the powers of his heart amid all the bright lessons of the universe which tell him of the goodness of God; but never could one soul have been saved had not God himself undertaken the work. This is an important idea.

Salvation becomes a very different thing to me when I see it flowing from the operations of God—operations above and beyond all his ordinary operations on matter and on mind! It attaches me to the Deity by a new principle. It shows me God himself making for me a new system and a new world! It attaches an infinitely higher value to my salvation, and attaches me to my Redeemer as *my Lord and my God.* And I feel alike bound and inclined to be as much more grateful and devoted on this account, as I should be for my power of walking, if a miracle, and not nature, had given me feet.

2. In this sketch of salvation furnished in the text by the Holy Ghost, the *Origin* of salvation is mentioned: it is the *rich mercy* of God. This is the origin of the Gospel method. God acts in *mercy, in rich mercy,* when he saves sinners like us. It is not in justice, though not contrary to it. It is not goodness merely. It is goodness of a new and peculiar kind. Mercy is the exercise of good-will toward those who have not merited good-will. And the mercy, the *rich mercy* which saves us, is the exercise of God's good-will toward those who have merited anger and punishment. This is peculiar to the Gospel system and operations. There is nothing like it any where else. When I go out among the works of God, and witness a thousand operations which diffuse happiness over his fair and bright creation, I see testimonies enough that God is good. I find no contrivance or operation designed wholly, and working wholly to produce unhappiness. True, I find hearts bleeding, and know the sensibilities which make them bleed were planted in them by God. But I know, too, that the same sensibilities are needful as qualifications for felicity; and that a heart which, in such a world as this, could not be sad, could not be happy. Moreover, I find proofs enough within me and without me, that there is such a thing as the joy of grief—something like many recollections of the past, as sweet as they are mournful to the soul. And especially

I find in the clustering, though qualified felicities of the world, that its Maker has done much to make it happy. I find direct proofs of this. All the utilities of the vegetable world, for example, could have been compassed by God if no Divine pencil had touched, with rich and sweet coloring, the blossoms of the spring-time. Those hues of beauty which do so much to please the eye are not needful for fruits or timber. God could have caused both without them. In such things; in the thousand tasteful adornings of his universe; in the felicities of the wild-bird that carols on the wing; in the felicities of the beast upon his sunny hills; of the inhabitants of the sea, who sport from its azure surface down to the depths of the ocean's bed; we find indisputable testimonies of the goodness of the Deity. These testimonies (I am not going to undervalue them) may be *tokens* of mercy. I mean they may be *hints* flung out to man to make the *inquiry*, whether in God their author there may not be goodness which shall reach to the sinfully unworthy. But nothing answers this inquiry. The earth, the heavens, are silent. In all the universe there is not the least item of proof that the goodness of God will ever save the guilty. This goodness—and it is *rich mercy*— is revealed solely in the Gospel. Salvation on this ac- count becomes a very different thing to me. I see in it the *rich mercy* of God. I see God, its author, operating in a new field, and on new principles, in such a *way* as he operates nowhere else; for I see the atonement of the Divine Redeemer, and the special operations of the Holy Ghost. This attaches me to salvation by a new tie, an unequaled demonstration of God's love for me. It gives me a new lesson about the Deity. It demonstrates to me, what all God's goodness to creatures on earth and to angels in heaven could not demonstrate. For it shows me that the Divine goodness operates to reach those deserving of punishment and anger. *Mercy*, rich *mercy* is the origin of my salvation. Nothing else could originate it. God never did any thing else like it. God acts here as he acts nowhere else; and I feel myself bound to him by a loftier principle than any which binds an archangel in heaven. If sin is the greatest evil, salvation is the greatest of all God's wonderful achievements. For me mercy operates: for me—a sinner, a wanderer from God, whom justice not only, but all God's *other goodness* would properly have left to the eternal wages of sin—rich mercy intervenes, and originates the salvation of God.

3. And God in this operation was moved by *love: For his great love wherewith he loved us*. My brethren, when we attempt *to reason* about the feelings of the Deity, we are exceedingly liable to err. The theme is too vast for us. We can never compass it. What should move God, how could we tell? We are only the creatures of a day, and soon perish. We are little and limited beings. We whose reason can proceed but a little way among *things seen and temporal;* we whose powers are baffled at every step; we erring mortals; we worms, dust and ashes; what could we tell about the Deity? How could we dive into the depths of the Infinite Mind, and tell what should move *that high and lofty one who inhabiteth eternity?* Hide, hide thyself in the dust, thou diminutive creature! Tremble and quail, thou guilty sinner! *As high as heaven, what canst thou do? deeper than hell, what canst thou know?* But stop! No. Lift up thy head, thou trembling mortal! The Gospel speaks to thee. Be not afraid. The Gospel tells thee what feeling it is that moves thy God. Thou, miserable wretch! thou, a

fearful trembling sinner! thou, whose sighs began with thy first breath, and will not cease till thy last breath has left thy nostrils; thou didst move the Infinite Mind! *God loved thee*, thou miserable sinner! The dark uncertainties of creation and providence are put to flight by the Gospel. GOD IS LOVE. We need not reason about the feelings of the Deity toward us. We *know* what they are. *The great love wherewith he loved us* beams on us its demonstrations from every page of the Gospel, and drives to a returnless distance the dark and distressful uncertainties which reason must always have left to hang like a pall around the nature of God!

Again, this attaches me to the Gospel. My salvation commenced in *love*. Not in might, not in majesty, not in any of those attributes of grandeur which fling such fearfulness and awe around the throne of God's almightiness! No, no. It began in *love*. This is what my heart wants—just what it wants. It wants *God* to *love* me. Nothing else will do. In a few days I am going to be cut off from all the endearments and sympathies of life. My friends, my wife, my children—if they live, I must die! I haste to the end. The grave is ready to receive me, and I sink into its bosom! Neither in that cold spot nor in the country beyond it can the loves of the world reach me! In that country I shall possess these same sensibilities, my spirit will be such that I shall want something to love, and want some being to love me. Earthly loves may do very well for me here. They may still the throbbings of many an anxious hour, smooth the pillow for my dying head, and let me know that the clay I am forsaking shall have a decent burial. But for my eternity no love but God's will do for me. If he can love me, sinner as I am, and I can know and love him, then I am perfectly assured that nothing shall ever arise in the mighty roll of eternal ages that shall dash my joys, and make me a miserable creature. This is enough. To have my God love me is enough. The Gospel assures me that he *has* loved me, and loved me though a sinner ; and has given an infinite and bloody demonstration of that love; *the* demonstration—the *only* demonstration which could ever satisfy my heart in respect to his love ; namely, that his love has made a precious SACRIFICE for me. And, now, if my faith embraces that love, I can look for the sympathies, and kindness, and tenderness of my God and Maker, in all the exigences which may betide me, from the death-bed where earthly loves forsake me, onward to the remotest ages of eternity. This attaches me to God by the right bond and right demonstration. It satisfies my hopes and my heart when I know the *great love wherewith my God loved me. Even when we were dead in sins,* adds this Sketch of the Holy Ghost. It is the fourth idea.

4. The love of God reached us when we were in a most unworthy and miserable condition. We were *dead in sins.* Two ideas are included here. One is, that our transgressions deserved, and had incurred the penalty of the law of God, eternal death. The other is, that sin had put out the life of the soul, removed from it all qualifications of spiritual existence, all power of doing and enjoying any thing agreeable to God, and in which the soul of man finds its best and highest portion. Such is man. He is a *dead* man. He is dead to holiness, dead to heaven, dead to God, dead to all the interests which fill up the eternity that awaits him ! He can enjoy many delights. Amid the things of the world he can gratify his tastes, and fill up the little hour of life with day-

dreams of pleasure vanishing one after another, at the touches of truth and his own experience. But he can not enjoy God, and can not enjoy himself but little. His own mind often troubles him, and he becomes his own tormentor when he realizes partially, as sometimes he must realize, that in his irreligious course he is doing much and suffering much to gain nothing but a winding-sheet, a coffin, and a grave; and beyond these a *fearful looking-for of judgment*, indignation and wrath, tribulation and anguish! He does not love his God, and can not enjoy him. Without this salvation, he must have all his *good things in his life-time;* and then it would be better for that man if he had never been born.

Salvation is wrought out for this guilty and unworthy creature. And *such,* my dear brethren, *were ye. But ye are washed, but ye are sanctified, but ye are justified, in the name of the Lord Jesus and by the Spirit of our God.* The love of God reached you when ye were in that guilty and unworthy condition. And this afternoon we are going to rejoice in it, and sing about it—

> " 'Twas love that kept the throne,
>   And wrath stood silent by,
>   When God's eternal Son came down
>   To groan, and bleed, and die."

I hope you will be able to sing happily, and in all the sweetness of a Divine hope. Ye ought to be. The order in which the Holy Ghost has placed this idea in the text is most consolatory—God *loved us even when we were dead in sins.*

I have often thought that if it were not for two ideas in the Gospel, half the anxious world would be driven to despair. This is one of them: *Even when we were dead*

in sin, the great love of God reached us. AND, IF IT
REACHED US THERE, IS IT EVER GOING TO FAIL US? Blessed, blessed argument! I declare to you that if salvation
were not published to me as thus gratuitous, thus gracious—God loving the sinner where he might most righteously have sent him to perdition—I should often find all
the light of my hope going out under the oppression of
the fear that I had sinned beyond the reach of all the
mercy of God! In my heart what ingratitude! what
forgetfulness of God! what pride! what coldness! what
vanity! what hardness after all the mercies he has shown
me! But when I remember this preaching of the Holy
Spirit: *God loved us when we were dead in sins;* I HOPE HE
WILL LOVE ME STILL. This is one of the ideas.

The other is linked with it. *He that spared not his own*
SON, *but freely delivered him up for us all, how shall he not*
with him also freely give us all things? These two ideas
are enough. Despair has no business to afflict a creature whom God loved, WHEN THERE WAS NOTHING IN
HIM TO BE LOVED—when he was *dead in sin!* and
despair has no business in a world which has furnished a
cradle and a cross for the Son of God. I may have
Christ for mine; and if I have him, I have all that a sinful and guilty creature can ever want.

> " The Lord 's my shepherd—I 'll not want ;
> He makes me down to lie
> In pastures green ; he leadeth me
> The quiet waters by."

5. Hence the fifth idea of this Sketch of salvation is
its *operation : Hath quickened us together with Christ.*
The meaning of this is that *God quickens* believers (or
makes them alive from their spiritual death) in regenera-

tion just as really as the dead body of Christ, torn and
mangled, and laid in the tomb, was made alive again.
His resurrection was a copy of theirs, and theirs is on
account of him. They live in him. When he rises they
rise. *Because he lives they shall live also.* Oh what bright
and blessed links in this chain of salvation which lifts us
to heaven! Jesus Christ is the head of the church and
representative of his people. He is God's pledge *to*
them. He became their surety. The Father accepted
him as such, and the demonstration that he fulfilled all
the demands upon his suretyship was to be found in
his resurrection from the dead. He rose the conqueror
of death, and laden with the spoils of the grave; and
the same Divine power by which he came back from the
dead, operates when a sinner is regenerated and made a
new creature in Christ.

This operation has been occupying some of your
thoughts, while you have been preparing for this communion season. You have been considering the Divine
life in your souls. You have been looking back upon
the past, and remembering what you were.

One of you has been saying: Years have rolled on
since I first became a communicant. Grace met me, I
hope, a great while ago. But it *was* grace. There was
nothing in me then, and there is nothing in me now by
reason of which I could ever live to God, and hope to be
purified and live with him in heaven. The more I see
of my heart, through all this course of years, the more
experimental proofs I find that just *by the grace of God I
am what I am.*

Another of you has been saying: This hope of mine
is the work of God I am a *new creature,* and *God's workmanship in Christ Jesus.* Once I was far different from

this., I neglected religion; I did not love God. I was worldly. I was envious. I was covetous. I was proud and unforgiving. But now I can forgive my bitterest enemies. I love God, and love his service. I can give up the world and take Jesus; and I humbly hope that he who has begun a good work in me will perform it until the day of Jesus Christ.

Another of you has been saying: A few years since, I thought the world was every thing. An ardent boy, my heart panted for riches, honors, pleasures. My thoughts were all occupied about the world. I plunged into it. I forgot God! I forgot death! I neglected prayer! I was bound toward perdition! But grace rescued me from my dreadful delusion and peril! God opened my eyes and led me to *seek first the kingdom of heaven.*

Another of you has been saying: A little while ago I was a wild, giddy girl! I cared little for the love of God! I lived for the pleasures of the world. If I prayed at all, it was by constraint, and not from the attractions of holiness and the love of my God. But grace saved me. It was God's own operation. He sent the message which opened my eyes to see the precipice on which I was sporting, and down which it is a thousand wonders that I had not plunged! He opened my heart to the love of Jesus; and made me know that this love is better than all other loves. Oh, I would not go back to the world:

> " Jesus, I my cross have taken,
>   All to leave and follow thee.
> Perish every fond ambition,
>   All I 've sought, or loved, or known;
> Yet how blest is my condition,
>   God and heaven are still mine own."

Another of you has been saying: I am now going to

the communion-table: I do hope in the mercy of my God. Only a few days ago I was struggling with this dark and dreadful heart! It would not break, it would not bow! I saw I was lost, *dead in sin*, an enemy of God, but my heart would not yield! All was a wilderness to me! My thoughts quarreled with God's law, with its awful penalty, with its strictness, with my own helplessness, and even with the system of free grace and the offers of the Holy Spirit to aid me! I was too proud and self-righteous for these! But truth pressed upon me. The light of my hope went out, and I expected to have made my bed in hell! But my God saved me! He sent from above: *He took me, he drew me out of many waters*, and put peace into this bleeding heart!

The preparation you have been making for this afternoon has reminded you that your salvation was the operation of God.

I hope it hath done more than this. I hope it hath brought you to the

6th Idea of this sermon of the Holy Spirit: *Hath raised us up together, and made us sit together in heavenly places in Christ Jesus.*

There are two ideas included in this EXALTATION of the believer with Christ. The one is that of the *covenant;* the other is that of *experience.* You may take your choice. They are both fit for the communion-table. The one is, that just as surely as God hath raised from the dead and exalted the Saviour to heaven, just so surely will he bring the believer there. This is so certain, on the promise and covenant of God, that this exaltation is spoken of as bestowed already. It *is* bestowed. It is given in the everlasting covenant of God to every one that embraces, in faith, his Son. And no matter what obstacles and sins may seem to oppose, what wildernesses must be traveled over, or what Red Seas or Jordans must be passed, the believer shall at last reach heaven, just as certainly as his Saviour has got there—as certainly as God is true. This is the idea of the covenant. Christ, the covenant head, is in heaven, and that is Jehovah's pledge, in the sight of men, angels, and devils, that where *he is* believers *shall be also.*

The other idea is that of *experience.* I can but name it now. I hope I need not do more. I hope you will come to the Lord's table this afternoon in such a frame of soul that you will know what it means to *sit in heavenly places in Christ Jesus.* You *will* know, if YOU HAVE GRACE ENOUGH TO ENJOY GRACE ABOVE EVERY THING ELSE, delighting in God. The experiences of grace are the exaltation of the believer. They are such when he feels that it is better for him to be a believer than to be any thing else. Then the soul is lifted to communion with God. It experiences those communications of grace which lift it away to another world, and loses itself in the depths and enjoyment of that love which the Father has manifested to us in the gift and crucifixion of his Son. Then the believer loses sight of the world. It has faded from his view as he has been lifted up into the sight of the heavenly city. He resembles Peter on the mount of transfiguration : *Lord, it is good for us to be here.* He wishes never to go down again : *Let us build three tabernacles.* Blessed experience, to be permitted to enjoy through Christ a holy delight in God, and the tenderness of a heart-intimacy with him ! I would rather be a redeemed sinner than any thing else—delivered by love from going down to eternal burnings. Angels can never love Christ as a redeemed sinner loves him. He has never done for angels what he has done for poor sinners. In their songs of personal gratitude, there is no verse about Bethlehem. There is no tale of bloody memory such as the Christian sings in the garden of Gethsemane. And if angels *stand in his presence*, surely a redeemed sinner may come nearer still; may lie at his feet and lean on his bosom, and look up in his face and sing,

"Love I much, I 've much forgiven!"

This is the idea of experience included in the believer's exaltation.

Both these ideas are fit for the communion-table. We come there to enter into covenant with God; and we come there as redeemed and forgiven sinners to indulge our hearts in loving him *who first loved us.* These two ideas are the believer's exaltation, for these things are the most like heaven of any thing that lies on this side of the river of death. Let us see:

In heaven the soul has got home to God; and sins, and fears, and death done with, it feels perfectly secured for all that it can ever want during the ceaseless life-time of eternity. In the *covenant*, the soul enters into that same security here. The covenanting believer has all he wants. *All things are* his. *Life, death* is his; for he is Christ's. Nothing can harm him any more. *All things shall work for his good.* He shall never shed a tear too much, nor have a trial too sad, nor die too painfully or too quick. Hear his *covenant* song:

"Man may trouble and distress me,
  'Twill but drive me to thy breast;
Earth with trials hard may press me—
  Heaven will grant me sweeter rest."

In heaven the redeemed soul has the full enjoyment

of God. It is filled with his love, and is like him. The believer then *walks with Christ in white;* and, remembering Calvary and the cross, he joins in the anthem of redemption: *Unto him that loved us and washed us from our sins in his own blood.* In his experiences here the believer resembles this. They are a foretaste of heaven. They make him resemble heaven. They make him holy while they make him happy. If in these experiences you come unto the *banqueting-house* this afternoon, you will have something of that sweet, and deep, and solemn, and satisfying joy which you are going to have when grace has conducted you to your heavenly home. You will be *seated in heavenly places in Christ.*

But you can not always be here. The vacant seats which death has made in your circle at your communion-table, warn you that your last communion is coming. Well—let it come.

There is another item in this sermon of the Holy Spirit: *That in the ages to come he might show the exceeding riches of his grace, in his kindness toward us through Jesus Christ.*

7. This is the glorious and eternal *purpose* of the plan of our salvation. There is something most consolatory in this idea. I know not how to express it. But I see in it what is elsewhere expressed, that God purposes to save me *for his own name's sake;* that, in *the ages* of eternity, *the exceeding riches of his grace in his kindness toward us through Jesus Christ* may show the glory of the grace of God to an astonished and adoring universe!

My salvation would be a very different thing to me if its purpose were not thus taken from the Deity himself. But now I see God is interested in saving me. It will be his *highest glory* to save such poor sinners. Angels

18

may manifest his might, but blood-bought sinners will manifest his love! *In the ages to come*, angels and the archangel shall see it with infinite and eternal wonder! *For he hath created all things by Christ Jesus* TO THE INTENT *that unto principalities and powers in heavenly places, might be made known* BY THE CHURCH—(a body of redeemed sinners)—*the manifold wisdom of God.* A redeemed sinner is a miracle, and will be a miracle to all eternity! In the bosom of God, and sprinkled with the blood that bought him, there angels will wonder at him; and *he* will wonder, and adore, and love for ever, on account of the *exceeding riches of grace*, the KINDNESS and LOVE *of God through Jesus Christ* our Lord. Oh! I can not despair of heaven! Sin, unworthiness, weakness, devils, can not make me despair! My salvation commenced from the very depths of the Divine nature, the unfathomable LOVE *of God;* and the full accomplishment of it shall be that which will give the brightest luster to the diadem of the King of kings! If I could *not* hope that God would save me for *my* sake, the Gospel still would let me hope that God *will* save me for his own sake; and hence *I will hope*, for the greater my sin, the greater God's own glory in saving me! My prayer shall take that argument—and I can use it any where this side of the belly of hell: Save me for thine own name sake! Glorify thyself—glorify thy Son—by bringing me home to heaven.

To that heaven, my dear people—to those ages to come—this Sketch of Salvation, drawn by the Holy Ghost, calls you to look forward. I told you I could not preach to you; but let this text preach. Are you ready for that heaven? Are you preparing for it? Is the Divine life, into which you profess to have been *quickened,* vigorous and growing in your souls? Do you enjoy God? Do you realize your exaltation, your high felicity and glory in being Christians, the beloved children of God, and redeemed by his love? Are you happy in Christianity? This afternoon you are coming to its central scene—the death of the eternal Son of God to save *you* from hell! *He* loved *you.* When you were *dead in sin* he loved you and *gave himself a ransom for you.*

Does your heart love him? Do you embrace this salvation of God as the best and highest portion you are ever to enjoy? And can you now send out your anticipations, with the text, to the eternity of saints? Can you go up upon the top of Mount Calvary, and, amid the rending rocks, the vinegar, the gall, and the spear, the darkened heavens and the dying prayers of the Son of God, can you say: I take this Saviour—this blood for my own? And then, going out upon the top of Mount Olivet, and lifting your eyes after the ascending Saviour, going to *his* God, now *your* God, and *his* Father, now *your* Father, can you exclaim, He has gone *to prepare a place for me; he will come again and receive me to himself.*

God grant it to you *according to the exceeding riches of his grace, in his kindness toward us through Jesus Christ.*

Christ Stricken.

[SACRAMENTAL.]

For the transgression of my people was he stricken.—ISAIAH, liii. 8.

IT is probable that the mode of expression employed in the prophetical writings has some regard to the manner in which it pleased God to show the prophets what was yet to come. He gave them knowledge of futurity; for the benefit of his church through all generations, he led them to make record of their knowledge. And it is reasonable to suppose that the style of the record was influenced by the way in which their knowledge came to their mind.

That way we can not explain. It lies beyond us. God inspired them, and he has not seen fit to tell us by what machinery, or whether by any, he led them to know facts still hidden in the dark bosom of a vailed futurity.

But there are some expressions connected with this subject which lead us to suppose that God gave the prophets a view—an eye vision—of the future. They are sometimes called *seers*. They are said to have had *visions*. This indicates that their knowledge came, not by *hearing*, but by *sight*. And it is probable that God spread out before their eye a picture—that he painted, mapped futurity for them—made it pass before their eye; and after they knew his revelation, they wrote it down.

Isaiah was a *seer*. He had his *visions* of futurity. He knew their truth. He had visions of many sorts. And you may have noticed, perhaps, in reading his prophe- cies, how, when he comes to any matter which pertains to Christ, there are three things which give to his style a new cast—a peculiarity.

First, there is an *elevation* about it. His mind rises— his words rush like a torrent—as his language labors and staggers under the mighty significance with which it is loaded.

Second, there is a *clearness* about it. It has a splendor as of the sun. He seems to have stood, not in the mid- night, but in the noonday of futurity, all the darkness of coming centuries lifted away.

Third, there is an *amplification* about it. When the prophet comes upon the time of the Messiah, he lingers upon it; he seems reluctant to leave it. He clings to it with unwonted tenacity. He can rush over centuries— he can dispose of them with a single dash of his pen ; he can sweep on by kings, and crumbling thrones, and dying millions, and sinking ages of Time's great march; but when he comes down to the period of the *Star in the East*, he pauses—he lingers—he exemplifies—his mind moves backward and forward from Bethlehem to Cal- vary, from Calvary back to Bethlehem ; he follows the track of Christ and never loses sight of him till he is laid in the tomb. And from the spot of that entomb- ment he takes the key-note of his song of exaltation. He sees salvation. He sees the redeemed church radiant with glory. *Awake, awake, put on thy strength, O Zion; put on thy beautiful garments, O Jerusalem, the holy city.*

. . . *Shake thyself from the dust, O Jerusalem; loose thyself from the bonds of thy neck, O captive daughter of Zion. . . . Break forth into joy, sing together, ye waste places of Jerusalem, for the Lord hath comforted his people. . . . Sing, O barren, break forth into singing. . . . Enlarge the place of thy tent and let them stretch the curtains of thine habitations. Fear not, thou shalt not be ashamed, for thy Maker is thy husband. The Lord of Hosts is his name; and thy Redeemer, the Holy One; the God of the whole earth shall he be called.*

These are the prophet's peculiarities of style as compared with himself, whenever he comes upon the times and trials of Christ. You may find them all exemplified in the connection of our text. We can not now examine it for you. Take the lesson alone. Begin with the fifty-first chapter and end with the fifty-fifth, and you will see what we intend.

The text comes in where the prophet comes to the period of Christ; comes thus elevated, clear as the sun, and disposed to linger on the bright vision—bright to *him* and to every redeemed sinner, but dark and dreadful to the Victim from whose shame and throes and tomb all this light arises, to spread over time and over eternity.

For the transgression of my people was he stricken. Isaiah had seen it. God had showed it to him as he rolled back the heavy midnight which lay upon slumbering centuries. Hence his language is that of history. He *was* stricken. To Isaiah it was all passed, as he turned from his vision to his pen and his faith, and he makes the record, not as a Jew, not as a prophet, not as a man, a being of time simply, but as a soul lifted above centuries that died at his feet, as the ocean waves die on the shore.

For the transgression of my people was he stricken.

If an ordinary reader has any doubt about the significance of this text, the inspired writer of the Acts of the Apostles has put it beyond all question. This is the *place of the Scripture* which the Ethiopian was reading to whom the Spirit sent Philip. You will find part of the seventh and eighth verses of this chapter quoted in the eighth chapter of the Acts. What the Ethiopian could not understand, was, of whom Isaiah was here speaking. Philip told him. He *began at the same* Scripture and *preached unto him Jesus.*

He explained the whole passage. He showed the fullness of salvation and the extension of the Church in gospel times promised in the Scriptures which the Ethiopian had been reading, as in the last verse of the fifty-second chapter: *so shall he sprinkle many nations.* This made the Ethiopian think of professing his faith as a Christian and being baptized, and Philip baptized him.

In the efficacy of Christ's *death* the Ethiopian believed. It was *Christ* who *was stricken.*

For the transgression of my people. This explanation is very specific: *my people*, not others, it would seem. We can not stop here to unfold this idea, and explain how general and how limited was the atonement made by Jesus Christ for sinners. Conflicts of opinion on this subject are easily reconcilable to all truly Christian and enlightened minds. Every body confesses that the expiation made by Christ for sinners was sufficient for the whole world, if the whole world would trust it. All agree, therefore, in the unbounded nature of the sacrificial offering. Every body confesses that all sinners will not be saved by this expiation, and that, therefore, when *God laid on him the iniquity of us all,* his covenant election, his determination, extended no further than *his people.*

All agree, therefore, in the certain aim of Jehovah in this transaction.

Every body confesses that the offer of Christ to sinners is made freely in the Gospel, *without money and without price.* All agree, therefore, in the warrant for a sinner's faith, that sinners may take and trust him if they will. Every body confesses that none of God's people will ever be saved by the expiation of Christ without repentance, faith, and holiness. All agree, therefore, in the necessity of personal religion. These are agreements enough.

If, on the one hand, any believer chooses to look upon the whole world in view of Christ's death, and mourn that so many have *trodden under foot his blood,* and will finally perish as *despisers of his grace,* how shall we reprove them? If, on the other hand, any believer chooses to look back upon the eternal covenant of grace, wherein Christ's people were given to him *before the foundation of the world,* and view Christ's death as a fulfillment on his part of the condition of the covenant, how shall we reprove him? How shall these two believers reprove one another? Do they not agree? Or, if not, are not those points wherein they disagree points beyond the range of revelation, and, therefore, beyond the obligations of faith, points to be understood only when we shall no longer *see as through a glass darkly,* no *longer see in part and prophesy in part.*

My people: God called the whole nation his people sometimes, and whether he means this here, or means only those who shall finally be his in heaven, the general doctrine of the text is not altered.

The doctrine is that of an expiation for sinners, made by an innocent Victim substituted in their place. He was *stricken for them. He laid down his life for the sheep.* He died to *redeem them that were under the curse.* The sufferings of Christ were expiatory of sin. They were penal sufferings. Christ died not merely to rescue us from the ruin into which we had fallen, but from the punishment which we had merited. This is the doctrine of the text.

The religion of Christianity consists very much in believing in and being affected by THE DEATH of Jesus Christ in a proper manner. Toward that one offering all eyes ought to be turned. Toward it all the prophecies and ancient symbols look. There all the promises center. There hope begins for sinners. There God meets them, his *anger being turned away from them.* It is his *death* that saves—not his life. Paul would preach nothing but *Christ and him* CRUCIFIED, *slain for us.* Our most solemn ordinance memorializes his dying. We have none to memorialize his birth.

Indeed, no living man knows the time of his birth. History has not preserved it, and God has not told it. It is wrapped in profound mystery, just as if God would hold our eyes steadily fixed on his death. And he was born, he became man, too, not for the sake of living, but for the sake of dying, that he might *taste death for every man.*

We have often been compelled to pause, and tremble, and shrink back, when we have come upon the borders of this theme. It is too mighty. It seems to lie beyond us. It is the great work of God in redemption, and is the mother of the spiritual faith and spiritual feeling of his people; and we know full well that faith and feeling can go beyond words. And, therefore, we have been afraid, painfully afraid, that any ideas we could utter, instead of aiding you, would clip the wings of your faith and damp the ardor of your feelings, and hold you back from soaring to God. Let your hearts and your aids of the Holy Spirit, gained by prayer, compensate for the imperfections of language and our ideas.

For the transgression of my people was he stricken. In the substitution of an innocent being to suffer in the room of the guilty, (and especially such a Being as Jesus Christ,) and in pardoning and accepting the guilty into favor on that account, there is something which seems to stagger the human mind. It appears a departure from all our common ideas of justice and propriety. It appears to set God himself before us in a character almost the opposite of his own declarations, as the friend of the holy, and as taking vengeance upon the wicked. He here seems to contradict himself: He punishes the innocent and lets the wicked go free. Not only so, but the innocent is a Divine Person—the Eternal Son of God; and that *He* should be the stricken sufferer increases the matter of amazement. Still further is our wonder and difficulty of mind enhanced when this act stands alone—when nothing else like it is seen in all the movements, and all the revelations of God.

My brethren, we have no disposition to diminish this singularity. It has all the wonderfulness you have ever attributed to it. It stands alone. God never did any thing else like it. Here we approach a strange matter. And it is no wonder that minds have been staggered when they have aimed to grapple with this infinite and amazing revelation.

But we certainly shall fail of the just and real essence of the Christian religion in our hearts, if our hearts do not have faith in just this expiation; and if our minds can not compass the whole amazing matter, we may hope at least to have some gleams of illumination, like the lightning's flash on the dark bosom of the storm.

Let us see:

I. The wonder of this punishment for sin laid upon an innocent and Divine Being, accords with our best conceptions of God.

The most just conceptions that we ever have of the Deity is that of an incomprehensible Being. He is infinite, and therefore beyond mind. It is necessary to conceive of him in this manner. This is what distinguishes our just conceptions of God from our just conceptions of any other beings. Other beings are limited. Our imagination can soon work its way up to the boundaries of their strength, their wisdom, their intelligence, and all there is about them. God is unlimited. Far on as our imagination may travel, it gets no nearer to the boundaries of God. He has none. At the very last stages we are as far off as when we began. God does not come in to be weighed and gauged among the analogies of his universe.

You perceive the conclusion. The high wonder of this expiation agrees with the infinitude of God. It is like him. He is his own analogy. A suffering Christ is an infinite wonder; and, therefore, the wonder of the doctrine of an expiation for sinners by the sufferings of the innocent, instead of being a reason for our incredulity, is really a reason for our faith. Those ideas of justice which we have from the legal transactions among men, among the little and limited interests of a contemptible world to be burnt up, and among the relations soon to sink down for ever into the ocean bosom of eternity, have no right to come in as measure, and gauge and limit, for the justice of that *High and lofty One who inhabiteth eternity.*

This expiation by the *stricken* victim has relation to him. *His* rights were violated. *His* justice must be maintained. The interests of all our eternity were periled. Our relations with God himself were broken up.

As we conceive of the *power* of God, we are satisfied with no limit, and no analogy. If we speak of him as *laying the foundation of the mountains, taking up the isles as a very little thing, or guiding Arcturus and his sons,* we employ the mountains, the isles, and the stars, only as aids to our feeble conceptions, as stepping-stones to help us on. They are not the measure of God's might. It has no measure. It has no resemblance. God's will is his power. He can work without means, and do one thing just as easily as he does another.

As we conceive of God's *intelligence* we are satisfied with no limit, and no analogy. He reads hearts. He knows all things at once. He knows them without means. He never studies, never reasons, never employs one thing to aid him on to another. By direct inspection he sees into all things; yea, indeed, he knows all things, *without* inspection, by the eternal models of them existing for ever in the purposes of his own mind.

As we conceive of God's *presence,* we are satisfied with no limit, and no analogy. He does not move from one place to another. He fills immensity with his presence. *If we ascend up into heaven, he is there; if we make our bed in hell, he is there.*

As we conceive of God's *existence*, we are satisfied with no limit and no analogy. He did not begin to exist like every thing else. Eternity is his life-time. Centuries die at his feet, to him just the same as vanishing moments. With him *one day is as a thousand years, and a thousand years as one day.*

Such is God in all things. It may be difficult for our minds to take in these conceptions, but we can have no just idea of God without them. He is his own analogy —every where infinite, and every where beyond comparison.

And now, when we are called upon to view him and trust him in the matter of saving his people, we have but to give him his own high place, and let him be God, without limit and without resemblance. Glory to him that he is so. The innocence of the Victim, and the person of the Victim, and the expiation of the Victim, all accord with the incomprehensible God. *Great is the mystery of Godliness—God manifest in the flesh, seen of men, believed on in the world, received up into glory.* The expiatory suffering, named in the text, accord with all just conceptions of God. Beyond us, and peculiar in every thing else, he is beyond us and peculiar in the great atonement.

II. Our God has different modes of giving intimations of himself. We can not learn all that we are able to know of him in any one spot, or by any one transaction. To lead us on he has employed grades, and built one scaffolding above another, (some of them yet to be knocked down and burnt up as rubbish.) There is matter which came from nothing at his bidding; and in this world, where his winds howl, and his flowerets blush, and his snows sleep in their white, we may learn something of his control over matter. We may lift our eyes beyond this world, and as we look out upon the planets' blaze, and the planets' march—on Mazzaroth, and Arcturus, and Pleiads, we may add to our knowledge of God's government over material things as we walk along that pavement of sapphire, studded with the diamonds of his morning stars.

Beyond this mere matter there is *mind*. The kingdom of intelligence is more glorious than the kingdom of matter. Reason, memory, taste, imagination—that mysterious thing which we call mind—here is something wherein God takes another step, and gives another intimation of himself. The study of his wisdom may last us for ever.

Beyond mere intelligence there is a kingdom of *sensibilities*. The affections—love, hate, enmity, grief, hope, joy—what indescribable wonders do these words suggest! Here is another leaf of God's endless book—another stepping-stone to aid our conceptions of him.

Still beyond, there is a *moral* kingdom. Intelligence and sensibility both belong to it, and come into mysterious play when the moral feelings mingle with them. In this moral kingdom, wherein, by conscience, convictions, and moral sensibilities, the creature carries along with him the machinery for his felicity or his woe, we have another intimation about God. Angels that *excel in strength*, fallen spirits reserved under chains of darkness, belong to this moral world—a world of wonders.

The world of grace has still higher. Redemption—the salvation of sinners—is not a matter of mere creation, or mere government, or recovery from ruin merely; it is a matter of mercy to the sinning and the punishment of sin. This matter evidently lies beyond all others.

And now, when we *have such* a matter, and when all along, in the fields of materialities, and intelligence, and sensibilities, and moral nature, we have seen God rising higher and higher out of our sight, and wrapping himself round with clouds which our eye can not penetrate, have we not reason to rejoice that in this last field of God Almighty, where sin is punished and sinners are saved, there is just the carrying out of the systems we have seen all along? We see God making good his own analogies. They demanded, not resemblances in the things themselves, but a perpetual gradation. Mind is not like matter. Sensibility is not like cold intellect. Conscience takes hold on the soul with a strength of its own. And forgiveness of sinners, while sin is punished, is another step. And shall we refuse to take it? I mean, rather, shall we refuse to let God take it and let our faith follow him? *Stricken for my people* is just the amazing thing which the rising gradations of God demand. Matter, mind, sensibility, conscience, pardon, will surely allow us to go on to atonement and glory. We must not *limit the Holy One of Israel.* The suffering of a Being, innocent in himself and infinite in his mysterious person, agrees with the analogies of God.

And even if you take any one field of God's works, you may find there a similar invitation to an adoring faith in the atonement made by stricken Innocence. What does our unbelief in such an atonement demand? What are its difficulties? Does it not demand of God that he shall stop before he has acted on a field where our limited intellect can not comprehend him? As he works, unbelief does not lay hold on his skirts to be lifted, but to draw *him* back; and refuse to let him go beyond us, and have a field where the blaze of his glory shall dazzle the eye of his insignificant creature! We should not venture such an action on any other theater of God's working.

When the keen eye of modern Science has traveled out to the utmost verge of visible things; and the rapt astronomer fixes his gaze on the last star his glass can reach; and beyond all is blank—an infinite vault of space—an unbounded ocean, where, to his eye, no sun or comet sails—no matter sleeps—no being moves ; shall he stand there, and while rapt in amazement at the myriads of worlds, and suns, and systems he has passed, shall he affirm there is none beyond—that he has reached the end of the march of God Almighty? Shall he not rather look back on the amazing worlds he has passed, and call up their eternal arithmetic to make him believe that he has not compassed the Eternal yet? that out beyond him, deep in unfathomable space, other worlds may wheel, and other suns burn, and other creatures move, by the will of the living and self-existent God? And, when all along he has seen variety giving glory to uniformity—when the moons of Jupiter are more than our own, and the belts of glory around Saturn give him such an unequaled evening sky—shall he not be prepared to believe that in the far higher fields of a moral glory there is some-thing which no analogy has touched, except the analo-gies of God; some spot wearing the high imprint of God's peculiar hand; some place, field or system, where mortal knowledge must give place to immortal amaze-ment and adoration? That place is Calvary—that field is the Church—that system is salvation for sinners through the sufferings of a *stricken* substitute. God, that smote him, herein goes beyond man, out of our sight, and calls on faith to follow him. This is the height of his adorable wonders—the place where he is like himself—the peculiarity and the last step of an ascending series. *One star differeth from another star in glory ;* but the Star of Bethlehem outshines them all—and *shall* shine in the skies of eternity when other stars have gone out.

III. The mystery, the wonder of this redemption of sinners, by *stripes* laid on Christ, accords with us, as well as it accords with God.

We are sinners. See what sin hath done. Some symbols of its mischief are visible. It blasted paradise! It fell on the cursed earth! It forged swords for battle! It hath sprinkled tears all over this world! It hath plunged the daggers of grief deep into every heart! It hath spread death-beds, and built coffins, and dug graves! And these are only symbols of its dreadfulness. That want, that deep want in the human soul, of some hold on God, some feeling of security as we stand amid tears and tombs here, and look out into the midnight of another world, goes beyond these symbols. Oh! if we could have that hold on God, we could die a thousand deaths, after wiping the death-sweat from the brow of our last friend! And this feeling of human want reaches its last anguish when conscience is whetted into its keenness, and our poor soul sees it is justly cut off from God and worthy of his indignation! Sin has broken up our relations *with Him.* Our Creator, our final Judge, is against us! No earthly offending can compare with this. The law which sin has broken is God's law—the law for the immortal spirit—the law for

eternity to come! Eternity! Oh, eternity! mind staggers under the weight of that idea. To last on *for ever*—
and last a sinner, cut off from God, and no more at
peace with myself than with him—to feel eternally the
gnawings of the *worm that dieth not* and the wrath of
God! Sooner come annihilation! A thousand-fold
sooner let God lift up his hand upon me and extinguish
my existence for ever!

Now, in the presence of these symbols, these wants,
this sin which has no analogy, which has broken up our
peace-relations with God, this conscience, these agonies
of a fearing spirit, and this dreadful eternity—what shall
be done? What shall God do for us? What do we
want him to do. Want him to do? Just what he has
done. We want him to meet our infinite fears with his
infinite offers. To meet our worst woes with his ineffable grace. We want him to *show* us while we stand
trembling before *his* justice, that something has been
done which that justice can not find fault with—something which can cope with all the malignities of sin—
something which shall wave the peace-branch over the
door into eternity! He has done it. It is his own
work, on his own authority, like him, and just *because* it
has such wonders about it as the innocence and the
mysterious person of a suffering Christ, our faith can
trust it. Where we most fear, God is most wonderful.
The excellence and the innocence of the sacrifice as the
ground of *our* peace, show us that the august redemption
perfectly assorts with the ineffable woes and wants of
our sinful condition.

But we must leave this matter of argument. Other
items may come up, if God will, at another time.

For the transgression of my people was he stricken. Herein God was more wonderful and mysterious than comprehensible. The uses we ought to make of this subject are not trivial.

There are those who have no living faith in this atonement, and who will not come to the memorial of it this afternoon. Why? Simply because of two things— things more of heart than of the understanding: First, they have low and groveling ideas of God—ideas very much confined to his earthly things, and his natural attributes. They can think of his power, and see it in the everlasting hills. They can talk of his wisdom, and think they are talking very well about it when they unfold the sciences and laws which belong to this material earth and the material heavens! Poor fools! This is only the beginning! *not* the beginning—it is only an emblem, a dim symbol, a shadow! This earth shall be burnt up. The time hastens when these heavens shall be no more. God shall *create a new heaven and a new earth, wherein dwelleth righteousness.* In righteousness, in his moral and spiritual kingdom, in his glory and honor; and if depraved souls were not so earth-bound and groveling, their ideas would be absorbed in the moral excellences of God, and move first toward the issues of a coming eternity. They would seek first the kingdom of God. They would let go of earth; they would let the sun and stars go out; they would reach forth toward a spiritual God and a spiritual eternity—the hope and the home for the soul!

The other reason is, that they do not justly realize their condition and necessities as sinners. If men have inadequate notions of God, they will have inadequate notions of sin. If they have inadequate notions of sin, they will have inadequate notions of Christ; and then there will be nothing seen in their condition to *drive* them, and nothing in his character to *draw* them, to his infinite sacrifice. Oh, if they had any thing like a just idea of what it is to be a sinner, they would look to the sacrifice of Christ with amazing gladness and gratitude! If they did not feel that they might come to his table, they would get as near as they could, and look on, and wonder, and wish, and pray! But they are ignorant of both God and themselves; and, therefore, are not constrained toward the best thing that God has to give them —an interest in the blood of his Son! When that Son shall have *made up his jewels* he will say to these groveling and unawakened souls: *Behold, ye despisers, and wonder, and perish.*

Pause, pause sinner, tread not under foot that blood! that blood! This is the height of all God's wonders! It comes toward the depths of all your wants and woes. It offers you life and immortality. God's very heart, his heart of kindness and love, has embarked in it; and if, as you stand before death's door, and trembling before God's thunders, you reject this Christ, it had been *better for you if you had never been born!* Repent, flee to Christ, and live! Flee *now*, while that throne is a *throne of grace.* It shall soon be taken down, and God will rear the throne of eternal judgment! There you stand! time gone! the world gone! communion-tables gone! How will you answer it to him *then,* that you are not at his table to-day?

But the tenderness of this subject to believers is as remarkable as its terror to unbelievers. *For the transgression of my people was he stricken.* This was the great wonder of God! an adorable wonder! The Victim! Oh, the amazing Victim! Jesus Christ was not a mere man. Nor was he an angel. He is the Son of God who *thought it not robbery to be equal with God.* He is *the brightness of the Father's glory, and the express image of his person. He upholdeth all things by the word of his power.* When he came into the world, God said, *Let all the angels of God worship him.* Isaiah calls him the *mighty God.* The Psalmist rendered him the homage of adoration, when he exclaimed: *Thy throne, O God, is for ever and ever; a scepter of righteousness is the scepter of thy kingdom. Thou, Lord, in the beginning hast laid the foundation of the earth, and the heavens are the works of thy hands.* This adorable Being became a man—a poor man—he *had not where to lay his head*—a *man of sorrows and acquainted with grief.* In the agony of the garden, when his soul was buffeting the billows, he *sweat as it were great drops of blood falling down to the ground.* On the cross he uttered such a death-wail as never burst from other dying lips, *My God, my God, why hast thou forsaken me!*

Believer, you know what all this was for. And now I want to ask you some questions. When you think of God, of the greatness of his works, of his ten thousand worlds, of his infinite majesty, will you ever be afraid any more that he will not care for you and condescend to your littleness? Will you ever hesitate to tell him your fears, your wants, your heart's hidden anguish, and to *expect* him to lend his ear to your suppliant cry? Will you ever hesitate to *draw near* to him and lean upon his bosom, and pour your tears of mingled penitence and love at his feet? Oh, remember, this wonder of God in the atonement, this greatest of his wonders, this wonder which reaches beyond all the exhibits of him in matter, in mind, in feeling, in morals—this wonder was wrought just for you—for you, a poor sinner, and child of the dust! It is the majesty of God which sweeps down to you. Will you ever doubt any more, and hold back your heart, since such a Friend has died for you, and your grace and salvation is God's highest glory?

At the table of the covenant you may call up all your sins, all your unworthiness, all your worldliness and pride and obstinacy, and repent over them in hope. Your transgressions, what numbers of them come floating over your memory! what wanderings from God! what worldliness! what pride and selfishness and vanity! what ingratitude! what unbelief! But they can not cut you off from God! *For the transgression of my people was he stricken.* If you feel yourself that poor and unworthy sinner, to forgive whom and commune with whom would be one of God's most amazing wonders, you are the very communicant whom he will take into covenant with himself. Your unworthiness is the very plea that his stooping majesty wants from your lips. Believe, adore, and wonder and love.

But you can not be here always. Your race is partly run. And if, as you look forward toward the *swellings of Jordan,* nature trembles, and you feel that it is no small matter to meet that conflict, the nature of our subject assorts with your necessity. You do want much: dying is no trifle. But you can not want more than Christ has to give you. *Fear not, thou worm Jacob! When thou passest through the waters I will be with thee; and through the rivers, they shall not overflow thee; when thou walkest through the fire thou shall not be burnt.* The wonders of Christ's death meet all the wants and wonders of your own dying.

You will aim to feel this this afternoon at his table. Not this only. From these hights of privilege, you may look forward to something more glorious. Jesus Christ, in the end, will be the *great wisdom of God*, and in the brightness of his coming indicate the gloom of his crucifixion. *Every eye shall see him.* Behold, *he cometh in the clouds of heaven.* See his retinue! See those *ten thousand times ten thousand that stand before him!* See those *twenty thousand chariots of the Lord!* The dead raised. *Lift up your heads, ye saints, your redemption draweth near. When he who is your life shall appear, then shall ye also appear with him in glory. Ye shall be changed into the same image from glory to glory. Ye shall be like him, for ye shall see him as he is.* And now, *caught up* to be *ever with the Lord;* entering that *house of many mansions,* you will have not the faith, but the eternal demonstration, that Christ being *stricken for the transgression of his people,* assorts both with your blessedness and with the wonderful glory of God. For you shall love him for ever, and be like him for ever: and *you shall hear the voice of many angels round about the throne, and the elders, and the number of them ten thousand times ten thousand, and thousands of thousands, singing with a loud voice, Worthy is the Lamb that* WAS SLAIN, *to receive power, and riches, and wisdom, and strength, and honor, and glory, and blessing. And every creature which is in heaven* will be heard *saying, Blessing, and honor, and glory, and power be unto him that sitteth upon the throne, and unto the Lamb for ever.* It is enough for our full faith: the glory of redemption is the glory of heaven! Who *can* despair? what sinner can refuse to believe, and repent and love? *For the transgression of my people was he stricken.*

Christ Delivered Up.

[SACRAMENTAL.]

He that spared not his own Son, but freely delivered him up for us all, how shall he not with him also freely give us all things ?—ROMANS, viii. 32.

IN general, the Gospel founds its encouragements for believers and for unbelievers on precisely the same platform. There is scarcely a particle of difference. Saint or sinner, the same doctrines are rung in his ears. Saint or sinner, the same invitations are poured round his heart. Believer or unbeliever, the same great atonement is held up before his eye. Hearts, all hearts are expected to be influenced by precisely the same announcements, and they have the offer of precisely the same Christ, in the same way and for the same purpose. This afternoon there will not be an unbeliever away from the communion who is compelled to be. Every one of them has precisely the same offers as the children of God. Every one of them has precisely the same promises. They will turn their back upon the Lord's table for no other reason than their unbelief in God's love and in his Son. All there is wanting, all God demands of them, all they need do to annihilate the distance between themselves and the children of God, is just to close in with God's offers in faith, and let that faith in Christ which justifies them conduct them at once to holiness and to the comforts of hope.

On the other hand, no believer, in this wilderness of his pilgrimage, ever arrives at such a state as not to need precisely the same considerations which God addresses to unbelievers. His faith is demanded the same as theirs; his love, his penitence, his whole heart. His hope and his holiness are to grow by the embracing acts by which they commenced at first. He is just to embrace Jesus Christ for his own; and there is not a sinner who hears me, now in the high road of his rebellion, his face set toward hell, who has not precisely the same privilege.

The argument of the text, therefore, which we shall attempt to unfold, is just as much addressed to unbelieving hearts as to believing ones. The unbelieving will reject it. They cast it off from them. They do not want it. If they have any anticipations about religion at all, they propose to themselves some other starting-point in the race of salvation than just beginning by faith in the things which God hath done to save them. But believers will be as likely to welcome the argument as unbelievers to reject it.

I. Let us look at the nature of the argument.

II. Let us examine some of the particulars embraced in the grounds of it.

III. Let us take the encouragement of its conclusion.

I. The nature of this argument is very simple. It is addressed to believers, and designed to meet the discouragements which so often assail them. These discouragements are numerous; and, as one after another comes up, either in fact or amid the expectations of fear, it often happens that the believer's heart becomes the seat

19

of sadnesses which have no parallel and admit of no description. Some of you understand them very well. You
have known what it is to walk in dark places. Your
light has sometimes forsaken you. You have questioned
whether it were possible that God should deal with any
one he loves as he hath dealt with you ; and your desponding temper employed the darkness without you to
put away the last ray of hope that cheered the heart
within you. Sometimes you have been cast down under
an oppressive sense of the Divine justice ; and the more
clear were the views you had of God, the more you
thought that his character was all embarked against you.
Your sin, your unworthiness, the trials before you, your
coming death and the judgment beyond it, have cast a
melancholy over your contemplations, and your heart
has bled under the anguish of your conclusion that you
knew not, after all, whether he cared for you or what
should become you.

In reference to all such ideas, the argument of the text
is constructed. The Apostle knew, as well as you do, the
difficulties we have to contend with. In this chapter he
mentions some of them : *Condemnation, the law of sin and
death, the sufferings of the present time, the bondage of corruption, groaning within ourselves.* And then he turns,
(just as a believer must, if he would not sink into a useless despair), simply to his God. *If God be for us, who can
be against us ? He that spared not his own Son, but freely
delivered him up for us all, how shall he not with him also
freely give us all things?* We are going to want many
things. We scarcely know how much. Between us and
heaven lie many trials, it may be, and we can not come
up to the solemn revelations of the final judgment without battling the dark billows of death ? But now our

discouragement may give place to hope, and our distrust may yield to faith, if we can but see clearly that our God hath already done for us MORE than all that which we hereafter can need. He hath done it. He hath given us his Son. This is the greater gift. All else we can want bears no comparison with this. If we have accepted this gift, and doing so have conspired with God in his designs; if we have received at his hand already a benefaction, which swells beyond the measure of all other benefactions, on what principle is it that God can ever refuse to us any thing or all things? Since he hath done for our salvation such a work, and since we have commenced our march at his call; since he hath already done *more* than now remains to be done, will he give us up and let us perish when we need only some minor benefactions to secure us as the trophies of his own glorious work? It can not be. We know of no principle on which God can act, we can conceive of none, which should prompt him now to refuse a believer the benefits he needs.

If you were a culprit in prison, and the clemency of legal authority should pity your confined and enfeebled condition, and pronounce your pardon, and the messenger who brought it to your cell should find you a cripple and unable to go out through the opened door of your prison-house, would you not *expect* that the same clemency which had flung it open for your going forth to the free air of heaven, would also reach its aid to the crippled limbs whose misery moved the compassion which pardoned you? If it would furnish no such aid, on your bed of straw and musing upon your crippled limbs as you lifted your hopeless eye to the opened door, you would execrate the mis-named mercy that had pardoned you! you would say there was no mercy about it! you would ask, Why torment me with an offer impossible for me to accept? There is a Holy Spirit for you as well a crucified Christ.

If you were an undutiful son, whose extravagance and profligacy had plunged you into misery and want, and the fatherly affection which you had abused should follow you still, and the strength of that affection should not only send you a message of forgiveness, but should prompt your offended father to sacrifice the most valuable of his possessions to relieve you from the debts of your profligacy, that you might be free and return to him, could you have any thought that the same affection, when you *wished* to return, and when you had worked your way back to the door of the paternal mansion and stood there in want—could you ever think that same affection would refuse a morsel of bread to your hungry lips? This is the nature of the argument. It proceeds on what God hath done—on the ground that he hath done the most wonderful thing which needs to be done, and on that account there is the most abundant reason to trust him for all the rest.

II. Let us look at some of the particulars embraced in this argument. Take them in the exact order of the text:

1. *He that spared not his own Son.* It was *God* whose benevolence originated the gift made to us. It was God, acting beyond all his other works—beyond all nature—in a new way—in his redeeming work—beyond all his creation and common providences. If the plan and foundation of our salvation had their origin any where else, they would be very different to us. We could exhaust a crea-

ture. We could exhaust an angel. A moment ago, when I was speaking of the pardoned prisoner and the profligate son, some of you felt the failure of the figure. You realized its feebleness: you did right. We do want something of God which can not be suitably imaged by all the clemency and power of his creatures. If I could trust his creatures under such circumstances of imprisonment and profligacy, it would be but a faint image of what it means to trust my God. As a sinner, I can hardly conceive of the extent of my wants. I have offended God. I have done the worst thing I could do. I may not, indeed, have reached the highest degree of crime possible for me, but it would have been impossible for me to do a worse thing than offend God. My sin hath broken his law, and its just penalty is *everlasting punishment—fire prepared for the devil and his angels!* I want pardon. I want some ground of assurance that I can have it. I want to see how it can come to pass that sin, a thing which tore angels out of heaven and turned them into devils in hell, can be forgiven unto me, and I can be restored to the full favor of God. I ask not angels to undertake for me. I would not trust them—either their wisdom or their works. I can not draw upon my own powers. My mind is too entirely limited to understand what the violated government of God must demand in order that a sinner can be forgiven. My feeble understanding can not gauge the dimensions of offense in the Divine mind against sin. Still less could I trust any created power in the universe to make any compensation for me—any atonement. Whose powers could hope to grapple with the difficulty of appeasing an angry God? Who could pay hell? Who could scale heaven and take it by violence or just demand? But God has himself commenced for me. My salvation originated there. Where lay the offense of sin, deep in the heart of God, thence sprang the plan and the affection which have come to my relief. *God forbid that I should glory save in the cross of our Lord Jesus Christ.*

These ideas run through the whole Bible. Men are very much prone to measure sins side by side with one another. God does it very little. The idea is hardly in the Bible. Sin, all sin, is such an offense that the difference between the evil of one sin and that of another, as committed against God, is scarcely worthy of mention. If I am *a sinner*, that is enough. That fact cuts me off from all hope—from any thing to be derived from law and from all creatures in the universe. Hence you may notice uniformly in the Bible these two strange things to an unconverted man : first, that it never sends him to any of his own powers for relief, but sends him directly to God ; and second, that it makes not a particle of difference between the call it gives to one sinner and the call it gives to another. Great sinner or little, he must *be born again*, or not *see the kingdom of God.* Great sinner or little, he must repent—must *believe* in Christ ; he must lift his *cross and follow* him. Great sinner or little, if he will do this, he will not fail of salvation. His help is in God. And one idea in the ground of the argument before us is, that God himself hath risen over our lost world, and undertaken for our salvation. One sinner is as welcome to forgiveness as another.

2. A second idea is, the idea of *the gift* which God made to the world. *He spared not his own Son.*

There is a method of conceiving of God which may be very natural to us, but which is very unjust. An unregenerated sinner is very apt to employ it, and so far as I know does employ it, through all the stages of his unregeneracy. He employs it in his deepest speculations, and what is still worse, he will carry it along with him in those moments of conscience and contemplation—moments of feeling and fear—when he kneels before God to deprecate his anger and implore the favor of his pity and love. Even a regenerated sinner, in his times of darkness, and amid the besettings of unbelief, falls back upon this erroneous and unhappy mode of conceiving of God. It is a mode which divests him of all resemblance to those common sensibilities which constitute bonds of affectionate reliance and attachment. It is a mode which despoils him of the just attractions of his character, and represents him to our cold and closed hearts as little else than infinite power, and infinite justice, and infinite understanding. Some of you will apprehend, very justly, what we mean when we tell you that in all your trembling attempts at peace with him you never approach him—you never pray to him as a Being of emotion and tenderness—you never expect to succeed with him at all on the ground of the affections of his own heart. You think, you feel, you act, you pray, as if God had no heart, and had no business to have one. Now, there may be, indeed, something in the infinity of his perfections which, overawing the mind, tends to produce this conception; but there is *more* to produce it in the darknesses, distrusts, and deceptions of sin. The recoilings of a conscious guiltiness, the unrelentings of a sullen depravity, are ever unwilling to conceive of God justly. They weave an excuse for themselves out of their perverted idea of the Deity,—to them an intellectual, holy, authoritative, but heartless Deity, whom they can neither trust nor love, and who can not love them. And even a feeble and timid faith is very slow to put aside all this evil, and clothe God with the affections that belong to him. *God is love.*

Now, to meet this misconception, the idea of God's gift of his Son stands so prominent in the text. His *love* to sinners prompted the gift. God would have us measure that love by the love he bore to his Son. He loved his Son. It would have been a very different thing for God to have given any thing else. A sacrificed world, a sacrificed angel, legions of angels sacrificed to the object of our redemption, never would have been such a demonstration to correct our misconceptions of God. He could have done nothing else *so* to evince his regard for us. There was his love for his Son, his own and only Son, his *beloved* Son (as the Gospel emphatically expresses it), struggling in his heart with the love he bore to poor sinners. Nothing else would do. He must yield his Son, or give up the sinners. The sinners must sink to hell, or the love God bore to his Son must give way— give way, so far as Christ's humiliation was demanded. The love of the sinners prevailed, and this demonstrates, that over even sinners, God is no mere cold-hearted governor, but just as really exercises fond and tender affections for them as he exercises such affections for his only and beloved Son. *God is love*—love toward sinners—not more King than Friend and Father.

3. The other idea grows out of this. It may be the same perhaps. Perhaps to give his Son to the world would have accomplished nothing even in the way of proof, and would have been accounted nothing if he had *not* given him to the humiliation of the manger, the law, the temptations of the devil, the sorrows of life, the crucifixion and the tomb. However this may be, there is a

distinct stress laid in the Gospel upon these wonderful
and humiliating distresses. God gave his Son to all
these. There was a two-fold reason for it. One part of
it was found in the government of God—the other part
was found in the nature of the sinner himself. Sin had
broken and dishonored the government of God. That
government was infinitely important, and could not be
given up. God himself could not spare it; it was necessary to his perfections, and, therefore, necessary to his
own infinite blessedness or felicity. He would no longer
be *the blessed God* if his government could be dashed into
pieces and sinners offend him with impunity. The
universe could not spare it. The felicities of moral
existence in all worlds, (greatly at the present moment,
and entirely in the end), depend upon their conformity to
that moral government which originates in God's nature,
and is appropriate to the nature of all moral beings. It
would be a most horrible thing if God would do what
sinners in this house this moment want him to do—
give up his moral government and fling out full license
and impunity for sinners to do as they please. Such
license would ruin them. Other worlds are spectators
of this. The same government which sin hath violated
here extends there. Heaven is a holy place and a happy
one, because law, LAW reigns there in the efficacy of a
loved obedience—and hell is an unholy place and a
miserable one, because law, LAW reigns there only in
the just penalty it inflicts upon an unrelenting disobedience. There may be other worlds, now, like this,
passing through a period of probation, and cognizant
of what God is doing here. In them, and in heaven,
among those mighty intelligences denominated, *thrones
and principalities and powers*, sin might have broken loose

19*

to do its mischief, if God, in redeeming sinners here, had not demonstrated an infinite attachment to his law. Hence the great Redeemer took the law-place of sinners. He bared his head to its thunders. He became a man. He was born in poverty and danger. He lived in toil and in tears. He had *not where to lay his head.* The Devil tempted him. And though he was holy, though he was the *beloved Son of God*, the Father himself looked on and saw it all. He took him at his willing word. He took him instead of sinners. He let loose upon him the demands of infinite justice, and now every moral being in the universe that knows it, knows by what wonderful distresses of a Holy Being, the law was *magnified and made honorable.* No spectator in the universe can look on the cheered soul at our communion-table this day, or look up to those seats where other souls, once here, are now communing with Christ in heaven, and thence derive any encouragement to sin. The distresses and death of Christ hold up the penalty of the law before every spectator, and sustain the moral government of God, though sinners live and shall *live and reign with Christ* in his kingdom.

The other part of the reason for the Saviour's distresses, we said, was to be found in the nature of the sinner himself. We can not unfold all this. We have not time. We will only try to explain what we mean. And we *do* mean, that the most difficult thing which we know any thing about among all matters of persuasion, is just to persuade a sinner, truly sensible of his sins, that God cares much about him, and is so willing to forgive and save him, that he may instantly give up his sins and trust his soul in the good hands of God. Tell him this and he will not believe it. Let the *Gospel* tell him as *though God did beseech you by us, we pray you in Christ's stead be ye reconciled to God ;* and the hardened sinner not only, but even the distressed and tearful sinner will be slow to believe, and slow to trust a promising God. He thinks he may not. Sins make him afraid. Sinfulness fills his gloomy heart with dark suspicions of God. He imagines somehow he is shut out. One poor sinner, now I trust redeemed, who will be at the communion-table this afternoon, said to me lately : "I never knew till you told me that I might fly to Christ *now*, and just as I am. That amazed me. I was such a stranger to him. You told me to give God my heart just as it is. That surprised me. I thought you did not know me. Fly to Christ just as I am ? To Christ now ? Such a stranger to him ? Give God my heart *just as it is ?* I had never thought any thing about Christ ! He had always been last in my thoughts, as one to resort to *after* I was religious—and fly to him *first ?* Fly to him now ? Stop trying, and he do all ? Impossible ! You did *not* understand me ! My powers seemed stunned ! It was entirely new truth to me." So she thought then. But she has learnt better now. She comes to the communion-table now believing in his welcome, and not expecting any longer to receive any benefit except by him. *Before* she believed, she says: " I can not describe my ineffectual efforts to grope and feel after Christ through thick darkness. I could not find him. I could only cry, Jesus, Master, have mercy on me, and ask him to take my heart—for I could not give it to him—and make it for me what I could not make it myself. I never knew the promises were for *me*, until you told me. I thought they were not for me." " Not for you ?" said I. " It is the lie of the Devil !

They *are* for you if you want them. It is the very act of faith to take them and trust Christ to do all he has said." Another poor sinner will be *away* from the communion-table this afternoon, detained from the place of her heart's longing, " because (as she said) she *can not* go there with such a sense of her unworthiness, and such a fear that she should not walk worthy of her profession." I said to her: " Suppose it were all different with you; suppose you had *not* a sense of your unworthiness and *not* a fear of being unfaithful—could you go then?" "Oh no!" was the answer, "that would not be the right feeling." But she comes not to that bread and that cup. You see how difficult it is to persuade sinners to trust in God as one who cares for their souls. Bitter tears will be shed to-day by those whose unbelieving hearts, or hearts of little faith, keep them from the communion of God.

Now Christ passed through all his distresses, if not *for the sake* of carrying the persuasion of faith to such hearts, at least in such a relationship to them that his distresses meet all the horrid gloom of their fears. Their doubts and distance from God, and distrust and gloom, arise from sin. Sin is an offense and has a penalty. When Christ undertook to atone for it he looked all its penalty in the face. God gave him up to all his humiliation, agony and death. He put him into the sinner's nature. He put him into the sinner's place. It would not have been enough to have God love the world, and to have the Son of God come into it and go out of it in any other mode than as he did. A sinner's gloom not only, but a sinner's just sense of sin would give rise to a fear, an awful and just fear, of the penalty of the violated law, if Christ had not grappled with the penalty himself. A sinner's sense of unworthiness not only, but the spiritual light of his just convictions, would have kept him back from trusting in God, would have fostered his gloom and his unbelief, if he could not have seen that God loved him well enough to give his Son to death, and that that death, in the presence of a silenced law and a guilty soul, had opened up the free way for a sinner into the favor of God. Every body knows the mercifulness of the Deity. Every body talks about it. The heathen do. They always did. But the mere naked idea of the merciful disposition of God neither persuades any body to faith nor to sanctification. That idea does not reach the secret place of persuasion in a heathen's heart, nor in the heart of our cold and careless friends around us. It never will. Hearts need to see God in Christ. Hearts need to realize the extent of his love for sinners by all the tearful demonstrations of a satisfied justice and a reconciled God, which lie between the manger of Bethlehem and the garden-grave of the man of Arimathea. Let them see this, let them realize it, and the most gloomy disposition in the world will be ready to exclaim, Guilt, do your worst—law, do your worst—justice, death, devils, do your worst! *If God be for us, who can be against us?* The most distressed disciple in the world, yea the most distrustful and unworthy heart in the world, will then break forth into singing, and mingle faith and love with a sense of unworthiness in the penitential tenderness of its song:

> " Alas ! and did my Saviour bleed,
> And did my Sovereign die ?
> Would he devote that sacred head
> For such a worm as I ?"

It is not a little remarkable that among all the supports

of unbelief, and all the suggestions of the gloomy inge·
nuity of despondency, we never hear a whisper of doubt
about the merits of Christ or the sufficiency of his sacrifice. No, not a whisper. To every heart Christ seems
enough. Guilt, unworthiness, despair, can not look on
him without confessing there is a way open to the heart
of God and into heaven.

These are the particulars embraced in the ground of
the argument. God so loved the world. God spared
not his Son. God delivered him up for us all, to take
our place when he made *his soul an offering for sin. When
we were yet enemies Christ died for us.*

And the ground of the argument is deep and broad
enough for,

III. Its sweeping conclusion: *How shall he not with
him also freely give us all things?* We can ask nothing
now which does not sink into insignificance as we take
our stand on Calvary amid the scenes of the crucifixion.

We are sinners. We are great sinners. We need the
forgiveness of God. That forgiveness is now the freest
thing in the universe. God loves to forgive sinners.
He loves to save them. He loves to put honor on the
redeeming blood of his Son. Repent and trust, and the
benefits of that blood are all your own.

We are unworthy sinners. How marvelous has been
our obstinacy! Looking back to the days of our youth,
and following along in recollection the line of our devi-
ous life, what a multitude of unworthy acts and affections come up to our mind! What counsels we slighted! What tender and touching warnings were lost upon
us! What forgetfulness of God! What envy, selfishness, and ambition. What disobedience to parents!

Our father's love, our mother's prayer, cry out against us! Looking into our hearts now, what do we find there to recommend us to God? What worldliness! what insincerity and unbelief! what coldness! Ah! were it not for the memorial of this afternoon, tears might for ever dim our eyes, and grief, and shame, and despair, find an eternal abode in our hearts! We are unworthy. Christ is infinitely worthy. *How shall not God with him freely give us all things?*

The argument is perfect. Its ground is wide enough for its conclusion. God himself has nothing more precious to give. Be it the province of your faith to embrace Jesus Christ for your own, and then *all things are yours. All things.* Of course we can not name them all.

We want many things. Evidently God is offended with this rebellious world. The very things he is doing terrify us, and we want some overbalancing testimony to meet the sadness of circumstances. We behold a world full of misery—blood flowing—tears falling—elements seem to war against us—and not far off is the winding-sheet and the deep solitude of the charnel-house! No matter. God has done greater things than turning our trials and tombs into mercies. Be it ours to weep when God will, and die when God will. *All things shall work together for good to them that love God. All things are yours, for ye are Christ's and Christ is God's.*

On the very spot where a sinner's fears gather, Jesus-Jehovah seems to have shed the light of his own glory. A sinner's fears gather round the bed of death. Blessed be God, Jesus Christ died. If he had not, and I did not know he died *for me*, I should feel something wanting to the provisions of my redemption. I know better now. *Precious in the sight of the Lord is the death of his saints.* Jesus Christ died; and when he bids me memorialize his death, he does all that can be done to dissipate the fears of my own. Oh! if he died for me, I can afford to die! He has been there before me, and if I am his he will be there with me!

Into the world to which we are rapidly moving, Jesus-Jehovah has gone before us. If he had *not*—if he had not appeared at that tribunal where I must stand shortly, and pacified it with the sufficiency of his atonement, and extended his redeeming dominion over the world I am soon going to inhabit, I should feel that something was wanting. Nothing is wanting now. The man of Calvary is the *Prince* of Peace upon the throne. As I open my eyes in the immortal world, I shall see the reigning Redeemer in his glory ; I shall behold *in the midst of the throne a Lamb as it had been slain.* I shall behold the *four living creatures,* and the *four-and-twenty elders falling down before him, and casting their crowns at his feet.* I shall hear the ascriptions of praise from lips once polluted as my own, *Unto Him that loved us and washed us from our sins in his own blood.* If I want immortality and heaven, Jesus Christ is enough for me to trust in : I want no more.

My brethren, memorialize his death this afternoon in the fullness of faith and love, and God *shall freely give you all things* in this world, and the world to which you go. You will soon be there. God grant that this ordinance may aid to prepare you. It will, if you lift the cup in humble penitence and faith, and say : *He that spared not his own Son, but freely delivered him up for us all, how shall he not with him also freely give us all things ?* God help you to do so. *Amen.*

Rejoicing of Faith.

In whom, though now ye see him not, yet believing, ye rejoice with joy
unspeakable and full of glory.—1 PETER, i. 8.

THE Apostle was here speaking of Jesus Christ. It
was *he* in whom this believing was exercised; it
was he of whom the Apostle says, *though now ye see him
not.*

In this passage the Apostle was addressing believers,
Christians, the true followers of our Lord Jesus Christ.
He mentions a part of their Christian experience. He
did not hesitate to mention it. He knew very well what
it was. It is not probable that any one had told him:
indeed, the contrary appears quite evident. As we learn
from the first verse of the chapter, he was writing to the
saints, the strangers *scattered abroad throughout Pontus,
Galatia, Cappadocia, Asia and Bythinia;* and it seems
quite evident that he could not have learned, by any
human testimony, the experiences of believers spread
over such extensive regions of country. Yet he does not
hesitate to describe their experience. How did he know
it? How could *he* tell how they felt—what they
thought, or hoped, or feared? How could he venture to
describe hearts which had never been described to him,
and venture all his reputation and influence on the accuracy of that description? I do not believe that we have
any occasion to resort to the idea of inspiration for an

answer to these questions. Inspired, unquestionably he was; but he knew all that he affirms about the experience of these Christians on quite another principle. He knew it because he knew his own. He knew it because he knew the powerful workings of Divine grace in human hearts. He knew it just as any believer of much faith and experience would know now in what manner any other believer, who was a *stranger* to him, would be affected under particular circumstances into which his faith had conducted him. There is scarcely a believer in the world who would not venture to speak just as Peter speaks here. If any one of *you* should hear of a man, or a multitude of men, who, on account of their attachment to true religion, had been expelled from their native country, been despoiled of their goods, and been flung into other straits and difficulties, and yet would not yield up their religion, but stood firm in the midst of all these trials—there is not one of you who would hesitate to affirm, that is a happy man, those are a happy people. You would feel confident that the God they had honored had not deserted them; and though they might be *now for a season in heaviness through manifold temptations*, yet that they are happy and rejoicing Christians. You would begin to doubt your own Christianity, if you could hesitate to say so of them. On the same principle Peter speaks. He knew what faith was, and what it would do. He knew what God was, and what he would do. He knew what a tried heart was, and how under the tearful and heavy trials of its fidelity, its strength would grow, as its burdens grew, and the inward light grow brighter, as outward skies grew more dark and terrible. Hence Peter (just on this ground probably) does not hesitate to describe the experience of these *strangers*, affirming of them that they *rejoice with joy unspeakable and full of glory.*

These *strangers,* as he calls them, were in difficulty. Their faith had brought them into difficulty. They were *scattered abroad* over strange and wild countries. Because they would not deny Christ, the enemies of Christ expelled them from their homes. It was a sore trial. No man who has never been an exile from his home and country must even undertake to describe it. He can not. There is an anguish in severing the heart-strings which bind us to our native land unlike any other anguish. Other lands may receive us, richer soil be under our feet, brighter skies be over our heads, and blander breezes fan our cheek; yet, after all, the exile will have a sense of dreariness and desolation, his heart will sink within him, and gladly would he turn back even to his native rock. All this you can faintly apprehend, but yet none but the experienced can know the touching sorrows of an exile's heart. Such sorrow formed a part of these believers' trials. In the sixth verse our Apostle tenderly adverts to it: *Now for a season,* says he, as if he would encourage them it should not last long, *ye are in heaviness through manifold temptations.* And then still further to soothe a sorrow which nothing *could* eradicate, he names to them the reason for this afflictive dispensation: *That the trial of your faith, being much more precious than gold which perishes, though it be tried with fire, might be found unto praise, and honor, and glory, at the appearing of Jesus Christ, whom, having not seen, ye love; and in whom, though now ye see him not, yet believing, ye rejoice with joy unspeakable and full of glory.*

These believers were happy. They were very happy. Notwithstanding all their troublous and terrible circum-

stances, they were very happy. They *rejoiced.* Their joy
was one of peculiar kind; but we should be very bad ex-
positors of the Scriptures' preachings if, since the Apostle
says it was *unspeakable,* we should attempt to measure
its dimensions, or give a full delineation of its particulars
or its character. It can not be delineated. It is beyond
words. It can be known only by experience, and such
experience, too, as, I am afraid, lies beyond the most of
us. If there were not in our religion some passages of
brightness and blessedness, which no words can unfold,
some extension beyond language, some power and enjoyment beyond description; the facts of our religion
would not comport with its theory. According to its
theory, it is supernatural. It claims to be of God himself.
It maintains that God commences it by his own regene-
rating power in the heart, when he answers a sinner's
prayers; that God carries it on by the Holy Spirit in the
souls of believers, when he *works in them that which is
well pleasing in his sight;* and it maintains that even here,
in this infancy of a Christian's existence, there is the
commencement at least of the same qualities and joys
which shall constitute the full of the immortal spirit's
bliss all along the ceaseless roll of interminable ages in
the world to come. Such is its theory ; and if its expe-
ience were all describable, its theory and experience
would not accord. Hence the Apostle justly calls a part
of this experience *unspeakable.* It can not be described.
Words can not describe it. They may go a little way,
but it will go beyond them. Religion will have both an
elevation and a minuteness which no language can tell.
It ought to have. It reaches into eternity. It constitutes the everlasting portion of the soul. It fits for
heaven. And after an inspired Apostle, even, has ex-

hausted the power of words, and reached the end of every possible delineation, he is compelled to leave the portraiture unfinished, to receive by experiment what it could not receive by description—as it is *unspeakable and full of glory*.

This ineffable excellency of our religion is a very common idea in the Scriptures. And it is well worthy of our most profound consideration what particular thing it is that the Scriptures so commonly mention as being *unspeakable*, lying beyond the power of description. You need not go beyond the text for an example. It is Christian *joy* that is *unspeakable*. This is just like the rest of the Scriptures. They do not often represent any thing of personal religion as indescribable, except that which belongs to the religious affections. They explain, almost to the full, religious principles, religious practices, religious doctrines, religious aims, religious conscience; but when they come to the matter of the religious affections, they go but a little way. They soon lose themselves in the unfathomable depths of the religious sensibilities—in the ineffable exercises of a believer's heart. If there were no other proof than this of the verity of experimental religion, of the reality of a *new heart and a new spirit*, as constituting a part, and a vital part of Bible godliness, this alone would be enough. Language labors and fails in the detailing of the religious sentiments. If I may speak so, it describes them only on the outside. It can not unfold the whole interior. There is something *there* which beggars description. If there were *not*, we should doubt the reality of a *new heart and a new spirit*, and the reality of a believer's direct communion with God.

The text tells us the mode, or cause, or origin, of this felicity which it names. The spring and ground of it all is faith—just faith in our Lord Jesus Christ : *in whom believing, ye rejoice.* If there had been no *believing*, there would have been no rejoicing. Faith excites the religious affections. Faith in the heart will produce love in the heart. To lean upon God is the very way to learn to love him. *Faith worketh by love.* I can not now enter into that subject. I only wish you to remark the fact, how the text attributes the joy of these Christians to the faith of these Christians.

And now I lay down this principle, to which I ask your extended attention, namely, that faith, just faith in our Lord Jesus Christ, is sufficient to make believers happy ; that the exercises of faith are enough, under all troublous circumstances, to guide them to an *unspeakable* but real felicity.

Allow me to enumerate a few ideas to illustrate and substantiate this.

1. I allege the experience of ancient believers. I affirm, that as certainly as their faith lasted, their felicity lasted. You can find no exception. There never was an exception. They were often troubled. Storms beat upon them. The furnace burnt upon them. Enemies triumphed over them. They endured all you can imagine the Apostle to mean by his *manifold temptations.* But though they were *in heaviness*, they were happy. They were always happy, if faith did not give way. Job was an example. Job says amid his sorrows, *I know that my Redeemer liveth.* He seems to have known as much redemption as you or I do ; and his experience is a withering rebuke upon the silly notion of some of our theological book-makers, that the Old Testament saints knew little of the doctrine of immortality : *I know that my Redeemer liveth ; and though after my skin worms*

destroy this body, yet in my flesh shall I see God, whom I shall see for myself, and mine eyes shall behold. Job had faith, and Job was a happy man. Asaph was an example. Asaph says: *It is good for me to draw near to God: I am continually with thee.* This was faith. *Thou shalt guide me with thy counsel and afterward receive me to glory.* Asaph had faith, and Asaph was a happy man. David was an example. David says: *As for me, I will behold thy face in righteousness; I shall be satisfied when I awake with thy likeness.* David had faith, and David was a happy man. Paul was an example. He had trials enough, surely, to have crushed him, if he could have been crushed. But he says: *None of these things move me. I am persuaded, that neither death nor life, nor angels, nor principalities nor powers, nor things present nor things to come, nor hight nor depth, nor any other creature, shall be able to separate us from the love of Christ.* What faith! and what remarkable felicity! Stephen was an example. Led forth to the spot of his execution by an infuriated rabble, he kneels in the midst of the shower of stones that his murderers hurled upon him (what a place for calm prayer! what a strange place! and what a strange prayer!): *Lord, lay not this sin to their charge.* Happy man! The happiest man on the ground! Unagitated, forgiving, calm, hopeful, he died with that prayer on his lips which shall make your own death happy, if you have faith to offer it: *Lord Jesus receive my spirit*— and *he fell asleep.* He had strong faith: he was a happy man.

2. We allege the experience of modern believers. It may not, indeed, furnish such lucid examples, but it sustains our position, that faith and felicity are invariably linked together—and that weak faith and woeful in-

felicity are so far the attendants of each other, that aside from weak faith (or entire unbelief) there is no such woeful infelicity in the world. I give you a challenge: I challenge you to produce a single instance of the failure of faith to do all we have claimed for it. You can not produce one. You may find some unhappy Christians— a great many, for aught I know. I suppose you can. But when, why, are they unhappy? Never are they unhappy, only when faith fails, or is feeble or staggered. As ministers, we become acquainted with a vast amount of misery. I would not harrow up your feelings, by any attempted detail of it. It is ineffably varied. We see men crushed under the disasters of life—strong men trembling like an aspen leaf, when their reverses are such that they know not where they shall get bread for their wives and children. Such men have come to us by night (no uncommon thing) to tell a tale which they would not tell you in your counting-houses. We thank them for it. Such a visit puts an honor upon us: no, not on us, but on the Christianity in whose service we minister. We see persons desolate—the last friend dead—not a tried heart left on earth to soothe their sorrows by the sympathy of its own. We see people in pain—sick and dying people. But we *never* see an instance of the failure of faith to do all we have claimed for it. It can, it does make men happy. Faith never fails in its efficacy, only when it fails in itself. If it is not feeble, or staggered, or interrupted, it never fails. Let me make a confession to you, if it is to my own shame. In the early part of my ministry, I used to aim very often to soothe the afflicted and encourage the darkened and depressed by a reference to natural principles, such as the courses of this world, the common lot of life, the uselessness of repining, the mercies still left, or some such thing. I have done with all that. I do it no more. It never did any good. It only dammed up the currents of grief for a little while, to become the more deep and dreadful, when they burst away the frail barrier. It never carried healing to the grief-spot of the heart. It only smothered the fires of trial, to burn the more fiercely and more deeply too, when, in a little while, the heart should find they were only smothered. I hope I have done with all that. I have learnt its inefficacy. If I can not lead to the exercises of faith, I can not do a smitten heart any permanent good. If I can make an inactive faith active— or a weak faith strong—or a trembling faith confirmed— or bring a wandering faith back, then I can make an unhappy man a happy one. His tears may flow; but they have lost their bitterness—they will not burn and blister as they did. His heart may not cease to bleed; but it loves the bleeding—all that is left after the balm of Gilead has been applied to the gash. I only aim, therefore, in some way, to bring in faith, and let its exercises do the comforting. I only stand by and look on.

And now, if you blame this practice, I summon to my defense your own observation and your own experience.

What have you observed? What did a miserable man or a depressed one ever tell you? Did he ever tell you that his faith was strong and his heart uncomforted? No such thing. Quite the contrary. Tears of misery have flowed when faith has faltered. They have turned into tears of joy, when faith conducted to God.

What have you experienced? Some of you have had trials, and deep ones. You would have been unworthy of the name of *human*, much more of the name of *Chris-*

tian, if they had *not* been sad ones to you. But I challenge the darkest day you ever saw, the saddest chapter of your memory, the severest recollection you can call up, if you were not a comforted man, or a happy and comforted woman, just as certainly as your faith held on to its God. I challenge all your memory to say, if your faith had not faltered, or did not lie inactive in all those seasons when you were the most wretched and uncomforted. If you are a believer, and have ever been tried sorely, you know it is so.

Then, let no man blame us when we would employ this only antidote to human sorrow. Let no husband stand by and be dissatisfied when, at the sick-bed of his dying wife, we aim to waken a faith which shall comfort her. Let no friend be afraid we shall injure the sick man when we try to infuse into his unbelieving heart a little of that faith which *alone* can either fit him to die in peace or bear his pains with a composure which shall aid his recovery. Away with such folly! These fears of injuring the sick by the only means which really *can* compose and comfort them, are all the foolish fears of ignorance, and worldliness, and unbelief. It is universally true that faith tends to make men happy; and that, if it is only in just exercise, it will bring felicity along with it every where.

3. Faith tends to make men happy because it has good ground for solacing every misery. So full of trial is this miserable world that to be free from distressful apprehension is no small good of itself. When faith can only turn over the world upon the hand that really wields it, and leave it there as a firm faith does, how many dark days turn into bright ones; how many dreadful apprehensions, how many corroding cares, how many agitating

perplexities, just melt away from the heart and leave it peace. The future is God's. He may take care of to-morrow. Enough for us to pray : *Give us this day our daily bread. I will both lay me down and sleep, for thou only makest me to dwell in safety.* Oh, what an inestimable privilege, that in this changing and dark world, not knowing what a day shall bring forth, not knowing whether the efforts and industry of our youth shall supply us with a competence in old age, and not knowing whether we shall live to see old age at all, and not knowing at what moment some gathered but unseen storm may burst upon us—what an inestimable privilege is faith, that we may commit into the hands of an offering and faithful God, all those dangers, and difficulties, and feared disasters which we have not skill to shun or courage to meet. This is the privilege of faith. It solaces care, and fear, and anxiety. It puts this uncertain world into hands that can manage it. It makes the world God's, and God a father. And if our fears, as well they may, grow still more troublesome as we think of another world, it does the same thing with that which it has already done with this—it leaves it with a trusted God. Here, then, thou child of uncertainty and anguish, sink thy woes! Here dry thy tears! Here dismiss thy gloomy apprehensions ? Trust that God who hath made provision for both thy worlds, and half thy burden shall instantly drop from thy heart. Because,

4. Faith furnishes us an *infinite resource.*

No man can tell all his wants. If he could tell the present, he could not tell the future. Every man is a sinner, and sooner or later must meet a just God. Every man has an immortal soul, and knows not how soon its eternal destiny will be fixed. We are not afraid to affirm that a very large portion of our unhappiness, at least the unhappiness of every reflecting mind, comes from a sense of our insufficiency to attain the materials for our happiness. Nor are we afraid to affirm that the felicity of every reflecting mind must be extremely limited, unless it has hope in the infinite power and good-will of God himself. Our weakness, our ignorance, our sins, the insufficiency of our attainments to make us happy, and the no less insufficiency of our dearest friends to do for us what we need, are things which fill our thoughts with no small anguish. But faith leads us to God as an infinite and certain resource. Just mark some of the particulars which faith includes, as it comes to the covenant offer of God on the ground of the great atonement.

(1) It is God himself who hath done it. *He* has provided for me, a helpless and unworthy sinner.

(2) He has done it under the promptings of his own *kindness and love.*

(3) He has done it by the sacrifice of a Victim sufficient for all that I can need as a sinner, and such a sacrifice as perfectly demonstrates to me—*first*, that God has an infinite good-will toward me, and *second*, that he will not fail to give me any thing else which I may need, since he hath given his Son.

(4) He has already accepted the sin-offering. The tomb of Jesus hath been opened and emptied, and he has gone back into heaven, *having accomplished eternal redemption for us.* What grounds for faith! What invitations to it! As surely as I believe all this, I can not but believe that infinite resources are provided for me. I can not ever want. It is impossible. If Christ is mine, all is mine. So every true believer knows and feels when his

faith is in full exercise. He must be a happy man, for his resources are inexhaustible. Hence,

5. Faith makes men happy because it furnishes aid for our most trying difficulties. It overcomes the world, for example—the world whether frowning to frighten or flattering to seduce us from our fidelity. The world must undermine our faith before it can daunt us; it must undermine our faith before it can clothe this world with such seductive charms as to draw us into its embraces. Oh! how many Christians have been made unhappy, have *pierced themselves through with many sorrows*, because their faith has been so little that they loved the world so well! If they had had faith enough to refuse to be conformed to it, to renounce its riches, to despise its smiles, to stem the torrent of its fashions, they would not have been compelled to look back upon their life and find it half barren of any evidences that they had loved and served God. What a canker their gold becomes! what a curse their honor! what a torment their worldly friendships, when they have about done with life and are looking after evidences that they are going to inherit life everlasting! Faith, if they had lived by it, would have made them happy. It would have held them above the world. It would have taken away the world's power to draw them within its fashion, and fan into flame the *passions that war against the soul*. It would have spread over the whole map of their life bright evidences that they had walked with God, and are soon to inherit the pilgrim's seat and sing the pilgrim's song when his toil is over.

6. Faith tends to felicity, because it hightens the bliss of every fit temporal enjoyment. It adds the delights of sentiment to the delights of sense, and a higher senti-

ment to the enjoyment of the most exquisite taste. This might be illustrated in a thousand particulars. Take one only. There are such things as *tokens*, and they are some of the heart's fond treasures. In themselves they are useless things, yet they are most useful. They are valueless, yet most valuable—yea, valuable *because* they are valueless. Being valueless, they are evincive of an affection beyond price. They are tokens, and have in themselves nothing to tempt to forgetfulness of their token character. They go beyond sense, and utility, and all calculation, and address that species of sentiment which diffuses its felicity in the inside of the heart. The little ring placed on your finger by your dying mother has a token value to you which the arithmetic of gold could not measure. Now, a man of faith finds the world full of such tokens, and his faith enhances the blissfulness of all his tastes. The summer rose that makes us happy with its blushes needs to be seen with an eye of faith, or more than half its beauty and our blessedness in admiring it is lost. Faith makes it a token, a token of God—a token of tenderness that is felt toward us in another world—a token of that paradise whose roses shall never wither, and where no rude blasts shall spoil the pencilings of God's fingers. The man who has this faith has more than sight amid the beauties of his garden. He has sentiment. He has taste elevated and tokens cheering leading away to that garden of eternal bloom.

Just so of all else here. The felicity keeps pace with the faith. It is not that the man has been fed—that is not his joy—but that God has fed him; not that he has been defended, but that God has defended him; not that he has picked up along his path many a fragrant blossom to cheer him, like a half tasteless and quite heartless Deist, who sees no soul in a floweret—but that One who cares for him has placed them there, has scattered them along his path on purpose to have him find them and be happy. Faith *will* find them, and faith will make him a happy man. Especially,

7. In one word more, because faith never stops short of heavenly-mindedness, if it is really exercised at all.

How can that soul be unhappy whose treasures are laid up in heaven? whose tastes are themselves heavenly? whose delight is to rise on the wings of contemplation, or on the wings of prayer, and, holding communion with God, look over all the delights of paradise soon to be its own? This is our privilege as Christians. If we *believe*, we *shall see the glory of God.* The last tear will soon be dried, the last struggle soon be over. Safe housed in the eternal city, we shall sin, and suffer, and die no more. Blessed anticipation! Glorious prospect! *Return unto thy rest, O my soul, for the Lord hath dealt bountifully with thee.*

My brethren, if we are not happy Christians, it is not the fault of our circumstances, but the feebleness of our faith which makes us so. Be it our prayer; *Lord increase our faith.*

The Lamb Slain Worshiped in Heaven.

And they sung a new song, saying, Thou art worthy to open the book, and to loose the seals thereof: for thou wast slain, and hast redeemed us to God by thy blood, out of every kindred, and tongue, and people, and nation.—REVELATION, v. 9.

THE book of Revelation abounds in the most amazing and stupendous imagery; and what was designed to be taught to us by the imagery herein employed, is often not a little obscure. And it would not, therefore, be safe for us to adopt any great and important principles of religion from these descriptions alone. We might understand the figures employed here; and the unusual nature of them and the stupendous strangeness, might very naturally lead us to draw upon an excited imagination for the sense of them, instead of resorting to the severe carefulness of sober reason. But when we affix to the imagery of this Book no meaning or sentiments of religion which are not taught to us in unfigurative language in many other parts of the Scriptures, we are in no danger of being led into any error by the splendor or strangeness of the imagery employed.

And when we find precisely the same doctrines and sentiments which are taught in other parts of the Scriptures, carried out here in the visions and imagery which come before us in the stupendous dress of another world, and find that these unusual descriptions are employed for no purpose of representing *new* things, but that they simply carry out into the eternal world and the field of wonder what we have already been led to know in this world, and by the language of simplicity, we have an additional confirmation of our sentiments; we perceive then, that when the curtain which hides another world is lifted, heaven has the same ideas as earth, and Christ *there* has his exaltation on the same ground as his people have ascribed it to him here. This may have been one of the reasons for the singular composition of this book.

In the chapter which precedes the one before us, John was favored with a magnificent and amazing vision. *I looked, and behold a door was opened in heaven, and the first voice which I heard was as it were of a trumpet talking with me, which said, Come up hither, and I will show thee things which must be hereafter.* Immediately John obeys the voice, and passing through the open door into heaven, he beholds the throne of God, *and one sat on the throne. A rainbow is round about it. There are four-and-twenty elders clothed in white raiment, and they had on their heads crowns of gold.* There were *lightnings and thunderings and voices—and four beasts full of eyes before and behind, giving glory and honor and thanks to him that sitteth on the throne.* And, uniting in this act of worship, *the four-and-twenty elders fall down before him that sitteth on the throne, and worship him that liveth for ever and ever, and cast their crowns before the throne, saying Thou art worthy, O Lord, to receive glory and honor and power, for thou hast created all things, and for thy pleasure they are and were created.*

This is the worship of heaven. It is most comprehensive. It includes the idea of the great design of the existence of all things. And it was appropriate to him. He was now to receive a prophet's lessons. He had been called into heaven to be shown *things which should be hereafter*. The Spirit was going to instruct him in those mysteries of Divine Providence which lay in the future, which regarded the destinies of the Church and the world, and reached down through unknown ages to the final consummation of all things. What he was to know was contained in a sealed book, *sealed with seven seals*, and held in the *right hand of him that sat upon* the throne. The book contained the grand MYSTERIES of God—the explanation of the reasons why God made his creatures, and *how* the glory and honor he was receiving were finally to accrue to him at the final winding up of the agitated scenes of this world. Who shall read *such* a book? A challenge is given in heaven—given by *a strong angel* to the whole universe, to furnish a being who is *worthy to open the book and unloose the seals thereof! And no man in heaven nor in earth, neither under the earth, was able to open the book, neither to look thereon.* Aside from Jesus Christ and his redeeming work, the whole universe of God is a dark and unfathomable mystery. And this dark and dying world especially furnishes such mystery and strangeness, that no eyes *can look thereon* and understand God at all, or understand his dispensations at all, aside from Christ acting in his great work of redemption. Every infidel that breathes may very well unite his tears with those of John : *And I wept much because no man was found worthy to open and to read the book.* Anxious as we may well be to have a just under-standing of the things which we behold ; aside from Christ, God, the existence of creatures, earth, death, time, the use of the world, and the reason for its end, will all be utterly and painfully inexplicable. As John was overwhelmed with the painful emotion—no man to *read*

the book or even look thereon—one of the elders saith
unto him : *Weep not*; *behold the lion of the tribe of Judah, the
root of David hath prevailed to open the book and to loose
the seals thereof.*

This was Jesus Christ. *He* was *to open the book.* He
was promised to be a descendant of David, of the tribe of
Judah. That was the regal tribe—the tribe of kings and
conquerors, whose preëminence was designated by the name
of *lion*, which was attached to it from the time probably of the death-prophecy of the old patriarch, Jacob.
Judah, said the dying patriarch, *is a lion's whelp; from the
prey, my son, thou art gone up : he stooped down, he couched
as an old lion; who shall rouse him up.* Judah was the
head tribe in war; and its kings, like David, were types
of an incomparably greater King, who should vanquish
Satan and all the powers of darkness, should save his
people, and reign on the throne of Heaven for ever, after
the last earthly throne was crumbled into pieces.

John was waiting to see who should *open the book* and
reveal the grand mystery of God. *And I beheld, and lo !*
—it would seem by this expression that John was very
much surprised. He was expecting the appearance of
some amazing personage, clothed with overwhelming
majesty, to take the book out of the hand of God on the
throne. He had been oppressed with the idea of the
sealed book, and had *wept much, because, neither in heaven,
nor earth, nor under the earth,* one could be found to open
it. He had been told that the *Lion of the tribe of Judah*
should accomplish this ; and while he looked to see some
majestic and amazing appearance, he was surprised at
what appeared. What did he see ? *And I beheld, and
lo ! in the midst of the throne and of the four beasts, and in
the midst of the elders stood—a* LAMB *as it had been* SLAIN,

and HE *came and took the book out of the hand of him that
sat upon the throne.* Strange manifestation! No wonder
that John was amazed! A LAMB, an emblem of weakness, of mildness, innocence, and suffering—a LAMB
with marks of recent slaughter upon him—one that had
been SLAIN, but is still alive—such a being comes up
to be the first object of wonder amid the grandeur and
worship of heaven! *He* takes the book *out of the right
hand of Him that sat upon the throne; and when he had
taken the book, the four beasts and four-and-twenty elders fell
down before the* LAMB, *having every one of them harps and
golden vials full of odors, which are the prayers of saints;
and they sung a new song, saying, Thou are worthy to take
the book and open the seals thereof, for thou wast* SLAIN *and
hast redeemed us to God by thy* BLOOD. Christ unfolds the
wonders of God. The death and the redemption of
Christ are here presented as the grand matter which explains the universe, and which prompts that act of adoration in heaven in which all the creatures of God are
employed.

This is the explanation of the text. With this the
heart of the true Christian accords. The more he knows
of Christ in his amazing work of redemption, the more
he is amazed at the adorable wonders of his grace.
Christ—Christ SLAIN, explains the universe, explains
God, explains death, explains heaven, and satisfies the
heart. This opens the seven-sealed book. This manifestation of redeeming love animates the worship of
heaven : *And I heard the voice of many angels round about
the throne, and the beasts and the elders; and the number of
them was ten thousand times ten thousand and thousands of
thousands, saying with a loud voice, Worthy is the* LAMB THAT
WAS SLAIN *to receive power, and riches, and wisdom, and*

strength, and honor, and glory, and blessing. And every creature which is in heaven, and on earth, and under the earth, and such that are in the sea, and all that are in them, heard I, saying, Blessing, and honor, and glory, and power, be unto him that sitteth upon the throne and unto the Lamb for ever and ever. This is the explanation of the text. We have, therefore, this great TRUTH or DOCTRINE:

The death of Christ for the redemption of sinners, constitutes the distinguishing peculiarity of his work, and the high ground for his adoration.

Let us name to you *six* ideas about this doctrine:

1. Like the chapter before us, the Scriptures every where teach us to regard *the death* of Christ in a peculiar manner.

While the Scriptures have recorded the history of his birth, of his life, of his sufferings, and conversation, they have manifestly done this only in explanation of his character and to give us a just view of his amazing condescension; and all these things they concentrate to one point, as they gather them all around the crowning matter of the whole—his amazing death! Manifestly, Christ's business on earth was to die; not to live, but to die. He became incarnate that he might be able to die. The sacrament of the Lord's Supper, which you hope to celebrate on next Lord's day, is certainly the most solemn and affecting of all the ordinances of your religion; and it is just a memorial of his death. The Bible has not taught us to memorialize his birth, or his birth-day, his miracles, or any act of his life. Not a word of all that. The Scriptures would not make any appointment which could have any tendency to distract our minds, or to divide our hearts between the example of his life and the atonement of his crucifixion. In that one thing,

in his crucifixion, centers all that engages the faith of the
sinner to be saved by his grace.

No careful and candid reader of the Bible (as it seems
to me) can doubt for a moment that the sacred Scriptures
attach to the *death* of Christ a peculiar and supreme importance.   They do never speak of it as merely one of the
things to command our admiration, nor do they speak of
it merely as *that thing* which carries out and crowns his
character.   Uniformly and every where they speak of it
as THE thing of his Divine mission, to which all other
things were merely incidental and subordinate.   When
Paul was about to die, he could say : *I have fought a good
fight, I have finished my course.   His* work was done.
His business on this side the shores of heaven was to be
done in the acts of his *living ;* and he had done it.   He
was now *ready to be offered up.*   But Christ could say no
such thing.   Quite the contrary.   *His* work on this side
the shores of heaven was to be done in his dying ; and
hence, just on the eve of his crucifixion, and knowing
well that he was soon to die, and *willing* to die, he says :
(quite unlike his great Apostle,) *I have a baptism to be
baptized with, and how am I straitened till it be accomplished.*
Amid his perfect and sinless services, as he did the will
of his Father in his life-time, not a word escaped him to
manifest that he had done, or even *touched,* the great
work which he came to accomplish.   Amid his unshaken
contemplations of the glory which he was about to
have in heaven with the Father, and which he had had
with him *before the foundation of the world,* not a word
escapes him to indicate that he had purchased it yet.
The thing to be done is always *before* him—not behind.
And not until he had been through the agonies of the
garden, the mock trials of the court, and the mock adu-

lation which gave him *a reed* for a scepter and *thorns* for a crown—not until the sneers and jibes of his murderers had ceased, and his life-blood was pouring from his opened veins, and vanquished death had found his dart shivered into pieces as it struck him—not until then could he exclaim: *It is finished.* Dying finished it. Dying was the burden of his work. *A Lamb as it had been slain* is the object of worship in heaven. Hence,

2. The manner in which he met death was peculiar. He met it as no living man could have expected; as no righteous man that we know of ever did. The grace of the Divine promises extends to that hour. *Blessed are the dead that die in the Lord. The righteous hath hope in his death. Precious in the sight of the Lord is the death of his saints.* How, then, would you expect a good man to die? How would you expect Christ to die, who lived without sin, if a life of holiness was his main work here, and if he had no more of difficulty to encounter with the king of terrors than falls to the lot of the righteous? He had more. And hence he quailed at the prospect. He did not give back—but he quailed. He was willing to die. He would not accept deliverance. A word would have brought more than twelve legions of angels from heaven. But, no, he would not give back: *The cup which my Father giveth me, shall I not drink it?* says he. And this very fact (his willingness to die) makes his agitation of soul the more wonderful, as he trembled at the prospect. Willing to die, ready, he still trembles, *sweats great drops of blood falling down to the ground;* in an agony he prays: *Father, if it be possible, let this cup pass from me.* Certainly this was very peculiar for a righteous man. Stephen did not die so. Kneeling calmly down amid the showers of stones his murderers

hurled at him, he died without a groan, his soul cleaving
the vault of heaven on the wing of that prayer: *Lord
Jesus, receive my spirit.*   Manifestly, the death of Christ
was very peculiar.

3. Hence the sacred Scriptures uniformly speak of this
death in a manner totally different from that in which
they mention the death of and other being.

It was nothing extraordinary that a good man should
die—or that the character and course of a good man
should bring death upon him, he becoming a martyr to
the truth, and sealing the message of his living lips with
the unchanged affirmations of his dying lips.   Isaiah
had died so, and others of the prophets before Christ;
and Stephen, and James, and others of his disciples, died
so after him.   It has been common.   This is one of the
trials which may sometimes be expected.   The track of
the Church through the pathway of centuries was marked
by the blood and the unburied bones of the martyrs.
Jesus Christ himself foretold all this, and the mention of
such dying is a very familiar matter in the New Testament.

But the Scriptures never mention any of these deaths
as they mention Christ's.   They are never spoken of
as a propitiation for sin—as a sacrifice—as procuring redemption by blood.   In this respect there is a plain
and indisputable contrast between the language of the
Bible about the death of Christ and its language about
the death of others.   Isaiah, Abel, Zecharias, Stephen,
Peter, James, Paul,—not one of the whole army is
spoken of as making atonement for sin, or any procure-
ment of eternal life.   But, on the contrary, the death
of Christ is uniformly mentioned, as having such an
intention and such a result.   *He was wounded for our
transgressions ; he was bruised for our iniquities ; the chastise-*

*ment of our peace was upon him ; by his stripes we are
healed. He bare our sins in his own body upon the tree.*
We are said to be *bought with his blood—to have redemption
through his blood, even the forgiveness of sins.* The Lord
*hath laid on him the iniquity of us all. He tasted death for
every man.* Not a single syllable like this in all the
Bible is ever applied to the death of any other being
that ever died. So that there is a perfect and entire contrast and contrariety between the Bible mention of Christ's
death and its mention of that of the martys. Paul has
himself employed this idea : *Was Paul crucified for you?*
Hence,

4. On the ground of this death, the Scriptures found
the argument for even the common morality of life.
They *do* found it here. They never expect any other
foundation to avail. The death of Christ was an infinite
exemplification of love ; and the spirit of Gospel morality is distinguished from that of a cold-hearted philosophical morality by having its foundation in love : remember, not in mere utility, but in love. Hence, the
Bible expects of every believer that he shall have his
baptism of spirit and the animation of his life by the
contemplation of the death of Christ and drinking in the
sublime spirit of his crucifixion. If, for example—what
shall I say ? no matter what—the argument is extended
in the Bible over the whole field of an earthly morality—
you may take example in any thing—if *husbands* are to
love their wives (and scarcely any other earthly duty can
be more important), if they are to *love their wives* they
are to take their measure from Christ in his death—*love
your wives even as Christ loved the Church and gave himself
for it.* If—no matter what, the argument goes every
where—if Christians are to *love one another*, they are

called on to do it *even as Christ hath loved us, and given himself for us, an offering and a sweet savor unto God.* In that dying love is centered the perfection of all the spirit that a Christian needs. *Herein is love, not that we loved him* (even a philosophical morality may lead to the laying down of one's life for his friends), *but that he loved us and gave himself for us when we were yet enemies.* And then, beyond this, if, as creatures of God and bound to an immortal destination, we owe duties to our Maker and Judge, they take their spirit from the same bloody and blessed fountain. With exultation and rapture indescribable Paul exclaims: *The love of Christ constraineth us, because we thus judge, that if one died for all, then were all dead, and that he died for all that they which live should live henceforth, not unto themselves, but unto him who died for them and rose again.* And when Paul would embody in one short sentence every thing he wanted for his converts whom he loved, he prays that they may *know the love of Christ which passeth knowledge.* This principle is universal. It extends every where. The evidences are thrown around us in all the Bible fields, that the Divine writers would have us take the spirit of our conduct just from *the dying* of Christ. Hence,

5. The Holy Scriptures uniformly expect to affect us most, and to furnish us the highest lessons of holiness, by affecting our hearts with the contemplation of the death of Christ. They want faith to fix there: *Christ loved me and gave himself a ransom.* They expect to furnish an antidote to the love of sin by leading us to faith in him who died to expiate it. They never expect to affect our hearts much by chapters of statistics on sin's evil, like some cold and calculating political economy. Their philosophy lies deeper; and let the would-be reformers

of the world know it lies infinitely beyond them. It
expects to make hearts most happy, and souls most
heavenly; life most pure, and death most peaceful; sinners most like God, and most fit to meet him—just by
influences drawn from the crucifixion and felt at the foot
of the cross. Because,

6. This death of Christ is an incomparable manifestation of Divine love, and hence is calculated to have an
unequaled moral influence. It stands solitary—on a
platform of its own—heaven-high above all other Divine
manifestations. All else must yield to it. The *rain
from heaven and fruitful seasons*, which witness for God,
the sun in his pavilion of glory, the stars in their fields
of blue, are infinitely beneath it. These, all these, tell us
no story of an infinite and sacrificing condescension of
love to enemies. Angels, before they saw this, had seen
offices of love, and some of them had been sent even to
earth on its high mission as *ministering spirits to minister
for those who shall be heirs of salvation.* But never before
had they seen its sacrifices and the extent of its condescension. In no other instance did love ever "stoop so
low, or endure so much." In no other instance did it
ever operate so freely, or reach so far. Never was humiliation so deep, or agony so dreadful. He who *thought
it not robbery to be equal with God took upon him the form
of a servant, and became obedient unto death, even the death
of the cross.* Nothing demanded it of him. He was under
no obligation to do it. Not a tongue in the universe
could have blamed him if he had not done it. The victims of sin from earth might have gone down in the track
of the fallen angels, and Divine holiness and justice
would have been for ever satisfied and untarnished, as
the last sinner died and went to his doom. But the love

of God would not have it so. Jesus Christ would not
have it so. Though he saw betwixt himself and the salvation of sinners which he contemplated, an arrayed
army of horrors—a tearful life in frail human nature—
buffeting, and scourging, and spitting—an agony of soul
—a battle with the prince of darkness, and that, too,
when *forsaken* of the Father—yea, when the Father himself should lift the sword to smite the head of his Son,
still he said, *Lo! I come to do thy will.* The Victim was
ready, and new adoration awoke in heaven!

This dying love of Christ was a new spectacle to the
universe—it was a new manifestation of the heart of its
God. Christ only, and Christ as a *Lamb that was* SLAIN,
could open the seven-sealed book and arouse the adoring
rapture of an astonished heaven. *Before* this time it was
known what power could do—a universe was held up on
the fingers of God. Before this time it was known what
justice could do—as sinning angels were *reserved under
chains of darkness.* But it was *not* known what LOVE
could do. Christ told that story, and gave a new view
of Jehovah to an adoring universe. He who was most
majestic became most mean—the *Ancient of days* became
the babe of a span long—the owner of all heaven became a poor man that *had not where to lay his head*—he
who was most glorious and happy became *a man of sorrows and acquainted with grief,* and coming off victorious
over shame and poverty, over cursing and ignominy, the
bitterness of death and battle with devils, he comes up
into heaven with the blood of his own slaughter upon
him, the triumphant demonstration that *God is* LOVE.
This is a new aspect of the heart of God. Its beatings
were never so seen before, and never will be any where

else. No wonder that this display of sacrificing love for sinners is influential:

> "From the highest throne of glory,
> To the cross of deepest woe;
> All to ransom guilty captives,
> Flow, my praise, for ever flow."

Divine love perfectly triumphs, and Divine justice is perfectly satisfied. The majesty and the pity of God meet. God is great by being good. He has shown the utmost hatred of sin, and his inflexible attachment to his holy law, in the very same transaction where he shows his mercy and unparalleled love. *The Lion of the tribe of Judah* maintains his honor and his dominion over a universe of hearts, by becoming the *Lamb that was slain.* Grace reigns, God is glorified, and sinners live. *Thou art worthy to take the book and to open the seals thereof, for thou wast* SLAIN *and hast redeemed us by thy blood.*

With this adoration in your hearts, prepare to take into your hands the *cup of* blessing on the next Lord's day. Christ, the wonder of heaven, is the Redeemer of sinners.

The conclusions from this subject may perhaps aid your adoration. We name a few ideas.

1. This is the adoration of heaven. Jesus Christ has appeared there, *a Lamb as it had been slain,* and in that character receives for ever the admiration and worship of the heavenly inhabitants. Hearts on earth ought to assort with hearts in heaven over every contemplation of the atoning sacrifice of the Son of God.

2. As love constitutes the mode in which God seeks to save us, and at the same time constitutes the highest manifestation of his unfathomable perfections, the religion, whereby we hope to be at peace with him, must very

much consist in the same kind of affection. It is God's
love which solicits your hearts. Lay aside your servile
fear. You may even forget God's majesty if you can,
all of it which does not come to your mind as his majesty
appears in heaven, clothed in the unequaled grandeur
of a bloody redemption. Open your heart to God, just
where God opens his heart to you. Consent to love him
as his child. Love loaded the cross with its Victim :
let love weep and adore and trust and sing at the foot of
it. Such a Saviour, the wonder of heaven, ought to
attract all hearts ; and such a Saviour, such a wonder,
ought to be enough to convince the guiltiest sinner on
earth that grace can save him. Hence,

3. There is no occasion for that gloomy despondency
which sometimes feels that it *may not* confide in Christ,
because it has nothing but a heart to offer. Christ wants
nothing but your heart. It is love Divine which has
tempered and whetted and polished the *sword of the
Spirit.* Let it penetrate your heart. Be won by the love
of Christ. You *may trust* in his sacrifice, and that trust,
whatever your dark mind and trembling conscience may
whisper, shall do *more* than any thing else you can
render, to honor him on the very point where his glory
is greatest. And more : Jesus Christ seeks your heart,
even more solicitously than he seeks your conscience
even. Do you not see that he would conquer you by
his love, alone stronger than death ? Be heart to heart
with Christ. It is the first thing he asks, and if not *all*,
it is the life-spring of all the rest. We are saved by faith.

4. You need not fear to worship Christ. He is
worshiped in heaven. And not only so, but his bloody
work as our Redeemer is the crowning glory of God,
seen when the seven-sealed book is opened and the *new*

song in heaven begins—never to end.   Adore, where angels adore.   Bow in supreme homage before the LAMB, in company with the four-and-twenty elders who are round about the throne.

5. Finally, what unequaled humility and penitence become us at the communion-table!   Not our own, but his—not there by merit, but by love and mercy—brands plucked from the burning—some of us taken recently out of the whirl of the world—and all of us, not in hell as we have deserved, but now heirs of heaven : abundant are the reasons we have to exclaim with adoring humility and love, *Thou wast slain, and hast redeemed us to God by thy blood.*

A Pastor's Sketches 1 & 2
by Dr. Ichabod Spencer

"*A Pastor's Sketches* is a sobering and challenging reminder that the Holy Spirit is the true agent of conversion. This book is urgently needed today when so much of our evangelism is patterned after current marketing methods. It has deeply convicted me to always seek to be in tune with the Holy Spirit as I minister to others." **Jerry Bridges**

"Dr. Spencer's *Sketches*, reprinted after a lapse of many years, are a veritable treasury of pastoral wisdom. They will amply repay careful reading by pastors and serious Christians in our day." **Maurice Roberts**

"The Spencer extracts are superb and will be of great benefit when printed. This is very sobering but enlightening material. It is quite contrary to much of today's practice and all pastors need to read it." **Peter Jeffery**

"Spencer is a master at flushing sinners out of hiding and directing them to Jesus Christ for salvation through Spirit-worked, simple faith. The responses he makes to inquirers is, in the main, biblical, doctrinal, practical, and experiential. His perceptive counsel certainly has produced much fruit. *A Pastor's Sketches* is a compelling read for pastors and Christian workers; its pages contain the nuts and bolts of biblical evangelism." **Joel R. Beeke**

"The republication of Spencer's sketches gives a rare opportunity for contemporary pastors, who have few if any models of pastors who understand the 'work of evangelism.' These sketches show a doctrinal depth and an experiential savvy perfectly meshed in one who had the cure of souls as his passion." **Tom Nettles**

"Ichabod Spencer was gifted by God with a passion for the pastoral care of souls. Any pastor desiring to shepherd the sheep, or to see God's elect drawn to Christ, will find page after page of wise and sage counsel in this work. It is practical, pious, personal, and precious." **James White**

List Price for each volume **$12.95**
Purchase both from SGCB for **$22.00**

Solid Ground Christian Books
Call us toll free at **1-877-666-9469**
E-mail us at **sgcb@charter.net**
Visit us on the web at **solid-ground-books.com**

SGCB Classic Reprints Series

In addition to the *Spencer Sermons* that you hold in your hands, SGCB is excited to announce our intention to bring back several classic volumes that have been out of print for too long. Here are our present titles:

The Church Member's Guide by John Angell James was once the most popular book in both the UK and the USA for instructing Christian's in their privileges and responsibilities as members of the body of Christ. Many are familiar with Calvary Press' booklet *The Duties of Church Members to their Pastors*, which is simply one chapter from this invaluable book. It would be a great tool for those who teach New Member's Classes, or Discipleship Training classes, as well as those desiring to know their responsibilities as members of the Church of Jesus Christ.

Christ in Song: Hymns of Immanuel compiled by Philip Schaff, best known for his massive *History of the Christian Church,* is an outstanding devotional tool that traces the Life, Ministry and Worship of our Lord and Savior Jesus Christ through all the ages of the Church. There are 600 pages of praise to our Lord from the greatest Christian hymn-writers and poets who have ever lived. The response to the announcement of this reprint is unprecedented in the ministry of Solid Ground Christian Books.

First Things by Gardiner Spring is a two volume set that is also very rare. Spring is best known in our day for the Banner of Truth works *The Power of the Pulpit* and *The Attraction of the Cross*. He is also known to many by his small volume *The Distinguishing Traits of Christian Character*. Most recently Soli Deo Gloria has reprinted his treatise entitled *The Mercy Seat*.

These volumes set before our minds the foundation upon which all life is built, as recorded in the opening chapters of Genesis. In a day in which these chapters are being challenged even in so-called evangelical churches and seminaries, Spring takes us back with absolute assurance that we are reading genuine history. Every page is filled with pure spiritual gold.

We plan to publish *Silent Times* by J.R. Miller, *The Life of J.R. Miller,* by John Faris, *The Lord our Shepherd* by John Stevenson, *The History of the Work of Redemption* by Jonathan Edwards and many more, as the Lord enables us to do so. If you have an interest in these titles, please let us know.

Solid Ground Christian Books
Call us toll free at **1-877-666-9469**
E-mail us at **sgcb@charter.net**
Visit us on the web at **solid-ground-books.com**